Documents on Contemporary British Government

I. British government and constitutional change

Documents on Contemporary British Government

I. British government and constitutional change

EDITED BY
MARTIN MINOGUE

*Senior Lecturer, Department of
Administrative Studies, University
of Manchester*

CAMBRIDGE UNIVERSITY PRESS

CAMBRIDGE
LONDON   NEW YORK   MELBOURNE

Published by the Syndics of the Cambridge University Press
The Pitt Building, Trumpington Street, Cambridge CB2 1RP
Bentley House, 200 Euston Road, London NW1 2DB
32 East 57th Street, New York, NY 10022, USA
296 Beaconsfield Parade, Middle Park, Melbourne 3206, Australia

First published 1977

Printed in Great Britain at the
University Printing House, Cambridge

Library of Congress Cataloguing in Publication Data
Main entry under title:
British Government and constitutional change.
(Documents on contemporary British Government; v. 1)
Bibliography: p.
1. Great Britain — Politics and government — 1964-
— Sources. I. Minogue, Martin. II. Series.
JN234 1977.B65   354'.41   76-26374
ISBN 0 521 21437 8 hard covers
ISBN 0 521 29148 8 paperback

For Lizzie

Contents

ix   *Contents*

Preface

This is the first volume in a two-volume selection of documents related to government in Britain. This volume illustrates the main characteristics of the system of government, with an emphasis on significant areas of constitutional change; the second volume deals with the local government systems of Britain (England, Wales, Scotland and Northern Ireland) and their reorganisation.

The past thirty years is taken as the principal reference period, but the majority of documents in both volumes comes from the past decade, which has witnessed a remarkable and unprecedented series of reforming investigations across the whole field of governmental activity, and into the system of government itself. The chief reason for the concentration in these volumes on the formal structures of government is that the analysis and reform of these structures has occupied the centre of the political stage in recent years. Moreover, the system of government more readily lends itself to documentary analysis than the less formal parts of the political system, and it would have been impossible, for reasons of space, to deal adequately with political parties, pressure groups and elections within the scope of the present volume: it may be that a separate sourcebook is needed to cover these areas. Clearly an understanding of the political context of structural and constitutional changes is essential to either description or analysis of those changes, and the business of relating governmental structures and arrangements to political institutions and processes is part of the task of teachers and students of politics and government everywhere. This documentary selection is, therefore, intended to be complementary to the best existing texts and commentaries on British government and politics. The intention is to give students the opportunity to make more direct acquaintance with the basic materials of British government than the burgeoning supply of instant textbooks either allows or encourages. Too often the student thinks of official documents as dull, incomprehensible or insignificant. Sometimes they may be all of these things, but more frequently they are lively, readable and make crucial contributions to policy formulation. This selection is published in the hope that students will be stimulated to turn towards these primary sources of information, and away from the easy 'crammer' which all too often oversimplifies what is complex, renders anodyne what is fascinating, and imposes an unreal order on a shifting, disorderly process. It is my view that if students become accustomed to familiarity with the primary documents, they will not only learn to make their own judgements about source material, but will derive from their studies an enhanced enjoyment and enthusiasm for further enquiry.

Undeniably the attempt to select from a mass of documents has pitfalls for the unwary. Documents cannot be properly understood if divorced from their political and administrative context; extracts may give an incomplete or partial impression of the content of a particular document. The need to compress the selection into the confines dictated by the publisher and the market inevitably compels the editor to make arbitrary decisions about which documents, or parts of documents, to include or exclude. Accepting these strictures, I would emphasise firstly, that the documents are intended to supplement the secondary reading material and lecture programmes, which will provide the basis for any course in British government; secondly, that I have attempted to provide brief contextual material which will serve to link together the selected sources in a reasonably coherent manner, but would expect the more detailed interpretation of the sources, and their context, to be provided by lecturers responsible for courses (and this allows for differing interpretations of the same material, where textbooks frequently impose a particular approach); thirdly, that in selecting from documents, I have tried to reduce the elements of arbitrariness by making lengthy rather than brief selections and by concentrating on documents which seemed to have a more permanent rather than an ephemeral character; and finally, I have tried to illustrate the wide range of sources which contribute to the formidable mass of official publications: White Papers, Green Papers, departmental reports from special working parties, Royal Commission reports, parliamentary papers, commentaries by pressure groups, contributions from individual policy-makers — the range of sources is enormous and fascinating. But the sheer volume daunts the average student, and even when it does not, considerable problems of access may remain. The present selection is intended to provide more convenient access to these sources, and at the same time to stimulate an appetite for more extensive use of the basic materials for the study of British government. (Note: 'British' and 'Britain' are taken to include Northern Ireland throughout these volumes, though technically they do not.)

I wish to offer my thanks to Quentin Skinner for helpful criticism of the Introduction, and more generally for the intellectual stimulus and friendly encouragement he has given me for many years; to James Craig, who always has interesting things to say about British government and politics; to the staff of the John Rylands Library, Manchester University, for considerable help in locating documents; to Marjorie Marchant for help with the typing and preparation of material; to my publisher for sympathetic flexibility over deadlines; and to my wife Lizzie for her comments upon the Introduction and for constant encouragement and support. Any faults are my own.

Introduction

I

'We must be satisfied with the soup that is set before us, and not desire to see the bones of the ox out of which it has been made.'

(Dasent, *Popular Tales from the Norse*)[1]

Although the British constitution is in form unwritten, it has attracted many pens, which have produced many words of exposition and interpretation.[2] It is not the purpose of this brief introduction to add yet another commentary; the intention is rather to emphasise those lines of constitutional development which are still of some practical significance and to provide an essential historical context for the political and administrative changes of the last thirty years.

The bare bones of the British constitution are provided by the major political institutions: the Executive, centred on the Crown; the Legislature, centred on the House of Commons; and organised political parties, which link together the executive and the legislature. But we can not really see what the constitutional body looks like until the bones are fleshed out. The Executive, for example, is an immense complex of administrative organisations, legal structures, political concepts, influential groups, and powerful individuals. Parliament is a more orderly but intricate arrangement of law-making machinery and political power relationships; political parties are rarely monolithic, often disorganised, and have lives outside the central political arena which impinge upon the way in which they behave inside that arena. Above all, these institutions have no real existence except in terms of the behaviour of the people who inhabit them and make them work, whether well or badly. Yet the way in which people operate political institutions is determined partly, at least, by the values which they attach to these institutions and by a high level of common agreement as to the nature and significance of these values. The values are often shared on the basis of a common understanding as to the rules by which the political institutions are expected to be operated. Where there is no common agreement, or where that agreement breaks down, we shall find an area of constitutional conflict or uncertainty, which will be settled or clarified only by a resolution of the political conflict.

1 Quoted in J. R. R. Tolkien, *Tree and Leaf* (Allen & Unwin, 1975), p. 25.
2 Two useful recent works which relate constitutional developments to the political and governmental system are T. C. Hartley and J. A. G. Griffith: *Government and Law* (Weidenfeld & Nicolson, 1975); and Peter Bromhead: *Britain's Developing Constitution* (Allen & Unwin, 1974).

It is the existence of this informal process of constitutional rule-making which gives the British constitution its curious combination of structural rigidity and behavioural flexibility. Many of the constitutional 'rules' (or conventions) change constantly as politically powerful groups adjust their relationships, both to each other and to their constituencies, in response to a changing political environment. These adjustments may produce changes in attitudes towards the role and operation of major political institutions, creating an atmosphere in which the common agreements may be renegotiated or enlarged. It is often extremely difficult to detect this process at work, but we invariably see the outcome in the form of a political action which reveals to us that a constitutional ground-rule has been reformulated. There is an interesting correspondence of method here between legal and political changes. Just as our free institutions have been said legally to have broadened down from precedent to precedent, so we can see that those institutions have also broadened down politically from precedent to precedent: each political reformulation becomes a new constitutional precedent. For example, it became clear with Mr James Callaghan's election to the leadership of the Labour party in 1976 that the monarch no longer had an effective power of choice of Prime Minister during a Labour administration. The Labour Party's attitude had been proclaimed in these terms after 1957, when the monarch was able to choose between two Conservative contenders for Prime Ministerial office; but the constitutional precedent was 1976. It is difficult to imagine, politically, that the Conservative Party would not now follow this precedent. But we cannot be certain until the situation arises in practice, and specific action confirms a new political value which is commonly accepted by the competing political groups.

On the other hand, constitutions are not always, or even often, a plain man's guide to the real world of politics. It has been said that the function of political culture is 'to eliminate troublesome enquiries by offering readymade directions for use, to replace truth hard to obtain by offering comfortable truisms, and to substitute the self-explanatory for the questionable'.[3] Our view of the constitution, of the ground-rules within which the serious enterprise of power politics is conducted, is a significant part of our political culture; and if the ready-made directions for use provide us with a palatable constitutional soup, and truisms which may be comforting as well as comfortable, then we could do a good deal worse. These truisms will at least give us some indication of the existence or otherwise of a common constitutional tradition, manifested by the perceptions people seem to have of the present political system and of past political events. It is difficult to know what the outlines of such a historical tradition would look like or how pervasive it might be. We can see more readily what have been the perceptions of influential groups and actors: and it is not surprising then to discover the existence of different, partly conflicting, interpretations of a 'common' constitutional tradition. In short, politically active groups are, either specifically, or in the very broadest sense, ideological: and their interpretation of past events will often be conditioned by their present

3   Alfred Schütz, Collected Papers II (Martinus Nijhoff, 1964).

intentions or future ambitions. The 'Whig' or the 'Tory' interpretation of the British constitution is likely to tell us more about Whigs and Tories than about our constitutional history.

Are there any comfortable truisms? It is dangerous to pen generalisations which are made to apply equally to the circumstances of the sixteenth and the twentieth centuries. It is almost equally misleading to talk of the 'nineteenth century constitution' or the 'seventeenth century constitution' if there is any implication that these are unique entities which bear no relation to each other. Perhaps the least misleading general proposition is that in the past four centuries there have been recurring problems in the government and politics of Britain, which have been constantly reformulated in terms of the conflicts, philosophies, political configurations, and social and economic structures of successive generations. One crucial ingredient in each reformulation has been the reception and interpretation of the previous formulation, and the associated political events and ideological debates. But another crucial ingredient is the pressure for change, the necessity to adjust ideological interpretations and political rules to the ebb and flow of social and economic movements. It has been suggested that what gives strength and permanence to our Constitution is its adaptability, its capacity to bend without breaking; an alternative view is that the Constitution simply reflects a highly developed political consciousness in a society which has been constantly sensitive to the need for change on a predictable, peaceful basis, and has created the political machinery required for the purpose. The first view sees a primary role for the Constitution itself; the second view sees the Constitution as merely a reflection of political developments. Both views underestimate the extent to which violence, or the relentless exercise of overwhelming power, have been significant at crucial points in our political history.

From the standpoint of 1976, some parts of our constitutional history seem more relevant than others. Three areas of concern today have been enduring features: relations between the executive and the legislature, the control of the executive, and the relation between the individual and the state. Two other features have been relatively newer problems: the scope and complexity of the state bureaucracy and the efficient discharge by the state of a very wide range of obligations; and the creation of representative democracy, and the associated organisation of mass political parties, a phenomenon which has transformed the earlier relationships between executive and legislature.

The executive and the legislature

A leading constitutional historian writes: 'The essence of the Constitution today is the temporary entrustment of great powers to a small Cabinet or body of Ministers (who are members of one or other of the Houses of Parliament) who are formally appointed to office by and dismissible by the King, but who are politically responsible to the electorate, through the House of Commons, which is periodically elected on a wide popular franchise, and who are legally responsible under the Law, and who are served by a corps of permanent civil servants.' It is a formula, he states, which was 'the fruit, not of any theoretical speculation, or of any profound fore-sight, but of long experience of what works and what does not'.[4] What are the ingredients of this formula?

All constitutions are principally concerned with a definition of the executive power in the state, with the question of which persons enjoy executive power, and crucially with questions of control and limitation of the executive power. There is generally an attempt to balance the need for effective government and the desire for limited government. Executive power in English history had always resided in the monarch; and much of English constitutional history is the story of how the monarch exercised this power, how constitutional restraints on autocratic mon-archical authority developed primarily through Parliament, and finally how effective monarchical power was transferred to leading political groups centred on Parliament, but organised into a governing Cabinet of Ministers, with a strong first Minister or Prime Minister. The old royal prerogatives still exist in form; but in practice they are exercised either by the Prime Minister, or the Cabinet, or by Parliament acting in accordance with the decisions of a Cabinet collectively responsible to it. The monarch's Privy Council, so strong an instrument of royal government in Tudor times, still survives, but again, it acts only in accordance with Cabinet decisions.

How did the monarchy lose its authoritative position? This is simple to describe, more complicated to explain. The landmark is the 1688 revolution, which more properly is a 'revolution' spanning the period from approximately 1629 to 1714. It is sometimes described as a bloodless revolution, but there was ample blood-letting in the Civil War of the 1640s, when Monarch and Parliament took up arms against each other; the King lost not only the war, but his head, and with him effectively died the notion that Kings were divinely ordained and could not be replaced by subjects (although the legitimacy, as opposed to the reality of such replacement continued to be debated well into the eighteenth century). Despite the royalist (and Stuart) restoration of 1660, power had shifted significantly to subjects who could control Parliament, and the 1688 revolution institutionalised this fundamental shift in relations between the executive and the legislature. This still left the monarchy with significant powers, and substantial authority, but from this point on there was a gradual if unsteady process of attrition of both powers and authority. The eighteenth century saw the full development of Cabinet government, and the transfer of chief executive status from the monarch to the most prominent of his advisory ministers. Associated with this was the development of the principle that Ministers were, both individually and collectively, answerable to Parliament for their policies and their actions. Neither Cabinet, nor Prime Minister, nor these notions of ministerial responsibility, have a legal place in British constitutional arrangements; but they were the central facts of political development within the readjusted framework of government provided by the revolutionary settlement.

4 S. B. Chrimes, *English Constitutional History*, (4th edition, Oxford University Press, 1967), p. 9.

Walter Bagehot, writing in 1867, was the first to define Cabinet government as the 'efficient secret' of the British constitution,[5] but since then the debate has focussed on the position and powers of the Prime Minister.[6] This debate is closely linked to the analysis of executive control of Parliament through the operation of a rigid two-party system in which the political leadership of the majority Parliamentary party forms the Cabinet.

The struggle between the King and his subjects operating through Parliament considerably predates 1688. But it was the settlement of 1688 (specifically the 1701 Act of Settlement) which established the formal supremacy of Parliament over the executive, and supplied the practical strength of Parliament, which is its regular and continuous existence. But in discussing parliamentary control, we have always to ask, who controls Parliament? And although there have been periods when Parliament was genuinely independent in its composition, for the most part the executive has found ways of dominating Parliament through control of a majority of its members, or because of a common identity between those who were prominent in the executive and those who were prominent in the legislature. The introduction of fully representative democracy in the nineteenth and twentieth centuries (1832, 1867, and 1884 Reform Acts, and legislation in 1918 and 1928) might have been expected to reinforce Parliament. In practice, it stimulated the deliberate organisation of national political parties which competed for control of Parliament, and therefore of government. Since independent action by a Parliamentary majority would henceforth serve only to embarrass or displace the governing body which constituted the leadership of the Parliamentary majority, such action soon ceased altogether. Today, the executive controls Parliament with little real difficulty, and the complexity of modern legislative activity often means that 'the real debate is taking place outside'.[7] Approximately one-third of the ruling party in the House of Commons will be members of the government; the remaining backbenchers have little scope for effective action against the executive. Richard Crossman, then Leader of the House, once expressed this powerlessness directly to his own Labour Party backbenchers: 'If I give you people desks, telephones, and secretaries, you will begin to think you are running something, and believe me, you are not.'[8] It is the consciousness of the contemporary imbalance between the legislature and the executive power which has stimulated so much recent concern for parliamentary reform. Part of the concern has been to make Parliament more democratic, by restricting or altering the powers and composition of the House of Lords (ironically, one of the few cases where executive intentions have been frustrated by the legislature). But the contemporary themes are the efficient operation of Parliament and effective scrutiny of the activities of the executive. Procedural

5   W. Bagehot, *The English Constitution* (1867; see Fontana edition with introduction by R. H. S. Crossman, 1963).
6   See A. King, ed., *The British Prime Minister* (Macmillan, 1969).
7   R. H. S. Crossman, in H.C. 539, 1966–7.
8   R. H. S. Crossman, quoted by John Mackintosh M.P., in *Specialist Committees of the House of Commons: have they failed?* (The Waverley Papers, Edinburgh University Press, 1969).

reform has been seen, rightly, as the prerequisite for effective scrutiny. The pursuit of these aims produces a dilemma neatly expressed by a witness to the 1970 Select Committee on Procedure: 'When you strive for greater efficiency you are interfering with the right of an opposition, which is to delay. To achieve a balance between the two is beyond anybody's comprehension . . . most of the delays that we complain about are the rightful delays of free people in a free society using the instruments that we fashioned for them.'[9]

Democracy or bureaucracy

One defence of the imbalance between the executive and the legislature is that government must be allowed to govern, and that the efficient administration of public affairs is just as much in the interests of the citizen as the ability to obtain redress or to restrain executive action. The question of efficiency has been a surprisingly constant factor in English constitutional history. The early struggles between Parliament and the Crown frequently hinged on the question of the control of supply and taxation; and in practice this implied a concern that the Crown should not with impunity indulge in reckless or extravagant expenditure, though it was the propensity for monarchs to do just that which gave Parliament some leverage in this long negotiation. Although Charles I managed quite effectively for eleven years without parliamentary financial support, he was finally obliged to grant redress of grievances in return for badly needed finance: this redress took the form of several measures intended to restrict the royal prerogative, and to entrench the idea of a permanent legislature in some degree of balance with the executive. The constitutional proposals of 1641 were soon overtaken by the Civil War, but provided a significant guide for future constitutional debates. The greatest single landmark was the 1689 Bill of Rights, which in effect listed James II's abuses of power, and declared them illegal. The executive accepted explicit restrictions upon its power, and the principle of Parliamentary supremacy was beyond dispute. But the revolutionary settlement also made clear that power had not simply been transferred from the Crown to Parliament; there had rather been a readjustment of the balance between these branches of government to reflect the changed realities of the political relationship between the old monarchical 'party' (the Tory party) and the parliamentary 'party' (the Whig party). Henceforth the political conflicts between these parties would focus on the Tory wish to preserve an essentially moderate constitutional compromise, and the Whig desire to give the broadest possible construction to the settlement in terms which would further extend parliamentary powers while permitting government to continue with reasonable despatch. Crudely expressed, the political balance between Crown and Parliament rested on their capacity for mutual obstruction: the Crown could dissolve Parliament at any time, and Parliament could refuse finance to the Crown at any time. The main requirement, therefore, was a system of political bargaining which would ensure

9   Lord Maybray-King, in H.C. 538, 1970–1.

that these ultimate powers were not often used. In the eighteenth century, 'the politics of influence' became central to the maintenance of a constitutional balance, and underlay the development of political interests and factions and their coalescence into two major political parties. At first the organisation of political groups was founded on patronage; today, though political patronage still provides some lubrication for the wheeling and dealing of inner party politics, it is ideology, or at least common identity which provides the cement for party construction; and the creation of mass electoral politics through a reforming sequence beginning in 1832 and ending only in 1928 stimulated political parties to orient themselves both ideologically and organisationally to the new electorate. Today this means that a member of Parliament, though constitutionally representative of his whole constituency and its electorate, is in practice elected not as an individual but as a party supporter who must give that support when required to in Parliament. The electoral system tends to reinforce the position of the two major parties (now Labour and Conservative), who from time to time exchange the offices of Opposition and Government. Each administration is formed by the leadership of the majority party, until such time as another general election is held.

A useful consequence of this two-party system of parliamentary government is that government is relatively stable, and the transfer of power between political groups is achieved in a peaceful and orderly manner; conceivably this is the principal function of our present Parliament. An adverse consequence is that Parliament is insufficiently independent of the executive to exercise effective restraints upon executive power. The true relation between the exercise of executive authority and the restraint by the legislature of executive action is made obscure by the operation of one of the principal constitutional conventions, the responsibility of Ministers to the legislature. This convention played a significant part in institutionalising the shift of power from the monarch to Parliament and is central to the notion of the political responsibility of Ministers to the people. Two developments have conspired to weaken the effect of this convention. First, the development of party government, which means that Ministers are in essence answerable only to their own party. Secondly, the expansion of the activities of contemporary government to a point where Ministers are technically answerable for an enormous range of bureaucratic activities of which they can have no actual knowledge. Moreover, the scope and complexity of policy-making in public affairs means that civil servants are closely involved in the formulation and presentation of policy proposals. Yet Parliament has no way of compelling civil servants to answer questions about policy; and no way of obtaining redress from civil servants who have been in error.[10] The weakness of the convention is now widely acknowledged, except by Ministers and civil servants, who have a vested interest in retaining a useful device for the diffusion of legislative scrutiny. When constitutional procedures become a shell for some other

10   The classic instance is Crichel Down, when the Minister of Agriculture was compelled to resign, and senior officials found culpable by a public enquiry suffered nothing more punitive than a transfer to other departments. For an account, see R. D. Brown, *The Battle of Crichel Down* (Bodley Head, 1955).

reality, they become dangerously archaic, obstruct the progress of constitutional change, and bring constitutional procedures into disrepute.

The state and the individual

This point leads directly to the problem of government which has been a feature of constitutional growth since earliest times: the problem of control. All constitutional activity in the end relates to the wish to limit the arbitrary authority of powerful individuals or groups and to prevent the unrestricted exercise by individuals or groups of the formidable powers of the state. The growth in the scale of operations of the modern state and its penetration of most areas of individual activity have given a special character to the problem of control in the twentieth century. Earlier in English history, the struggle to control arbitrary authority centred partly on Parliament, partly on the assertion of a system of law which provided some degree of protection to the individual. The operation of the rule of law and the principle of equality before the law have been the main safeguards of individual rights, which nowhere find explicit expression in constitutional terms. The judiciary and the courts occupy a significant role in upholding the rule of law, and one of the central features of the revolutionary settlement was the entrenchment of judicial independence by the 1701 Act of Settlement. Today, the rule of law is so much part of British political culture that people are rarely fully conscious of the benefits of such a system; by comparison, constitutions elsewhere which make considerable formal provision for the protection of individual rights and liberties have failed to give full protection in practice, because of the absence of a deeply-embedded tradition of rule of law. Nonetheless, there is cause for concern about the individual citizen's relationship with the state in contemporary Britain. In the face of bureaucratic action, the citizen has two traditional channels of redress: through the courts and through Parliament. Yet the weakness of Parliament in relation to the executive makes it an uncertain support for the aggrieved citizen, and the complexity, delays, and expense associated with the judicial process makes it an unlikely resort for the average citizen. In the absence of a system of clearly defined public law, or of clearly defined and readily available channels of redress against the state administration, the average citizen may feel helpless, frustrated, baffled, or alarmed.[11] There is the clear danger that the citizen will feel alienated from the state, despite the considerable benefits derived from large-scale government. The distrust of government and its servants is not new: and perhaps a healthy distrust of big bureaucracies is a natural and self-protective posture. But government itself could do much more to obtain acceptance and co-operation. British government is bedevilled by secretive attitudes to its own work, a 'secrecy . . . founded on a fear of effective criticism'.[12] The 'King's government' has always been secretive; and the

---

11   The attitude survey carried out by the Royal Commission on the Constitution (and summarised in their *Report*, Cmnd. 5460, 1973) provided evidence that these feelings are widespread.
12   J. A. G. Griffith, *Parliamentary Scrutiny of Government Bills* (Allen & Unwin, 1974), p. 257.

'King's servants' have always employed the rule of confidentiality in their own interest as much as in the interest of the state. But undue secrecy is not in the interests of the modern state and its citizens, not only because of the fragility of the instruments of redress against arbitrary executive action, but because the complexity of public affairs requires considerable openness in the policy-making process. Secretiveness has damaging effects upon the executive itself: 'Very often a "secret" classification on a paper is no more than a way of drawing attention to its importance; and a draft with no security marking has little chance of being taken seriously. It becomes more important to keep one's thoughts on policy confidential than to get them right.'[13] Perhaps this has always been so: but getting policy right is today more significant for larger numbers of people than was the case when policy-making was the province of autocratic monarchs and a few trusted advisers. The very scale of contemporary government and its activities makes more necessary a precise definition of the powers and obligations of the state, and the rights and duties of the citizen. Statute law provides only a partial definition; and the arguments for a new Bill of Rights look stronger as government expands. Control and restraint of the arbitrary exercise of state power remains a central concern of British constitutional debate, but just as the relation of state to subject has taken new forms, so must there be new forms of restraint and new instruments of redress; alternatively we must follow a sound tradition and adapt the old forms and the old instruments to new situations and new requirements.

II

'Something new is necessary for every man and every nation. We may wish, if we please, that tomorrow shall be like today, but it will not be like it. New forces will impinge upon us; new wind, new rain, and the light of another sun; and we must alter to meet them.'   (Walter Bagehot)[14]

Political institutions are like people in one respect: they have a long life, marked by growth, progressive change, ageing, and decay. But unlike people, political institutions can be rejuvenated, and so live longer; we might say that in the process they become new institutions, and so re-enter a familiar cycle. But they might in many respects retain some of their earlier forms or characteristics, so that the reality of the new institution is clothed in older garments. Such discontinuities of form and content can be misleading to the ordinary observer; yet this apparent discontinuity fulfils a useful practical purpose: it enables changes to occur and be accepted with the minimum of social and political dislocation. People accept what is new more readily if it has a comfortingly familiar appearance. But the discontinuities of form and content are a headache to the political scientist, anxious to disentangle the 'real' from the 'unreal' characteristics of political systems. Indeed many political scientists decide to ignore the 'unreal' elements and concentrate on the 'real'

13 S. Brittan, *Steering the Economy: The Role of the Treasury*, (Penguin, 1971), p. 63.
14 W. Bagehot, 'Physics and Politics', *Collected Works*, vol. VII, p. 76.

elements in political systems. In doing so, they make an over-confident jump to the position that formal institutions are mere superstructures of real political systems and have no useful place in the analysis of political systems. This view results from the tendency to treat political institutions as if they had no history. That this tendency arises from a laudable desire to understand and explain political phenomena 'as they really are' does not alter the fact that impatience with the history of 'things as they are' is a sort of intellectual illiteracy. It is an approach which, apparently pragmatic, leads unerringly to a level of abstraction far removed from actuality; an approach which, searching for clarity, leads only to obscurity or opaqueness. The failure derives from the inability to comprehend the real life of formal institutions, their reflection of political values and ideas, and the essential continuity of this interaction over long periods of time. The process by which changes occur involves both formal and informal phenomena; the informal phenomena invariably provide the basic material of change, but the formal phenomena often provide the crucial evidence of the reconstitution of that material. In short, we frequently recognise change by the formal appearance; though we can only explain change by analysis of the informal process, which is likely to be compounded of social, economic, political and intellectual events and movements.

Change in British government over the past thirty years has been astonishingly many-sided. There have been major changes in the organisation of central government, the administrative machinery for planning public expenditure, the management and structure of the Civil Service, the structure of local government, the machinery for redress of grievances, Parliamentary committees and procedures, the internal organisation of public corporations, the health and water services, and not only in the whole national structure of constitutional government, but in the external relations of the national structure. The whole period might be described as a period of transition from one clearly defined and understood, but outdated system of government, to a new system of government as yet shadowy and imprecise, were it not for the surprising fact that all these changes in our governmental arrangements have been emphatically unsystematic. Change has been spontaneous and piecemeal, in some areas quite drastic, in other areas only marginal. At no point has there been any appearance of a master design into which the many pieces of the jigsaw could be fitted. Perhaps the notion of a master design is unrealistic, since to obtain such a controlling scheme of things would have required a massive political negotiation and a remarkable degree of consensus over a wide range of constitutional and administrative issues. Yet in a political system, by definition, even one change in one part of the system must have consequences for related parts, and (logically) for all the other parts. In a controlled process of change, the consequences for the whole system of a change in a part of the system must be predicted if the outcome expected from the change is to be the actual outcome; otherwise the process of change will do no more than produce unanticipated consequences and leave the system in disarray. It is not difficult to imagine the problem of controlling the process of change when many reforms take place simultaneously, or in rapid succession. The more piecemeal and *ad hoc* the process, the more unpredictable and uncontrollable will be the final outcome. The 'new' system, produced by pressures to reform an outmoded system, will in practice be a certain formula for continued and everlastingly haphazard, reformulation.

To set this out is to describe the reform process in British government not only over the past thirty years, but to some extent in previous 'reforming' periods, notably the 1830s and thd 1870s and 1880s. To describe the process in these terms is apparently to condemn it. But the condemnation of actual events serves little explanatory purpose; it is more important to explain why the process should wear such an air of uneasy inevitability. The explanation is to be found in the nature and operation of the British political and administrative process, and in the strength of British political cultural traditions. In the first place, a strongly marked political culture is inevitably conservative: hence the (already remarked) attachment to familiar forms, whatever changes of content might be taking place. Linked to this is the inherent conservatism of large-scale and complex organisations (such as British governmental structures exemplify). Lindblom's view that in such structures, the rate and scope of change must be marginal and incremental rather than total and radical, is manifestly accurate, if philosophically unsatisfactory.[15] The process of contemporary governmental reform in Britain appears to match all the requirements of the incrementalist concept: that problems will be repeatedly attacked rather than solved; that solutions will be remedial, moving away from observed difficulties rather than towards agreed objectives; that policy-making and analysis will be socially fragmented, and will go on at a large number of points simultaneously; that the analysis of consequences will always be incomplete; and crucially, that decisions will be shaped by what existing power structures will tolerate. In short, in a relatively stable political system, the intrinsic qualities and internal constraints of administrative and political processes will be the crucial determinants of political and constitutional change.

From that point, it is a short step towards the understanding of the structural nature of political and constitutional change in Britain. An examination of the major contemporary changes indicates an obsession with structural forms: we wish to improve the quality of local government, of health services, of Parliamentary effectiveness, of the whole system of government: in all cases, we have sought a solution in structural reorganisation. Structural change is the favoured device of the incrementalist decision-maker, because it is possible thereby to produce the appearance of change without the reality. Invariably, the people who inhabit the new structures will be the people who inhabited the old structures, and they will often bring with them their old preconceptions and behaviour, soon learning to mould the reformed structures to unreformed intentions. But structural solutions also

---

15   C. E. Lindblom's construct of *disjointed incrementalism* envisages a bureaucratic organisation in which past policies are continued with the least possible modification to suit
changing circumstances. The basic assumptions are that rational decision-making is
impossible; that even if a theoretically rational choice can be established, it cannot be
implemented; and that decisions will be geared to the existing power structures, rendering
major innovation unlikely. See *The Intelligence of Democracy* (New York, Free Press,
1965) and *The Policymaking Process* (Prentice Hall, 1968).

reflect a basic error of analysis, where analysis concentrates on the defectiveness of structures. This proneness to a pre-emptive form of diagnosis puts the whole body politic at risk, and emphasises the most significant weakness in the British reform process, that is, the tendency to define in formalistic and organisational terms problems which fundamentally are political and ideological. There is a curious reluctance to explore a range of political and ideological alternatives, to choose between these alternatives, and only then to create a structural pattern to give effect to clear political choices. This is not to say that political choices are not in evidence; indeed, it is the political configurations which determine what types of structural reform are acceptable. Local government reorganisation is the clearest example of a reform process in which the considered proposals of a relatively impartial Commission were transmuted into arrangements more in line with the views and wishes of politically powerful groups in local government. Proposals by a Constitutional Commission for the limited devolution of government to Scotland and Wales are undergoing a process of implementation dictated almost entirely by the political calculations of the major parties at Westminster; proposals for reforms in the machinery of redress of grievance have consistently been watered down in response to the cynical reluctance of a powerful executive to have itself too closely held to account. Indeed, the reform of government constantly stumbles into a *Catch 22* situation where government is in need of reform, but it is an unreformed government which is required to introduce reform. This sort of situation produces a species of lip-service reform which leaves inviolate the fundamental issues involved in the relation of modern government to society, and provokes a series of marginal (or 'incremental') reforms which have no systematic or planned relationship. A comment attributed to Petronius, writing in A.D. 66, describes the situation exactly: 'We trained hard, but it seemed that every time we were beginning to form up into teams, we would be reorganised. I was to learn later in life that we tend to meet any new situation by reorganisation, and a wonderful method it can be for creating the illusion of progress while producing confusion, inefficiency, and demoralisation.'

It has been suggested that incremental change is all that is possible in the administrative world of political man. If this is so, then we can never hope that radical social change can be achieved through reform of our political institutions, and this is what political and constitutional change is about, if it is about anything. The reform of local government in Northern Ireland demonstrates that institutional change *can* be radical, if the political climate is complaisant. But it also retails to us the bitter lesson of experience, that radical institutional change is always more likely to be generated by an unstable political system than a stable one; and this too often means that the benefits of institutional innovation are neutralised by the uncertainties of political conflict. The unstable political system is most likely to stimulate institutional change, and least likely to safeguard new institutions. Stable political systems are more likely to safeguard innovations, but less likely to produce them. For these reasons, it may be that we should regard incremental changes within stable political systems as the only viable type of administrative reform; and it is worth remembering that a series of incremental changes can, in the long run, produce fundamental changes: that they will always be sloppy and unco-ordinated may be the price to be paid for the continued existence of stable institutions. It is less important that the train should be on time than that we should be free to travel.

What's wrong with British government

'The constitution . . . of England must be to inquisitive men of all countries . . . an object of superior interest.'   (Hallam, 1818)

There has been ample material from both participants and academic commentators on the defects of the British system of government, but the attitude survey specially commissioned by the Royal Commission on the Constitution provided evidence that most people are frustrated by the complexity and impenetrability of government, alienated by its remoteness, and worried by what they see as undemocratic tendencies.

See also **46, 47**.

1 THE COMMISSION ON THE CONSTITUTION

Extracts from *The Royal Commission on the Constitution 1969–73* (The Kilbrandon Report, Cmnd. 5460, 1973), reprinted by permission of H.M.S.O. These extracts are from the Majority Report.

266. In our efforts to determine the nature and extent of dissatisfaction we have had a great deal of help from our witnesses, many of whom have had first-hand experience of government, at all levels from the Cabinet downwards, while others have devoted their lives to study of the problems with which we are concerned. But we decided at an early stage that in addition we should do what we could to find out the views of the general public. We therefore commissioned the Government Social Survey to arrange for an attitude survey to be carried out on our behalf . . .

267. . . . . The questions were confined to the themes of participation, nationalism and devolution, which seemed to us to be the most important when the survey was commissioned.

268. This limitation meant that to all intents and purposes the only specific 'solution' put to those being interviewed was some kind of devolution. The answers given to questions about devolution reflected a fairly widespread interest in some moderate degree of change in this direction, and this finding has influenced our thinking. It must be recognised, however, that if a person is dissatisfied, and he is presented with only one suggested remedy, then he may be expected to take a generally favourable view of that remedy, whatever it is, even if he has given no previous thought to it. This factor, taken in conjunction with the specialised nature

of the subject and the technical limitations inherent in all attitude surveys, suggests that the survey results should be used with caution . . .

269. Using all the information available to us we have tried to track down the main sources of dissatisfaction with government. Inevitably these overlap and run into one another, but nearly all the complaints of substance seem to spring either from the centralisation of government in London, or from developments in the operation of government which have tended to run counter to the principles of democracy . . .

CENTRALISATION

270. We have described in Chapter 8 the enormous increase in the scale of government in recent times, including the advent of the welfare state and the assumption by government of responsibility for ordering the economy. The greater volume and complexity of government has inevitably increased the importance of the central co-ordinating role. There is a feeling in some quarters that only those at the centre can know all that goes on, and that only they are properly qualified to assess all the possible repercussions of taking any particular action. They must therefore have the last word. The contrary argument is that while the growth in the volume of government has increased the power of those at the centre, it has resulted in ever greater demands upon them and made it quite impossible for them to have a full grasp of all that is going on. In trying to reconcile the many conflicting interests it is all too easy for them to finish by pleasing no one. The recipients of their edicts out in the regions have become uneasy about the quality of the decisions being taken, and have come to question the need for the centralisation of so much power in London.

271. Discussions with a large number of people, especially those engaged in public life, have given us a clear picture of the typical complainant. He is a man of ability and experience, connected with an important local authority or perhaps with some regional body such as an economic planning council. He knows his locality well, and is confident that the solution which he and his colleagues propose for a particular problem is best for the people living there. He may well have gone to the trouble of visiting London to explain his views. But often, and not infrequently after what he considers to be an unreasonable delay, he learns that his proposed solution is not endorsed by the central government. Possibly the decision is conveyed to him by a junior official, and it may be based on professional or technical advice which appears to him to be no more, and perhaps less, authoritative than that available locally. He suspects that the matter has not received the same quality of attention in London as he and his colleagues have given to it locally, and he is perhaps frustrated because the decision is based on factors of which he has little direct knowledge and which he is not fully competent to dispute. He is left with the feeling that the obvious and commonsense thing to do has been vetoed, and that if those in London had been as familiar with local circumstances as he is the result might have been different.

272. This picture of the typical complainant — and there are others not so much

in the public eye — is illustrative of a feeling that there is too much control from London over things which people in the regions regard as primarily their own concern. It has been put to us that the United Kingdom is the largest unitary state in Europe, and among the most centralised of the major industrial countries of the world. While not all our witnesses accepted that the consequences of centralisation are necessarily bad, the predominant view was that government is too centralised in its operations to deal properly with the whole range of functions which are now its responsibility. Such over-concentration of responsibility was said by one witness, quoting an expression originally used to describe the centralisation of government in France in an earlier age, to produce a state of constitutional ill-health characterised by 'anaemia in the extremities and apoplexy at the centre'.

273. The fact that these complaints are made does not mean that regional critics are careless of wider national considerations. They realise that they cannot always have things their own way. But when people in other regions see that year by year the South East of England prospers, apparently regardless of the economic climate, whereas, despite the operation of regional policies designed to help them, they do not, they naturally begin to question the system and to ask whether the economic and social policies being applied are the best that can be devised to meet their particular needs.

The allocation of public expenditure

274. We received from representatives of local authorities and regional economic planning councils frequent complaints about the allocation of public expenditure in the regions. What these people seem to want more than anything else are a fair share of public funds for their regions and a voice in determining its allocation to the various services so as to ensure that regional as well as national considerations are taken into account.

275. On the question of fair shares their knowledge about what the various regions of the country are getting is incomplete, and there is insufficient information published to enable them to work it out. On the allocation of funds within the region they are largely in the hands of the central government. Because the government is responsible for managing the economy, and for ensuring that national policies and national standards are applied, it exercises considerable influence over the allocation of all public expenditure. But people in the regions complain that allocation at national level often fails to produce a commonsense result on the ground. Priorities between the various services — education, roads, hospitals and so on — are decided by the Cabinet. A balance is struck at national level, and this is broadly reflected in the allocation of expenditure to the various services throughout the country. Under this system the Cabinet might agree, for example, that there should be a special drive to improve facilities for primary education, and a particular authority might be given permission to build a new primary school. But what if everyone locally is agreed that a new road or hospital is much more urgently needed than a new primary school? In such circumstances — which are evidently

not unusual – people in the particular locality feel that they should be able to forgo the school for the time being, and have the road or the hospital instead.

276. The central government, however, will not normally allow public funds to be switched from one service to another in this way, at least between the 'key' services for which it accepts special responsibilities for determining standards and co-ordinating developments. It considers that, if such transfers were permitted, national policies for the various services might be undermined. If a number of authorities decided to use their primary school allocation for other purposes, the intended drive on primary school building might peter out; and the additional use of funds on roads and hospitals would in effect change the order of priorities decided by the Cabinet. Looked at from a national point of view it would also upset the balance of fairness in services between one area and another. In the eyes of Whitehall an area which chose to build a road instead of a primary school might not have so pressing a need for new roads as some other areas; and those other areas might not be able to use their school allocation on roads because their need for schools was even greater.

277. And so, for these reasons, regional preferences may be subordinated to national policies, and on occasion the results may seem nonsensical to local people. While they do not ask for more than their fair share of public funds, they do not see why they should not be given greater discretion to spend it in the way desired by the majority of local people. Local authorities already have some discretion to allocate expenditure among the various services for which they are responsible, and there have been changes in this respect while we have been sitting; but this dis-cretion is said to be much circumscribed in practice, while a large part of public expenditure in the regions is not under local democratic control at all.

Lack of co-ordination between government departments

278. Another cause of complaint is that the central government is so large that its right hand does not know what its left hand is doing. Whitehall is said to speak with too many voices, and not to co-ordinate its activities sufficiently to ensure that the operations of the various departments fit in with one another and make sense in regional terms. This is another consequence of looking at everything on a service or functional basis at national level. What some people want to achieve is a regional view. Subject to the overriding needs of national economic control, they would like to see the central government in London confining itself to laying down general policy, leaving the lesser policy issues and detailed administration to be dealt with locally. In this way they would hope to achieve a blend of government activity more in keeping with local wishes.

Civil servants in the regions

279. Although representatives of the regional economic planning councils were at pains to commend the work of the civil servants on the regional economic planning

boards, other witnesses said that many civil servants stationed in the regions were too junior, and that the more senior appointments tend to be filled by older men towards the end of their careers. With one or two exceptions, officers working in the regions were said to have insufficient authority and discretion to settle things on the spot. Too much was governed by central policy or had to be referred back to Whitehall. And however identified an officer might become with the interests of the region in which he worked, his first loyalty was inevitably to his own department. Apart from any other factors, that was where his promotion prospects lay. In discussions about possible governmental arrangements at regional level, the point has often been made to us that the civil servants responsible for administering regional affairs should be answerable to some regional authority. And it has been suggested that the country as a whole would be better served if a tour of duty away from London were to be regarded in the civil service as a normal and desirable feature of the able officer's career.

Political life in the regions

280. It was put to us that the lack of administrative authority in the regions and the concentration of government power generally in London mean that political talent in the regions is not given a proper chance to develop. Those likely to be most effective in helping to develop a rich and full life for a particular region will usually be men and women who themselves belong to that region and are the most talented people in it. The complaint is that at present only a small minority of them are used in government. Able people tend not to enter public life because they cannot see that they will be able to achieve anything worthwhile. Some able people who were attracted to service on the regional economic planning councils when they were first set up in 1965 quickly lost interest when they found that they were given no real authority or influence. In this respect our system of government has been compared unfavourably with that of West Germany, where there are positions of considerable political power at the regional level and it is not uncommon for able men to move either way between national and regional politics.

281. People concerned about the lack of a strong political life in the regions argue that if political power could be transferred to the regional capital, then other centres of power — commercial, industrial and cultural — would also be attracted to it, as they are now attracted to London.

282. The point is made, however, that regional political power in the formal constitutional sense could still be practically useless unless it were to be accompanied from the centre and throughout the administrative machine by a new style of thinking, positively favourable to devolution and based on co-operation rather than the exercise of central authority. One of the most common complaints by local authorities is that, although in theory they have considerable freedom of action in the services which they administer, in practice their options are heavily circumscribed by the need to conform to national policy and by Ministerial edicts, often extending to quite minor matters — school building plans and minor traffic regulations are

just two of many examples. And there is unease in local authority circles about the way in which some Parliamentary Select Committees have begun to concern themselves directly with matters which fall within the statutory responsibility of the democratically elected local councils.

Imposition of uniformity from the centre

283. Many witnesses felt that one of the most unsatisfactory consequences of centralisation was that regional diversity was dwindling. It is said that national policies and standards, imposed from the centre supposedly to ensure fairness between one region and another, tend to produce a uniformity which is inconsistent with the retention of a distinctive regional character. On the other hand there is evidently widespread pressure in some fields for the same treatment to be given to all.

284. This is an important question which we have not been fully able to resolve. It is important because one of the main purposes of any system of devolution would be to allow free local choice, which implies variety; and if the public at large did not really want variety there would be much less point in devolution.

285. The evidence on this issue is conflicting. Government departments told us that nearly all the pressures they get are for uniformity, not against it. The typical complaint is that in some way the provision in one particular case is not as good as in other cases. There is a general underlying assumption that everyone in the country is entitled to the best that is going; and it seems that if variety means less for some than for others it is not wanted. On the other hand, as we have already indicated, many people with responsibility in the regions would like to be given freedom to do things in their own way.

286. The attitude survey suggests that on this question members of the public at large are fairly evenly divided. When respondents were asked whether they thought that the standards of the various social services should be the same in every part of Great Britain, or that each region should be allowed to set its own standards, 53 per cent favoured uniformity and 44 per cent regional discretion. Some parts of Britain which are generally thought to be among those most interested in devolution actually showed a desire for uniformity above the average.

287. The answers given to questions about devolution showed that in Great Britain as a whole 61 per cent of respondents appeared to favour at least a moderate degree of devolution involving more regional responsibility for taking decisions. But half these people would withdraw their support for devolution if it meant that people in other regions would be 'better off financially' than they were; and, not surprisingly, of the 30 per cent still in favour of devolution in those circumstances, two-thirds said that they would change their minds if it meant that they would be 'actually worse off financially' than at present, thus leaving only 10 per cent of all respondents still in favour of devolution regardless of the material consequences.

288. On the question of uniform standards there is obviously a strong feeling

that government should be 'fair' as between one citizen and another. This feeling shows itself in the pressures brought to bear on Westminster and Whitehall. On the other hand the desire for 'uniformity' does not appear to be as great as is often assumed. It may be that the central government, having grown accustomed to ensuring uniformity in some important fields for good and sufficient reasons, also imposes uniformity in other fields out of habit or convenience, and not because the people have manifested any particular desire for it. In those matters which touch the life of the individual very closely, such as the level of social service cash benefits, most people probably do want a reasonable degree of uniformity. It would not seem right to them if, for example, old age pensioners in one part of Britain were to be paid more than those in another part. But in those broader matters which individuals tend to know little about, and in which they have no ready standard of comparison — such as the provision of schools, roads and hospitals, and the standards to be adopted in building them — they may well have no particular desire for uniformity. Their local representatives who deal with these things in practice do not seem to want it. In some fields there are already substantial variations in the level of service provided by different local authorities. And in many fields exact parity of treatment is not practicable.

Congestion in Whitehall and Westminster

289. It was suggested to us that centralisation has led not only to dissatisfaction in the various regions of the United Kingdom but to congestion in the central institutions of government. Indeed this congestion, and the administrative difficulties to which it gives rise, are an important contributory cause of regional discontent. Because Whitehall is trying to do too much the quality of its decisions is said to be adversely affected. Another point made is that while opponents of devolution say it would lead to yet more civil servants, no one has attempted to measure the administrative costs which now arise from over-centralisation — from the duplication of work at different levels and from the ever-increasing time and effort that has to be devoted to co-ordination within the huge government machine.

290. The effects of centralisation on Parliament itself are also much spoken of. It is said that Parliament has become overburdened, and that its procedures are increasingly inappropriate for the volume of present-day business. There is a shortage of Parliamentary time for necessary legislation, and too much has to be left to delegated legislation, which, while being technically authorised by Parliament, in practice receives less Parliamentary attention than it should, in some cases none at all. We have been told that time is nevertheless wasted on minor matters of a kind with which Parliament ought not to be concerned. To the severest critics — often businessmen primarily engaged in the control of large commercial enterprises — Parliamentary procedures seem irrelevant to the efficient despatch of government business. They think it is impossible for Parliament as it now operates to exercise a proper degree of control over essential matters.

General assessment of complaints about centralisation

291. We have recorded the principal complaints that arise from the centralisation of government in London. They are by no means the only views put forward. Some people consider that in an advanced industrial society, concentrated in a few relatively small islands, government must necessarily be mainly from the centre. They say that the social and economic life of the country is so closely integrated, and that the issues of government are so complex, that there is little scope for the dispersal of government power. Although there are exceptions, this opinion is widely held among people with first-hand experience of central government. Some of them might be thought to have a vested interest in maintaining the *status quo*, but their experience must be set against the comparative ignorance of public affairs of a good many of those who hold a contrary view. There is a tendency for the pro-centralist view to be supported also by trade unionists, partly perhaps because they are themselves largely organised on a national basis. Some think too that the interests of ordinary working people and of under-privileged groups will be better protected by a strong central government than by relatively weak regional governments.

. . . . . .

294. Moreover, government institutions are themselves aware of the difficulties which centralisation has produced, and they have for some years been taking action to overcome them. Certain important central government departments have been re-organised to improve co-ordination. The process of hiving off government activities to agencies outside the civil service has begun. Local government is being reformed so that it will become the responsibility of fewer and bigger authorities, thus increasing their negotiating power *vis-à-vis* the central government; and the many different controls over local authorities are being studied with a view to eliminating those that are not strictly needed. Parliament, as we noted in the last chapter, is concerned to improve its own workings. It has to be recognised that, in all these efforts to solve their organisational problems, government institutions are in a much more difficult position than big business; they have many conflicting interests to serve, and no one overriding criterion such as profitability to guide them.

295. Our conclusion, however, is that despite these attempts to improve matters, the degree of dissatisfaction produced by centralisation remains substantial. People working in government, feeling that they are in the best position to form a balanced view, and that they are doing their best to mitigate what they regard as the inevitable evils of any modern system of government, tend to underestimate the strength and quality of the dissatisfaction. On the other hand, many of those who complain tend not to have thought out very fully the implications of a more regional system of government. These implications are many, but one question in particular would need to be answered before any proposals for regional devolution could be safely embarked upon. How far is the general public prepared to accept that matters which are now decided at national level, and subject to representations through Members of Parliament, should in future be finally disposed of at regional level,

with the inevitable consequence of more marked variations in standards between one region and another? The greater the regional discretion, the less guarantee there will be that citizens will be treated alike in all parts of the country in matters which affect their daily lives. The electorate might be prepared to contemplate regional devolution, but it is important that its full implications should be appreciated. In the course of discussing various schemes of devolution we shall later examine more closely what would be involved.

THE WEAKENING OF DEMOCRACY

296. We now turn to complaints about the various ways in which people think that democracy is being weakened. Some of these complaints amount to allegations that the formal machinery of democracy is not working properly; others arise from a more general feeling that the reasonable expectations of a society living under a democratic system of government are not being satisfied. We deal first with the more specific complaints.

The backbench Member of Parliament

297. Members of Parliament appear to be regarded on the whole as sympathetic to the views of ordinary people, and as effective champions of constituents in difficulty. But it is widely thought that the present system does not provide them with sufficient useful work or give them any great satisfaction. Many people are under the impression that the Members' main function in Parliament is to vote for their party. According to this view the rigidity of party discipline has brought the backbench Member more and more under the control of the party whips, turning debate into what one eminent Parliamentarian has described as a ritual dance. It is said that Members are frustrated by their inability to influence the making of policy, and that as a result they tend to seek greater opportunities to interfere with and criticise government. It is suggested that they should have a more constructive role, so that they would not merely act as an irritant to government departments but would advise the administration in the formative stage of policy making. Members of Parliament have themselves complained that at present practically everyone is consulted at this stage except them, and that they are brought in only to be presented with decisions already formulated in draft legislation.

298. The majority of respondents in the attitude survey — 55 per cent — thought that Members do not have enough power and influence over the decisions that are made; and judging by our other evidence the support for this view among informed observers is even greater. There is a feeling that the Member of Parliament has become devalued as the people's representative, and that he ought to be given the status and facilities accorded to his opposite numbers in countries such as the United States. The resources of government departments have far outstripped those available to him. The business of government has become bigger and more expert, and he has been left behind. He is said to have insufficient information and

opportunity to exercise any substantial influence over the policy decisions of the executive.

299. The contrary view is that Members of Parliament do still have considerable power, and that at best the complaints are exaggerated. It is easy to see how the exaggeration can arise. The fact that so few Members appear willing to question the party line in public, much less vote against it, lends support to the notion that they are merely acting under party orders and have little influence on the government as individuals. It is not generally appreciated that the influence of Members is largely brought to bear in committees and party meetings operating off the floor of the House, usually without publicity, and that important Parliamentary votes are often preceded by much pressing and canvassing of individual opinions. Behind the scenes the Member of Parliament is still someone to be reckoned with. Although government policies and draft legislation may be prepared without his participation, they are decided in the light of what Members generally can be expected to support; and their views are sometimes sought in the preparatory stages of legislation through the medium of debates on reports of independent committees or Government Green or White Papers.

300. Although critics often refer to the small amount of influence exercised by the ordinary Member, it seems to us that the real complaint is that the kind of influence which he exercises is increasingly inappropriate for government on the modern scale. Changes in his role are under way, but his influence is still regarded as largely negative. His strongest power is one of obstruction and criticism, and it can be exercised only in relation to what is put before him or comes to his notice. In an age of experts and new management techniques, some Members at least would like the opportunity to be more professional, and to have more direct influence over the many decisions which affect their constituents. They are not content to await their chance as Ministers, but want to be able to participate in government in a more constructive way as backbench Members. In this the weight of general opinion seems to be on their side.

Other criticisms of Parliamentary government

301. It has been suggested to us that the need of the party in power to preserve a majority in the House of Commons from day to day actually results in undemocratic government. The argument is that a small minority on one wing of the government party can, and has quite often been known to, frustrate the wishes of the majority of Members. Because the government needs to retain the support and sympathy of this minority of its Members in order to stay in power, it sometimes draws back from policies which it knows to be right and which on a free vote would be supported by a majority of the whole House. It is said that if individual decisions could be dissociated from the need to maintain the government in power by majority support, there would be greater freedom of executive action and debate. More extensive use of free votes would result in some government measures being rejected; but in that way the democratic process would be properly at work, since if

a majority of all Members is against a government proposal that ought to be taken as a fair indication that the proposal is wrong. Stability under a free voting system could be preserved by appointing the government for a fixed term of four or five years. Many people think that this would help governments to develop their policies more sensibly, in the light of long-term interests, instead of being as at present unduly preoccupied with current decisions and short-term interests.

302. Fixed terms would also remove another constitutional feature to which many people have objected, the Prime Minister's power to call an election at the moment of his choice. This is thought to load the scales too much in favour of the government of the day, particularly since the advent of public opinion polls. Another factor in the timing of elections is the ability of the government to manipulate the economy so as to give it maximum advantage. There have been further suggestions to the effect that the Prime Minister should be appointed by Members of the House of Commons on a majority vote, or be directly elected by a separate poll of the whole electorate.

303. These are the complaints that have been brought to our notice; they may fairly be said to reflect a feeling of resentment that the people's representatives in Parliament are, from day to day, too little in control of what is going on in government and that the electorate is given an opportunity to change its representatives only at the time most favourable to those already in power.

The growth of *ad hoc* bodies

304. A number of our witnesses expressed strong disapproval of the growth of what are generally referred to as *ad hoc* bodies — that is, bodies appointed by the government to execute or advise on particular specialised functions. As we noted in the last chapter, there are now some hundreds of these bodies. They encompass a wide range of government activity, including the nationalised industries, broadcasting, health, education, regional planning, water resources, countryside preservation, forestry, tourism, culture, sport and many other fields. The principal complaint is that they are not democratically elected and in practice are often not accountable to anyone.

305. The complaint comes mainly from representatives of local authorities. The authorities are critical of the way in which they, the elected representatives of the people, have been passed over when the administration of new government functions has been decided upon. They consider that many of the functions given to *ad hoc* bodies, particularly those of an executive kind, ought instead to have been allocated to them. The ways in which the health services and (in England and Wales) the water services are now being reorganised, with some functions being taken away from local authorities and placed under appointed bodies at the regional and local level, have occasioned widespread dissatisfaction, as being out of keeping with the declared intention to strengthen local government. Many local authorities also resent the fact that the regional economic planning councils are not rooted in local government.

306. The complainants say that because the central government is functionally organised it is naturally predisposed to think in terms of functional nominated bodies when new government responsibilities have to be allocated. It is recognised that in the past the geographical areas covered by local authorities have sometimes not been suitable for the new functions to be performed, or that the authorities have been too small and not sufficiently well served by good calibre councillors and staff to inspire confidence in their administrative and technical ability to exercise the new functions satisfactorily. But with the reorganisation of local government into larger and more powerful units, and with improving efficiency, local government leaders think that in future there should be much less reason for setting up *ad hoc* bodies. They believe that many of the functions which have to be performed below the level of the central government should be well within the capabilities of the large new authorities, acting either individually or working together in small groups to cover an area of regional size.

307. The burden of the evidence we have received is that the drift towards government by nominated bodies has gone too far. It is generally felt that where these bodies perform functions which cannot sensibly be performed by a democratically-elected body, they should at least be made answerable to such a body in some way which will ensure that the views and the pressures of the electorate are brought more directly to bear on their activities.

Other complaints about the weakening of democracy

308. The other complaints about the weakening of democracy are inter-related. Before dealing with them individually it will be helpful to outline the general picture into which they fit. We are here moving into a vaguer area of discontent. People are uneasy about the working of government, often without being quite sure who or what is to blame or what needs to be done to remedy the situation. The unease arises from a general feeling that the reasonable expectations of a society living under a democratic system of government are not being satisfied. In varying degrees people are disenchanted with government because, although it is elected by the people and is supposed to serve their needs and wishes, in practice it has developed a momentum of its own which seems to leave them out of account. Consequently there are complaints that government is remote from the people and too much carried on in secret, and that it has enlarged its activities at the expense of individual freedom without giving effective guidance to the public on how to deal with the multitude of government organisations and without providing adequate machinery for appeals against administrative decisions and for the remedy of grievances. People tend to feel that government is not in touch with them, and is not sufficiently sensitive to their views and feelings. So much now happens between elections, or appears not to be influenced by the outcome of elections, that the right to vote for a Parliamentary candidate once every five years or so has come to seem an inadequate expression of the democratic will.

309. Not all of these complaints are strictly related to constitutional reform in

the sense that they might be remedied by the creation of new institutions or by other legislative action. But they are at the very centre of the relationship between government and people and cannot be ignored in any discussion of constitutional questions. In the paragraphs which follow we attempt to explain a little more fully what the problems are.

Participation and communication

310. At the time of our appointment there had been much discussion of a desire for greater participation in government. There had not emerged any clear idea of the form which that participation should take, and one of our most difficult problems has been to determine what 'participation' might mean in practice and how strong and widespread the desire for it is.

311. Greater participation could be achieved by giving existing elected representatives more control over what government is doing, or by increasing the numbers of elected representatives, or by providing for more involvement in government activities in particular fields by persons not necessarily elected but in some way representing the general public. It could also take the form of more prior consultation with people affected by government decisions, or better communication generally between government and people so that the electorate was made to feel less remote from government. Participation could be more effective still if there were greater opportunities for it to be exercised locally; many people would be able to play an effective part in government only in their own localities, and there they would be knowledgeable and understanding about local issues and readily accessible to those affected by their decisions.

312. The strength of the desire for all these different kinds of participation cannot be precisely gauged. The evidence and other information available to us does not for the most part clearly distinguish one from another. There is certainly a substantial demand for a greater measure of control by existing elected representatives, which is the first method of increasing participation. That much is clear from what we have already said about the workings of Parliament and about the activities of *ad hoc* bodies.

313. There are also some indications that it might be desirable to increase the numbers of elected representatives, which is the second method. There is the desire, mainly expressed by people involved in local government, to replace appointed bodies by elected bodies wherever possible. There is also the demand, not unanimous but substantial, for new elected assemblies in Scotland and Wales. And while there is not the same clear evidence of such a demand in the regions of England, it is argued by some respected advocates of devolution that a latent demand exists. Yet, despite the increase in the scope, scale and complexity of government, the total number of elected representatives at all levels is actually being reduced. This will be the effect of the current reforms of local government and it is causing some concern, at least to people in local government.

. . . . . .

315. Some people who would not consider elective office might be prepared to serve in a more limited way. One such way would be to share in the third kind of increased participation we have mentioned — more involvement in government activities by bodies representing the general public. In many quarters non-elected bodies are unpopular, but there will continue to be a need for bodies performing advisory or consumer-watchdog functions, or fulfilling an appeal role, and it will not be practicable for all such bodies to be directly elected. Many of our witnesses, particularly those representing some English regions, were, for limited regional purposes, generally happy with a pattern of representation which included no directly-elected persons but which reflected a wide range of non-government interests such as industry and the trade unions, education and so on, and allowed for some indirectly-elected representatives from local government. In this more limited field of participation the demand is probably not so much for more direct election as for more effective influence. People do not like to be appointed to government advisory bodies and then find that their advice is ignored.

316. That leads on to the next possibility — more prior consultation with those actually affected by government decisions. This could be achieved through representative bodies or through direct contact with the public. The complications surrounding the idea of greater consultation are admittedly immense. All fields of government and all types of decisions are concerned, from important constitutional issues which some people would like to see subjected to a referendum down to quite small planning decisions which may nevertheless have a marked effect on people's lives. We can only record our opinion that, whatever the difficulties may be, there exists a widespread desire for more consultation.

317. Finally, there is the more elusive concept of general communication between government and people — a state of mutual trust and understanding which enables each to appreciate the position of the other so that the people on the one hand will recognise the difficulties of government and the limitations on what it can do, and government on the other hand will be fully and continuously aware of what the people think about it and expect of it. We believe that in this sense there is at present a wide gap in communication. This belief is explicitly supported by the attitude survey and there are echoes of it in our general evidence. Several witnesses suggested that the chief fault of government is its inability to communicate directly and simply with the people. One essential element which seems to be missing is a demonstrated willingness on the part of government to listen as well as to inform. Put simply, the contention is that government needs to do more to discover and understand the views and problems of ordinary people. It should reach out more to maintain contact with the individual . . .

318. Whatever its precise nature and strength may be, the desire for increased participation and communication has not yet crystallised into general support for a particular set of constitutional proposals. Although some proposals are contained in our evidence, the public at large evidently has no clear idea of what needs to be done. There is a vague and diffuse feeling of dissatisfaction with government in general, and some evidence that people think the system could be improved; but,

with the exception of devolution and possibly also of the proposal for a referendum on entry into the European Communities, no specific constitutional ideas have attracted popular support. Popular support for devolution, in the sense that there is a wide public interest in it and it is commonly spoken about at election time, is largely confined to Scotland and Wales. Although the attitude survey suggests that people in the English regions could also become interested in some kind of devolution, so far their interest in it does not constitute a popular demand. And popular interest in a referendum on entry into the European Communities, although according to our impression fairly widespread throughout Britain, arose out of a particular and transient situation and against the background of referenda being held in other countries faced with the same decision. It did not appear to be part of a general and continuous demand for referenda on all important issues.

Secrecy in government

319. In recent years one aspect of communication that has attracted specific complaint is the alleged lack of openness in the conduct of government policy making and administration. It is almost a matter of general agreement that, leaving aside security issues, too much government is carried on in secret. At least, few seem prepared to argue to the contrary. The most outspoken critics say that secrecy in government, although represented as being in the public interest, is often merely in the interest of Ministers and civil servants. They contend that executive secrecy in a much-governed country denies the knowledge which is essential for an informed public opinion, and inhibits effective scrutiny and criticism of the government and administration. Green Papers — that is, government papers of a consultative nature, introduced a few years ago as a step towards more open debate of government policy — have been criticised as being almost as firm in their conclusions as White Papers, and as tending to push the government's favoured solutions. There is a demand for more open government and administration which would encourage wider public debate in the light of full information before conclusions are reached. While it is recognised that this might sometimes cause delay, it is said that in practice the increased public debate would be likely to relate mainly to policies which were in any case of a long-term nature.

320. While there is substance in these criticisms, we think that the expectations of some critics are probably unrealistic. The whole question of secrecy is bound up with delicate problems of diplomacy and practical administration which cannot simply be ignored in the interests of more open government.

The undermining of civil liberties

321. Another complaint is that institutions of government are exercising more and more power over the individual without adequate safeguards being provided to ensure that they treat him fairly. It has been put to us that the law relating to civil liberties and the right to redress leaves scope for the unchecked abuse of adminis-

trative discretion; and that where there is provision for the remedy of individual grievances it is often not effective in ensuring that justice is done. Ordinary people tend to be confused by the wide range of government institutions, and are said to have difficulty in discovering, let alone defending, their rights. The attitude survey suggests that a substantial minority have at some time had specific grievances which have either not been dealt with satisfactorily or have not been presented, often because the individual was reluctant to tackle the organisation concerned or did not know where to go.

322. Fears about the encroachment of government on the freedom and rights of the individual have led to various suggestions for reform. Some advocate a general Bill of Rights — a basic code of rights and freedoms which the citizen could fall back on in all circumstances — and others a comprehensive system of administrative courts to which the citizen could appeal when aggrieved by a government decision which went against him. Another suggestion is that the scope and powers of the Parliamentary Commissioner for Administration should be extended. More generally, it has been pointed out that if the modern tendency towards the hiving off of government functions to separate agencies continues, the case for introducing additional checks on administration to protect the individual citizen would be even stronger.

. . . . . .

CONCLUSION

324. We do not wish to give the impression that we have found evidence of seething discontent throughout the land. We have not. Although the people of Great Britain have less attachment to their system of government than in the past, in our opinion it cannot be said that they are seriously dissatisfied with it. Some dissatisfaction is to be expected, particularly in view of the wide and growing ambit of government responsibility. Because the lives of people are now so much more affected by government than in the past, there are many more potential grounds for discontent. Other advanced countries face similar problems, and for similar reasons. That is no justification for concluding that the problems are insoluble. But it seems inevitable that in picking our way through the field of complaints we shall find some that arise from defects which will simply have to be tolerated, and others that arise from defects which are incapable of cure by changing the machinery of the constitution and which can be made more tolerable only by changes in attitude and practice. No system of government anywhere ever did or ever will leave the people with nothing to grumble about. But many of the complaints relate to defects which can at least be partially remedied. And some sources of complaint which have not so far given rise to particularly vigorous or widespread protest nevertheless contain the seeds of more serious dissatisfaction which may arise in future if remedial action is not taken.

. . . . . .

The present situation

1230. For reasons already discussed people have tended to become disenchanted with government. Their trust in it has been weakened. They are bewildered by it and are not confident that it is operating in a truly democratic way, responding properly to their own views and feelings.

1231. There may be little justification for this attitude to government. Probably most of those engaged in it can justly claim that all their work is conditioned by a respect for what the public thinks. Their lack of responsiveness may be more apparent than real. It is interesting that in dealing with this problem the attitude survey concludes that there is on the part of the people 'a *felt* lack of *communication*'. The implication seems to be not that government does not wish to communicate, but that whatever effort it may have made has not been successful, since people still feel it is out of touch with them. The report says:

> 'There are two aspects to this problem; not only a feeling of lack of communication from local and central government about what they are doing but also a feeling that those in government are not aware of the views of the ordinary person, that they ought to be more aware of them and react to them. What people seem to be feeling a need for is not simply more opportunity to make their views known to those in government (important though this is); the man in the street considers that his rulers should be more positively concerned to know what his problems and his views are.'

If, as we believe, this conclusion is right, the general disenchantment with government may be largely attributable to a failure in communication. Government must demonstrate more clearly to the people that it is willing to put itself in their shoes and to listen as well as inform.

1232. Who exactly is it who is required to demonstrate this willingness and to show more positive concern for the people? When people say that 'government' is remote and out of touch with them, against whom is the complaint directed? Is it Ministers? Is it politicians generally? Or is it officials working in the departments and agencies of government? The roles of politicians and officials are very different and must be considered separately.

Politicians

1233. We include under this general heading Ministers of the Crown who are in control of government. In the eyes of the general public they are politicians first and Ministers second. Their role in government is paramount but temporary. Next year they may be in opposition. It seems that in the public mind politicians, in and out of office and regardless of party, have acquired a corporate image.

1234. Politicians are legitimately concerned with communication for party political purposes, and in their party role they do not expect a very sympathetic hearing from that portion of the electorate which supports their opponents. It is part of our democratic system that it should be so. Nevertheless, as a body and irrespective of their political views, they ought to be generally and continuously respected for the value of the work they do and the way they go about it. It is important that they should be looked upon, in this sense, as trustworthy custodians of government. If they are, people will be encouraged to develop confidence in the institutions of democracy, and will more readily identify themselves with government and feel less remote from it.

1235. We are not here concerned with whether all the complaints made about our system of Parliamentary democracy are well founded. For our present purpose the relevant fact is that they exist. In varying degrees they indicate a mistrust of the present system. And in the minds of the complainants this mistrust can hardly fail to be associated with the elected representatives who both work the system and have power to change it for the better. If, for example, people have indeed gained the impression that the procedures of Parliament are antiquated, ritualistic and inappropriate for the present day, that Members of Parliament are required to engage in criticism for its own sake, lack real influence and have little positive function except to vote for their party, that the will of the majority in Parliament may be frustrated by the need to preserve party alignments, and that, more generally, the Parliamentary franchise gives the people inadequate control, then, whether or not their impressions are a true and fair reflection of the facts, they will tend to hold politicians responsible for what they believe to be wrong, and politicians will find it difficult to gain their trust. It is for politicians themselves to judge the volume and validity of the complaints and where necessary to correct false impressions or consider remedial action. We are concerned only to make the point that if people believe the system to be faulty they will lack trust in those who are running it, and communication on day-to-day matters of government will be made all the more difficult.

1236. It is sometimes the duty of politicians not to respond to popular feeling, but to go against it. They are elected to use their own judgement on behalf of the people. The only sanction which governs them is the risk of not being re-elected. But it seems that Parliamentary elections may no longer be sufficient to satisfy people that government is accountable to them. Elections are held infrequently. In many constituencies the outcome is usually a foregone conclusion, and whatever the result it is hardly likely to indicate where voters will stand on the multitude of issues which will be dealt with by government in the ensuing years. People therefore have a need for their elected representatives to keep in continuous touch with them, so that government, though for the time being in full control, may at least be exposed to the force of democratic opinion and be required to explain the reasons for its decisions.

1237. It might be argued that government is already exposed in just that way through press and radio, and through the now overwhelming influence of television. These media do undoubtedly provide one of the most important links between government and the people. If people nevertheless feel that government is out of touch with them and lacks understanding of their problems, it may be that some part of the remedy is to be found in a changed approach by the media. It could be that they now put out information about government in such volume or in such a way that most people are unable to absorb it and abandon the attempt to do so. Or their particular selection of news and comment may not be such as to reflect adequately either the feelings about government which are uppermost in people's minds or the concern and efforts of government to take those feelings into account. The media do not of course exist simply to act as a forum for democracy. They have other roles, such as the provision of entertainment, which are not in any sense political. But in view of their enormous influence, the effects which they have on the relationship between government and people may need to be better understood.

Public officials

1238. Although politicians are responsible for government and play a prominent part in controlling it, the great bulk of its work is dealt with solely by officials. For many people it is the great mass of departmental machinery which is largely responsible for conveying an impression of remoteness and lack of concern. Indeed it has been suggested to us from within the civil service itself that much might be done to reduce alienation from government by improving communication between the citizen and the various departments and agencies of government.

1239. In the past this has been seen as presenting a number of difficulties with constitutional implications. Departmental officials are responsible to their Minister and for the most part act only in his name. They have no separate authority of their own which would enable them to respond to the public in a less inhibited way. Officials working on policy are not usually authorised to discuss it with the public or with the news media, since this might cause embarrassment to Ministers or be considered discourteous to Parliament. In some cases secrecy is maintained also to avoid commercial speculation or to safeguard national security. Such restrictions on publicity have made it difficult for officials to open their minds to people outside government and reveal themselves as fair and trustworthy people with a genuine concern for the interests of the public. If they cannot somehow be revealed in this light people will tend to assume that they are remote and insensitive planners, maintaining secrecy for their own purposes.

1240. In the executive offices of government departments, where most contacts with the public take place, much of the work is governed by national policies and by the desire to ensure that citizens in the various parts of the country are treated alike. Scope for the individual approach may be limited, and officials for the most part have to apply and defend laws and rules for which they are not responsible and which in fact they may not like. The more able among them are therefore handicapped in their efforts to respond to the public in a helpful way. The less able may retreat into formality, or display impatience which can do lasting harm. And in practical terms the situation is much the same in local government offices. For reasons such as these a good many people have come to expect from officials the kind of response which is adequate but unsatisfying; and when they receive a more encouraging response it does not seem to alter their expectations for the future. They know little of the effort that officials put into government or of the attention given behind the scenes to individual needs.

1241. It is desirable therefore that communication between officials and the public should be improved. But is it realistic to hope that officials performing often unpopular tasks on the authority of someone unseen can be viewed by the general public in an appreciative way? We think it is. The departments and agencies of government have a continuous and long-term function. Each is in touch with the public for limited purposes requiring a certain kind of relationship which can be built up over a period of time. With greater attention to the impression that government is creating, with less formality and more personal contact, officials might appear in a more true and sympathetic light and in practice might become more openly and personally responsible for what they do. Such an improvement could only be brought about from within the service itself. Admittedly it might in some fields add to the cost of government. It could not be achieved without staff adequate in numbers and calibre, since a responsive attitude can hardly be expected from an official who is continually under pressure or one not fully qualified to accept the responsibilities of his office. Much might, however, be accomplished simply by devoting greater attention to communication skills in the recruitment, training and deployment of staff.

The attitude of the people

1242. We have emphasised that communication is a two-way process. The gulf between government and people cannot be bridged by the actions of government alone; the people themselves have an important part to play. They have a duty to exercise their franchise and other democratic rights and to know broadly how government works, appreciating its difficulties and the limitations on what it can do. Their pressures on government should be founded in a responsible attitude and a sense of obligation towards the community. If it is true that higher educational standards have made people more critical and demanding, they should also have made them more understanding and responsible. Complaints about the gap between 'them' and 'us' tend to overlook that the people classified as 'them' are for the most part ordinary citizens doing their jobs to the best of their ability. Except in relation to the specific work they do they also belong to 'us'.

1243. A greater knowledge and understanding of government may well be a key requirement. We have noted the apparently widespread ignorance in Scotland and Wales of the existence and functions of the Scottish and Welsh Offices. We have no reason to suppose that the knowledge of similar matters in England is any greater. It may be that the practical workings of government should be taught as a necessary part of secondary and higher education. Perhaps television and radio could be used more effectively to show people how government is run and give them a chance to comment on it. Education about government is a delicate matter, fraught with political difficulties. But politics often intrude when they are not wanted or necessary. For example, new measures tend to be explained on radio and television by Ministers, who are inevitably concerned with political advocacy. This task might on some occasions be performed in a more useful and acceptable way by the neutral officials whose job it will be to administer the new measures.

Conclusion

1244. The difficulties of communication between government and people have long been recognised, but in recent times two new factors have emerged. These are the enormous growth in the scope and complexity of government and the almost continuous introduction of change. These factors have caused government to acquire the image of a huge insensitive machine with an ever-increasing momentum of its own. There is therefore a growing desire for it to be in some way humanised and brought back into closer contact with the people.

1245. It is possible to take the view that people have come to expect too much of government, that since it is they who have pressed government to do more and more they must leave government to get on with the job and accept the consequences, one of which is the remoteness of government from the individual; and that in any case communication is bound to be imperfect in human institutions and it is unwise to encourage expectations of any real improvement. But neither people nor government seem to take this view. There is evidence that both would like a closer relationship and believe it to be possible. If that is so the future can be approached in a more optimistic spirit. Although a good deal of what government has to do will never be popular, it should be possible to increase the general understanding and trust between government and people to an extent which is well worth striving for . . .

Section II
Parliament

'If the public could nightly see all that passes within our walls, I fear the reverence now so rife towards our respected selves would be woefully diminished . . . there are many men who have actually been scared into silence.'

(J. A. Roebuck, Member of House of Commons, 1833)

The weaknesses of Parliament, and the need to improve its procedures and effectiveness, have been a consistent theme in the post-1945 period: parliamentary reform has been regarded as a critical area of constitutional concern (2, 3). There have been numerous — largely unsatisfactory — attempts to rationalise the complex procedures of Parliament, but the principal activity has been constant review of and experiment with the arrangements for scrutiny of the Executive. The most important types of scrutiny are the examination of departmental administration (4, 5) and the control of public spending programmes (4, 6). Many reformers hoped for more effective scrutiny by specialist committees which would concentrate on the activities of individual departments (5), while the more conventional arrangement was to focus on an area of activity which involved more than one department. The advantage of the specialist committee is that individual departments may be held to account more directly than under the conventional system. The 1969 Report of the Select Committee on Procedure heralded the introduction of a system of scrutiny of public expenditure and administration which enjoyed the advantages of both approaches, replacing the old Estimates Committee with a new Expenditure Committee, with sub-committees divided in terms of blocks of work with a rough correspondence to the activities of groups of departments, and a general sub-committee able to range over the whole field of public expenditure control (6). But the executive have shown a disinclination to continue experiments with committees corresponding to individual departments: perhaps this is an indication of the effectiveness of such committees (5).

Another Parliamentary defect to which reformers have pointed is the complex and confusing legislative process, which has come under great strain as government legislative programmes have continued to expand. In July 1971 the Select Committee on Procedure reported on 'The Process of Legislation', dealing with procedural problems, the difficulty of controlling delegated legislation, and the need to improve the capacity of private Members' Bills to reach the statute book. The Committee also proposed the use of pre-legislation committees, of which there was an example in 1973 in relation to sexual discrimination. The Committee's proposal for a further review of the legislative process was taken up by the appointment of the Renton Committee, which has recommended that legislation needs to be pro-

cedurally less confusing, and more clearly drafted, if laws are to be aptly administered and widely understood (7).

A less publicised aspect of reform relates to Members of Parliament, many of
whom have close links with external bodies, and some of whom have extensive
business interests: these connections raise the possibility that external pressures or
pecuniary self-interest could unduly influence the Member in the performance of
his Parliamentary duties. The decision to have a compulsory public register of
Members' interests was a response to concern over this problem. (8).

A major issue of Parliamentary reform since the turn of the century has been the
existence and power of the House of Lords. Since the Parliament Act of 1911
limited the capacity of the Lords to delay Commons business, there have been
three reforms. The Parliament Act of 1949 reduced the period of delay in business
from two years to one year; the Life Peerages Act of 1958 introduced the creation
of Life Peers; and the Peerage Act of 1963 allowed hereditary peers to renounce
their peerages. The Labour administration of 1966 attempted to introduce a
thoroughgoing reform of the Lords, but was frustrated by the widespread opposition
of both back-benches, although the reform proposals were substantially agreed by
the leaders of all parties (9). The Labour Left preferred abolition of the Lords,
while the Tory Right feared the wholesale creation of Labour peers. The issue can
now be expected to lie dormant until such time as the Lords again contrive to
frustrate the legislative intentions of a Labour government, which is always a possibility in the last year of a Parliament.

Despite the great efforts that have gone into attempts to reform Parliament,
there has not really been a commensurate improvement in Parliament's effectiveness. The reason lies partly in diffusion of aims among reformers, uncertain about
the proper functions of Parliament, and partly in the control which the executive
exerts over decisions about specific parliamentary reforms.

Other appropriate references are 1, 20, 40, 41, 49, 58, 59, 60.

2 WHO GOVERNS BRITAIN?

Extracts from *Who Governs Britain?* by David Owen, M.P., published by *The
Guardian*, 6 Feb. 1974; reprinted by permission of the author. This article is an
example of many critical commentaries on Parliament by back-bench Members.
David Owen is now Minister of State in the Department of Health and Social
Security.

The real problem stems from a growing awareness that Parliament has little power.
Constitutional historians emphasise the separation of powers between the execu-
tive and the legislature in the United States and the fusion of powers in the
British Parliament. This distinction leads many to conclude that because there is a
fusion of power there is also a sharing of power between Government and
Parliament.

The truth is that this supposed power sharing is a facade. What little sharing there might once have been is already substantially eroded. Power could be reclaimed, but it would be a painful process. No Government will easily give back power to the one body that is charged with the responsibility of challenging its authority. No political party will readily accept its own members assuming an independent stance.

When one first enters Parliament, it is surprising to find that the majority of members are content to allow the erosion of power to continue. There is an occasional uprising and an assertion of independence, but apart from the younger members, little sustained enthusiasm for a sharing of power. Predominantly this is because to share power involves responsibility. It involves the acquisition of detailed knowledge which is demanding both in time and effort. It is more comfortable and less time consuming to cling instead to the illusion of power and to forgo its reality.

Parliament is never happier or the benches fuller than when it is debating generalities. It is rather frightened of detail, or specifics, finding security in the embrace of the party whip and in the simplicity of the polarised view. Parliament as presently constituted refuses to come to grips with the complexity of modern government. It appears unable and unwilling to stimulate a more balanced and informed public viewpoint. To challenge the pervasive influence of Government effectively Parliament needs to be seen as an independent force with an authority of its own. The present serious economic and industrial crisis has its roots in a much deeper political crisis. Behind the sloganising and such bogus issues as who governs the country lies the real issue of how the country should be governed. Defenders of the democratic parliamentary system invoke its benefits with pompous rhetoric, but there is far less readiness to recognise democracy's inherent limitations.

There is, fortunately, today a rather wider recognition than even a few months ago of the benefits of conciliation and compromise. Not only are they the natural manifestations of democracy, they are its very cement. Divisions and confrontations are rightly seen to erode democracy at its foundations. Yet division stems from attitudes that believe in and perpetuate polarisation. The parliamentary structure at present seems to many to institutionalise divisions, elevate dogma and foster confrontation . . .

. . . . . .

. . . Participation is rightly judged as a deeply serious political issue. But we mock participation when politicians invoke public opinion polls one day and ignore them the next. When they invoke referenda when politically convenient and then drop referenda when inconvenient. A plebiscitary democracy is fundamentally different from parliamentary democracy and it is hard to see how the two can run in harness. Parliament and government undoubtedly need to develop a far greater sensitivity to people's aspirations and demands . . .

. . . . . .

It is an advantage of our present system for government ministers to be MPs to be subject to questioning and answerable in debate. It is a strength for the Government to be formed from the majority party in the House of Commons and for the Prime Minister to owe his position to his ability to command support not only of the party outside but also the majority of MPs in his own party. It is in contrast a weakness and not one which is inherent in the system that government has gained a position of near total power over Parliament.

It is able to push through the legislature almost every decision large or small. This sometimes works in favour of the party outside Parliament and ensures the preservation of the mandate but it can just as easily operate against the mandate and against the view of the party outside. It is a weakness of our present system that the Whips have been able to rely on an automatic vote of their own MPs. That they can so blatantly manipulate Parliament by fostering the myth that almost all votes are issues of confidence. It is an abuse that Prime Ministers can threaten to call elections with conviction if at any time it appears that they can win through without having any justification in terms of time served or lack of support from their own MPs.

The vote in Parliament which should be the highest manifestation of democracy has become a charade. It is taken on a purely party basis far too frequently and then operates automatically. The formal vote should be the occasion for exercising judgement and thought, undertaken when a Government has refused to reconsider its position . . .

. . . . . .

We need urgently a structure for our parliamentary democracy which will better reflect the collective wisdom of Parliament. Free voting in the House of Commons over the last decade shows surprisingly progressive results. In the present crisis there is a majority for conciliation. Backbench MPs, of course, influence the policies of their own front bench and while some undoubtedly underestimate this influence, supporters of the existing system often cynically exaggerate its strength. The influence is not unreasonably strongest when reinforcing the known views of the party outside.

The bluntest view of the present system is provided by Dick Crossman, himself a former Leader of the House. 'The Labour MP is a GI in a political army whose rifle is his vote. He was sent there as one vote to the majority. That's all he was sent there to do in terms of the party and in terms of most of his constituents.' The remedy lies with the electorate. They can and should demand from their own MP qualities of judgement, independence and vision. MPs cannot all be generals or even aspiring generals but they should not be GIs either.

. . . . . .

One carefully fostered myth that needs to be demolished is that all Government decisions are made by Ministers. As the scope of Government has grown, so the doctrine of ministerial responsibility for all decisions has been devalued. A multitude of decisions involving millions of pounds and deeply affecting people's lives are made under the authority of Ministers, but these decisions have never been discussed or presented even indirectly to Ministers. This area of civil servant decision-making rather than that of major Cabinet decision-making could comprise the most fertile territory for Parliament to establish greater control over Government.

The main weakness in the present parliamentary structure which militates against any sharing of power is the knowledge gap existing between Ministers in the Government and MPs generally. It is this knowledge gap above all which is the root of so many of the violent swings in policy occurring, often overnight, when Opposition make the transition to Government and, more slowly, when Government settles back into a long period of Opposition. At present, while in opposition, political attitudes are all too frequently formed through ignorance of the possible expenditure limitations that face Government. Oppositions are peculiarly susceptible to extra-parliamentary pressure. This party pressure is wholly legitimate and is one of the most powerful influences for change without which Parliament and Government would become far too susceptible to the bureaucratic embrace.

Parliament, however, cannot abdicate from a responsibility to challenge both Government and political parties. At present it has to be admitted that even if the fullest facilities existed for closing the knowledge gap there are too few MPs who actively want to participate in the type of detailed analysis that such work would entail. The individual MP who wishes to participate finds the current research and secretarial facilities woefully inadequate. No one looking back over the last 10 years of British politics can fail to be staggered by the artificiality and posturing of much of parliamentary debate.

Both major parties have adopted policies in government very different from those espoused in opposition. In trying to find an explanation it is too simple to seek refuge in the old slogan that it is the duty of an Opposition to oppose. In some areas there has been a remarkable degree of bipartisanship – Northern Ireland being perhaps the most striking example. But over prices and incomes policy, regional policy, state intervention in industry, foreign policy and defence policy, there has been a ludicrous record of inconsistency. Consistency is not always a political virtue. Politicians must be ready to change their position and learn from experience, but all too frequently changes in policy have not reflected new realities but an inadequate assessment of existing facts, not new attitudes but a narrow, partisan and frequently very transient interpretation of political advantage. Public disillusionment feeds on such a diet.

3 PARLIAMENTARY REFORM

Extract from *Reforming the Commons*, a pamphlet by the Study of Parliament Group (Political and Economic Planning, 1965); reprinted by permission of the publisher. The Study of Parliament Group is an influential group of university teachers and Parliamentary officers interested in the study of Parliament. This extract expresses a reforming philosophy which is widespread in and out of Parliament.

'Parliamentary reform' too often has meant to each Member or publicist one or more hobby horses to be ridden with skill and panache, like Don Quixote's horse, in all possible directions at once. But the work of Parliament should be looked at comprehensively.

Parliament has to be seen as a practical working system. One thing cannot be changed without involving consequences, often unexpected and unwanted, in others. Nothing can or should be changed unless M.P.s are quite clear what it is they have and what it is they want to have.

The British system of government has been uniquely stable because it has been able to combine strong government and strong opposition — effective Parliamentary and public criticism. Thus the Group's evidence showed no sympathy for those few 'romantic reactionaries' (in all three parties, let it be said) who might wish to return to the almost mythological mid-Victorian days of 'the rights of the private member'. Governments must govern, but they will govern better if subject to a kind of scrutiny and criticism which is in fact performed at the moment by Parliament but only in an excessively piecemeal, random and unsystematic manner. That is why the Group based its evidence on the assumption that for a long time effective 'Parliamentary control' has meant not mainly the threat of overthrowing the Government in the House but also the process of informing the electorate, influencing the government by inquiry and debate and scrutinising the administration.

So the evidence of the Study of Parliament Group did not argue for great changes in the basic character of British institutions or of the procedures of Parliament, still less for any fundamental change in the balance of power between Parliament and the executive. They urged rather 'the need to relate together systematically a fair number of changes of detail which have seemed for a long time ... no more than the commonsense of the matter of maintaining the repute and power of Parliament' ... So eager was the Group to keep the horse in front of the cart, that governments must govern, that it stated its basic case in this way:

> 'We consider that there is a strong case for streamlining the passage of legislation, but only if the consequence is to give the House more time, facilities and procedural devices with which to obtain the information that Members require and to study, scrutinise and criticise both the working of the whole machinery of government and the factual assumptions on which policy decisions are made.'

It could indeed be argued that the House quite simply spends too much time considering legislation and too little on the scrutiny of administration. So if none of these contemplated changes is of any great novelty, yet the need for such changes is nonetheless very great. For there is no denying the growth of a scepticism about Parliament which is not entirely a product of ignorance of how antique forms obscure modern realities. It results more from a deep-seated anxiety that Parliament has ceased to perform efficiently its role — however that be conceived — within the constitution ...

4 SELECT COMMITTEES

Extracts from *Select Committees of the House of Commons* (Cmnd. 4507, 1970);

reprinted by permission of H.M.S.O. This Green Paper, published by the Heath administration, reflected in part the important 1969 Procedure Committee report on Scrutiny of Public Expenditure and Administration, in part the current attitude of the executive to 'departmental' committees. The proposals in the Green Paper were supported by the Labour Opposition, and so commanded wide support in the House of Commons.

The proposals of the Select Committee on Procedure

8. In a Special Report to the House in December 1968 the Select Committee on Procedure announced their decision to make further enquiries into the methods of examination and control by the House of Commons of public expenditure and of the choice of priorities in the planning of it. The result of their enquiries was the first Report from the Committee for the Session 1968—69 which was ordered to be printed in July 1969.

9. The Committee recommended that the Estimates Committee should be changed to a Select Committee on Expenditure, whose Order of reference should be — 'To consider public expenditure and to examine the form of the papers relating to public expenditure presented to this House'. The new Committee should have a General Sub-Committee of sixteen members (some of whom would also be members of the functional Sub-Committees) and eight further Sub-Committees (each of nine members) which would be neither 'subject' nor 'departmental' but 'functional', and which would have the following Order of reference —

'To consider the activities of Departments of State concerned with . . . (naming a functional field of administration) and the Estimates of their expenditure presented to this House; and to examine the efficiency with which they are administered.'

It was suggested that subjects might be allocated to the eight Sub-Committees on the following pattern —

Industry, Technology, Manpower and Employment;
Power, Transport and Communications;
Trade and Agriculture;
Education, Science and the Arts;
Housing, Health and Welfare;
Law, Order and Public Safety;
Defence;
External Affairs.

10. The role of the General Sub-Committee would be to scrutinise the projections of public sector expenditure as a whole after an annual debate on the Expenditure White Paper and to consider the adequacy of the material provided and to give an account to the House of the work of Sub-Committees. It would guide the work of the Committees as a whole and co-ordinate the enquiries undertaken with the work of other Select Committees. The tasks of each functional Sub-Committee would be threefold —

(a) It should, first, study the expenditure projections for the Department or Departments in its field, compare them with those of previous years, and report on
any major variations or important changes of policy and on the progress made
by the Departments towards clarifying their general objectives and priorities.

(b) It should examine in as much detail as possible the implications in terms of
public expenditure of the policy objectives chosen by Ministers and assess the
success of the Departments in attaining them.

(c) It should enquire, on the lines of the present Estimates Sub-Committees, into
departmental administration, including the effectiveness of management.

11. The Committee recommended that the Public Accounts Committee and the
Select Committee on Nationalised Industries should be retained and should continue to exercise their present function. They recommended that the House should
decide on the future of the Specialist Select Committees in the light of their Report
and as the occasion arose.

The achievement of the Specialist Committees

12. Some assessment of what the Specialist Committees have achieved is necessary
as a preliminary to considering what should be done for the future. This is not to
pass judgement on the work of individual Committees, but rather to ask whether
this form of Parliamentary scrutiny has been so far justified by results as to warrant
its continuance and whether there are any changes which experience suggests to be
desirable. It must be borne in mind that it is less than 4 years since the first of the
Committees was appointed; given the novelty of the task it was not to be expected
that the full potential of this form of proceeding could be realised in so short a
period. The promise which the Committees hold for the future is therefore at least
as significant as what they have already achieved.

13. Considering first the contribution which the Committees have made to the
functioning of the House, it must be conceded that when − too rarely − their
reports have been debated, the degree of interest shown by other Members has
sometimes been disappointingly small. This may suggest that the House has yet to
learn how to make the most of its Committees − 4 years is a very short period in
the history of Parliamentary institutions − but it is no test of their usefulness. The
indirect contribution which the Committees have made to the quality of debate
and of Questions by making Members better informed cannot be measured, but it is
beyond dispute that they have acquired a growing body of expertise and have
brought together in their reports, for the benefit of the House and the public generally, a valuable body of fact and opinion on some important issues. Further than
that the Committees have, in the course of their enquiries, opened up new channels
of communication between Parliament and interested bodies and individuals
throughout the country. To take an example, the Select Committee on Science and
Technology took evidence from a wide variety of people and representative bodies
including Government Departments, nationalised boards, public corporations,
public companies, learned societies, universities and the Confederation of British

Industry; they met representatives of local authorities and of the Services, and others directly concerned. Members of the Committee travelled in Europe and the United States of America, and visited many places in the United Kingdom in order to make on the spot assessments.

14. It is as yet too soon to assess the contribution which the Committees have made to the formation of outside opinion and their influence on Government policy. But there is no doubt that reports of Committees have attracted widespread publicity in the press and other media and have done much to stimulate discussion of current problems. The influence of the Committees on the formation of new policies is more subtle and in many cases will not be visible for some time to come.

15. This represents a considerable achievement, the more so when account is taken of the difficulties under which the Committees have laboured. New institutions of this sort need time to find the most appropriate style and the Committees have been hampered in the planning of their work by the fact that they were appointed only for a session at a time, and did not know what their expectation of life was. In some cases also, particularly in the case of more technical inquiries, the work of Committees has suffered from shortage of supporting staff.

Proposals for the future

16. The choice would seem to lie in effect between accepting the full recommendations of the Select Committee on Procedure; retaining and developing the system of Specialist Committees along with the Select Committee on Nationalised Industries; and some course intermediate between the two. Although the Select Committee on Procedure recommended the retention of the Select Committee on Nationalised Industries and expressed no view on the future of the Specialist Committees, the Government believe that these Committees could not continue to exist as they are now alongside the proposed comprehensive Expenditure Committee because the combined demand on the time of Members would be much too heavy and the overlap between their fields of inquiry too great.

. . . . . .

18. The recommendations of the Select Committee on Procedure would provide a clean cut and comprehensive solution and avoid any repetition of the difficulties associated in the past with the setting up and standing down of Specialist Committees. There is certainly a need to reorient the work of the Estimates Committee to take account of the 5 year projections of public expenditure in the White Paper and some strengthening of the Committee would be necessary to enable it to discharge this responsibility adequately. But although almost all policies find expression in expenditure at some point, it does not follow that their examination is always best approached from this angle; under such a system subjects with small expenditure implications may not receive the attention that they deserve. Moreover the functional structure of Sub-Committees proposed by the Select Committee on Procedure could not well provide for the consideration of subjects such as Scottish Affairs and Race Relations which cut across this whole basis of classification. And

a Select Committee on Nationalised Industries, able to range over the whole of their activities, would seem a more effective instrument for scrutinising the public corporations than Sub-Committees of an Expenditure Committee, which would be directly concerned only with the corporations' capital investment; it also better reflects the constitutional relationship between the industries and Ministers.

19. These considerations suggest that there would be advantage in a dual system which provided for the retention of the Select Committee on Nationalised Industries and some Specialist Select Committees alongside an Estimates Committee somewhat enlarged in numbers and transformed into an Expenditure Committee. It appears to be the general view that 'subject' Committees are to be preferred to 'departmental', because their inquiries are not inhibited by the artificial limits of departmental responsibility, and the Government do not intend to recommend to the House the appointment of any more departmental Committees . . .

20. The Estimates Committee would be restyled the Expenditure Committee, with suitable amended terms of reference and a membership of, say, 45. These changes would enable the Committee to focus its attention on public expenditure rather than on the Supply Estimates and to examine a wider selection of the issues arising in this field. Because the new Committee unlike the Estimates Committee, would not be barred from considering the policies behind the figures, there would be occasions when it would be appropriate for Ministers to give evidence before it, as they have before the Specialist Select Committees.

21. The new Expenditure Committee should presumably have the same permanent status under the Standing Orders of the House as the Estimates Committee now enjoys; but it would introduce an undesirable rigidity into the structure to afford the same status to the Specialist Committees. It is, however, important for the effective working of the Committees that they should know over what period to plan their work and the Government would propose to make clear on moving for their first appointment that they envisaged the Committees on Science and Technology, on Race Relations and Immigration and on Scottish Affairs as continuing for the remainder of this Parliament, subject in the case of the last named to any reconsideration made necessary by constitutional developments.

22. In the last Parliament the work of the various Select Committees was coordinated by an unofficial liaison group composed of the Chairman of the Committees, presided over by the Chairman of the Public Accounts Committee. The group also played a valuable role as a link between the Government and Select Committees generally as well as providing a forum for discussion of matters of common concern to Select Committees and the Government believe it should continue.

23. The proposals outlined in this memorandum are concerned with Select Committees of the House of Commons only. But there is also scope in the Government's view for making more use of Joint Committees of the two Houses of Parliament to consider matters which are not controversial in the party political sense; such Committees might facilitate the progress of law reform Bills. The Government are considering proposals for this purpose.

Conclusion

24. A system of Select Committees on the lines set out in the foregoing paragraphs, co-ordinated by the proposed group of Chairmen of Committees, would in the Government's view provide an effective machinery of scrutiny without in any way impairing the responsibility of Ministers to Parliament or detracting from the importance of proceedings on the Floor of the House. The proposed system would be flexible and capable of ready adaptation to changing needs and would represent an important development in the structure of Select Committees. It would provide for the increased scrutiny by Parliament of the longer-term projections of public expenditure which the Select Committee on Procedure saw to be desirable, while building on the foundations laid in the last Parliament by the Specialist Committees. The House would have the opportunity of watching the Expenditure and Specialist Committees in operation side by side and at a later stage would be able to decide in the light of practical experience whether to deploy more of its Select Committee resources in the one direction or the other.

25. Any system of Select Committees must make additional work for Ministers, their Departments and, of course, for Select Committee members themselves. It increases the pressure on the parliamentary timetable and the risk of controversy over the proper limits to the confidentiality of the decision-making process. But this is the inevitable price to be paid for the significant strengthening of the parliamentary system to which the proposals in this paper are addressed.

5 SPECIALIST COMMITTEES

Extracts from *Specialist Committees in the House of Commons: have they failed?* by John Mackintosh, M.P. (The Waverley Papers, Department of Politics, University of Edinburgh, 1969); reprinted by permission of the author. John Mackintosh is a leading advocate of specialist committees and was a member of the controversial Select Committee on Agriculture which was appointed in 1966 but wound up in 1968.

Before examining the record of these Committees, it is worth recalling the major reasons why they were so consistently advocated by reformers and why they were successfully resisted till 1966. Many diverse arguments were used to support the proposal but the main point was relatively simple. The House of Commons had steadily lost influence over the executive because of the increasing strength of the party system. In the nineteenth century, the House had dismissed governments without having to face a general election, it had sacked individual ministers and had introduced and carried bills against the government and had taken government measures and defeated or rewritten them. The main two signs of this power were that the House controlled its own timetable and could force a Government to disclose full details of its policies even in such sensitive areas as foreign policy and defence.

All this was altered as the mass electorate voted more and more according to party labels and thus gave the party leaders, that is the Prime Minister and his colleagues, direct control over the MPs. The Government used this control to force the House of Commons to surrender decisions about the timetable to the executive and to give up the House's power to appoint select committees and to order the publication of government papers. Gradually the Commons became reduced to registering the results of general elections and to passing virtually all the legislation put before it. Under these conditions, the Opposition uses the House to explain to the public its case against the Government, while ministers use it to put over their policies. The only influence remaining to the House occurs in special situations when government backbenchers manage to convince the Cabinet that it is in the government's own interest to modify some proposal and such cases of influence are hard to pin down because there are so many other pressures brought to bear on ministers.

Facing this situation, the reformers appreciated that it was not possible to go back to the more open and independent voting of the mid-nineteenth century. Nor was there much use producing more time for backbench contributions if the time-table itself was in the hands of the Government. Direct control over ministers could scarcely be restored to MPs since they had no secure base, no independent position in their constituencies which would enable them to resist party pressure. But ministers are still influenced by public opinion and by the need to win general elections so that the House of Commons could be given a slightly larger place in the decision-making process if, without in any way tampering with party loyalties, it could find out and publicise the real choices open to the Government at any particular time. For instance, in the field of agricultural policy, if the House knew what options were being considered when farm prices were fixed each year, they could understand the alternatives and appreciate the various forces so that the public could learn what was happening and see what return it was getting for the money expended. In this way, the Commons could be given investigatory functions which would: (a) open up an issue allowing outside opinion to focus on the problem before a decision was taken, (b) inform MPs so that debates and questions in the House would be more relevant and therefore testing for Ministers, (c) force Departments and pressure groups to explain their assumptions, do the necessary research and justify their decisions, and (d) bring public attention back to the Commons as it was the place where these investigations were made, as debates then became more informed and as the outside interest groups and the public in general found that pressure through the House could occasionally persuade governments to modify their policies.

To all those, mainly academics, who had thought about the problem, this seemed to be the only way forward. Moreover the standard objections, coming mainly from politicians, appeared to be misguided or trivial. First there was the 'we do not want to be like the French (pre-1958) or the Americans' response, which could be dismissed as an unreal fear since the British political system was quite different from the French or the American and the effect of investigatory committees would therefore be quite different also. Then there was the suggestion that these committees would become involved in policy disputes, start making recommendations and even try to steal executive authority from the Ministers. The obvious answer was that while the party system remained no Minister need pay any attention if he did not want to. The existing committees (on Estimates and Nationalised Industries) realised this fully and therefore avoided making themselves looking foolish by pronouncements on sensitive party issues. Finally there was the curious argument that the House as a whole would resent any attempt to derogate from its position as the ultimate arbiter on policy questions. This seemed the most flimsy objection since it is generally accepted that the House does not exist as a corporate body actually taking decisions on important matters apart from the government. This is why it has not, in practice, resented encroachment by the existing investigatory committees. In any case, the real encroachment is coming from the stream of advisory bodies and commissions being set up by successive governments just because the House is not in a position to investigate problems and produce informed recommendations . . . The reason why these threadbare contentions carried the day until 1966 is that they were not the real explanation for the opposition. It is not always appreciated that politicians groping for a counter-argument often reach back for out-of-date constitutional maxims which seem to cover their position (as when a Minister not wanting to disclose something in a recess says it is his duty to make his first report to the House of Commons).

The real reasons underlying the opposition to select committees are powerful and come from several quarters in the House of Commons and from Whitehall. In the first place, it is mainly outsiders interested in the democratic process who consider that the Commons' primary function is to act as a check on governments between elections and who therefore assume that this is one of the main objectives of MPs. In fact the vast majority of MPs do not accept this. Ministers, shadow ministers and the throng of would-be ministers on each side regard the House as a place where the government defends its position and the Opposition, far from any desire to alter existing policies, wants to make its case to assume in full the same set of governmental powers after the next election. And for the remainder, the bulk of MPs who do not expect to go any further up the political ladder, they likewise have little desire to alter existing policies. On both sides, they are loyal supporters of their front benches and they see the Commons as an extension of the struggle for power which takes place at elections. For all these groups, the idea of select committees of the specialist investigatory kind seems a foreign intrusion into the set-piece confrontations which, for them, is the life of politics.

Moreover, in a sense, they are right in that it is disingenuous of the reformers to keep saying (as most of them have done) that they had no intention of altering the relations between the executive and the House of Commons. If this was true, there would be no point in making the proposals . . . Instead of fixing up legislative proposals in cosy conclaves with the pressure groups and then coming to the House with a 'take-it-or-leave-it' approach, there would have to be public explanations and discussions at a formative stage in policy-making. To introduce such extra and less predictable considerations would mean more work, the strain of increased uncertainty, civil servants would have to learn the new technique of public exposition before rank and file MPs on committees and ministers would have to be able to face much more searching cross-examination than can ever take place under the rules of Question Time . . . In addition, many MPs have other more personal reasons for reacting against these reform proposals. For the ambitious backbencher, the task is to impress ministers and particularly the Prime Minister, for this service on select committees is of no use unless the MP becomes a thorn in the government's flesh and then the impression created is detrimental. Moreover most MPs, ambitious or not, are very jealous lest any colleague should steal a march on them. Clearly no member can serve on more than one or two committees and it would be most galling for some backbenchers to feel that they were being outshone in debates or simply not being called by Mr. Speaker because other MPs either knew more or had a prior claim to speak by virtue of service on the appropriate select committee. In general, MPs are political animals and far more interested in scoring political points than in understanding the administrative processes and narrow options open to any government. Ministers, for their part, find it easier to dismiss broad political attacks than to rebut a careful dissection of their precise choices while many of the orators in the House prefer such broad, if fruitless, attacks to detailed attempts to influence or alter governmental decisions. Politics in part depends on the capacity to sharpen up differences, to paint pictures that are almost caricatures, while government is often the laborious process of explaining how little movement is possible and again the fear that MPs on committee will get so involved in comprehending the latter that they become incapable of the former is understandable.

It is important, therefore, to appreciate that select committees of the kind under discussion were not appointed in December 1966 because the House of Commons overwhelmingly wanted them or forced them on the Government. Probably only some sixty to eighty Labour members, mostly of the 1964 and 1966 intakes, were definitely in favour with a far smaller number of Conservatives in support. The Committees were introduced because the Prime Minister felt they were part of the reforming image the Labour Party was trying to acquire in those years, because he thought they would keep some of the more restless among the new intake happy and because both the Leader of the House and the Chief Whip were (by December 1966) committed Parliamentary reformers . . .

The opponents of the system came from several sources. Some Cabinet ministers, such as Mr. Michael Stewart and Mr. Richard Marsh, felt that Parliament was a power struggle and these committees became, in effect, engines for criticising the Government thus simply aiding the Opposition. They believed that the task of the majority was simply to support their front bench. Some of the supporters of the system had perhaps failed to think out its full implications. Even Mr. Crossman at times talked as if the best thing for the Committees to do was to go off and think up new ideas or document projects which might be of use to the executive rather than to insist on pressing a particular department, week in and week out, about its conduct of affairs.

In this respect some senior civil servants certainly found the Committees hard to take. The departmental committees wanted to discover whether different sections of Whitehall had different views or different priorities. They wanted to know what arguments had gone on prior to decisions being taken. One method of getting this information was to ask whether adequate thinking had been done before new policies were undertaken. All these questions and indeed the whole approach flew in the face of deeply ingrained civil service practice, senior officials having been trained to give the impression that Whitehall was entirely united on every ministerial policy and that all prior research and consultation had pointed to the identical conclusion. Nothing was more exasperating for committee members than to know privately that a terrible battle had taken place in a ministry or between a ministry and the Treasury only to find that not a hint of this or of the issues involved would be admitted in evidence before the Committee. Moreover, the objective of the MPs was not to get ammunition with which to attack the minister, but to find out the arguments and the extent to which alternative policies had been considered. The Fulton Report (published in 1968) argued in favour of more openness by the civil service, but this was a new departure and hard to carry through so long as the doctrine of collective responsibility remained in full force. As a result, when officials giving evidence denied that there had been any debate within the Executive or alternatively put aside all policy questions as suitable only for the minister, mutual antagonism developed, the Committee often resolving the difficulty by calling for a paper on the point at issue. This only made matters worse as busy officials found themselves committed to preparing numerous documents, some of which required considerable research, and they may have suspected that the documents were not really wanted by the MPs and might never be read. There is evidence that a number of civil servants complained to their ministers that they could scarcely fulfil their normal duties because of the burden imposed by the committees . . .

It seems clear that a number of the most senior departmental ministers and officials made their opposition to scrutinising committees clear to the Prime Minister. Some of the ministers resented the committees because of specific clashes, others more as a matter of principle, while the heads of one or two of the public corporations protested that they could be put through the mill both by the Committee on Nationalised Industries and by the Committee on Science and Technology. Finally, among the adverse forces, the Whips Office, though headed by a reformer, Mr. John Silkin, began to have its doubts. The problem that worried them, they said, was the manning of committees. By this, they did not mean the select committees which were always oversubscribed, but the fact that MPs used service on these committees as an excuse for not attending the less interesting (for government supporters) standing legislative committees.

So, adding up the balance in a pragmatic way, this whole experiment raised little or no outside interest. It was a politicians' problem and had the support mainly of the newer Labour MPs, while it antagonised many ministers and senior civil servants. If the Government as a whole, or the Prime Minister in particular, had had any long-established views in favour of reform, that would have settled the question. As it was, the Government was characterised by impatience with backbenchers and their desire to play a more positive role, while the Prime Minister's early background and training in public life has often made it easy for him to identify with the civil servants' viewpoint. For these reasons and despite considerable support in the columns of the quality press, the cause of parliamentary reform and of the select committees, particularly those attached to specific departments, lost ground in the way that has been described.

6 PARLIAMENT AND PUBLIC EXPENDITURE

Extracts from Sir S. Goldman: *The Developing System of Public Expenditure Management and Control* (Civil Service College Studies 2, 1973); reprinted by permission of H.M.S.O. This booklet is based on lectures given at the Civil Service College by a former senior Treasury official. This extract is an account of developments in the arrangements for Parliamentary scrutiny of public expenditure.

... Parliament's increasing concern with the inadequacies of the traditional techniques of public expenditure control in face of the far-reaching developments already described produced the inquiry into Treasury control of public expenditure by the Select Committee on Estimates in 1957. The report of this Committee in 1958 is a landmark in the system's evolution. Though a good deal of it is concerned with older and more traditional aspects of Treasury management, such as prior sanctions to expenditure or delegated powers, and a questioning of the Treasury's need to maintain detailed scrutiny of departmental expenditure, there is much that is forward-looking in the report. As important as anything was its emphasis on control over policy as the key aspect of Treasury control over public spending and the correlative need for early and continuous participation by the Treasury in the formation of spending policies or programmes by departments.

The Committee also laid especial stress on the need for reviews of policy, by which it meant study of those aspects of programmes where expenditure did not or had not varied much over time, to ensure that inertia did not lead to the uncritical acceptance of spending when the original object had changed or disappeared ...

On forward looks, the Committee praised the work that had been done on defence expenditure and its three-year projections but criticised their absence on the civil side. In its comments on this the Treasury again challenged the Committee's strictures. It claimed that three-year estimating was in fact standard procedure, that it played an important part in the Treasury's oversight of public expenditure policy and was regularly reported on by the Chancellor to the Cabinet. Here, too, the Treasury's defence does not at this time sound convincing. All who were then involved in these matters know that the three-year estimates were on the whole regarded as something of a nuisance and engaged little of the attention of departments or the relevant divisions of the Treasury itself. Certainly they were no real forerunner of the Plowden five-year forecasts . . .

All this reflected a fair degree of general dissatisfaction, and any subsequent investigation such as the Committee recommended, basing itself on its analysis and in particular on the weaknesses and gaps it had identified, would no doubt have made some radical recommendations for improvement. In the event however the Plowden Report raised the level of discussion to an entirely new plane and its proposals marked a decisive break with all that had gone before.

Too much has already been written about the Plowden Report for more to be required here. Its decisive contribution to the development of the system of public expenditure management and control can be stated in a few words. What it advocated was a system of long-term assessments, based on five-year rolling programmes for all departments, covering the whole field of expenditure, and considered against the background of the medium-term prospects of the economy and thus of the resources likely to be available from which demands of the public sector had to be met.

Other points made by the report, less crucial but still important, were its stress on stability of public expenditure decisions and the need to avoid chopping and changing of programmes which was wasteful of resources and productive of inefficiency; on the need for improving the instruments for measurement and analysis of public expenditure; and on the importance of better machinery for taking collective decisions by ministers. The Committee also attached weight to the inter-relation between public expenditure and growth of the economy . . .

It is something of an historical accident that publication of the Plowden Report should have coincided with the financial and balance of payments crisis of 1961. Major technical advances had taken place during the preceding few years, for example in the definition of public expenditure, its classification into main blocks, application of the concept of constant prices, clarification of what was meant by 'current programmes' of departments, the place of the contingency allowance and the relative price effect. When the crisis of 1961 broke therefore the skills, experience and techniques were all available to permit the drawing up of the first Public Expenditure Survey of the kind recommended by Plowden . . .

(v) *The devaluation trauma and reappraisal, 1967–68.* Devaluation in November 1967 made necessary a major reallocation of national resources from public and personal consumption to exports and the balance of payments . . .

Some adjustments to programmes took place immediately on devaluation but these were only precursors to the real thing. This was contained in the Prime Minister's statement of 16 January 1968 and embodied in the simultaneous White Paper on *Public expenditure* (Cmnd 3515). All main details of the economies are set out in the White Paper: in defence a major reduction in commitments outside Europe, a cut in the size of the forces and in purchases of equipment, and reduced spending on infrastructure in the United Kingdom. In civil expenditure no increase in social service benefits in 1968–69 and a limit on the next uprating to cover price increases only, maintaining the real purchasing power of benefits but no more; reductions in the rate of housing subsidies, and limiting the rate support grant to local authorities by restricting the acceptable increase in expenditure deemed to be eligible for grant over the next two years to only 3 per cent above 1968–69. In total cuts amounting to £330m in 1968–69 and £360m in 1969–70 were announced, which still left expenditure to grow by a good deal more than GNP in 1968–69 though by substantially less in 1969–70.

This was a change in trend of a monumental kind which could only have been achieved by major alterations in policy. In securing them the whole machinery of the public expenditure control system was thrown into action and employed for the first time at full stretch involving all departments and ministers and the inter-departmental instrument of PESC now much tried and tempered by experience over the years.

. . . . . .

The January 1968 statement and subsequent action were unique in the history of public expenditure up to that time in that they represented a major readjustment of governmental priorities quite different from the relatively modest changes up and down in departmental programmes which had occurred so far. The central feature of the operation in administrative terms was that for the first time comprehensive control over public spending based on clearly defined objectives covering both the earlier and later years of the quinquennium was substituted for indicative planning five years ahead, and was buttressed by determined arrangements for monitoring expenditure against firmly based departmental programmes.

. . . In the Green Paper on *Public expenditure: A new presentation*, May 1969, anticipating some of the Committee's probable recommendations, the government undertook to produce a White Paper in the late autumn as the first of a series embodying proposals set out in detail in the Green Paper. The importance of this commitment was that henceforth all decisions on public expenditure whether in total or on individual programmes would be reflected promptly in material to be presented to Parliament and public. This introduced an entirely new element into the system of public expenditure management, and one likely to play an increasingly important role.

. . . . . .

There are two sides to Parliament's intervention in this field. First there is its probing of the activities of the Executive in managing public expenditure. This has usually taken the form of enquiries by a Select Committee – either Procedure or Estimates (now Expenditure). Secondly there are Parliament's own attempts to organise itself so as to match developments taking place within the Executive and in part the result of its own pressures and recommendations. A remarkable fact that requires explanation is Parliament's relative success and effectiveness in the first of these roles, and the difficulty it has experienced so far in achieving the same degree of success in the second. This leaves the future somewhat uncertain, though not without hope given goodwill, common sense and a measure of luck.

. . . [The Select Committee on Procedure in 1968–69 which returned once more to control of public expenditure and its administration as a subject for study.] In its Report in the spring of 1969 the central problem was clearly stated (paragraph 8): 'Expansion of government activity into many new fields and an extension of the time-scale on which plans for public spending now have to be made have not been matched by corresponding developments in the financial procedures of Parliament.' The Committee went on to make many radical proposals for changes in the activities of Parliament and the material to be made available to Parliament by the government to permit these activities to be pursued. At the same time it took note of and welcomed government intentions for the future as set out in the Green Paper on *Public expenditure: A new presentation*, which had been submitted as official evidence to the Committee. In particular it commended the proposal to issue an annual White Paper comprehensively disclosing the government's policies and programmes for public spending and the suggestion that this be followed by a regular debate. The Committee went on to say, 'Your Committee believe that the annual discussion on public expenditure foreshadowed in these proposals could and should come to occupy as important a place in Parliamentary and public discussion of economic affairs as that now occupied by the annual Budget debate.' It followed this by a number of suggestions concerning the substance of the White Paper most of which were in fact adopted in the first issue of December 1969.

The Committee's recommendation in favour of publication of the medium term economic assessment including all price and income forecasts embodied in it proved too radical for acceptance by the government. On the other hand its proposal that the Estimates Committee be expanded and converted into a Select Committee on Expenditure with functional sub-committees, including a general sub-committee, to cover the whole field of public expenditure apart from those aspects already under scrutiny by other committees like the Select Committee on Nationalised Industries, was adopted, though in modified form, by the subsequent Conservative government.

There was a fortuitous element in the coincidence of the Select Committee's enquiry and the government's internal study of the system of public expenditure management and control which culminated in the Green Paper of May 1969. But the Committee's existence and its known direction of thought undoubtedly influenced the government's determination to advance on lines set out in the Green Paper. To this extent Parliament once again played its catalytic role, helping to break down resistance to change and furthering progress.

This role has been continued by the Select Committee on Expenditure, the successor body to the Estimates Committee. Though it has been in existence for little more than a year it has already made a number of useful proposals about the form and content of the annual White Paper, a large proportion of which have been adopted and put into effect. Among principal points have been its emphasis on the importance of clear comparisons between estimates of programmes and actual expenditure under them and the need for detailed analysis and explanation of the reasons for disparities and for variations in programmes themselves so as to distinguish policy from estimating changes. The Committee has also made much of the need to pay attention to the objectives of programmes and to the importance of devising measures of 'outputs' or results of expenditure.

. . . . . .

As analyst, critic, stimulant and innovator, Parliament's role in the development of the system has been important and must be freely acknowledged. When we pass from this to the second aspect of its activities – its own internal response to this evolution – the story changes. I have already referred to the importance attached by the Select Committee on Procedure in 1969 to an annual debate on the White Paper, foreshadowed in the preceding Green Paper. Since then there have been three such debates on the three Papers issued so far, leaving aside special occasions like the debate on the government's major policy document, *New policies for public spending*, in October 1970. No-one however generously inclined could describe them as other than disappointing. The Expenditure Committee itself has continued to stress how vital it regards the White Papers and Parliamentary debate on them. In the Report of its General Sub-Committee dated 29 July 1971 (H.C. 549) one reads: 'We feel that the importance of the Command Papers and Parliament's discussion of them cannot be over-stated. The Command Papers contain the core of the government's policy and reflect its overall social and economic strategy. Similarly the debate on the Command Papers should provide the main opportunity for the case of the legislature to be brought to bear on the programmes of the executive. It should be among the most important events of the Parliamentary year . . . ' (a strong echo of the Committee on Procedure's words in 1969). The Committee went on to stress that the basic issue for discussion is the government's whole choice of priorities.

. . . . . .

To some extent the range and complexity of the White Paper inhibits understanding and thus dampens debate and controversy. Elaboration in the White Paper itself, in part, as I have shown, a response to demands of the Select Committee on Expenditure, is a factor. Excessive concentration on technicalities by speakers in the debate of December 1971 provoked Mr Douglas Houghton to describe it in terms that justify repetition: 'It has not been a political debate but a discussion between practitioners, craftsmen, accountants, quantity surveyors and forecasters. It was described to me as being like a gathering of bridge enthusiasts. It has been a debate between those who have become more or less accomplished in the art of financial prediction, a highly sophisticated financial edition of Old Moore's Almanack.' There may be some exaggeration here but it is difficult to withhold sympathy entirely from Mr Houghton.

It can be argued that too great an effort is required from ordinary Members to grasp in its entirety a subject so large and complex involving more than £25,000 million of expenditure and over twenty major programmes. It has also been claimed that the issues raised are not sufficiently controversial or not presented in a sufficiently controversial or provocative manner. They are too much based on fact . . .

It is also hard for Members to answer the question: 'If you want more of this what are you willing to give up; and if you will not give it up in the public sector are you willing to abandon it in the private sector by accepting an increase in taxation?' This sort of approach tends to dampen emotion and defuse controversy. It would thus fail to attract the large mass of Members, leaving only the specialists to whom Mr Houghton referred.

. . . . . .

This account would not be complete without some reference to the work of the sub-committees of the Select Committee on Expenditure and the problems this has raised. Apart from the General Sub-Committee which has been active in dissecting the White Paper and suggesting changes and additions, the sub-committees' contributions so far have been modest. In practice they have not accepted the Select Committee on Procedure's advice in their 1969 Report in which it was recommended that sub-committees should devote their attention to the general implications of each major programme first and to follow this by examination in detail. Instead with few exceptions they have concentrated on particular issues of varying interest and importance. A clear need has emerged for more effective co-ordination of sub-committee activities, a task which might well be assumed by the General Sub-Committee, though this could create problems . . .

. . . . . .

There is a problem here whose resolution will require care and common sense. In announcing its acceptance of the idea of a select Committee on Expenditure to replace the Estimates Committee the government in its White Paper of October 1970: *The Select Committees of the House of Commons* (Cmnd 4507) declared that 'the new committee unlike the Estimates Committee would not be barred from considering the policy behind the figures' (para. 20). It also acknowledged that in view of this change in practice Ministers might have to be called to give evidence (since there were clear limits beyond which officials could not go in discussing the origins and justification of government policy). The new committee and its sub-committees on the one hand and the government on the other are clearly feeling their way towards an acceptable interpretation of this expanded function. One difficulty is that the concept of 'the policy behind the figures' is not unambiguous. It does not define whether the Committee's 'consideration' could come before policy has been settled; nor whether it can expect to be allowed to pass judgement on government policies after the event and to participate in the consideration of alternatives. There have been signs from the Committee that some of its members wish to see its powers and functions extended so that it would come actively to participate in government policy-making, both in establishing objectives and the choice among alternative methods of achieving them.

It is highly doubtful whether the White Paper reference to 'considering the policy' was intended to be interpreted in this way. Thus two past Chief Secretaries to the Treasury giving evidence to the Select Committee agreed that there could be no question of publishing the PESC Report, the basic document on which decisions on public expenditure plans and programmes are taken. The government's intention was almost certainly to invite the Select Committee to consider policies as set out in the White Paper and reflected in already settled programme estimates; and beyond this to reserve the right itself to decide when to encourage discussion of future policy either by the Select Committee or by the public at large (through Green Papers or other media). Consciousness of the Select Committee's existence and activities is bound to produce a greater willingness on the government's part to invite such participation and to expose its thinking on policy options more freely . . .

7 THE RENTON REPORT ON LEGISLATION

Extracts from *The Preparation of Legislation* (The Renton Report, Cmnd. 6053, 1975); reprinted by permission of H.M.S.O. This investigation derived from the 1971 Procedure Committee Report on 'The Process of Legislation'; these extracts describe the existing legislative process and discuss the need to make legislation more intelligible to the ordinary citizen and to Members of Parliament, and more manageable to those involved in the administration and application of legislation.

OUTLINE OF PRESENT LEGISLATIVE PROCEDURE FOR PUBLIC BILLS

Government bills

Introduction into Lords or Commons 4.1 The Government decide whether a Bill is to be introduced first into the House of Lords or into the House of Commons. Finance Bills are always introduced in the Commons, as are most Bills which are regarded as politically controversial.

Procedure in the House of Commons

Introduction and First Reading 4.2 A Government Bill introduced in the House of Commons is presented by a Minister. On presentation the Bill is formally read a first time and ordered to be printed. The Bill is then published and becomes available to the House and to the public. It is usual for a Bill to have attached to it an Explanatory and Financial Memorandum, or an Explanatory Memorandum if the Bill has no financial effect. The Memorandum includes a forecast of any changes in public sector manpower requirements expected to result from the passing of the Bill; it must be framed in non-technical language and contain nothing of an argumentative character. A Government Bill brought from the Lords is deemed to have been read a first time and ordered to be read a second time in the Commons when a Minister informs the Clerks at the Table of his intention to take charge of it.

Second Reading 4.3 When Members and the public have had time to consider the Bill (and, if the Bill is urgently required, in a much shorter time) a day is appointed for the Second Reading. The debate on Second Reading is concerned with the main principles of the Bill as a whole, but reference to alternative methods of achieving the objects of the Bill is permitted. The debate normally takes place on the floor of the House, and at its conclusion the Bill is given a Second Reading (whether un- opposed or on a division). It could be rejected, in which case nothing more would be heard of it. Bills relating exclusively to Scotland usually have their Second Reading debate in the Scottish Grand Committee, which includes all the Members representing Scottish constituencies. Similarly a small number of non-controversial Bills are sent for discussion of their principles to a Second Reading Committee, consisting of 16 to 50 Members nominated for each occasion having regard to Members' qualifications and the party composition of the House. The Committee report to the House whether they recommend that the Bill be read a second time or not, and the House decides without amendment or debate whether or not to accept the Committee's recommendations.

Committee Stage 4.4 When a Bill has received a Second Reading it will in most cases be sent to a Standing Committee; although for various reasons, especially when a Bill is of a constitutional nature, it can have its Committee Stage on the floor of the House. Standing Committees consist of from 15 to 60 Members who are specially appointed for each Bill so as to reproduce as nearly as possible the party com- position of the House. A money resolution providing the necessary funds must have been passed on the floor of the House, after the Second Reading of the Bill, before any clause that makes a charge on public funds can be taken in Committee.

4.5 The Committee Stage is the main opportunity for detailed consideration of a Bill, and the stage at which most amendments are moved. The proceedings are sub- stantially the same whether this stage is taken in a Standing Committee or in Com- mittee of the whole House. The Committee goes through the Bill clause by clause, first considering amendments to the clause (selected by the Chairman in his dis- cretion) and then debating the motion that the clause, or the clause as amended, 'stand part of the Bill'; the Chairman may, however, rule that there shall be no debate on 'clause stand part' if in his opinion the principle of the clause has been adequately discussed in the course of debate on amendments. After the clauses of the Bill have been disposed of, proposed new clauses are similarly dealt with, followed by the Schedules to the Bill and proposed new Schedules, and finally the preamble, if any, and the long title. Changes in the sequence of consideration may be made if the Committee so decide. Most 'Scotland-only' Bills are committed to a Standing Committee composed mainly of Scottish Members.

Report Stage 4.6 When the proceedings of a Committee of the whole House on a Bill are concluded, the Bill is reported to the House at the next sitting. In either case, a later day is usually appointed for its further consideration at what is called the Report Stage. (A Bill reported from a Committee of the whole House without amendment proceeds, however, directly to Third Reading.) At the Report Stage, the entire Bill is open to consideration: new clauses and Schedules may be added and amendments made (the new clauses being taken first), but no question is put on each clause that it stand part of the Bill unless it be a new clause. The Speaker's selection of amendments and new clauses for debate tends to be stricter than at the Committee Stage. All Government amendments will, however, normally be selected, and any non-Government amendments on subjects to which the Government had at the Committee Stage promised further consideration. When all amendments have been disposed of the Bill goes to Third Reading.

Third Reading 4.7 The motion for the Third Reading of a Bill is normally put immediately on the conclusion of the Report Stage, and the question is put without debate unless notice has been given by not less than six Members of an amendment to the question or of a motion that the question be not put forthwith so that there may be a debate. Debates on Third Reading are becoming rare, but where one does take place it is limited strictly to the contents of the Bill. Only minor verbal amendments can be made to a Bill on Third Reading: if material amendments are necessary the order for Third Reading must be discharged and the Bill recommitted to allow the amendments to be introduced in a resumed committee proceeding.

Procedure in the House of Lords 4.8 House of Lords procedure is, broadly, similar to that in the House of Commons. When a Bill is brought from the Commons or introduced into the Lords, the First Reading is moved forthwith and the Bill goes through the same stages as in the Commons. The main differences are that any amendment tabled may be moved and there is no selection of amendments. There are no Standing Committees and Bills are normally debated in Committees of the whole House, but sometimes suitable Bills are sent to a Public Bill Committee. There may be a Report Stage even where no amendments have been made in Committee, and amendments may be moved then and on Third Reading. Although all Bills have to be passed by both Houses, in effect financial legislation is not scrutinised in detail by the House of Lords. The Lord Chancellor is available to advise the House on English legal points arising in the course of the consideration of Bills, but normally no Scottish Law Officer is a Member of the House. In 1969, during the Labour Administration of 1964–70, this difficulty was obviated when the then Lord Advocate was created a Life Peer and was then available to advise the House on Scottish legal matters during the remainder of that Administration's term.

Amendments made by second House 4.9 The procedure in either House for the consideration of amendments made to one of its Bills by the other House is essentially the same. If the first House agrees to all the amendments a message is sent to the other House to that effect. If not, a message is sent which may contain either reasons for disagreement or amendments to the amendments made by the second House and consequential amendments to the Bill. The second House may agree with the first House, or disagree and insist on their own amendments, and may in either event make further amendments; a message is sent to the first House accordingly. A single exchange of messages is in practice usually sufficient to secure agreement, but if agreement is not reached before the end of the Session the Bill is lost, unless the Parliament Act is invoked in the next Session.

Royal Assent 4.10 When a Bill has been finally passed by both Houses, Royal Assent is normally notified separately to each House in accordance with the provisions of the Royal Assent Act 1967, though Royal Assent may on occasion still be pronounced by Commission in the presence of both Houses. It is still possible for Royal Assent to be declared by the Sovereign in person in Parliament. The last occasion was in 1854.

Private Members' Bills

Procedure in the Commons 4.11 A Private Members' Bill is a public Bill promoted by a back-bench or Opposition Member, or brought from the Lords after being promoted by a private Peer. Its progress depends largely on the extent to which it receives some of the restricted amount of time allowed for Private Members' business. In recent Sessions 12 Fridays have been allotted to Private Members' Bills in the House of Commons. Priority in debate on these Fridays is determined by a ballot (for Commons Bills) held soon after the beginning of each Session. In addition as soon as the ballot Bills have been presented (and given a formal First Reading) and a date has been named for their Second Reading, Members may seek leave to introduce Bills on Tuesdays and Wednesdays by a motion under the '10-minute rule' procedure which allows one speech of approximately 10 minutes' duration for the proposal and one such speech against it. If the motion is carried the Bill is given a formal First Reading. After the ballot Bills have been presented, Members may also introduce Bills on any day by a simple written notice of presentation. On presentation such Bills are likewise given a formal First Reading. A Private Member's Bill is in practice unlikely to make progress in the Commons if it is opposed by the Government. Subject to that, it follows the stages described above for Government Bills.

Procedure in the Lords 4.12 In the House of Lords it is the privilege of any Peer to present a Bill without notice and without moving for leave to bring it in, and it is most unusual for any objections to be raised at that stage. Though the Government can oppose the Bill in debate, it is for the House to decide what progress the Bill shall make; this is equally true of a Private Member's Bill brought from the Commons. The Lords will always take up a Private Member's Bill that has passed the Commons, but may alter it substantially, or, on occasion, reject it.
. . . . . .

THE CRITICISM

Introductory

6.1 Our terms of reference imply a widespread concern that much of our statute law lacks simplicity and clarity. This concern has been expressed to us in evidence by the judiciary, by bodies representing the legal and other professions, by the Statute Law Society, by non-professional bodies and by prominent laymen familiar with the problems of preparing legislation. First, let us try to assess the strength and substance of the criticism.

6.2 The complaints we have heard may be broadly grouped as follows:

(a) *Language*. It is said that the language used is obscure and complex, its meaning elusive and its effect uncertain.

(b) *Over-elaboration*. It is said that the desire for 'certainty' in the application of legislation leads to over-elaboration.

(c) *Structure*. The internal structure of, and sequence of clauses within, individual statutes is considered to be often illogical and unhelpful to the reader.

(d) *Arrangement and amendment*. The chronological arrangement of the statutes and the lack of clear connection between various Acts bearing on related subjects are said to cause confusion and make it difficult to ascertain the current state of the law on any given matter. This confusion is increased by the practice of amending an existing Act, not by altering its text (and reprinting it as a new Act) but by passing a new Act which the reader has to apply to the existing Act and work out the meaning for himself.

. . . . . .

FACTORS TO BE TAKEN INTO ACCOUNT IN SUGGESTING REMEDIES

7.1 In subsequent chapters of this Report we examine various remedies to deal with such of the criticisms recounted in the previous chapter as we think are valid. Before solutions can be considered however, it is necessary to take account of several factors which have an inescapable effect on the situation.

The mass of legislation

7.2 A prodigious mass of statute law is enacted each year by Parliament. Some idea of the current flow of new legislation can be obtained from the number of pages added to the statute book in the three decades from 1943 to 1972. The figures are:

1943 to 1952	15,600
1953 to 1962	11,000
1963 to 1972	18,000
The total for 1973 is	2,248

These figures give some measure of the burden on Parliament and on the Government machine over the past thirty years. The accumulation of statute law is formidable, and figures worked out in 1965 showed that the 'live' statute book consisted then of some 33,000 pages of current law, parts of it dating back 700 years.

7.3 There is hardly any part of our national life or of our personal lives that is not affected by one statute or another. The affairs of local authorities, nationalised industries, public corporations and private commerce are regulated by legislation. The life of the ordinary citizen is affected by various provisions of the statute book from cradle to grave. His birth is registered, his infant welfare protected, his education provided, his employment governed, his income and capital taxed, much of his conduct controlled and his old age sustained according to the terms of one statute or another. Many might think that as a nation we groan under this overpowering burden of legislation and ardently desire to have fewer rather than more laws. Yet the pressure for ever more legislation on behalf of different interests increases as society becomes more complex and people more demanding of each other. With each change in society there comes a demand for further legislation to overcome the tensions which that change creates, even though the change may itself have been caused by legislation, which thus becomes self-proliferating.

7.4 Although matters of policy and the legislative programme are not within our terms of reference, we feel entitled to comment on the volume and scope of the legislative output of Parliament, because these matters have a direct influence on the form of Acts of Parliament. The more legislation there is and the more such legislation tries to deal with complex situations, the more likely it is that it will itself be complicated and therefore difficult to understand. It may be said that some degree of complexity and indeed obscurity may be the price we have to pay if society feels it necessary to satisfy the demands for more and yet more statute law. For our part we would point out that the price is a high one and we would urge that it should not be paid too readily. It is of fundamental importance in a free society that the law should be readily ascertainable and reasonably clear. To the extent that the law does not satisfy these conditions, the citizen is deprived of one of his basic rights and the law itself is brought into contempt. Whatever may be the pressures to increase the volume and extend the scope of legislation, it is our firm view that legislation which is complex and obscure may for that very reason be oppressive . . .

The problem of expressing complicated concepts in simple language

7.5 Ideally statutes should be written in ordinary straightforward English that can be readily understood by lawyers and laymen. However, although there is a discernible trend towards a more colloquial style in current statutes (which we welcome), it is not possible to deal in simple non-technical terms with subjects which are themselves technical and involved. Ordinary language relies upon the good offices of the reader to fill in omissions and give the sense intended to words or expressions capable of more than one meaning. It can afford to do this. In legal writing, on the other hand, not least in statutory writing, a primary objective is certainty of legal effect, and the United Kingdom legislature tends to prize this objective exceptionally highly. Statutes confer rights and impose obligations on people. If any room is left for argument as to the meaning of an enactment which affects the liberty, the purse, or the comfort of individuals, that argument will be pursued by all available means. In this situation Parliament seeks to leave as little as possible to inference, and to use words which are capable of one meaning only . . .

The conflicting needs of different audiences

The needs of the user 7.6 The user of the statute book who turns to it for information about the way in which the law affects his or his clients' interests should be able to find this information without undue trouble. There will of course be certain Acts which are not readily intelligible and it will usually be necessary for the layman to seek the advice of a professional lawyer. It should be possible for a professional adviser to find his way in the statute book without difficulty, and unnecessary obstacles ought not to be placed in his path. He has a right to expect that statutes should be drafted and arranged in a way which makes plain to him the relevance of the law, even of complex provisions, to the problems of his clients. From the evidence we have received however it is clear that the needs of such users of the statutes are not being met. We have paid particular attention to the views of the eminent judges who have discussed these matters with us because they, of all users, might be expected to give a balanced opinion as to how well or badly our legislation may be understood. We have discovered that even they often find it difficult to understand the intention of legislation passed by Parliament. If this is so, it is likely that practising lawyers find that the way in which the law is drafted presents at times an impenetrable barrier to understanding it; and we have indeed had evidence to this effect. If lawyers find the law difficult, how can the layman expect to fare? To the ordinary citizen the provisions in the statute book might sometimes as well be written in a foreign language for all the help he may expect to obtain there as to his rights and duties under the law. And this in an age, as we have pointed out, when the statute law has a growing effect on practically every sphere of daily life.

The needs of the Government

. . . . . .

(*a*) *Management of the legislative programme* 7.8 The average length of a Parliamentary session in recent years has been about 160 working days. Just under half of this time has, on the floor of the House of Commons, been devoted to the consideration of Bills (including Private Members' Bills), the remainder being taken up by general debates, supply and Private Members' non-legislative time. A substantial part of what is available for legislation is taken up by the Finance Bill; and when Private Members' Bills are also taken into account, the time available to the Government for its *own* programme (excluding the Finance Bill) is reduced to about 60 days. These 60 days allow for the discussion, mostly on second reading and report stages, of about 50 Government Bills of all types, including consolidation Bills. In practice therefore the amount of time at the disposal of the Government is commonly not enough to pass all the legislation for which a reasonable case can be made. This situation has two effects which are inimical to the satisfactory drafting of legislation from the user's point of view.

7.9 First, in the limited time available, it is of great importance to the Government that its Bills shall not be unduly held up by debate about their provisions. From the Government's point of view, 'Bills are made to pass, as razors are made to sell' (to use Lord Thring's aphorism), and if there are chances of getting Bills passed, they will be used, whatever the final result may be like for the user . . . The draftsman must therefore carry out his work with one eye to the drafting of proposals that will commend themselves to the favour of a critical legislature, and the other to the eventual product as it will appear in the hands of the user. Sir Courtenay Ilbert commenting in 1901 on the choice before a Minister when presenting a Bill had this to say:

'The Minister in charge of a Bill will often insist, and wisely insist, on departure from logical arrangement with reference to the exigencies of logical discussion. He will have considered how he intends to present his proposals to Parliament, and to defend them before the public, and will wish to have his Bill so arranged and expressed as to make it a suitable text for his speech. If the measure is at all complicated, he will desire to have its leading principles embodied in the opening clause or clauses, so that when the first fence is cleared the remainder of the course may be comparatively easy. In settling the order of the following clauses, he will consider what kind of opposition, and in what quarter, they are likely to evoke. He will prefer a few long clauses to many short ones, bearing in mind that each clause has, as a rule, to be separately put in Committee. His theoretical objections to legislation by reference will often yield to considerations of brevity. He will eschew technical terms, except where they are clearly necessary, remembering that his proposals will have to be expounded to, and understood by, an assembly of laymen . . . The draftsman has, of course, to bear in mind all these considerations'.

This is a classical description of the shifts to which a Government is driven by the need to get its legislation passed by Parliament whatever shape the Bill may be in when it receives the Royal Assent. Although the passage was written over 70 years ago it enshrines an attitude which still seems to have much influence, as the criticisms to which we have earlier referred amply bear out.

7.10 We recognise that any Government has a paramount interest in getting its legislation, and much other business, through Parliament; whether the legislation derives directly from a political commitment in a manifesto, or from the pressure of events, or whether it grows naturally out of the ordinary work of Government departments. Indeed, we concede that there is substance in the views advanced so long ago by Sir Courtenay Ilbert in the passage to which we have referred. But if shortage of Parliamentary time tends to lead to the enactment of measures which do not adequately meet the needs of those who have to use it, then one of two courses will have to be adopted. Either the flow of legislation must be staunched so that the draftsmen may have more time in which to make their Bills intelligible, or, if this is impossible, then in spite of the shortage of time, statutes must be enacted by Parliament in a form that will make it easier for them to be understood by those to whom they are addressed.

7.11 However, some Parliamentarians feel strongly that nothing should be done to hasten the legislative process. If there is now too much legislation, they consider that it would only make matters worse if the Government were to have at its disposal Parliamentary procedures and drafting practices which permitted even more legislation to be produced in a given time. The aim must therefore be to achieve greater clarity without removing from Parliament the power to legislate as it thinks fit, in the hope that such power will be exercised with restraint, responsibility and full regard for the need to achieve greater clarity in the drafting . . .

. . . . . .

The needs of Parliament 7.13 Members of Parliament in both Houses are busy people who have many exacting demands on their time. Although some are highly skilled in the law, most Members are not familiar with legal concepts. It is therefore in their interests that Bills presented to them for enactment should be in a form which is conducive to easy understanding of their effect. Mr Ian Percival QC MP who gave evidence to us stated: 'The more simple and clear a Bill is when presented to Parliament, (*a*) the better it will be understood, and therefore the better it may be considered and discussed; (*b*) the less time it will take, and (*c*) the more simple and clear it will be at the end'. We take this to indicate that Members of Parliament are just as keen to have a comprehensible Bill to consider as the users are to receive a comprehensible statute. It should not be supposed that, in considering draft legislation, Members are principally interested in scoring political points off their opponents with little regard for the final shape of a Bill as it leaves their House. On the contrary, Members often help to improve a Bill even when they are opposed to it. Nevertheless, 'simplicity' from the point of view of a legislator is not necessarily the same thing as it is from the point of view of a practising lawyer or a judge.

7.14 When a Member of Parliament is faced with a new Bill he wants to know two things about it fairly quickly. First, what the Bill is intended to do, and secondly how it affects the interests of the constituents he represents. It has until recently been assumed that it should be possible to gather this information from a study of the Bill itself, and that it should be the aim of the sponsor, whether this is the Government or a Private Member, to ensure that all the important information required is to be found within the pages of the Bill without the need to read existing legislation on the same subject. Ever since their Office was established in 1869, the Parliamentary Counsel, and their Scottish colleagues, have worked on the principle that, in the words of Lord Thring: 'It is not fair to a legislative assembly that they should, as a general rule, have to look beyond the four corners of a Bill in order to comprehend its meaning'.

8 MEMBERS' INTERESTS

Extracts from the *Report of the Select Committee on Members' Interests (Declaration)* H.C. 102, 1974—5; reprinted by permission of H.M.S.O. This Committee was appointed under the chairmanship of Mr Fred Willey, after the House of Commons had voted in May 1974 to establish a compulsory public register of M.P.s' pecuniary interests. Arrangements for a register have now been agreed, but the requirements for declaration are framed in a way which makes them less than penetrating.

1. On 22nd May, 1974 the House agreed to two Resolutions relating to the declaration of interests by Members:

(*a*) That, in any debate or proceeding of the House or its committees or transactions or communications which a Member may have with other Members or with Ministers or servants of the Crown, he shall disclose any relevant pecuniary interest or benefit of whatever nature, whether direct or indirect, that he may have had, may have or may be expecting to have.

(*b*) That every Member of the House of Commons shall furnish to a Registrar of Members' Interests such particulars of his registrable interests as shall be required, and shall notify to the Registrar any alterations which may occur therein, and the Registrar shall cause these particulars to be entered in a Register of Members' Interests which shall be available for inspection by the public.

. . . . . .

PART II – The Register

Purpose of the register 9. In carrying out his Parliamentary duties, a Member of Parliament is subject to many influences. He rightly is presumed to respond to the interests of his country, his constituency and his party. He is also properly subject to other influences which may affect his conduct as a Member of Parliament. Because, and only because, his Parliamentary actions may seem to be affected, a Member of Parliament is required to disclose any such pecuniary interest or benefit relevant to the Parliamentary action he is taking. The purpose of the register is to record generally and to give public notice of these interests and benefits which a Member enjoys and which might on occasion affect the discharge of his Parliamentary duties. The register is supplementary to and not in place of the obligation on a Member to declare his interests where the occasion arises.

10. A Member of Parliament must expect to be subjected to thorough public scrutiny in the performance of his public duties. He is also, however, a private individual and is entitled to a proper degree of privacy. His wife and children are equally entitled to such privacy. Accordingly, Your Committee reject the concept that the register should, in effect, consist of a Member's income tax returns and consider it unnecessary to require the amount of any remuneration or benefits received to be disclosed. Your Committee also recognise, as did the previous Committee, that the institution of a register can give no guarantee against evasion. In the end, responsibility must rest on the Member himself to disclose those interests that might affect his Parliamentary actions. He is, however, at all times answerable to the vigilance of his fellow Members and the public and the register will serve him and them in the discharge of his responsibility.

11. Your Committee recommend that the form for the register of interests to be sent to Members should contain the following definition: 'The purpose of this Register is to provide information of any pecuniary interest or other material benefit which a Member of Parliament may receive which might be thought to affect his conduct as a Member of Parliament or influence his actions, speeches or vote in Parliament'.

Scope of the register 12. Your Committee turn now to the classes of pecuniary interest or other benefit which are to be disclosed in the register. They wish to emphasise that the definitions they propose should be seen as broad guidelines within which Members should proceed with good sense and responsibility. In all cases of doubt the advice of the Registrar would be available. For the purpose of the register interests should be declared which date from the first day of the present Parliament.

13. Nine specific classes of pecuniary interest or other benefit are proposed. They are:
(1) remunerated directorships of companies, public or private;
(2) remunerated employments or offices;
(3) remunerated trades, professions or vocations;
(4) the names of clients when the interests referred to above include personal services by the Member which arise out of or are related in any manner to his membership of the House;
(5) financial sponsorships, (*a*) as a Parliamentary candidate where to the knowledge of the Member the sponsorship in any case exceeds 25 per cent of the candidate's election expenses, or (*b*) as a Member of Parliament, by any person or organisation, stating whether any such sponsorship includes any payment to the Member or any material benefit or advantage direct or indirect;
(6) overseas visits relating to or arising out of membership of the House where the cost of any such visit has not been wholly borne by the Member or by public funds;

(7) any payments or any material benefits or advantages received from or on behalf of foreign Governments, organisations or persons;

(8) land and property of substantial value or from which a substantial income is derived;

(9) the names of companies or other bodies in which the Member has, to his knowledge, either himself or with or on behalf of his spouse or infant children, a beneficial interest in shareholdings of a nominal value greater than one-hundredth of the issued share capital.

. . . . . .

Guidelines for Registrar

A. Status of Registrar (1) The Registrar shall be a senior officer of the Department of the Clerk of the House, to whom he shall be directly responsible.

(2) The Registrar shall act as Clerk to the Select Committee on Members' Interests appointed for each Parliament by the House.

(3) The Registrar shall act only under the authority of the Resolutions of the House and on the instructions given to him by the Select Committee from time to time.

B. Compilation and maintenance of Register (1) It shall be the duty of the Registrar at the beginning of each Parliament to send to every Member the copy of the form, agreed by the House, for the register of interests, together with a notice that the form should be completed and returned to him within 4 weeks of the Member taking his seat.

(2) The Registrar shall thereafter compile the Register which shall be put before the Select Committee who shall direct by what date it shall be laid before the House by the Clerk of the House and ordered to be printed.

(3) The Register shall be published as a House of Commons paper by Her Majesty's Stationery Office.

(4) The form for the register of interests together with the notice about the date of completion shall similarly be sent to every Member who takes his seat following a by-election.

(5) It shall be the responsibility of Members to notify the Registrar of any changes which may occur in their registrable interests within 4 weeks of the changes occurring.

(6) It shall be the duty of the Registrar to keep the Register up to date on the basis of the returns from new Members together with information given to him by Members of any changes in their registrable interests. He shall arrange for a revised Register to be published from time to time.

C. Access to Register (1) The Register shall initially be available for public inspection on Mondays to Fridays between the hours of 11 a.m. and 5 p.m. when the House is sitting and between 11 a.m. and 1 p.m. during recesses, except on public holidays, and during the month of August when it shall be available for public inspection on one day of the week. These hours may be varied from time to time by the Select Committee on the advice of the Registrar.

(2) Access to the Register by members of the general public shall not be permitted except by appointment. Any appointment made by telephone shall, save in exceptional circumstances, be confirmed in writing and at least 48 hours' notice shall be required.

(3) Before granting an appointment the Registrar shall require the applicant to furnish in writing his name and address.

(4) Members shall be able to inspect the Register without prior appointment on sitting days; during recesses an appointment shall be necessary.

(5) To enable Members to have access to the information contained in the Register outside the normal hours for inspection, the Registrar shall arrange for an up-to-date copy to be placed from time to time in the Library.

. . . . . .

E. Complaints by Members (1) Any allegation by one Member against another Member relating to the Register or to the disclosure of interests shall be in writing to the Registrar, who shall refer the matter to the Select Committee and shall furnish to the Member concerned details of the allegation.

(2) The Select Committee may hear both Members, together with other evidence, as they think fit and may then make a Report to the House together with a recommendation as to what action should be taken. Before making any such Report the Committee shall give the Member concerned the opportunity to make written representations and of being heard with such witnesses as he may desire to call.

F. Complaints by the Public (1) If any member of the public wishes to allege that a Member is in breach of the Resolutions of the House relating to registration or disclosure of interests he must make a complaint in writing to the Registrar.

(2) The Registrar shall inform any member of the public who wishes to complain that before taking any further action he should know that any communication between them is not covered by Parliamentary privilege or privileged at law.

(3) The Registrar shall have discretion to require from any member of the public wishing to make a complaint details of his name and address together with prima facie evidence as to the accuracy of his allegation; in the event of this not being supplied, he shall have the discretion to refuse to consider the matter further.

(4) If the Registrar is satisfied that a failure to comply with the Resolutions of the House has been established, he shall report the matter to the Select Committee.

(5) The Select Committee may, if they think fit, call for an explanation from the Member, to whom the details of the case shall be communicated by the Registrar.

(6) If the Member confirms that the allegation is true, the Committee shall forthwith make a Report to the House together with a recommendation as to what action should be taken.

(7) If the Member disputes the allegation, the Committee shall take evidence from such persons including the Member and his witnesses if he so wishes, as they think fit, and shall then after due consideration make a Report to the House together with a recommendation as to what action should be taken.

9 HOUSE OF LORDS REFORM

Extracts from *House of Lords Reform* (Cmnd. 3799, 1968); reprinted by permission of H.M.S.O. The Parliament (No. 2), Bill, framed to give legislative effect to the White Paper met substantial backbench opposition, and was withdrawn in April 1969 when the slow progress of the Committee stage threatened to paralyse the other business of the House of Commons.

4. The Government considers that any reform of the House of Lords should be based on the following propositions:
   (a) in the framework of a modern parliamentary system the second chamber has an essential role to play, complementary to but not rivalling that of the Commons;
   (b) the present composition and powers of the House of Lords prevent it from performing that role as effectively as it should;
   (c) the reform should therefore be directed towards promoting the more efficient working of Parliament as a whole; and
   (d) once the reform has been completed the work of the two Houses should become more closely co-ordinated and integrated, and the functions of the House of Lords should be reviewed.

5. The Government further believes that any reform should achieve the following objectives:
   (a) the hereditary basis of membership should be eliminated;
   (b) no one party should possess a permanent majority;
   (c) in normal circumstances the government of the day should be able to secure a reasonable working majority;
   (d) the powers of the House of Lords to delay public legislation should be restricted; and
   (e) the Lords' absolute power to withhold consent to subordinate legislation against the will of the Commons should be abolished.

6. The scheme which the Government proposes meets all these objectives and satisfies all these requirements. Its main feature is a two-tier House with 'voting' members who would be entitled to speak and vote, and 'non-voting' members who would be entitled to speak but not generally to vote. Membership would for the future be by creation alone and succession to a hereditary peerage would no longer carry the right to a seat in the House; existing members who sit by right of succession would lose their voting rights but would be able to remain as non-voting members for the remainder of their lives. Voting rights would therefore be confined to those on whom a peerage has been conferred but some of the peers by succession who are politically more active would be granted life peerages and so become entitled to membership of the voting nucleus. The government of the day would be entitled to secure for itself an adequate working majority over the opposition parties, although not a majority of the House as a whole when members who accept

no party allegiance are included. The present powers of the House would be reduced: in regard to public bills they would be replaced by a power to impose a period of delay of six months from the date of disagreement between the two Houses; and in regard to subordinate legislation by a power sufficient only to require the House of Commons to consider it again. There would remain a place in the reformed House for law lords and bishops, but the number of bishops would be gradually reduced from 26 to 16. The reform would not affect the judicial functions of the House or the wider aspects of peerage law, since these questions are outside the scope of a reform which is concerned with the position of the House of Lords as the second chamber of Parliament. The Government proposes that the reform should come into effect at the end of the present session.

. . . . . .

Functions of the House of Lords 8. Apart from providing the supreme court of appeal, the House of Lords at present performs the following main functions:

    (a) the provision of a forum for full and free debate on matters of public interest;

    (b) the revision of public bills brought from the House of Commons;

    (c) the initiation of public legislation, including in particular those government bills which are less controversial in party political terms and private members' bills;

    (d) the consideration of subordinate legislation;

    (e) the scrutiny of the activities of the executive; and

    (f) the scrutiny of private legislation.

All these functions have to be performed by Parliament, whether by the House of Lords or by the House of Commons, and in all of them except the last the House of Lords has in recent years made an increasing contribution and the volume of its work has expanded. Over the years it has evolved from a chamber which provided a check on the executive by its power to reject legislation to one which can still act as a check on the executive but does so through the detailed consideration of legislation and its scrutiny of administrative decisions. The House is however prevented from developing its full effectiveness by the problems of composition and powers which have bedevilled all discussion of its functions in recent years. Once these problems of composition and powers have been solved the functions of the House of Lords should also be reviewed and developed, but such a review cannot be profitably made until that time and it would in any event be more appropriately undertaken by the two Houses themselves. In making the present proposals, the Government has assumed that the functions of the House will remain broadly those set out above, but it has borne in mind that they might be extended and developed later. The Government sees this possibility of developing the functions of Parliament as a whole as the most positive ground for reform.

The present House of Lords — Composition 9. On 1st August 1968 the House consisted of:

(a)   736 hereditary peers by succession
(b)   122 hereditary peers of first creation
(c)   155 life peers
(d)   23 serving or retired law lords
(e)   <u> 26</u> bishops

Total 1062

In this paper, peers who sit by right of succession to a hereditary title are described as peers by succession; all other members of the house, that is categories (b)—(e) above, are described as created peers.

10. The membership of the House of Lords has increased steadily since 1900 when it was 590, because frequent new creations have been made and because until the introduction of life peerages in 1958 all newly created members of the House, except Lords of Appeal in Ordinary and bishops, were hereditary peers. The increase in the membership of the House has been accompanied by an increase in the number who do not attend: these now represent about one-third of the total.
. . . . . .

14. Since those peers who attend but take no party whip usually sit on the cross benches, they are commonly known as 'cross benchers'. They are a special feature of the House of Lords and include men and women with a wide range of backgrounds who for one reason or another prefer not to accept any party allegiance. The evidence shows that in speech and vote they do not adhere regularly to any party. Many have full-time occupations outside the House and for this reason they tend to come infrequently until they retire from their regular occupation; but after retirement many give a period of regular service to the House. Some of the most influential speeches by cross benchers have been made by those who come rarely. The evidence indicates that they do not possess any sense or corporate identity or act in any way as an organised group, and they resist any tendency for them to be regarded as such.

The present House of Lords — Powers 15. The House of Lords has the same right to initiate and revise legislation as the House of Commons (subject to the Commons' financial privilege), except for the restrictions imposed by the Parliament Acts of 1911 and 1949 . . . [T]heir effect in practice is that a bill to which the Lords are opposed can never be passed in less than 13 months from the original second reading of the bill in the House of Commons and in some circumstances the period could well be substantially longer. The effective delay which the House of Lords can cause is however much shorter than this, since the period of 13 months includes the time needed for the bill to pass through all its stages in the House of Commons after second reading and also the time which the House of Lords takes to consider the bill up to the point of disagreement. Nevertheless, dislocation of the parliamentary timetable can be caused at any time and, if a bill is not introduced until towards the end of a parliament, it may be lost altogether. Subordinate legislation, private bills and bills to confirm provisional orders do not come within the limitations of the Parliament Acts.

16. There has in recent years been an increase in the significance of subordinate legislation, with the result that the theoretical scope for the Lords to use their powers in order to override the Commons has in fact grown considerably since the passage of the Parliament Act 1911. Over a wide area, which tends to expand as the processes of legislation and of government become more complex, provisions supplementary to legislation are left to be made by subordinate legislation, that is by Order in Council or Ministerial order or regulation. The enactments conferring these powers normally include provisions for Parliament to supervise their use, the substance of which is either that an instrument made under the power may be annulled by resolution of either House or that such an instrument cannot come into force (or remain in force) unless approved by resolution of each House. Except in the fields of taxation and other financial matters, these provisions give parallel powers to both Houses. The Parliament Acts do not apply, and the House of Commons has no means of overriding a decision of the House of Lords which conflicts with its own. There can be no justification for a non-elected second chamber having co-equal power with an elected House of Commons in this important area of parliamentary business.

The case for reform 17. The present composition of the House of Lords gives it certain qualities which are particularly valuable to it in performing the functions set out in paragraph 8 above. The detailed consideration of legislation and the scrutiny of administrative decisions demand the presence of a nucleus of experienced parliamentarians who are able to devote a substantial part of their time to the business of the House; but its function as a forum for wide-ranging debate makes desirable in addition the presence of other men and women who have expert knowledge of or a special interest in the subject under discussion. The House of Lords provides a means of bringing both these groups together in Parliament. Nevertheless the House has two main features which are inappropriate to modern conditions: first, the right to vote can still be derived from succession to a hereditary peerage and second, the House still contains a permanent majority for one political party. The unsatisfactory situation which these features have produced is seen most clearly in the way in which the House of Lords has made use of its powers: although its formal powers are considerable, and have increased in scope with the wider use of subordinate legislation, in practice its final powers of delay over public legislation and of rejection of subordinate legislation have remained almost unused. These powers cannot however be disregarded since they give the Lords considerable influence, of which they make effective use in amending bills brought to them in the course of the ordinary legislative process of scrutiny and revision. Governments are naturally more ready to accept amendments on matters which do not involve major party political controversy, and the Lords' influence has therefore most frequently affected private members' bills and those government bills which have been less controversial in party political terms; but the Lords have nevertheless made their influence felt on party political issues, by governments both of the right and of the left.

18. Since the Conservatives have always in modern times been able to command a majority, the Lords' influence, and the threat of the use of their final powers, have naturally had a more important bearing on the major legislative proposals of governments of the left — for example, the delays forced upon the Labour Government on the Iron and Steel Bill 1949 — although for the same reason the threat to a government of the left cannot easily be brought into play without the risk of involving Parliament in a constitutional crisis. The same factors have applied to subordinate legislation: mention has already been made of the Lords' rejection of the Southern Rhodesia (United Nations Sanctions) Order on 18th June 1968, and there have been a few occasions on which orders have not been proceeded with because of known opposition in the House of Lords. But the fact remains that since 1914 the only bill actually passed into law against the continuing opposition of the Lords was the Parliament Bill of 1947, and on the single occasion since the Second World War when the Lords have rejected an item of subordinate legislation they did not persist in their opposition when an equivalent Order was subsequently introduced. The reason is clear: the composition of the House is such that the Lords cannot persist in their opposition to a measure upon which the Commons are determined without the risk of provoking a constitutional crisis. Nevertheless, the possibility that the Lords might use their formal powers remains a political fact with which every non-Conservative government must reckon, particularly after its third year in office, and which tends to undermine the effectiveness of the popular vote at an election. A situation in which the House of Lords is prevented by its composition from making an appropriate contribution to the parliamentary process cannot be satisfactory or even respectable at a time when increasing demands are being made on Parliament and there is widespread public concern that the country's parliamentary institutions should be made more effective.

19. To solve these problems some would favour a remedy which would abolish the House of Lords altogether, or alternatively would strip it so radically of its powers and functions that the House of Commons would become in effect the sole organ of parliamentary government. To adopt a system of single-chamber government would however be contrary to the practice of every other parliamentary democracy which has to legislate for a large population. More important, the case for two-chamber government in this country has been strengthened since the end of the Second World War by the growth in the volume and complexity of legislation, and also by the increase in the activity and power of the executive and in its use of subordinate legislation. Moreover, abolition of the second chamber would subject the House of Commons to severe strain, and paradoxically would result in less procedural flexibility and speed because of the need to guard against the overhasty passage of legislation.

20. Another remedy has been suggested which would leave the composition of the House unchanged but would reduce its powers. Such a remedy would transform the upper House into little more than a debating chamber, and at least some of its functions would have to be performed exclusively by the House of Commons. Again, additional burdens would be imposed upon the Commons which would be

difficult for them to sustain. Furthermore, if the House had no worthwhile function to perform, distinguished men and women would be reluctant to become members.
. . . . . .

Principles of reform 25. Two main principles emerge from the examination of these suggestions. The first is that if a reformed House is to have the influence which an effective second chamber requires, it must possess a degree of genuine independence. The present House has three characteristics on which such an independence could be founded: one is the fact already mentioned that a peer, having once become a peer, cannot be deprived of his seat; another is the participation of a considerable number of part-time members with wide interests and experience who can make contributions of high quality from time to time; and the third is the presence of a number of cross benchers who owe no allegiance to any party. The House is however prevented from exploiting these characteristics by the unsatisfactory features of its composition which have already been described – the hereditary principle and the permanent majority for one political party. The Government considers that these three characteristics should be preserved to give the reformed House the independence it needs, and to enable it to make a distinctive contribution of its own and not merely to duplicate the work of the House of Commons.

26. The second principle is that the reformed House, with all the qualities and opportunities it would offer, should be able to make an effective contribution to good democratic government. No government could however be expected to take advantage of them, or to encourage the development of the functions of the House, without reasonable expectation that its measures, although subject to proper scrutiny, would normally be passed without undue delay. It is therefore important that the government of the day should have a majority of the party membership of the working House sufficient for this purpose.

27. These two principles must inevitably conflict to some extent and it is essential that any proposals for reform should attempt to reconcile them as far as possible.

A 'two-tier' scheme 28. The need to reconcile these two principles led to the suggestion of a 'two-tier' scheme which would divide the membership of the reformed House into two groups, 'voting' peers and 'non-voting' peers. For the future, all new members of the House would sit by right of creation and not by right of succession to a hereditary peerage. Voting peers would constitute a 'working House' in whom the effective power of decision would reside. In particular they would be responsible for the bulk of the work arising from the legislative functions of the House: as indicated above, these duties require regular attendance and are not appropriate for those who can attend only occasionally. Voting peers would include every created peer who was prepared to accept, for the term of a parliament at a time, the responsibilities of regular attendance; in the first instance the number of created peers available to serve in the working House would be increased, to the limited extent necessary to create a viable House and to achieve political balance, by conferring life peerages on a number of those peers by succession who are active in the House.

29. The government of the day would have a majority of the party membership but, in order to preserve the measure of independence to which the Government attaches importance and to avoid the need for large numbers of new peers to be created at every change of government, it would not have a majority of the working House as a whole when those without party allegiance were also taken into account. It follows that the government's majority over the other parties would be small, perhaps ten per cent of the total of the opposition parties, and that it would not vary with the size of the government's majority in the House of Commons. It might be thought that the peers without party allegiance — the cross benchers — would thus hold the balance of power and would come to represent a new constitutional force; but it was pointed out in paragraph 14 above that they have no such sense of corporate identity at present. An incoming government would achieve its majority over the other parties by means of a suitable number of new creations during its first months of office: although this practice could theoretically produce an indefinite increase in the size of the voting House, studies have indicated that in almost any foreseeable circumstances the voting House could be kept, or soon restored, to an acceptable size if the older members retired as voting peers at the end of each parliament under a retirement rule (they would remain in the House for life as non-voting peers).

30. The 'second tier' would be composed of non-voting peers who would comprise all the other members of the House of Lords. The existence of this second tier would make it possible to bring into the House created peers who could not attend regularly but who would be able to make valuable contributions from time to time: they would include representatives of the professions, scientists, industrialists, trade union leaders and other leading members of the community, together with those experienced parliamentarians who had passed the age of retirement. Their presence would enable the House to consider and discuss with authority all aspects of national life. In order to preserve continuity and to limit the extent to which any individual's rights were taken from him, this second tier would also include, at first, those existing peers by succession who wished to remain in the House; but since they would not be entitled to vote, all connection between the hereditary principle and the power to vote would be severed immediately.

31. The Government proposes to retain the arrangements by which new members are admitted to the House of Lords and they would therefore continue to be admitted when created peers by the Queen on the recommendation of the Prime Minister. Alternative proposals such as nomination for the duration of a parliament have been rejected on the grounds that they would represent an unacceptable extension of the parties' powers of patronage. On the other hand, the Government has felt obliged to reject as impracticable a number of schemes which would replace the system of nomination altogether; and various methods have therefore been considered by which the amount of patronage implicit in the Government's pro-

posals might be limited or controlled. One suggestion was that the power of nomination should lie not with the Prime Minister but with some form of constitutional committee; but the members of a committee which possessed such a power would be placed in an extremely embarrassing situation and would be open to pressures and representations of a kind which would make it very difficult for them to do their work effectively. The Government does however see attraction in the possibility of a committee which, while possessing no power of nomination, would review periodically the composition of the reformed House and report, either to the Prime Minister or to Parliament, on any deficiencies in the balance and range of the membership of the House. Its members would include representatives of the political parties and persons without party political affiliations; a person of national standing but not necessarily with party political affiliations would be its chairman. Its reports would enable Parliament and the country as a whole to satisfy themselves that the powers of patronage were not being abused.

32. The Government takes the view that a two-tier chamber, organised and chosen in the way proposed, provides a sensible method of transition from a largely hereditary to a wholly created House without disturbing that blend of the active parliamentarian and the independent expert which gives the present House its special distinction and special qualifications for performing the functions assigned to it. It would otherwise be impossible to reconcile the two principles described in paragraphs 25 and 26 above, or to achieve a second chamber which would at once be strong enough for its legislative functions, and for the other functions which may be placed upon it in due course, and at the same time have amongst its members a sufficient range of knowledge to enable it to debate with authority any subject of public importance.

Powers of the reformed House 33. The Government considers that, in exercising the six main functions listed in paragraph 8 above, the reformed House must possess a real, if limited, power of delay whose use should not, as it would with the present composition of the House, risk precipitating a constitutional crisis. Since the government of the day would normally have a working majority, the actual use of this power would continue to be a rare event; but on public legislation generally a reformed second chamber should have a power of delay sufficient to cause the Commons and the government of the day to think seriously before proceeding with a proposal against the opposition of the Lords, and to encourage a government to seek agreement on any point of dispute which might arise between the House of Commons and the reformed House. On the other hand, it would not be right for a created House to be able to frustrate the legislative proposals of a government responsible to an elected House; and even if the House of Lords pressed its objections, it should be possible, provided the government had been warned of the objections and had considered its proposals again, for the House of Commons to carry them into law within a reasonable period of time.

34. With these principles in mind the Government proposes that if the Lords reject a public bill sent up from the Commons it should be capable of being presented for Royal Assent at the end of a period of six months from the point of disagreement between the two Houses, provided that a resolution directing that it

should be presented has been debated and passed by the House of Commons. The period of delay would be capable of running into the next session or the next parliament, and there would be no need as there is under the present procedure, for the disagreed bill to be passed again through all its stages in the second session of parliament. A straightforward power to impose a delay of six months has the double advantage of applying to the legislation of a government of any party at any stage of a parliament, and of being more readily comprehensible than the complicated provisions of the Parliament Acts.

35. On subordinate legislation, the Lords' present power of rejection is clearly inappropriate and unsuited to modern conditions. The Government has considered whether it might be possible to provide for a period of delay analogous to the period proposed for public legislation, but it has concluded that such a scheme would be impracticable in present circumstances because of the need for some orders to take effect immediately and because the concept of a period of delay is not part of the general legislative framework within which subordinate legislation is enacted. The Lords' power of outright rejection should therefore be replaced by a power only to insist that the government of the day should think again and, if necessary, that the House of Commons debate again and vote again upon any instrument to which the upper House has taken exception.

36. The Government hopes that the proposed reform of composition and powers will open the way to further developments in the functions and procedures of the House, and enable it to lighten the burden of the House of Commons and to play an increasingly valuable part in the work of Parliament as a whole.

10 PARLIAMENTARY STATISTICS

These tables are drawn, by permission of the publisher, from *The Times Guide to the House of Commons, October 1974* (Times Newspapers Ltd., 1974), reprinted by permission of Times Books.

The state of the Parties 1974

	February	October
Labour	301	319
Conservative	296	276
Liberal	14	13
Scottish Nationalist	7	11
Plaid Cymru	2	3
United Ulster Unionist Coalition	11	10
Others	3	2
The Speaker	1	1
Total	635	635
Electorate	39,748,531	40,083,286
Poll	31,333,226	29,188,606
Percentage	78.8	72.8

How the Nation Voted – October 1974

	Lab	C	L	Comm	Scot Nat. Pl Cymru	Others	Total
England: Electorate							33,351,228
Votes	9,694,579	9,416,158	4,878,948	7,032	—	193,953	24,190,670
MPs	255	253*	8	—	—	—	516
% of vote/turnout	40.1	38.9	20.2	—	—	0.8	72.5
Candidates	516	516	515	17	—	202	1,766
Scotland: Electorate							3,686,791
Votes	1,000,571	681,269	228,855	7,453	839,628	268	2,758,044
MPs	41	16	3	—	11	—	71
% of vote/turnout	36.3	24.7	8.3	0.3	30.4	—	74.8
Candidates	71	71	68	9	71	3	293
Wales: Electorate							2,008,744
Votes:	761,447	367,248	238,997	2,941	166,321	844	1,537,798
MPs	23	8	2	—	3	—	36
% of vote/turnout	49.5	23.9	15.5	0.2	10.8	—	76.5
Candidates	36	36	36	3	36	3	150
Northern Ireland: Electorate							1,036,523
Votes	11,539	—	—	—	—	690,555	702,094
MPs	—	—	—	—	—	12	12
% of vote/turnout	1.6	—	—	—	—	98.3	67.7
Candidates	3	—	—	—	—	40	43
United Kingdom: Electorate							40,083,286
Votes	11,468,136	10,464,675	5,346,800	17,426	1,005,949	885,620	29,188,606
MPs	319	277*	13	—	14	12	635
% of vote/turnout	39.3	35.8	18.3	—	3.5	3.0	72.8
Candidates	626	623	619	29	107	248	2,252

*Including the Speaker

Rise and fall of the Parties 1945–70

The following table gives the state of the parties after each election from 1945 to 1970; it also shows the size of the electorate and the percentage who voted.

	1945	1950	1951	1955	1959	1964	1966	1970
Conservative	213	298	321	345	365	303	253	330
Labour	393	315	295	277	258	317	363	287
Liberal	12	9	6	6	6	9	12	6
Independent	14	–	–	–	–	1	–	–
Others	8	3	3	2	–	1 (the Speaker)	2*	7*
Total	640	625	625	630	630	630	630	630
Electorate	32,836,419	34,269,764	34,622,891	34,852,179	35,397,304	35,894,054	35,957,245	39,342,013
Poll	24,978,949	28,769,477	28,602,323	26,759,729	27,862,652	27,657,148	27,264,747	28,344,798
Percentage	76.1	84	82.6	76.8	78.7	77.0	75.9	72.0

*Includes the Speaker

MPs' jobs, ages, schools

	Lab	C	L	Other		Lab	C	L	Other
Barristers	33	48	3	—	Oxford	60	80	3	1
Solicitors	10	11	—	3	Cambridge	24	73	2	3
Journalists	27	22	1	1	Other Universities	106	56	2	13
Publishers	—	3	—	1					
Public Relations	1	2	—	—		190	209	7	17
Teachers, lecturers	76	8	2	6					
Doctors, surgeons	6	3	—	—	Service Colleges	—	9	—	—
Farmers, landowners	—	21	2	3	Technical Colleges and				
Company directors	3	72	3	2	Colleges of Techno-				
Accountants	4	7	1	1	logy	34	2	2	1
Underwriters and									
brokers	1	16	—	—	Eton	1	48	2	—
Managers, executives					Harrow	—	10	—	—
and administrative	29	20	1	2	Other Public Schools	24	116	3	2
Other business	25	22	—	3					
Clerical and technical	17	1	—	—	Grammar	161	58	6	11
Engineers	29	3	1	—	Secondary or Technical	27	4	—	1
Trade union officials	19	—	—	—					
Party officials	3	4	—	—	*Elementary and Adult	7	1	—	—
Mineworkers	17	—	—	—	Elementary	54	2	—	1
Rail workers	4	—	—	—					
Other manual workers	7	—	—	—	*Including Ruskin College and National				
Publican	—	—	—	—	Council of Labour Colleges				

Age	Lab	C	L	Other	Total
Over 70	6	—	—	—	6
66–70	16	8	—	1	25
61–65	33	16	1	1	51
56–60	41	34	1	—	76
51–55	49	39	—	4	92
46–50	52	56	5	5	118
41–45	61	60	2	3	126
36–40	25	44	2	4	75
31–35	31	15	1	5	52
30 and under	5	4	1	4	14
Total	319	276	13	27	635

Section III
The centre of government

'Till the government of the country shall become a nucleus at which the best wisdom in the country contained shall be perpetually forming itself in deposit it will be . . . little better than a government of fetches, shifts, and hand-to-mouth expedients.   (Sir Henry Taylor, 1836)

Discussion of the organisation of central government has in the past concentrated primarily on the powers and organisation of the Cabinet and the Prime Minister (11, 12); more recently the emphasis has moved towards the co-ordination of the decision-making machinery of government and the capacity of this machinery as an instrument for effective policy planning and administration. A major tendency has been to reduce the number of Ministries by amalgamation of related departments, and in some cases 'giant' Ministries have been created to take advantage both of economies of scale and of the improved possibilities for policy co-ordination (13, 14, 15). The most successful innovations in central policy planning have been the Central Policy Review Staff (13, 16, 17, 19) and the machinery for the review and control of public spending over planned periods of time (16, 17, 18). This improved system of public expenditure planning and administration flows directly from the pathfinding Plowden recommendations of 1962, but owes a great deal too to public and political concern at the ever-increasing size and scope of public spending programmes, and to the contemporary emphasis on the efficient management of resources.

There has been no recent general review of the machinery of government, and perhaps the greatest weakness of the Fulton enquiry into the Civil Service was that it was not enabled to investigate the administrative system within which civil servants operate. Changes have often taken place on an *ad hoc* basis, in response to the particular views of different Prime Ministers, and it is perhaps significant that the most co-ordinated changes flowed from a full-scale investigation (Plowden, 1962). The centre of government remains, as it has always been, more impenetrable to the outside gaze than other parts of the political system, so that pressures for reform at the centre have been relatively muted. The Fulton Report on the Civil Service (1968) suggested that some of the tasks of government could be 'hived off' from the centre, but progress in this direction has been slow (22).
Other appropriate references are 6, 20, 21, 29 and 35.

11 ORGANISATION OF THE CABINET

Extracts from Patrick Gordon Walker, *The Cabinet* (Jonathan Cape Ltd., 1970);

83

reprinted by permission of the publisher. These extracts give an account of the Cabinet committee system and discuss the existence of 'inner Cabinets'. Mr Gordon Walker is a former Labour Cabinet Minister.

(1) Inner Cabinets The term 'inner Cabinet' is a misnomer. It is in no sense a Cabinet and must be distinguished from a Cabinet Committee. An inner Cabinet has no organic or set place in the Cabinet structure: it is no more than an informal, small group of friends or confidants of the Prime Minister drawn from members of his Cabinet. It is not formally set up; it has no papers or records; it is not served by the Cabinet Secretariat. An inner Cabinet as such has no power, no place in the hierarchy of political authority. It may, amongst other things, discuss questions coming before the Cabinet; but only to concert the advice the members of the inner Cabinet will tender to their colleagues. An inner Cabinet does not and cannot predigest the business of the Cabinet; nor set it aside or duplicate its work.

In regard to such a loose and informal thing as an inner Cabinet, the practice of Prime Ministers varies according to the predilections and perhaps the balance of opinion in the Cabinet. Some Prime Ministers have not felt the need for an inner Cabinet.

. . . . . .

Attlee in his first Administration made use of an informal inner Cabinet that consisted of Bevin and Cripps and, sometimes, Morrison. After the deaths of Cripps and Bevin, Attlee did not find close confidants among his Cabinet colleagues and became rather aloof.

Eden and Macmillan had no inner Cabinet. Each talked often to one or two individual Ministers about matters that concerned them and which might come to Cabinet.

Mr Harold Wilson in his early days as Prime Minister had an informal inner Cabinet — made up of Mr George Brown, Mr Callaghan and myself. We met on a number of occasions at Chequers: when we came together at No. 10, other Ministers were sometimes present.

In the very early days of the Labour Government we decided not to devalue and, a week or two later, to raise Bank Rate by 2 per cent.

In the interval between my leaving the Cabinet in January 1965 and rejoining it in 1967 Mr Harold Wilson had abandoned consultation with an inner group of Ministers.

. . . . . .

In the Second World War, as in the First, a full-fledged committee system was developed, but a more coherent one. This system became the basis for peacetime Cabinets from the end of the war onwards.

. . . . . .

The most important of these wartime committees was the Home Affairs Committee (which went under different names at different times). It became responsible for a major part of domestic policy. The 1944 Education Bill, the Government's most important piece of legislation, was settled in this committee and, as all the members and therefore the relevant departments were agreed, it did not go before the Cabinet.

Here was a striking example of a new principle in the Cabinet system: namely that a Cabinet Committee was parallel to and equal with the Cabinet. Within its jurisdiction and subject to possible reference to the Cabinet, a committee's conclusions had the same force and authority as those of the Cabinet itself.

In 1945 — in contrast to 1918 — the wartime system of committees was continued. Attlee was thus the first Prime Minister to have in peacetime a permanent structure of Cabinet Committees. He reorganized and simplified the committee system that he had inherited. In one category came the committees chaired by the Prime Minister himself. Attlee presided over the Defence Committee (which had during the Second World War displaced the Committee of Imperial Defence), the Economic Policy Committee, the Commonwealth Affairs Committee and the Nuclear Defence Committee.

In another category came committees presided over by other Ministers — sometimes the Minister principally concerned; sometimes co-ordinating Ministers without a department, like Morrison, Greenwood and Addison. The basic structure was as follows:

The Legislation Committee was responsible for allowing and supervising the drafting of Bills and determining the order of their introduction into the House: the Future Legislation Committee planned ahead for several sessions. An Economic Policy Committee was created with the task of overseeing planning, manpower and allied matters. A Production Committee looked after more short-term problems. An Agricultural Policy Committee was responsible for working out the annual Farm Price Review. These committees could appoint sub-committees.

This set free the Home Affairs Committee to consider the merits of all proposed Bills and other matters which did not fall to another committee or were not important enough to be taken direct to the Cabinet. In addition Bills due to go to the Cabinet in any case often came first before this committee.

By these means the merits of Bills and policies were considered before they came to Cabinet: some were settled in committees; committees were also responsible for the first draft of Bills, White Papers and the like.

Attlee introduced committees of junior Ministers presided over by a junior Minister to consider matters not of primary political importance. I chaired one such committee to keep Russian communist propaganda in various parts of the world under review, and to take or recommend counter measures.

The pattern established by Attlee was continued by subsequent Conservative Prime Ministers and became the standard structure of the Cabinet system of the 1950s and 1960s . . .

. . . . . .

The Prime Minister sets up and disbands committees, appoints the chairmen and members and sets the terms of reference. Normally, besides the Ministers departmentally concerned, some other Ministers are put on committees to ensure that policies are broadly considered. Ministers can be represented by their junior

Ministers. Often a non-departmental Minister is in the chair: indeed a Cabinet today needs some such Ministers for this purpose — probably about four.

Considerable arguments and even dispute can arise over these matters. A Minister may consider that his prestige or his departmental interests are involved: where various departments have overlapping interests there may be competition for the chairmanship of a key committee. When a Cabinet Committee on Prices and Incomes was set up in 1967, Mr Roy Jenkins, Chancellor of the Exchequer, and Mrs Barbara Castle, the Minister in charge of administering the policy, both claimed the chairmanship. The Chancellor was given the chair by the Prime Minister.

A major innovation made by Mr Harold Wilson was to raise the authority of Cabinet Committees.

Under Attlee and his Conservative successors many matters that were considered in a committee went afterwards to the Cabinet and were discussed over again. Any Cabinet Minister who did not get his way on a committee could, and often did, ask to have the matter referred to the Cabinet.

. . . . . .

In 1967 Mr Harold Wilson informed the Cabinet of his view that a matter could be taken to the Cabinet from a committee only with the agreement of the chairman. In exercising his discretion the chairman would consider the degree of disagreement in Committee or the intrinsic importance of the issue or its political overtones. In cases of dispute the question could be brought to the Prime Minister himself. Although this did not take away the constitutional right of a Cabinet Minister to bring any matter to the Cabinet including a question settled in a committee, in practice this right was greatly attenuated. This considerably reduced the pressure of business in the Cabinet.

. . . As with many constitutional innovations, including originally the Cabinet itself, an attempt was made to cast a veil of secrecy over Cabinet Committees. They came, however, to form so essential and structural a part in the working of the Cabinet that secrecy gradually broke down. It became widely felt that the public had a right to know at least the organization of the Cabinet system, which was the seat and centre of political authority in the country.

The 'Parliamentary Committee' set up by Mr Harold Wilson in 1968 is hard to classify. It possessed some of the characteristics of a Cabinet Committee. It consisted of about ten Cabinet Ministers presided over by the Prime Minister: other Ministers were called in when matters concerning their departments were under discussion: it was serviced by the Cabinet Secretariat with the usual agenda and conclusions. But it had no clear scope or terms of reference of the kind given to a normal Cabinet Committee. Its declared purpose was to enable a smaller part of the Cabinet to consider general political and parliamentary problems: it thus carried out some of the functions of an 'inner Cabinet' but was far too formal for such a group. In some respects it resembled a 'partial Cabinet'. In so far as this smaller group had effective power, it meant that for some purposes the Cabinet was smaller: this, as we have seen, involved a diminution in the Prime Minister's actual authority . . .

One judgement passed on the Parliamentary Committee is that it 'was evidently more of an expedient to help the Prime Minister than an administrative innovation'.

It seems extremely improbable that successor Cabinets will continue this experiment. It was in fact abandoned by Mr Heath in 1970. Neither the Parliamentary Committee nor its successor is, therefore, likely to enter into the regular structure of the Cabinet system.

Mr Crossman regards the evolution of Cabinet Committees as one of the factors in the 'passing of Cabinet government'. 'The point of decision . . . was now permanently transferred either downwards to these powerful Cabinet Committees or upwards to the Prime Minister himself . . . '

In fact the committee structure enabled a great deal more work to be transacted by Ministers: it permitted these to concentrate more than before on the co-ordination of policy between their own and other departments. The Cabinet was left freer for the more important decisions: much of the work that came before it was now better prepared. Sometimes, as for instance in the consideration of a White Paper that had come up from a committee, the Cabinet's work might be formal: but there was always some formal business before every Cabinet. Far the greater part of the Cabinet's work was anything but formal. Concentrated as it now was on the more significant issues, there could be prolonged argument before decisions were come to. Any matter of great importance that had been considered by a committee was brought before the Cabinet and on occasion a different decision made.

The preparatory papers and Minutes of every committee (except some that are considering secret matters) are circulated to Ministers who can if they wish raise points about them: though it must be added that the flow of paper is so great that a Minister often does not read these papers. However, his department will draw a Minister's attention to any matter that concerns it: and the Prime Minister, aided by the Cabinet Secretary, keeps an eye on the papers.

The committee system puts a great strain upon Cabinet Ministers who spend much of their working day at committees. But it greatly relieves the burden on the Cabinet. Present-day business could not be transacted by the Cabinet, were not much of the work delegated to committees.

The committee system not only enables Ministers not in the Cabinet to join in the settlement of policies on issues that relate to their departments: it also allows junior Ministers, in a way that was not possible before, to learn something about the working of the Cabinet system.

Above all, the use of committees has increased the efficiency of the Cabinet, without reducing its oversight and control over policy decisions.

12 PRIME MINISTERIAL GOVERNMENT?

Extracts from Patrick Gordon Walker, *The Cabinet* (Jonathan Cape Ltd., 1970); reprinted by permission of the publisher. Here the author contests the Crossman thesis of the replacement of Cabinet government by Prime Ministerial government, and suggests the operation of a 'partial Cabinet' system.

. . . . . .

Mr Crossman amongst others has argued that so great was the concentration of power in the Prime Minister that he in effect displaced the Cabinet. The 'point of decision' passed upward to the Prime Minister: the reality of the Constitution was now that Cabinet government had given way to Prime Ministerial government.

. . . . . .

Mr George Brown in his letter to the Prime Minister on leaving the Cabinet gave as his main motive 'the way this Government is run and the manner in which we reach our decisions' (*The Times*, March 16th, 1968). In his resignation speech in the House two days later, he elaborated this point. After speaking of the gravity of the situation, he went on: 'It is in just such a situation that it is essential for Cabinet government to be maintained . . . Equally it is in just such a situation that temptation to depart from it is at its greatest. Power can very easily pass not merely from Cabinet to one or two Ministers but effectively to sources quite outside their political control altogether.'

Mr Crossman's argument rests on two main points: first that the Prime Minister's control over the party machine inside and outside Parliament has raised him to unassailable supremacy, secondly, that Attlee decided to make the atom bomb and Eden to invade Suez without consulting the Cabinet.

Before going into the merits of these points, we should note that neither of them is as novel or as significant as is sometimes made out . . .

As we have seen, the Prime Minister's position as party leader was an important factor in the rise of his status and powers. But Prime Ministers dominated the political scene before Attlee and Eden. As early as 1882 *The Times* wrote of Gladstone that 'in the eyes of the Opposition as indeed of the country he is the Government and he is the Liberal Party'; and on another occasion that it was only occasionally, at official banquets, that the public was reminded that the Cabinet contained other members, beside the Prime Minister. Writing of this same period, A. J. Balfour said: 'Gladstone *was* the Opposition. It was he who scattered Disraeli's majority: and he did it alone.'

The power and status of the Prime Minister reached under Peel and Lloyd George were high points to which no other Prime Minister has attained. In 1848 Gladstone told Peel: 'Your Government has not been carried on by a Cabinet but by Heads of Departments each in communication with you.'

. . . . . .

Regarding the second point, that Attlee and Eden took major decisions without consulting the Cabinet — here, too, decisions of importance had previously been made by Prime Ministers outside the Cabinet.

. . . . . .

The question of Attlee's responsibility for the decision on the atom bomb and of Eden's for the decision on Suez involves consideration of the 'partial Cabinet'.

I use this term to denote a number of Ministers who constitute part only of the Cabinet but act for a time as if they were the Cabinet.

A partial Cabinet is different from an inner Cabinet in that it is an organized part of the Cabinet system. Typically a partial Cabinet is a standing or ad hoc committee presided over by the Prime Minister, which may — in matters of great moment and secrecy — prepare policies in detail and sometimes take decisions without prior consultation with the Cabinet as a whole. The Cabinet is in due course informed and consulted.

. . . . . .

The cases of Attlee and Eden were not . . . startling departures: they fit into a pattern that started earlier and continued later.

I myself knew about the decision to make the atom bomb. The use of the Woomera range in Australia was involved and as Commonwealth Secretary I was a member of the Cabinet Committee dealing with the matter. We were making decisions that were continuous, highly technical and which related to military and scientific secrets of other countries besides our own. There was no question of the Prime Minister alone making decisions. A number of senior Ministers shared in every decision. When the Minutes of the committee came before the Cabinet, the Prime Minister (as Mr Crossman puts it) 'did not feel it necessary to call attention to this item'. Why should he? The Minutes had been circulated to Cabinet Ministers, any one of whom could have raised the matter. Ministers receive many such papers on items in the Cabinet agenda. Owing to the composition of the Cabinet Committee there can be little doubt, had the matter been raised, that the outcome would have been no different.

The day after Nasser seized the Suez Canal a Cabinet Committee of seven was set up on July 27th, 1956 (consisting of the Prime Minister, Mr Butler, Mr Macmillan, Mr Selwyn Lloyd, Mr Head, Mr Lennox-Boyd and Lord Salisbury). This committee supervised detailed negotiations in the complex and rapidly changing developments of the next few months, which were also holiday months. The Prime Minister and the Foreign Secretary handled the details of Anglo-French military preparations. The Cabinet met on September 11th. On October 18th, the Cabinet was informed of the plan for the invasion of the Canal area. The Cabinet Committee drafted an ultimatum to Israel and Egypt. In meetings on October 24th and 25th the Cabinet made the final decisions and approved the terms of the ultimatum. At this meeting one Minister is said to have complained of the shortage of time for making decisions. But no Cabinet Minister resigned.

The same basic procedure continued under Mr Harold Wilson. The Overseas Policy and Defence Committee on a number of occasions worked out policies in detail before they came to the Cabinet — for instance proposals for defence economies and policy in Aden and elsewhere. Sanctions and the conduct of negotiations were supervised by the Rhodesia Committee. In November 1967 a group of Ministers met on a number of occasions to decide upon devaluation and upon the consequent deflationary measures. Final decisions were made by the Cabinet.

Thus the two concrete examples cited as proof of Prime Ministerial government (and other later examples that could be prayed in aid) turn out to be instances of partial Cabinets — which is something wholly different; for in a partial Cabinet a Prime Minister cannot act independently and in virtue of his office.

A partial Cabinet contains influential members of the Cabinet who can be said to represent it in the sense that collectively they carry very great influence within it. These members must be unanimous or nearly so before a partial Cabinet can function as such: otherwise there would be no certainty, and indeed little hope, of carrying the Cabinet. Dissenting Ministers might well insist on taking the issue straight to the Cabinet. In a partial Cabinet the Prime Minister's views might be rejected. Where there have been protests in the Cabinet against a partial Cabinet, these have been in reality directed against a particular policy rather than against the method by which it has been reached: this was so in 1911 and over Duff Cooper's resignation in 1938.

A partial Cabinet is the very opposite of Prime Ministerial government: it pre-supposes that the Prime Minister carries influential Cabinet colleagues with him, and that these will, with the Prime Minister, convince the Cabinet if policy is questioned when the Cabinet is informed. In fact Cabinets of all parties have accepted partial Cabinets as necessary, in proper circumstances, to the conduct of the affairs of the State: just as they accept, for the same reason, the selective distribution of telegrams.

Partial Cabinets, but not Prime Ministerial government, have become an accepted and established part of the Cabinet system.

(3) Checks on the Prime Minister Despite the rise of the Prime Minister there are restraints upon him that make Prime Ministerial government impossible.

Prime Ministers have on a fair number of occasions been overruled by their Cabinets both before and since the ascent of the Prime Minister in pre-eminence.

. . . . . .

Just as intangible factors enhanced the status of the Prime Minister, so they imposed a check upon him. The increased exposure of a modern Prime Minister on radio and television, which greatly raises his power when things are going well, may rapidly undermine his prestige when things are going badly. Indeed the mere passage of time may weaken his position through the overfamiliarity of the public with his manner and style of address. It may well be that the mass media of communication, which have helped to raise the Prime Minister to greater heights than his earlier predecessors, may also have shortened his political life in comparison with them.

. . . . . .

Although by the 1950s and 1960s the office of the Prime Minister had risen greatly in status, although the Prime Minister had acquired an authority different in kind from that of his colleagues, he was still not independent of the Cabinet. The Cabinet remained the sole source of political authority. On occasion and for a while a partial Cabinet could act in its name: but the power of a partial Cabinet always depended upon the assurance that a sufficient number of leading Ministers shared in its decision to secure the full authority of the Cabinet in the end.

A strong Prime Minister can be very strong. He can sometimes commit the Cabinet by acts or words. But he cannot *habitually* or often do so.

A Prime Minister who habitually ignored the Cabinet, who behaved as if Prime Ministerial government were a reality — such a Prime Minister could rapidly come to grief. He would be challenged by his colleagues in the Cabinet and on occasion overridden. Theoretically a Prime Minister could dismiss all his Ministers but then he would present his critics in the party with potent leadership: Mr Macmillan's mass dismissals in 1962 were generally held to have weakened him. Macmillan was less dominant in his new Cabinet than in his old. Future Prime Ministers may well, like Mr Harold Wilson, regard Mr Macmillan's 'slaughter' as an example to be eschewed.

A Prime Minister could not, and never does, behave as if he could govern on his own — because this would undermine his position. The attempt would be self-defeating: the Prime Minister would have less power than before he started to embark on Prime Ministerial government. He would be exchanging very real, very important and very distinctive powers for a mirage. Prime Ministers know this, whatever commentators may write — so Prime Ministerial government remains a matter of words on paper.

The truth is that the Cabinet and the party inside and outside Parliament do indeed find the Prime Minister an indispensable asset and that this gives him eminent power. But equally the Prime Minister cannot dispense with party, Parliament and Cabinet.

13 THE REORGANISATION OF CENTRAL GOVERNMENT

Extracts from *The Reorganisation of Central Government* (Cmnd. 4506, 1970); reprinted by permission of H.M.S.O. This White Paper heralded two significant developments: the merging of ministries into a number of 'giant departments' (though this was the culmination of earlier developments); and the creation of a new policy planning body, the Central Policy Review Staff, whose principal function will be to present an extra-departmental analysis of major options in key policy areas. C.P.R.S. reports go to the Cabinet.

A NEW STYLE OF GOVERNMENT: AIMS

2. This Administration believes that Government has been attempting to do too much. This has placed an excessive burden on industry, and on the people of the country as a whole, and has also overloaded the government machine itself. Public administration and management in central government has stood up to these strains, but the weakness has shown itself in the apparatus of policy formulation and in the quality of many government decisions over the last 25 years.

3. The Government intend to remedy this situation. The review of governmental functions and organisation which has been carried out over the last four months is intended to lay the necessary foundations. The aims in that review have been:

(i)   To improve the quality of policy formulation and decision-taking in government by presenting Ministers, collectively in Cabinet and individually within their departments, with well-defined options, costed where possible, and relating to the choice between options to the contribution they can make to meeting national needs. This is not confined to new policies and new decisions, but implies also the continuing examination, on a systematic and critical basis, of the existing activities of government.

(ii)   To improve the framework within which public policy is formulated by matching the field of responsibility of government departments to coherent fields of policy and administration.

(iii)   To ensure that the government machine responds and adapts itself to new policies and programmes as these emerge, within the broad framework of the main departmental fields of responsibility.

The fulfilment of these aims will improve the efficiency of government. This does not mean an increase in State power, nor any sacrifice of humanity and compassion in public administration. Indeed, the systematic formulation of policy and the presentation to Ministers of defined options for decision provides them with the opportunity for greater openness in government, and more responsiveness to the needs and wishes of the community and of individuals — in short, a new and better balance between the individual and the modern State. The Civil Service itself, as it is given clearer objectives and more sharply defined responsibilities, will find that the work of public administration will again become more satisfying and that relations with the public it serves will improve.

. . . . . .

5. . . . . The product of this review will be less government, and better government, carried out by fewer people. Less government, because its activities will be related to a long-term strategy aimed at liberating private initiative and placing more responsibility on the individual and less on the State. It will be better government, because the tasks to be done will be better defined and fewer in number, requiring fewer Ministers and fewer civil servants to carry them out.

. . . . . .

THE ANALYTICAL APPROACH

7. The basis of improved policy formulation and decision-taking is rigorous analysis of existing and suggested government policies, actions and expenditure. This analysis must test whether such policies or activities accord with the Government's strategic aims and, indeed, whether they are suitable for government at all. And it must test whether they are of greater or lesser priority than other policies or activities at present carried out, or likely to be proposed in the future; what is the most efficient means of execution; and whether their long-term effects are likely to accord with Government priorities and policies as they develop.

THE FUNCTIONAL APPROACH

8. Using the same approach to deal with the issue of the organisation of government departments, the object has been to ensure that the broad framework of the central machinery in terms of Ministerial and departmental functions complies with the Government's strategic policy objectives. In practical terms, this means the application of the functional principle as the basis for the allocation of responsibilities: government departments should be organised by reference to the task to be done or the objective to be attained, and this should be the basis of the division of work between departments rather than, for example, dividing responsibility between departments so that each one deals with a client group.

9. The basic argument for this functional principle is that the purpose of organisation is to serve policy. And policy issues which are linked should be grouped together in organisational terms. Furthermore, such grouping of related functions clarifies the lines of demarcation between responsibilities and saves duplication of effort between departments. It achieves economies of scale and avoids the diffusion of expert knowledge and the difficulty of co-ordination which organisation by area or by client group would involve. This grouping of related functions in unified departments has become the more important with the increasing complexity of modern society and, therefore, of government.

. . . . . .

The unification of functions

. . . The emphasis is on the grouping of functions together in departments with a wide span, so as to provide a series of fields of unified policy. This continues the trend towards unification of functions which has evolved in recent years and which may be seen, for example, in the Ministry of Defence and the Foreign and Commonwealth Office.

12. This offers a number of advantages:

(i)   A capacity within such unified departments to propose and implement a single strategy for clearly defined and accepted objectives.

(ii)   A capacity to explore and resolve conflicts both in policy formulation and executive decision within the line of management rather than by inter-departmental compromise.

(iii) A capacity to manage and control larger resource-consuming programmes, in terms both of formulation and administration, within departmental boundaries, making possible in turn more effective delegation of executive tasks.

(iv)   The easier application of analytic techniques within large and self-contained blocks of work and expenditure.

(v)   More direct identification to the community of the Ministers and departments responsible for defined functions, programmes and policies, more open communication between government and the public about these, and better opportunities to discuss and challenge them.

(vi)   A capacity to contribute more effectively to the formulation and development of the Government's overall strategy.

13. But these advantages will be offset if issues which warrant inter-departmental discussion are decided within the new unified departments without collective discussion by Ministers. This places an additional responsibility on departments, as well as on those in the central staffs, to ensure that the collective responsibility of Ministers is not eroded. Indeed, the two issues go together. The advantages of the unification of functions set out above are largely aspects of a single concept — the desirability of the comprehensive approach in government organisation. A department unifying a group of functions will be less open to the risk of being parochial and will, therefore, be more answerable to Parliament and the community at large. Equally it will have less need to fear for and defend its interests against other interests so that in the formative stages of policy it must and will be ready to discuss issues with other departments. In this way, the full range of facts and issues will be presented to Ministers for their collective decision.

14. The Government recognise that the mere aggregation of functions into a series of large departments would lead to problems of management because of the size and complexity of the top organisation apparatus. But these problems will be reduced by defining clearly the boundaries of the functional wings which will make up the large departments and the responsibilities, both Ministerial and official, of those who work in them. There will be a sustained effort to ensure that among those functions which remain a necessary part of central government, executive blocks of work will be delegated to accountable units of management, thus lessening the load on the departmental top management. These are, however, major changes and will take some time to bring about. Special attention will be also paid to the need to create within these large departments a satisfactory organisation for handling career planning and staff management.

The decision-taking process

15. The Government have also considered the machinery for decision-taking at the centre. It is here that changes are necessary to assist Ministers in assessing the relative priorities of departmental programmes and policies. Such changes must be designed to remedy the major difficulty which faces government in a modern complex society, which cannot be solved by good administration and management alone. It is the problem of policy formulation and decision-taking: how Ministers can have before them at the right time all the necessary information and the analysis to enable them to take decisions. Thus, the necessary basis for good government is a radical improvement in the information system available to Ministers.

16. To provide this essential basis it is important that there should be a capability at the centre for assessment of policies and projects in relation to strategic objectives, and the steps the Government are taking to improve their machinery for

this purpose are set out . . . below: they mark an important stage in the introduction of techniques which will assist Ministers in taking decisions, with the presentation to them of the information on a basis free from purely departmental considerations as the essential feature.

Stability

17. The considerable changes of government organisation outlined below will provide a firm basis on which the new techniques and the new approach to government can be applied to questions of policy and administration. The government do not foresee a further prolonged period of change and disturbance in the central machinery of government . . .

. . . . . .

COLLECTIVE ORGANISATION FOR POLICY-MAKING

Definition of Government strategy

44. The existing system of inter-departmental committees is designed to maintain the collective responsibility of Ministers for the Government's policies in each of the main sectors of governmental concern, by bringing together the differing views of Ministers and ensuring that the final decisions command the agreement of the Cabinet as a whole. For this purpose the system works well; and it is capable of continuous modification to meet the increasingly complex and technical character of the processes of government and administration in modern society.

45. In recent years, however, it has become clear that the structure of inter-departmental committees, each concerned with a separate area of policy, needs to be reinforced by a clear and comprehensive definition of government strategy which can be systematically developed to take account of changing circumstances and can provide a framework within which the Government's policies as a whole may be more effectively formulated. For lack of such a clear definition of strategic purpose and under the pressures of the day to day problems immediately before them, governments are always at some risk of losing sight of the need to consider the totality of their current policies in relation to their longer term objectives; and they may pay too little attention to the difficult, but critical, task of evaluating as objectively as possible the alternative policy options and priorities open to them.

46. The Government recognise that the task of producing a strategic definition of objectives, in the sense described above, is a new and formidable one and can only be approached gradually. They therefore propose to begin by establishing a small multi-disciplinary central policy review staff in the Cabinet Office.

47. This staff will form an integral element of the Cabinet Office and, like the Secretariat and other staffs in the Cabinet Office, will be at the disposal of the Government as a whole. Under the supervision of the Prime Minister, it will work for Ministers collectively; and its task will be to enable them to take better policy

decisions by assisting them to work out the implications of their basic strategy in terms of policies in specific areas, to establish the relative priorities to be given to the different sectors of their programme as a whole, to identify those areas of policy in which new choices can be exercised and to ensure that the underlying implications of alternative courses of action are fully analysed and considered.

48. The new staff will not duplicate or replace the analytical work done by departments in their own areas of responsibility. But it will seek to enlist their co-operation in its task of relating individual departmental policies to the Government's strategy as a whole. It will therefore play an important part in the extended public expenditure survey process described below, and it will also be available to promote studies in depth of inter-departmental issues which are of particular importance in relation to the control and development of the Government's strategic objectives.

Analysis of public expenditure programmes

49. The most important feature in the planning and control of public expenditure has been the development of the detailed and comprehensive annual Public Expenditure Surveys, linked with the medium-term economic assessments. Through these surveys, a rational and systematic basis has been developed for the broad allocation of resources to the public sector, and for detailed allocation to its component parts. The resulting system is a powerful instrument of demand management and financial control. It provides one of the basic elements in the information Ministers need to enable them to balance the claims of competing blocks of public expenditure.

50. However, there are two important respects in which it does not provide all the information that is needed for this purpose. It does not call for explicit statements of the objectives of expenditure in a way that would enable a Minister's plans to be tested against general government strategy; nor can it regularly embody detailed analysis of existing programmes and of major policy options on them. Much work has been undertaken in special ad hoc policy reviews and in long-term studies, but it has become increasingly clear that the public expenditure survey system should be further strengthened.

. . . . . .

14 GIANT DEPARTMENTS

Extracts from Sir Richard Clarke, 'The Number and Size of Government Departments' (*Political Quarterly*, 1972); reprinted by permission of *Political Quarterly*. This article traces the movement towards fewer and larger units of central administration, and the implications of these changes. The author was formerly a senior Treasury official, and from 1966—70 was Permanent Secretary at the Ministries of Aviation and Technology.

One of the most striking recent developments in government has been the emergence of 'giant' departments, of a size never before seen in peacetime. At the beginning of the First World War there were 18 main departments; twenty-one years later, in 1935, there were 23; twenty-one years later again, in 1956, there were 26; now there are 17 with civil service staff of 700,000. Foreign affairs, which only twenty-five years ago occupied four major departments, each with its own Secretary of State — the Foreign, Dominions, Colonial and India Offices — are now managed by one Foreign and Commonwealth Office (FCO) with its appended Overseas Development Administration. There is one giant Ministry of Defence, employing nearly 300,000 people (apart from military personnel and locally engaged staff overseas), which has absorbed the three Service Departments and has also now assumed responsibility for aviation research and development and military procurement, formerly a large part of the successive Ministries of Supply, Aviation, and Technology. The Government's relations with industry and commerce, apart from labour questions and agriculture, and including the nationalised energy and steel industries, the aircraft industry, shipping and civil aviation, are concentrated in a giant Department of Trade and Industry (DTI). The departments formerly responsible for housing and local government, transport and works, which have themselves gone through great changes in past years, have been replaced by a giant Department of the Environment (DOE). The old social service departments are in the Department of Health and Social Security (DHSS); and education and the Research Councils are in the Department of Education and Science (DES). Table I shows the changes in major departments over sixty years.

A decade of instability

There is no moment in the last decade at which the course changed. At the beginning of Mr. Wilson's Government in October 1964, one could have been excused for thinking that the trend was going the other way with the new Department of Economic Affairs and the new Ministries of Technology, Land and Natural Resources, Overseas Development, none of which survived seven years later.

. . . . . .

The real question is whether a small number of large departments is better or worse for the efficiency of the government than a large number of small departments. The issue is not whether large departments are better than small departments, but whether a few large ones are better than a lot of small ones. It is the management of central government as a whole that must be optimised, and not the management of any single part of it.

Scale of central government

We must therefore start from the size of the work of central government. There is wide agreement that central government, as we now have it in Britain, is too big a unit for efficient operation. To have one group of people, the Cabinet, responsible

Table I. Major Government Departments: 1914–1972

1914 (18 depts.)	1935 (23 depts.)	1956 (26 depts.)	Jan. 1972 (17 depts.)
Treasury	Treasury	Treasury	Treasury Civil Service
Inland Revenue Customs & Excise	Inland Revenue Customs & Excise	Inland Revenue Customs & Excise	Inland Revenue Customs & Excise
Foreign Colonies India	Foreign Dominions Colonies India	Foreign Commonwealth Relations Colonies	Foreign & Commonwealth
Admiralty War	Admiralty War Air	Defence Admiralty War Air Supply	Defence
Home Scotland Ireland	Home Scotland	Home Scotland	Home Scotland Wales
Lord Chancellor's	Lord Chancellor's	Lord Chancellor's	Lord Chancellor's
Trade Agriculture	Trade Agriculture Labour	Trade Fuel & Power Agriculture & Food Labour	Trade & Industry Agriculture & Food Employment
	Transport	Transport & Civil Aviation	
Works	Works	Works Housing & Local Government	Environment
Local Government	Health Pensions (War)	Health Pensions & National Insurance	Health & Social Security
Education	Education DSIR	Education DSIR	Education & Science
Post Office	Post Office	Post Office	Posts & Telecommunications

for the day-to-day conduct of the whole overseas and defence policy of the country, the course of the national economy including employment, growth, balance of payments, etc., and the situation and prospects of particular industries, the overseas economic and commercial policy, the expenditures of the public sector and the taxation required to pay for them, the provisions of the social services and the educational system, law and order, etc., presents them with too heavy a task, especially as their work in carrying out their collective Cabinet functions and their individual departmental duties is only a part of their daily responsibilities and preoccupations.

Can this load of decision-making at the centre be reduced? I can see no practical answer. It has been suggested that the Government should 'hive off' certain tasks to other public bodies or to the private sector; but virtually no progress has been made, for good reasons. Both parties accepted at the end of the Second World War far-reaching responsibilities for the course of the national economy; and they have since made their criticism of their opponents' performance and their own promises the centre of their electoral appeal. They could not now convince the public that the ability of government to carry out these responsibilities is not nearly as sure as the claims of twenty-five years ago required. Given the responsibility that they have assumed for the course of economic events, governments cannot devolve the work of running the public sector to independent bodies (so avoiding being continuously concerned with these problems in Cabinet) for they will always feel that they must be able to intervene in the nationalised industries and other public agencies in order to carry out policies for keeping the economy under control.

The pressure on the centre could be much reduced by handing over responsibility for education and the social services to elected regional bodies with the power to raise money by taxation; and having no 'national' policies for education, health and housing. The central government would then provide only the underlying legislative framework, and provide grants to the regional governments for them to spend as they thought best. But the experience of the last twenty-five years is that there is no regional consciousness upon which such a decentralised system could be based. Differences between standards provided by local authorities are regarded by the public and the experts in these fields as 'anomalies' which should be 'put right' by national measures, and not an expression of local choice and independence.

. . . . . .

Size of departments

Table II sets out figures about the size of departments, for which I am indebted to the Civil Service Department. They show the number of Ministers, the number of top-level staff, and the total staff, distinguishing between those engaged in central administration and those engaged in the provision of public services or the provision of services to other departments. The best indication of the size of the load and the burden on Ministers (which is the crucial question) is the number of Under-Secretaries and above, which is closely correlated with the number of staff engaged in central administration. These columns in Table II illustrate the difference of scale between the 'giant' departments and the 'conventional' departments.

. . . . . .

Classification by expenditure, which at first sight is a natural indication of load, is a misleading guide. Public expenditure in the only meaningful sense includes direct expenditure by departments (*e.g.* defence), expenditures from national insurance funds, expenditures by local authorities and other public bodies and certain expenditures by nationalised industries (all controlled to a varying extent by departments). The aggregate of expenditure coming within one department's purview does not determine the scale of the departmental effort required to handle it:

Table II. Ministers and Staff of Departments

	Ministers		Senior Staff			Total Staff	
	Ministers	Parly. Secs.	Permanent and Second Perm Secs.	Deputy Secs. and above	Under Secs. and above	Total Staff	of which Central Administration (thousands)
Giant Departments							
Foreign & Commonwealth	4	3	16	51	183	13	4.9
Defence	3	3	6	23	125	281	(19.0)
Trade & Industry	4	3	3	20	95	28	6.5
Environment	4	4	3	20	86	76	6.2
Social Services	2	2	3	12	57	76	7.4
Conventional Departments							
Scotland	2	3	1	6	33	11	4.0
Agriculture, Fisheries & Food	1	1	1	8	33	16	3.7
Home Office	3	1	1	5	32	26	3.3
Employment	2	2	1	6	28	33	1.7
Education & Science	2	2	2	9	27	4	2.2
Very Small Departments							
Lord Chancellor's Department	1	0	1	4	13	13	0.2
Wales	2	0	0	1	7	1	0.8
Posts & Telecommunications	1	0	0	1	4	½	0.3
Centre Departments							
Chancellor of the Exchequer's (Treasury Inland Revenue, Customs & Excise, etc.)	4	0	7	26	86	116	6.4
Civil Service Department	1	1	3	8	28	2	1.2
Cabinet Office	0	0	5	12	24	½	0.6

public expenditure on education is greater than that on defence, but it needs only a very small central government machine to deal with it.

. . . . . .

Coherence of a department

There is one definite limit to the size of a department under one Cabinet Minister and one Permanent Secretary. This is the coherence of the subject-matter of the department, for which the Minister is responsible to Parliament. The task of a Minister in charge of a department, whatever its size, is to formulate and express a political concept covering the department's entire field of responsibility. This concept determines his handling of the department's business in Cabinet and in Parliament, and informs all the department's activity. There is no place for a 'conglomerate'. Disparate subjects may be brought under one Minister, simply because none is important enough to justify having a Minister to itself. But the great Departments of State should be set up to deal with great subjects of State, with a Minister with a philosophy and a policy which embraces all his subjects and relates them together. There should be only one Minister in charge of each great subject of State, for if one tries to divide one great subject between two Ministers each with his own philosophy and policy, it is most unlikely that coherent government will result: it is probable, indeed, that some other Minister, or the Cabinet itself, will have to spend time mediating and adjudicating between them.

. . . . . .

Sectional interests

At the other end of the spectrum is the question whether the scope of some departments is too narrow. The danger of excessive narrowness is as great as that of excessive width. If the activities of a Minister and his department are focussed on one small sector of the national life, the interests of that small sector will get too much weight in the Cabinet and in government generally. This is not a question of 'vested interests' in the pejorative sense of the term, although these are always there, and are more difficult to deal with when the purpose of the department and the purpose of the 'vested interests' run closely together. The essence of good government is to appraise all sectional interests against the Government's concept of the national interest; and this cannot happen if some sectional interests are given too large a voice. This is not a matter of the size of the department. The dangerous combination is that of a powerful department with a narrow scope. A small department with a narrow scope is unlikely to be strong enough in the Cabinet and in Whitehall: the greater danger is that it will be ineffective.

. . . . . .

SPREAD AND SCOPE

The spread and scope of a department appear as the fundamental criteria which determine the limits of size. If the spread and scope are too big, the department becomes a conglomerate, which cannot work effectively in government. If the spread and scope are too small, the department either becomes an enclave carrying on its work in a backwater of public affairs or becomes the voice of a sectional interest, distorting the use of national resources and frustrating the sensible development of national policy.

Ministerial handling

Of equal importance to 'spread' and 'scope' is the problem of handling by Ministers. The new giant departments have teams of Ministers, at the head of which is *The Minister*, responsible to the Cabinet and to Parliament for the whole department — Mr. Davies for DTI and Mr. Walker for DOE. It is possible to have two Cabinet Ministers in one department. In the last ten years this has often been so in the Treasury and the Foreign Office, for good reasons; and in the 1969 Ministry of Technology there were Mr. Benn and Mr. Lever, and it worked well. But for giant departments generally it is in my view right to have one and only one; and if one Minister cannot cover the whole of the department's Cabinet business, I would say that this proved that the department was too large. In DTI and DOE there are three Ministers below *The Minister*, all Ministers with the rank and standing of men and women who are capable of dealing with the department's business, both in Parliament and with the customers outside. Below them again are Parliamentary Secretaries, bringing the numbers in each department up to seven or eight.

The Minister must clearly be able to handle the department's business in Cabinet; and he must be able to lead his team, guiding them on policy, supporting them when they run into difficulty, and knowing enough about the subjects with which they are dealing to handle them at a moment's notice in Cabinet, but in no circumstances superseding them in their negotiations with industries or local authorities or whoever the customers may be. This requires a somewhat different mix of qualities from those which top-ranking Ministers have usually needed in the past. The three subsidiary Ministers also have a difficult task, for they must both behave as responsible Ministers and cede the ultimate responsibility to *The Minister*. Formerly, men of this level would often have smaller departments of their own, which is a different kind of experience. The Minister in charge of a small department who was outside the Cabinet would try to distinguish himself by his conduct of his department and by pressing the department's sectional interests. In the new system, the subsidiary Minister must distinguish himself as a member of a team working over a large area, which is much more difficult. Rising politicians will certainly adjust themselves rapidly to this change in the requirements for promotion. This could lead eventually to better professionalism and teamwork in the Cabinet and fewer buccaneers; and for a country which can no longer determine the course of world events and must live by adapting itself quickly and easily to them, this may be a change for the better.

. . . . . .

Civil service problems

There are problems of civil service organisation and people at the top of the giant departments which are similar to those of Ministers. There will be fewer full Permanent Secretaries and more Second Permanent Secretaries, men of marginally lower rank and standing. The tasks of Permanent Secretaries change, with more emphasis on management and less on the details of policy, with more emphasis on the strategy of the whole department and Ministerial team and less on the day-to-day tactics. I do not believe that these considerations are limiting factors in their own right, as distinct from the limiting factors of scope and Ministerial handling. Nobody can survive in the top echelons of the civil service nowadays without great adaptability and ability to work in teams; and compared with Ministers, civil servants have the advantage of continuity and of not being in the firing line which makes it easier to see the changing situations objectively and adapt to them.

Managing giant departments presents problems, but I do not believe them to be significantly greater than those of managing the conventional departments of the past. The intractable problems are those of communication within the department, and of knowing what is going on and of influencing the thought and attitudes throughout the entire structure. But the conventional departments have been large enough for twenty-five years past to present these problems acutely, and the manifest need in a giant department to think and organise about this may lead to better results than were achieved previously when less attention was paid to this at the top. Similarly, the handling of staff — promotion machinery, training, career development, management services — may be better done in a giant department, where it obviously must be organised, than in a department of conventional size which tries to use the traditional informal methods which are excellent in a small organisation where the men at the top can have personal knowledge of everyone in the department but which are inadequate as soon as the department reaches what might be regarded as the 'normal' size in the 1950s and 1960s.

Resource allocation

The giant department must have an apparatus and procedure to determine its strategy and to allocate its resources. In a small department with only a few tasks, the Minister and the top officials can carry the strategy and priorities in their own heads. But sorting out the priorities of a giant department is very different; and one of the main reasons for having a giant department is to enable the Government's choices to be properly made. By joining the old Ministries of Transport and Housing and Local Government into one DOE, the Government could bring the decisions on housing, roads and other public infrastructure into one system, and bind these into an articulated programme. The 1972 DTI is responsible, like the 1969 Ministry of Technology, for a wide range of public expenditures for the support of industry and for industrial investment — civil aircraft projects, shipbuilding, nationalised industries' investment, nuclear reactor development, regional assistance and so on.

Bringing these together in one department makes it possible to try to apply the same criteria and policy throughout, so that the prospective return to the national economy from the investment of £10 million of public resources in each of them is reasonably similar. Only in departments of this size is it practicable to employ the special skills which are needed to make such comparisons.

. . . The last word throughout the public sector must always be with the political judgement, which embraces all the considerations which cannot be measured by the tools of the social sciences. It is sometimes argued that because the decision in the last resort is always a political one it is silly to spend a lot of resources and effort on serious appraisal. This view is in my opinion wholly mistaken. The point of the economic or social/economic appraisal is to get the considerations clear from the point of view of the national economy (*i.e.* the national economic interest), so that if the Government wish to bring other arguments to bear, the cost of doing so is definitely known; and to stop people from using wrong and untrue economic arguments to justify what they want to do (maybe on entirely legitimate grounds).

I emphasise this because it is in my opinion right for public expenditure decisions to be taken on political grounds, for that is what public affairs are about; and there are no 'correct' and 'non-political' methods of deciding how public money should be spent. What is wrong is to take public expenditure decisions without a clear understanding of the objective economic and social considerations as far as these can be determined, and of the cost of disregarding them. The more each department is required to set up the apparatus and procedures to sort out its own decisions and priorities in this way, and the more firmly it is laid down at the centre of government that the Cabinet will not agree to expenditure proposals unless this is done, the more likely it is that the political judgements will be made wisely and realistically . . .

Treasury control

With few and large departments, each capable of working out its own strategy, allocating its own resources, and settling its own problems within itself, the way is cleared for substantial external economies. The functions of the Treasury for financial control and of the Civil Service Department for civil service manpower control can be radically changed. These cease to be detailed day-to-day controls, and become much wider — allocation of resources between departments, examination of departments' own control and decision-making systems, laying down the groundrules for departments' operations, receiving regular performance and progress reports. In these questions of finance and manpower, the relationship between the Treasury and the Civil Service Department on the one hand and the giant department on the other becomes much more like that between a holding company and a powerful subsidiary.

In the last ten years, this relationship has changed greatly, following the Plowden Report on Control of Public Expenditure of 1961, but it is still a mixture between the 'holding company' concept and the old-fashioned detailed day-to-day control.

The full change cannot come until there are only a few main departments, each with its own effective organisation. But when this happens, it will greatly improve the machinery of government, for the Treasury and the Civil Service Department will then be able to concentrate on the proper work of the centre, instead of acting as censors and trying to do what the departments should do for themselves.

Less co-ordination

Another great improvement from the point of view of the centre happens because giant departments can solve their problems themselves without the need for co-ordination from the centre and without the need for an immense apparatus of Cabinet committees. Moreover, this should provide better answers, for the process of co-ordination and adjudication at the centre is essentially one of bringing in people who know nothing of a problem in order to get it solved; and the verdict may go in favour of the strongest Minister rather than the Minister who is right, and may indeed be decided according to fortuitous circumstances on the day on which the Ministerial argument takes place — what other questions are up for decision at the same time (and the possibility of package compromise), which Minister is momentarily in the ascendant and which in the dog-house, whether the co-ordinating Minister is tired or fresh and who has briefed him, etc.

Again, with small departments, there is a tendency for polarisation to take place: the protagonists, instead of genuinely seeking a sensible solution, take extreme positions in order to gain in a compromise settlement. For example, there may be a controversy between a nationalised industry and its suppliers of equipment: before the creation of giant departments, the former would be under the Minister of Power, the latter under the Ministry of Technology or the Board of Trade. Each industry would rely upon its own department and its own Minister to fight its case, if necessary to the Cabinet; and in practice the problem might never be solved at all. But when both are within the scope of DTI, they know that one Minister must take the decision; and both industries are then under pressure to seek solutions themselves.

Even when the number of departments has been reduced to the practical minimum there will still be overlappings of interests. But in general there will be two or perhaps three giant departments involved instead of five or six, and this immensely simplifies the task of discussion and settlement, and avoids the burden upon the centre of having to organise an endless series of meetings . . .

Gains at the centre

Seen from the very centre of government, the gains from all these factors are great. It becomes possible to have a smaller Cabinet, a perennial preoccupation of Prime Ministers. It avoids the awkwardness of having some departments with a Minister not in the Cabinet, an anomaly which is bad for their work (at the moment, the Ministry of Posts and Telecommunications is the only one). It avoids having some Cabinet Ministers who are always concerned to defend sectional interests; and it provides some large and exacting Ministerial jobs. It also reduces the load on the Cabinet by having fewer problems which engage the interests of many departments and thus occupy senior Ministers and the central machine; and therefore it enables the Cabinet to devote more time to its true (but often ignored) function of determining the strategy of the Government.

Advantage of giant departments

My conclusion is that the external economies from having a few giant departments instead of a large number of conventional departments are substantial if they can be attained. But this cannot be done by stealth. The improvements will not happen unless they are made to happen – the changed role of the Treasury and the Civil Service Department, the willingness of the Cabinet to allow the Ministers in charge of giant departments to settle issues within their own department and in consultation with each other instead of bringing them to Cabinet committees, the introduction to the Cabinet of systematic discussion of the Government's strategy. I have pointed out that these changes are not necessarily in the interests of all Ministers, for they introduce the concept of a deliberately thought out long-term Government policy and strategy and allocation of resources between departments to carry it out, which will by no means suit all Ministers.

The internal economies are less decisive, but my own opinion, which is backed by some experience, is that the giant departments can be run effectively, provided that the two basic conditions are met, *viz*. that the scope and subject-matter of the department's work makes a coherent whole, and that the scale and complexity of the work is within the capability of the department's team of Ministers to handle . . .
. . . . . .
. . . The overriding need is now a stability of structure for at least ten years, to let the new departments settle down and to enable the changes at the centre to be made gradually but steadily in order to realise the potential gains which are the justification for the change of system. This should not be contentious between the political parties. The idea that seems to have developed in the last ten years that a new Administration should change the machinery of government, which gives a party-political content to these changes and tends to make further changes inevitable at the next swing of the political pendulum, is unlikely to help any political party. Both parties gain equally from improvements in the machinery of government, and there is nothing in the present structure that is more appropriate to a Conservative Government than to a Labour Government. For both parties, as we have seen, changing the machinery of government is an expensive investment, the benefits from which can accrue only after several years of stability; and to regard such changes as a means of tangibly improving a Government's performance within the lifetime of one Parliament is likely to prove itself to be a mirage. It is greatly to be hoped, therefore, that the increasing academic and political interest in the machinery of government will not create a political atmosphere which makes this subject a field for political controversy and thus usher in a further era of continuous change.

15 MACHINERY OF GOVERNMENT CHANGES, 1952–74

This table, drawn from *Civil Servants and Change* (Civil Service Department, 1974), charts the origins and development of the five large functional departments created in 1970 and thereafter; reprinted by permission of H.M.S.O.

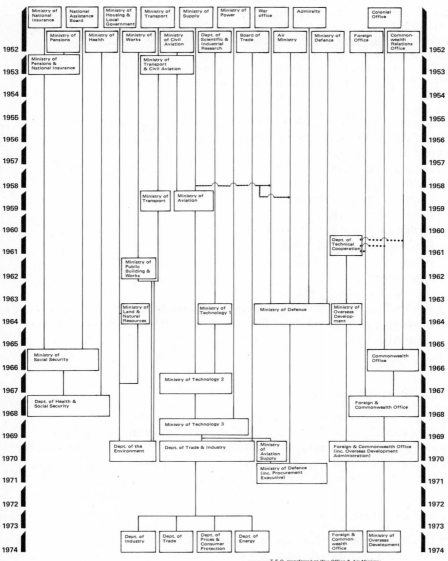

_____ T.F.O. transferred to War Office & Air Ministry
certain functions concerning the supply of equipment etc.
•••••• Act established Department which took over the
technical assistance work of the other 3 departments

16 THE PLANNING AND ADMINISTRATION OF PUBLIC EXPENDITURE

Extracts from Sir Richard Clarke, *New Trends in Government* (Civil Service College Studies 1, 1971); reprinted by permission of H.M.S.O. A major development in recent years, flowing from the recommendations of the Plowden Report of 1962, has been the establishment of machinery for continuous analysis and review of expenditure programmes. The institutional innovations are P.E.S.C. (the Public Expenditure Survey Committee) and P.A.R. (Programme Analysis Review); but, as these extracts show, all the main co-ordinative and policy planning mechanisms are involved, notably, the Cabinet, the Treasury, and the Central Policy Review Staff. These extracts are complemented by extract 17 below.

We are in sight of having nine (or perhaps ten) major departments in Whitehall, apart from the Treasury (and the revenue departments) and the Civil Service Department in the centre:

Foreign and Commonwealth Office (including Overseas Development) (FCO)
Defence (MOD)
Trade and Industry (DTI)
Environment (DOE)
Health and Social Security (DHSS)
Education and Science (DES)
Home Office
Employment (DE)
Agriculture, Fisheries and Food (MAFF)

The tenth is the Scottish Office, in an ambiguous position in this analysis, for its programmes, priorities and allocations are closely related to those of the English departments; and its activity is thus different in kind from the others . . .
. . . . . .

Organisation at the centre

We are here concerned with the shaping of the centre of the machinery of government — the Cabinet at the political level, and the Cabinet Office, the Treasury and the Civil Service Department at the official level. We are concerned both with the structure and the method of operation at the centre in itself, and the relationship between the centre and the nine major departments.

Size of the Cabinet

Beginning with the political side, the size of the Cabinet begins to decide itself. It will become a practical minimum of sixteen:

Prime Minister

Lord President
Chancellor of the Exchequer
Lord Privy Seal (Civil Service Department)
Lord Chancellor
Nine Departmental Ministers
Scotland
Wales

Prime Ministers may find it necessary or desirable to bring in more (at present, for instance, Mr Rippon, the Chancellor of the Duchy of Lancaster). There will be a number of Ministers outside the Cabinet carrying an equivalent pay and rank (notably the No 2s in the 'giant' departments); but it would seem unlikely that there will in future be any (such as previous Ministers of Power or Health) who might sometimes be in the Cabinet and sometimes out. From the point of view of the proper conduct of public business, the concept of a departmental Minister outside the Cabinet was never a good one. Such a Minister was at a great disadvantage (irrationally from the point of view of the relative importance of his and other Ministers' work) when bringing his business to the Cabinet; so the disappearance of such Ministers would be welcome. A future Prime Minister may, of course, change the departmental structure, and with it the Cabinet structure. But the advantages of stability of departmental structure have been emphasised, and are much greater with ten departments than with twenty; and the element of stability of Cabinet structure which would flow from this has much to commend it.
. . . . . .

Cabinet decision-making

By 'the Cabinet' here I mean the collective decision-making apparatus of Ministers, the Cabinet and its ministerial committees. This is a group of men and women of whom say 16–20 are Cabinet members and another 25 or so participate in the committee structure. They are people of diverse talents and backgrounds, mostly with considerable experience of political life, but, in the nature of things few will have knowledge in depth of the subject for which their departments are responsible.

It is sometimes thought that there is a close analogy between the decision-making in Cabinet and the decision-making of the board of directors of a company or any other executive group. There are certain common strands running through all committee work, but this analogy cannot be pressed very far. The width of the business of the Cabinet, with the only link between its various parts being politics and the responsibility to govern; the clamant pressure from events outside to take decisions, often with little time and altogether inadequate information; the intolerable load of business and activity upon every Cabinet Minister, and his dual responsibility both for his own department and his share in the Cabinet's decisions; the fact that most decisions must be announced immediately, and become the subject of public debate and criticism after publication, the fact that it is only rarely possible to explain the full reasons for the decision; the insecurity of the personal positions of the Ministers themselves, with never an assurance of more than five years' office (and that only very occasionally), and the continuous risk of sudden disappearance from the scene, often for quite unforeseeable and indeed irrational reasons.

Admittedly, if a great business organisation had to be run like this at the top, the results might be odd; but if these characteristics of Cabinet government were replaced by a system more like that of industry at the top, other kinds of difficulties would follow. The essential elements of Cabinet government must be taken as they are. On the other hand, it is clear that these special characteristics can lead to very bad decisions, and sometimes to avoidably bad decisions, and to reduce the incidence of these is one of the big machinery-of-government tasks. It follows that in setting up the organisation at the centre and the relation between the centre and the departments, we need specifically to try to eliminate the weaknesses in the system as they now appear.

In the problems which confront government, it is the political component (and not the technical component) which is decisive; and this is the component which the Cabinet is uniquely fitted to decide. The natural way to express this is as a direction or indication of the kind of action called for, and not as a technical decision in depth. It is the mass of technical decision-making which overloads the Cabinet and leaves them no time to consider the strategy of their policies or to clarify their political objectives.

So the purpose must surely be to have machinery which seeks to bring about a situation in which every member of the Cabinet is well equipped to take political decisions over the immense width of affairs the Cabinet has to deal with and within the instant time-scales involved – and by 'political' I mean the objectives, the value-judgements, the view of what public opinion will or will not stand – but leave the technical decision in depth to the departmental ministers. There is no clear-cut line which divides 'political' from 'technical'; but there is certainly a spectrum, and the great reduction in the number of departments should make it easier to move along this spectrum in the required direction. This is the heart of the matter; and the swamping of Cabinet business by questions for 'technical' decision – whether economic, industrial, diplomatic, social service, environmental – at the expense of 'political' decisions may well have been one of the main reasons why our governmental performance has appeared to have worked badly in the last decades.

Functions in the centre

The departmental structure at the centre is a combination of the Cabinet Office, the Treasury and the Civil Service Department (CSD). These three organisations, whose official heads hold the three top posts in the Home Civil Service, live very closely together, and although their interrelationships change over the years, according to different Prime Ministers and Chancellors of the Exchequer and the differing personalities at the top, it makes most sense to think of them as one group.

The functions are best considered not in terms of the units in the centre (which are intrinsically one group) but in terms of the related tasks, whichever unit does them. There is the self-contained central work — the Cabinet secretariat (with a co-ordinating role e.g. in defence and overseas policy); CSD's work in advising the Prime Minister on the machinery of government; and its responsibility for the civil service (pay, recruitment, structure, training, Civil Service College, etc.). Then there is the Treasury's work on the management of the national economy, on home and overseas finance, and, with the revenue departments, on fiscal policy; and its role in the co-ordination of economic policy. In each of these cases, the Treasury or the CSD or the Cabinet Office is the responsible department for doing the work, and draws on other departments for whatever help it needs, but in the end it must decide itself.

Centre and departments

The functions of the centre in relation to departments are entirely different. There is the central work on the department's objectives and priorities or Programme Analysis Review (PAR) and the analysis of issues for the Cabinet — done by Lord Rothschild's Central Policy Review Staff (CPRS) and the Treasury. There is public expenditure allocation (Public Expenditure Survey Committee, or PESC) and control — done by the Treasury's public sector divisions. There is the control of departments' staff numbers and manpower and organisation, senior appointments, management services — done by CSD.

Here the centre is dealing with the work of the departments, for which the departmental Ministers are responsible. Decisions must be taken which determine the constraints of money or manpower or other resources within which each department must work: these constraints must be determined by the Cabinet; and this is a joint process for the centre and the departments. After the constraints have been laid down, the centre must make sure that the departments comply with them: this, too, is a joint operation. Again, there may be disputes or incompatibilities between departments, and these have to be sorted out, by the centre and the departments together. The nature of the relationship between the centre and the departments is the crux of the ability of the whole governmental machine to work smoothly and effectively.

The relationship, as the Plowden Report on the Control of Public Expenditure said, 'should be one of joint working together in a common enterprise: it should be considered not in terms of more or less "independence" of the departments from "control" by the Treasury [and Civil Service Department], but rather in terms of getting the right balance and differentiation of function.'

With nine or ten large departments, all powerfully equipped to deal with their objectives, priorities, expenditure programmes and manpower, the nature of this relationship will inevitably become very different — notably in scale and detail of contacts and degree of supervision — from what it had been when there were twenty departments without such equipment.

We must note at once that there is potentially an issue of organisation at the centre, for parts of the Treasury, CSD and Cabinet Office (notably CPRS) are engaged on this joint work with only nine or ten departments; and this is potentially a source of friction. Before 1964, only one department — the Treasury — was concerned in this role; and although it is true that the two sides of the Treasury worked not much more closely together than the Treasury and CSD do now, there was only one Minister in charge of both, and there was geographical contiguity, which will not remain. Seven years ago, there was one department in the centre and 19/20 operating departments. Now there are three units in the centre and 9/10 operating departments, which is a most remarkable change.

The PAR-PESC operations

Before going into the implications of this, however, we must consider the substance of the relationships, and the practical tasks to be done. PAR and PESC should be seen as one very large operation, consisting of a number of stages, designed to enable the government to:

(a) create an overall strategy across the whole range of those of its policies which involve significant use of resources.

(b) establish the objective of each department and the priorities between them, considered over a five-year period, and in particular to determine which are the marginal objectives, affected by small changes up or down in the resources allocated to the department.

(c) determine the allocations between the departments, and so provide the resource framework within which each department can work.

(d) ensure that departments keep within their allocations, both of money and of civil service manpower.

(e) have an effective means of making day-to-day decisions within this framework of overall strategies, departmental objectives and priorities, and departmental allocations.

PAR and PESC are designed to become the basis of a new system of formulating and carrying out the government's policy . . .

. . . . . .

The procedure and the decisions are useless without a lucid and effective system for implementing them. Here is the greatest weakness in the present PESC system; and refinement is futile without the implementation system. This leads straight into the system of central financial and manpower control, i.e. the way in which departments manage their own spending and manpower, and the way in which the Treasury and the Civil Service Department manage the departments.

Departments' commitments

The decisions determining expenditure allocations cannot be said to commit the departments in any accounting sense of the term. If the departments do not themselves incur the expenditure, or are simply agents in paying out money to companies or to individuals in statutory schemes, they obviously cannot enter into such commitments. The decisions are neither 'rations' which entitle the department to the use of a certain amount of resources; nor are they like the conventional Estimates figures which express the state of an argument between the department and the Treasury about how much money the department would need, with the department able to ask for a Supplementary Estimate if the figure turns out too low, and surrendering the excess if the figure turns out to be too high.

If the system is to be viable, Cabinet decisions should, in my opinion, commit the departments to do their best, both in their own spending and in influencing that of local authorities, to keep the expenditure within the allocation; and to plan their forward policy on this basis. This is the basis upon which the department's work should be founded; and not, as it were, the automatic consequence of policies already laid down. The whole PAR/PESC system implies this. But the concept is not yet sharp enough to permit departments and the Treasury to handle this as the effective tool of financial operation. The conduct of expenditure business is an eternal dialogue between the department and the Treasury; and if the PESC allocation is the heart of it, as it must be, both sides must know exactly and precisely how they are going to work it.

Department—Treasury concordat

For this purpose, a formal concordat between each department and the Treasury is essential, to lay down precisely how both are going to work.
......

The right way to do this, in my opinion, is to break down the department's total expenditure in a manner that makes it possible to get sharper commitments in those areas which the department can control, and a more explicit statement of what it will do in those areas where it does not control. This develops a strategy for dealing with the whole of the expenditure. If the Treasury is satisfied with the strategy and with the department's internal procedures for giving effect to it, the corollary is that the need for Treasury control over the department's day-to-day transactions disappears. In other words, the 'concordat' sets out the department's expenditure planning and control system by which it intends to 'do its best' to keep within its allocation; and the extent to which the activities of the department under this system will need to be supervised by the Treasury.

Categories of expenditure

The right way to group the department's expenditures for this purpose is in terms of financial control systems, for example:

I   Expenditures reasonably within the department's control, and which can be programmed ahead.

II   Expenditures by the department of a nature that cannot be programmed ahead, because one cannot know what demands will arise and what they will cost.

III   Expenditures by the department under legislation, which cannot be altered except by changing the law.

IV   Expenditure by local authorities and other bodies outside the department's direct financial control.

The expenditures in Category I should all be included in a ration — a total figure, projected ahead as appropriate, with specific rules about how it is changed from year to year. The department undertakes to keep within this ration; and the proper course is for expenditure within this ration to be totally free from Treasury control . . .

The expenditures in Category II are more difficult to deal with. If their needs cannot be predicted five years ahead, it is clearly unrealistic to try to establish a 'ration' . . . Expenditures in Category II therefore must be handled *ad hoc* between the department and the Treasury. The overall allocation to the department must provide for this. The provision will depend upon the policy of the government and the expectation that expenditures will in fact have to be incurred but this cannot be expressed as a 'ration', and there can be no presumption either that the department would be 'entitled' to bring forward proposals up to that amount or that it would be debarred from bringing forward proposals costing more . . .

The expenditures in Category III are straightforward, though often very difficult to predict — the future cost of the agricultural price guarantees which depend upon the level of market prices and the size of the output, and the future cost of social security benefits, are examples. Here again, the idea of a 'ration' is irrelevant, for if the department has an open-ended statutory commitment it must honour it continuously. Likewise there is no need for Treasury control of the administration of such legislation, except, of course, to the extent that changes of the method of administration alter the cost by more than an agreed figure.

For Category IV, where the expenditure is not within the direct control of the department, e.g. local authority expenditure, the essential element is a process of discussion between the department and the Treasury to consider how the expenditure can be contained by indirect means, or, indeed, perhaps by changes in the law. The local authorities are responsible for about 25% of total public expenditure (as defined in PESC); and one cannot talk seriously about establishing objectives and priorities and allocation of resources without incorporating the 25% into the system. . . . . . .

Form of 'concordat'

The nature of the 'concordat' between the department and the Treasury described above is thus becoming clear. It would start from the five-year allocation for the department as laid down in the Cabinet's decisions and define how these will be changed from year to year, and the circumstances in which they can be changed at other times (e.g. demands by the Treasury for short-term cuts on grounds of national economic emergency; or demands by the department for additional allocation to meet some new large and unexpected requirement). It would define Categories I, II, III and IV in detail. It would determine the 'ration' for Category I, and the rules governing it, and the removal of 'Treasury control' within the category, and the arrangements for quarterly statements of commitments made and reconciliation with the ration, and provision for *ex post facto* checks. It would determine the 'estimated spend' included in the total allocation separately for Categories II, III and IV, and the minimum provisions for Treasury control under each.

But perhaps most important of all, for the time-scales of most government expenditures extend far beyond the normal spans of individual Ministers and the individual officials in specified jobs both in the department and in the Treasury, is the objective which both will seek to achieve. To carry out the economic objective of keeping within the allocation and planning the department's whole business on this basis, the first step after the allocation is decided must be a statement by the department of how it intends to operate in order to do this, and for agreement to be reached with the Treasury on it. Category I is straightforward when the 'ration' is fixed: in Category II, there is nothing to be done but await developments: but in Category III and Category IV there are real issues of strategy, on whether it is desirable to seek new arrangements, if necessary by new legislation, to limit the openendedness of particular government commitments, or of seeking new means of getting *de facto* control over public expenditures outside the government's direct control.

The obverse of providing for this serious and continuing dialogue between the department and the Treasury on the strategic issues of the control of the department's public expenditure and setting up forces which will enable it to be contained within its allocation, is the virtual abandonment of Treasury control and censorship of the department's expenditure in detail . . .

New system of expenditure control

The system of public expenditure control which we are now approaching stands the traditional system on its head. The traditional system saw the expenditure of a department (and indeed the total expenditure of the departments) as the sum of thousands of individual items; and thus the essence of the control of expenditure was the control of the items. The control of the items was delegated by the Treasury to the departments, partly in chunks brought together in sub-heads to which the Treasury's control applied, and partly in items of more than a specific size, which had to be submitted for Treasury approval individually. The dialogue between the Treasury and the department was in terms of items, not in terms of totals. The system which is developing, on the other hand, sees its focal point in the total − i.e. in the allocation − and the subject of the dialogue is, at one time of the year (early in the PAR/PESC process) and at another time of the year (immediately after the PESC decision) concerned with the total size of the department's expenditure and how it can be kept within a certain level − with the onus entirely on the department to deal with the items accordingly.

. . . . . .

. . . It will certainly inform the Treasury adequately of the way in which the department does its business; and enable the centre to take better decisions and make wiser proposals; and it will also inform the departments of the problems of the centre, and help them to make their own work more realistic and effective. In short, the new system will be much more constructive and relevant to the real problems of the management and control of public expenditure in the 1970s.

. . . . . .

Distribution of functions

I will recapitulate the functions in the terms of the discussion:
  (1) Cabinet secretariat — the normal Cabinet Office job, including some inter-departmental co-ordination.
  (2) Machinery of government.
  (3) Responsibility for the civil service.
  (4) Central work on departments' organisation, management and senior appointments.
      (2), (3) and (4) are all CSD functions. They are growing in size and importance, partly because they have been underadministered in the past, and partly because the methods of central control are changing from casework to examination of systems.
  (5) Analysis, allocation and control of departments' objectives, expenditure, and civil service manpower.
      This is the work of the Treasury Public Sector Divisions, the CSD Manpower Divisions and the Central Policy Review Staff. This will probably grow but with some change of balance between senior and junior staff.
  (6) National economy, finance, taxation — the normal work of the Treasury National Economy and Finance Divisions, with the Revenue Departments.
The problems arise at the interfaces between the centre and the departments, which is (4) and (5). This now engages all three central organisations; and I believe that there will be increasing pressure to have only one interface with the departments on this kind of work. Faced with nine strong departments, each able to handle its economic resources and manpower as described earlier, I doubt whether it will be practicable for the centre to continue to be split into three units each dealing individually with the departments . . .

. . . . . .

Divided responsibilities

How serious is the case likely to be for bringing together into one organisation the units in the Treasury, the CSD and the Cabinet Office that handle the centre's responsibility for managing and leading and organising and implementing the choices between the departments' objectives and resources and manpower? I would expect the case to become persuasive. There is a familiar dilemma in machinery of government, however, that the price of removing one difficulty is usually to create another; so the strength of the case is really important to judge.

I would note four potential sources of difficulty:

(i)   Departments greatly dislike having three separate contacts at the centre for closely related purposes; apart from the tiresomeness, it complicates their own organisation;

(ii)   Overlap in the handling of the PAR-PESC operation between the Treasury (and CSD) and CPRS;

(iii) Overlap and underlap between public expenditure control within the Treasury's and CSD's responsibility;

(iv)   The essential role of management and organisation in all questions of control from the centre.

Overlap in PAR-PESC

The functions of CPRS are bound to overlap those of the Public Sector Divisions of the Treasury. The staff will be composed of people some of whom will have different backgrounds from those who are doing the work in the Treasury, and their orientation will be different; but they will be performing the same function, which is to examine, question, analyse and relate together policy memoranda and projections of finance and resources; and to consider the inner consistency of each department's submission and its relation to the whole of public expenditure and the national economy. They will be doing some things that the Treasury does not do; and there are very good reasons for attaching them to the Cabinet Office and not to the Treasury, so that they can keep their different orientation. But the job in PAR-PESC operations is the same, and cannot be handled in duplicate with the departments without creating confusion in the centre and waste of time and frustration for departments.

. . . . . .

One may hope and expect that the Treasury and CPRS will work together and will not indulge in separate dialogues with the departments. But inevitably they will sometimes draw different conclusions, and will want to advise Ministers differently. This could create a dangerous rift in the centre. In public expenditure policy this should always be avoided, not because public expenditure is more important than foreign policy or defence or taxation — for it is not — but because a clash at the centre on public expenditure engages the discipline and viability of the relation between the centre and the departments, and threatens the authority of the centre and the control of public expenditure itself.

17 P.E.S.C. AND P.A.R.

Extracts from Sir S. Goldman *The Developing System of Public Expenditure Man-*

agement and Control (Civil Service College Studies 2, 1973); reprinted by permission of H.M.S.O.

Co-ordination of departmental programmes and presentation of advice to Ministers

The principal medium of inter-departmental co-ordination is the Public Expenditure Survey Committee (PESC) under Treasury chairmanship. This began more than a decade ago as a Treasury committee with representatives drawn from all departments, designed to ensure that advice to the Chancellor on public expenditure was fully informed of the position and views of departments, and to produce an agreed picture of the situation as seen by Treasury and departments together. Fundamentally these are still its main functions, though they have been elaborated and others added.

PESC is responsible for the assessment of programmes and their implications for public expenditure as a whole against the background of the medium-term economic analysis, and for producing the annual report for Ministers on which basic decisions on public spending are taken, and on which the subsequent White Paper is founded. It functions also as the main inter-departmental group for dealing with special exercises or developments in government policy in the public sector, for example, the latest reflationary operation. Finally it is the means through which contact can be kept and views exchanged on technical and theoretical problems.

The Treasury is mainly responsible for drafting the all-important annual PESC Report and for suggesting the principal issues that arise for Ministerial decision in the summer and autumn. This phase is vital for the Treasury since it is the moment when the revealed public expenditure prospect must be looked at against the total economic picture and the short- and medium-term problems that arise, and when the Chancellor needs to consider what the collective demands of spending departments mean for his fiscal and monetary policies, for prices and incomes policy and the inter-relation of them all. These factors will greatly influence the advice he gives to his colleagues in presenting them with the Report for their consideration. It is worth stressing that it is the Chancellor who is responsible for putting this Report to his colleagues, though all Ministers will have had access to it previously through their representatives on the PES Committee.

Though the system of inter-departmental discussion through PESC has worked with remarkable smoothness some difficulties remain. There will always be argument between the Treasury and departments about what constitutes their 'present programmes or policies' which need to be costed for inclusion in the total public expenditure picture. Uncertainty about future demands for particular services or facilities, mostly inherent and ineradicable, make any estimate hazardous. In practice this aspect of the system has functioned with less friction than might have been expected and serious differences of opinion have been infrequent.

However smoothly working has been the course of inter-departmental consultation and however sophisticated the techniques of presentation of the main issues for settlement to Ministers, it would be naive to think that public expenditure decisions involving perhaps major changes in the basic programmes of departments can ever be taken without a good deal of heart-searching in practice. Political and personal factors inevitably come into play and the temptation to avoid trouble in the short run at the cost of increasing risks in future is great. But if the temptations are there they are reduced by the comprehensiveness and quality of presentation of the issues to Ministers in the PESC Report and at other times.

The Treasury's role is also decisive in the development of confidence and trust among departments in day to day dealings and in the operations of PESC and its subordinate bodies. Relationships between the Treasury and departments cannot avoid an element of tension since despite an ultimately common purpose the immediate objectives of a department and of the Treasury are not identical. The one is concerned to defend its programme and the policy and objectives of its Ministers; the other is concerned to ensure that departmental programmes are well designed and economically deployed and that in total they conform with the requirements of economic policy generally.

. . . . . .

DECISION MAKING: PROGRAMME ANALYSIS AND REVIEW

The Treasury under the Chief Secretary is now responsible for managing the PAR programme. This is a major extension of its duties. It has involved setting up machinery parallel to PESC in the shape of the Programme Analysis and Review Committee (PARC) with a common chairman and substantial overlapping membership, extended to include officials specialising in programme planning as well as financial control. It has added work to the Permanent Secretaries' Steering Committee on Public Expenditure (SCOPE) which now deals with major conceptual and organisational problems thrown up by PAR. There has also been erected a Ministerial superstructure to deal with PAR reports and to supervise development of the PAR programme itself. All this activity requires to be serviced by the Treasury's public expenditure divisions and is a substantial addition to the burdens they carry.

In the United Kingdom this has been a common theme in most discussions of public expenditure going back to the report of the Select Committee on Estimates of 1957/58 and before. Underlying it is a desire to see stricter attention to: (i) establishing alternative ways of achieving given aims; (ii) better measurement of the costs of the various choices available ('inputs'); (iii) better measurement of the results of expenditure of resources ('outputs') so that valid comparisons with costs can be made.

There are two main types of decisions which have to be taken in the public sector, though the distinction between them is not hard and fast. First there are the larger decisions concerned with settling both the total scale of public spending and of the major programmes that comprise it. As I have shown these go closely together and in our system tend to be settled simultaneously. They involve big questions of economic policy and broad government strategy. In the public sector they come down in practice to questions of the basis on which cuts should be made in costed programmes when these exceed in total the level thought desirable for economic or other reasons, or the relative rate of expansion in the less frequent situations when growth is being sought. Secondly, there are the detailed decisions involving choices by responsible departments of the best means of achieving the ends they exist to accomplish, or of supplying the services they have to provide.

. . . . . .

. . . But by 1968/69 it had become clear to those concerned particularly in the light of overseas developments, that a greater effort would be needed to increase the rationality of detailed decision-taking, for its own sake and also because it was not unreasonable to hope that improvement here might make for sounder decisions in the larger field when it was a matter of judging the desirability of expansion or contraction of individual programmes to conform with wider economic or general strategy. This growing conviction coincided with arrival of the new government and of the group of businessmen familiar with programme analysis and review and its application in private business and commissioned to consider whether and how it could be introduced into government.

The result of this study was a recommendation in favour of a comprehensive plan to be introduced in stages but over a comparatively short space of time covering all programme expenditure of departments with regular appraisal of their progress backed by special analyses of particular sectors. Even those well disposed to the central concept of PAR however saw that its inherent complexities and the shortage of appropriate skills and experience within departments made a global approach hazardous.

. . . . . .

The central feature of PAR is that it is an approach to decision-taking which uses all existing techniques of cost appraisal and measurement and seeks to apply them to alternative methods of achieving determined aims. It would be wrong to regard it as an entirely new phenomenon. Indeed as with Mr. Jourdain who discovered after forty years that he had been talking prose, it is clear that many of the studies made by departments for a long time are PARs or have strong PAR-like characteristics. The contribution made by PAR theory is that it involves a higher degree of consciousness of what is being sought than existed before and a more deliberate search for options and alternatives. This is perhaps particularly true of the studies of current as distinct from new policies, where a special effort is required to look again at established practices to see whether they are still justified or should be replaced.

. . . . . .

The PAR programme makes new demands on departments, the CPRS (and CSD to a lesser extent), on Ministers, and finally on the Treasury itself.

It is upon departments whose policies are the subject of study that the principal burdens fall. The first requirement there is for trained and experienced staff. Analysis in depth of the problems under examination makes a big demand on existing resources. Training facilities have to be expanded. New costing systems have to be invented and appropriate measures devised of the results to be expected from the various options identified. So far the additional resources devoted to PAR have been comparatively modest though they are already putting a strain on departments which is bound to grow. This is likely to be the principal constraint on the development of PAR since there are distinct limits to the speed with which expert and experienced staff can be produced.

. . . . . .

PAR also makes new demands on Ministers. Perhaps the most interesting is that it requires them to be willing to submit important aspects of their departmental policy to the scrutiny of their colleagues and to defend both the analysis in PAR reports and their own choices among the options which the reports reveal. Ministers' readiness to operate on these terms is one of the main conditions for ultimate success of the new effort . . .

. . . . . .

Finally there is the Treasury's responsibility for providing the main stimulus behind the PAR programme; participating in the selection of PAR topics and discussions of the progress of individual studies; co-ordinating effort in PARC, SCOPE and elsewhere; advising the Chief Secretary on broad policy in this field; and Treasury Ministers generally on the policy implications of the PAR reports themselves.

The significance of PAR will grow as it is increasingly integrated into the main public expenditure control system. This is very much a matter of step-by-step evolution and should not be hurried. An early slogan was that 'PAR is the beginning of PESC' which meant that PAR analyses would need to be completed by a given time so that they might be incorporated into the costings of departmental programmes as these were drawn up for the annual PESC report to Ministers. But experience has shown this to be too restrictive. PAR subjects vary greatly not least in the time they need for proper study and reporting. The PESC cycle may make it convenient that decisions on some reports should be taken before the annual costing is completed. But it may be equally or even more convenient that they should be taken during the lengthy process of Ministerial consideration of the PESC report, that is as part of the main procedure for settling public expenditure programmes for ultimate disclosure in the White Paper. In this respect PAR reports or at least those concerned with current policy issues differ in no way from the many studies and reports which flow in a constant stream before Ministers for collective review and decision . . .

18 PUBLIC EXPENDITURE STATISTICS

Extracts from *Public Expenditure 1973–4 to 1977–8* (Cmnd. 5519, 1973); reprinted by permission of H.M.S.O.

Table 1.1. Public expenditure: 1973–74 and 1977–78

£ million at 1973–74 outturn prices including the relative price effect

	1973–74	1977–78	Average annual growth rate per cent
Defence and external relations:			
1. Defence	3,495	3,779	2.0
2. Overseas services	595	789	7.3
Commerce and industry:			
3. Agriculture, fisheries and forestry	590	384	−10.2
4. Trade, industry and employment	1,965	931	−14.4
Nationalised industries:			
5. Nationalised industries' capital expenditure	1,889	2,343	5.5
Environmental services:			
6. Roads and transport	1,628	1,798	2.5
7. Housing	2,169	1,818	−4.3
8. Other environmental services	1,519	1,789	4.2
9. Law, order and protective services	976	1,225	5.8
Social services:			
10. Education and libraries, science and arts	4,374	5,284	4.8
11. Health and personal social services	3,442	4,121	4.6
12. Social security	5,458	5,897	2.0
Other services:			
13. Other public services	447	462	0.8
14. Common services	443	583	7.1
15. Northern Ireland	791	841	1.5
Total programmes	29,781	32,044	2.0
16. Debt interest	2,950	2,500	−4.1
Contingency reserve	−	750	
Shortfall	−400	−300	
Price adjustments	17	−267	
Total	32,348	34,727	2.0

Table 2A. Public expenditure by programme in cost terms: 1968–69 to 1977–78
£ million at 1973–74 outturn prices including the relative price effect

	1968–69	1969–70	1970–71
Defence and external relations:			
1. Defence	3,362	3,054	3,122
2. Overseas services	444	437	423
Commerce and industry:			
3. Agriculture, fisheries and forestry	512	505	495
4. Trade, industry and employment:			
Investment grants	615	728	668
Other	825	753	760
Nationalised industries:			
5. Nationalised industries' capital expenditure	2,067	1,827	2,009
Environmental services:			
6. Roads and transport	1,181	1,212	1,276
7. Housing	1,545	1,460	1,453
8. Other environmental services	1,032	1,057	1,178
9. Law, order and protective services	659	689	770
Social services:			
10. Education and libraries, science and arts	3,284	3,371	3,572
11. Health and personal social services	2,565	2,639	2,869
12. Social security	3,348	3,575	3,821
Other services:			
13. Other public services	396	408	401
14. Common services	320	342	368
15. Northern Ireland	533	566	598
Total programmes	22,688	22,623	23,783
16. Debt interest	2,822	2,838	2,730
Contingency reserve	–	–	–
Shortfall	–	–	–
Price adjustments	1,324	1,197	929
Total	26,834	26,658	27,442

1971−72	1972−73	1973−74	1974−75	1975−76	1976−77	1977−78
3,235	3,300	3,495	3,553	3,635	3,693	3,779
443	528	595	609	678	732	789
546	497	590	544	402	385	384
519	310	235	111	48	18	4
847	1,228	1,730	1,589	1,266	987	927
1,902	1,915	1,889	2,129	2,305	2,323	2,343
1,231	1,360	1,628	1,699	1,749	1,778	1,798
1,248	1,524	2,169	1,977	1,839	1,844	1,818
1,213	1,317	1,519	1,511	1,594	1,656	1,789
825	917	976	1,024	1,097	1,162	1,225
3,758	4,112	4,374	4,529	4,764	5,012	5,283
2,973	3,254	3,442	3,584	3,759	3,930	4,121
4,430	4,991	5,458	5,725	5,799	5,854	5,897
449	568	447	446	461	453	462
397	441	443	470	517	534	583
634	721	791	808	810	819	841
34,650	26,893	29,781	30,308	30,723	31,181	32,044
2,683	2,640	2,950	2,800	2,700	2,600	2,500
−	−	−	150	350	550	750
−	−	−400	−300	−300	−300	−300
619	393	17	−154	−193	−231	−267
27,952	30,016	32,348	32,804	33,280	33,800	34,727

1. Governments come into office with a set of social objectives set out in political terms in a manifesto. Some of these objectives are expressed in very general terms (*e.g.* economic and social equality). Others involve specific improvements in individual programmes (*e.g.* increased pensions). Others again are designed to help particular groups in society (*e.g.* the disabled and the elderly).

2. It is in practice hard to translate the political aspirations and objectives of a manifesto into a coherent strategy for social policies which a Government can effectively implement. Resources are always scarce. Economic constraints and the constraints of the legislative programme limit the speed at which things can be done. There are limits to how fast the institutions both of central and local government can respond to change. Many of the most intractable problems affect more than one department, and involve central government, local authorities and other bodies. There is a serious lack of information about many social problems, and thus no reliable basis for assessing need or the effectiveness of provision. There is no effective mechanism for determining coherent and consistent priorities in the field of social policy generally.

3. All this suggests that a new and more coherent framework is required for the making and execution of social policies. In developing this the general aims must be to try to ensure that social problems, including the problem of poverty, are dealt with effectively; and that resources are concentrated where Ministers and Parliament judge they are most needed to meet objectives.

. . . . . .

8. The specific aims of this review are:
   (a) improved co-ordination between services as they affect the individual;
   (b) better analysis of, and policy prescriptions for, complex problems — especially when they are the concern of more than one department.
   (c) the development over time of collective views on priorities as between different programmes, problems and groups.

. . . . . .

Defects in social policy-making

12. Our consultations have suggested that the main defects seen in the present situation are:
   (a) it would obviously be impracticable for all social policies to be handled by one huge department performing the functions of all present departments and other bodies. Responsibilities are bound to be divided — for example, between agencies providing social security, job placement, personal social services, housing and health services. But these divisions can make it hard for central government to see and deal with people 'in the round';
   (b) the treatment of social issues should, in principle, be related to some broad framework of social policy. In practice, there is an inevitable tendency for them to be dealt with individually as they come to the forefront. This can allow different departments to put different emphases on different major

policy instruments — for example means testing, or helping the worst-off through 'positive discrimination', rather than through general improvements in programmes;

(c) Government needs better analysed and monitored information about the relative social needs of different groups, about the distributional effects of social programmes and policies and about the connections between the two. The links between policy-makers, social statisticians and other professionals could be closer. The part that research can play in policy-making is not always fully understood; existing research could be more effectively exploited;

(d) the Layfield Committee on Local Government Finance and the New Consultative Council on the same subject should lead to important improvements in the financial aspects of local government. But the Government should be able to respond rapidly to any proposals which they may make for improving the working relationship between central government and local authorities, who are the main agents in providing social services. For example:

   (i) the division of responsibilities within Whitehall should not impede the effective co-ordination of services at local level. This will become more important as local authorities improve the co-ordination of their own services by developing corporate management and other techniques;

   (ii) the trend towards giving greater discretion to local authorities, at least on questions of detail, is not easily reconciled with continuing attempts by central government to ensure that specific social problems are given high priority;

   (iii) there are wide variations not only in local standards of service, but in Whitehall's knowledge of these variations. If variations are to be kept within acceptable limits there may well be a case for at least doing more to monitor standards;

(e) even the best-conceived policies sometimes fall short at the point of delivery to their clients. An example is low rates of take-up of benefits or services. The reasons for this might include the attitudes of the intended beneficiaries, the behaviour of local officials or inadequate co-ordination with other services (cf. the multiplicity of overlapping local catchment areas for different services);

(f) many programmes lack adequate operational yardsticks. Without such information it can be hard to make proper comparisons between programmes and objectives, or to take informed decisions about priorities and phasing . . .

13. We now outline a work programme aimed at these problems. It rests on one key assumption: that if a 'joint' and more coherent approach to social policies is to have any chance of succeeding, departments and Ministers must be prepared to make some adjustments, whether in priorities, policies, administrative practices, or public expenditure allocations. For example, a study of a problem area might show that short-run remedial measures (department A) were ineffective unless supported

by long-run preventive policies (department B); this might require a shift of resources within B, or from A to B, or to B from elsewhere.

. . . . . .

A 'strategic' forum for Ministers

16. A longer-term and more coherent approach to social policy should help Ministers to operate more effectively and constructively. They need to be able to assess, more thoroughly than now, the varying needs, problems and opportunities in the social affairs field, and the likely effectiveness of different policies. They should meet from time to time to think about the strategy of social policy and not simply to deal — often at short notice — with a series of separate and probably unrelated issues.

17. A group of senior Ministers most closely concerned could meet in this way, say, every six months. The aim of these meetings would be not to reach executive decisions but to give an opportunity for broad discussions from which guidelines on priorities might develop. The background material for these discussions could include:

(a) the material which would be produced by improved social monitoring arrangements, including regular reviews of developments in the social field . . .
(b) the results of the periodic 'forward look' exercise, surveying likely forthcoming developments in social policy. (See next paragraph.)

Regular forward looks at forthcoming developments

18. The Central Policy Review Staff, in consultation with departments, has prepared a pilot version of a forward look at the social policy field. This lists the main items likely to be coming up to Ministers collectively in the next 12 months or so. It also makes more general comments on some broader issues which seem to emerge from this list. One of its main aims is to help Ministers and officials to look at impending decisions in a wider context, and to identify possible links and possible inconsistencies.

Social monitoring

19. A lot of work has been done in departments and elsewhere on improving social monitoring. Some aspects — especially evaluating the outputs and effectiveness of programmes — raise problems of measurement which in some cases may be insoluble. Nevertheless, there is clearly a need for a better transdepartmental information base for social policy. This would be an essential tool for regular Ministerial review of social policy, and would provide a better basis for determining priorities. It would also help in developing the concept of the 'social wage'.

20. Quite a lot could be done to extend work already in hand and to analyse and present more effectively material already available. Annex A recommends a pro-

gramme of developments which could be expected to produce first results quite quickly.

In summary, they are as follows:

(a) setting up in the Central Statistical Office a 'Social Group' of senior statisticians, on the lines of the existing Economic Group;

(b) regular reports on developments in the social field, with a series of key statistics showing trends in particular social problems and in the situation of different groups of the population;

(c) further work on monitoring the changing situation of more detailed subgroups, and the distributional impact of Governmental policies on these;

(d) more effective presentation of this material, or selections from it, to Ministers and senior officials.

Section IV
The government of the public sector

'Over the years, in relation to the railway industry, something has gone terribly wrong.' (Permanent Secretary to Ministry of Transport, 1967)

A cardinal political controversy in British government has been about the appropriate degree and forms of intervention by the state in the economic sector. A major impetus to state intervention came from the Labour Party's electoral victory in 1945, and its determination to secure what it regarded as the 'commanding heights of the economy'. But the philosophy of the 'public corporation' to some extent reflected a necessary compromise between principles of political control and economic operation; nationalised industries were to be free from interference in their routine management and administration but subject to overriding control by Ministers of policy. This distinction proved to be an over-simplification, and Ministers found a variety of opportunities to use their formal powers as potential sanctions, and as a foundation for the use of informal means of intervention and control (20). By comparison, parliamentary control was a blunted weapon, although the Select Committee on Nationalised Industries has produced much valuable analysis of this sector. However, the Committee's recommendations which were aimed at a clarification of the process of Ministerial control and a clearer system of public accountability for these industries (20) were largely rejected (21). The problems of reconciling the requirements of managerial freedom and political accountability remain and are bedevilled by the tendency of governments to use public sector industries as instruments in the short-term management of the economy (22).

Labour Governments have recently been concerned to extend Government influence in the private sector of the economy, especially in view of the considerable public financial resources made available to private industry as governments seek to stimulate investment and create employment in disadvantaged regions. The principal innovations here are the National Enterprise Board, with a capacity for direct intervention in the private sector, and Planning Agreements, in essence a system for the negotiation of Government relationships with key sectors of private enterprise.

A significant development in recent years has been the movement to obtain a voice for the consumer in numerous economic and commercial areas; the consumer concept has been broadened to take in the whole provision of goods and services by the public and private sector alike, and the consumer interest has found institutional reflection (24). The creation of a government-financed consumers' body, complementary to the Director-General of Fair Trading, and in the context of the creation in 1974 of a new Secretary of State for Prices and Consumer Protection,

129

means that consumers' representatives should now have the opportunity to make a significant impact on industrial and commercial practices.

20 MINISTERIAL CONTROL OF THE NATIONALISED INDUSTRIES

Extracts from *Ministerial Control of the Nationalised Industries* (Report from the Select Committee on Nationalised Industries, H.C. 371, I, 1967–8); reprinted by permission of H.M.S.O. Parliament's Select Committee on Nationalised Industries has an impressive record of informative and lucid reports, not only on individual corporations, but on matters of general concern. The Report on Ministerial Control met with criticism both from central government and from more detached commentators; yet its analysis of the organisational defects of the system of control of public enterprise remains cogent today, and the critics, acknowledging the problems defined by the Report, have failed to produce alternative remedies.

THE THEORY OF MINISTERIAL CONTROL

The obligations of Ministers and Boards

59. . . . there are many possible forms of nationalisation, implying varying degrees and methods of Ministerial control, turning particularly on the methods of financing the industries, the character and tenure of the Boards, the statutory powers given to Ministers and the method of staffing the industries – whether their employees are civil servants or not. Certain firm conclusions about Parliament's intentions regarding Ministerial control can therefore be drawn from the actual form of nationalisation that was adopted.

60. It was clearly intended by Parliament that Ministers should, to some extent or other, exercise control over the nationalised industries: for this was one of the major purposes of nationalising them. On the other hand it was equally clearly intended that the industries should benefit from some degree of managerial autonomy, and that some limits should thus be set to Ministerial control: otherwise there would be no point in establishing public corporations, with 'high-powered chairmen' and their own independent staff – they could have been placed, like the Post Office in the past, under the direct responsibility of Ministers. Hence the statutes imply a role for Ministers, but not one that extends to what has come to be called 'day-to-day management'. They also imply a limited degree of Parliamentary control; for example the industries' expenditure is not borne on the Estimates, and if the activities of Ministers are limited the extent of their Parliamentary accountability must be limited to a similar extent.

61. The statutes imply that the industries have two types of obligation. The first of these is that they must be responsive to the public interest. As has already been indicated, some authorities have argued that, in any event, they should be conscious

of the wider public interest, and in a sense this is true of all big concerns — public or private — or for that matter, of all citizens. However, apart from cases where the statutes specifically impose a public interest or social responsibility (such as London Transport's duty to provide an 'adequate service' or the electricity industry's responsibility for making supplies available to rural areas), the statutes do not *impose* on the Boards any particular duty to be responsive to the public interest. Any such duty that they may have derives from their subjection to Ministerial control.

62. The Committee will not attempt strictly to define 'public interest'. In broad terms it can be taken to consist of those wider issues, affecting the public at large rather than the industry itself, or its consumers, to which the industry might not have regard if it concerned itself only with its commercial success and were not required by Ministers to look beyond that single objective. Such matters would include not using monopoly powers to exploit consumers; taking into account the requirements of development outside those of any one industry (for example, railway services to development areas); considering social implications that might be neglected by strict application of narrow financial objectives (for example, avoiding road congestion or giving assistance to uneconomic pits to reduce redundancy among coal miners); co-ordination of industries' activities to reduce wasteful use of national resources; and adopting purchasing policies designed to help a home industry or to ease the balance of payments. The assessment of the interests concerned has been primarily a matter for Ministers . . .

63. The second type of obligation for the industries, implied by the statutes, is to operate as efficient commercial bodies. This derives partly from the extent to which they are left free of Ministerial control and, more specifically, from the requirement included in most of the statutes that they should pay their way taking one year with another . . . What is meant by 'commercial' is even harder to define than what is meant by 'public interest'. Although the phrase occurs often in the evidence it has been used to bear several different interpretations. At the minimum it must include being enterprising in seeking markets, discovering and exploiting technical advances, reducing unit costs wherever possible, and generally, as one witness put it, adopting a 'business-like' attitude. But to this some would add the main objective of the private business man, namely profit maximisation and expansion into other fields of activity. This latter interpretation can cause complications. The Committee will employ the term 'commercial' in the more limited sense.

64. These two obligations on the industry — to be responsive to the public interest and to operate as efficient commercial bodies — are not really reconcilable. Indeed, as previous Reports of the Committee have shown, they may be in conflict. For example London Transport have found that their two main statutory duties — to provide an adequate service and to pay their way — could not be reconciled. And both B.O.A.C. and B.E.A. have found, at different times, that their commercial judgement of what aircraft they should order clashed with the Government's judgement of what the public interest required.

. . . . . .

66. The fear is sometimes expressed that the acceptance by the Boards of these

two sets of obligations must result in confusion, both in their minds and amongst the wider public, as to where the duty of the Boards really lies, as to the criteria by which their success or failure should be judged, and as to who should be blamed when things go wrong. The Committee fear that these anxieties have been frequently justified. But they do not consider such confusion inevitable. They believe that given a proper institutional framework and proper relationships, within which the ultimate responsibility for every decision is made quite plain, it should be possible for the industries to fulfil both types of obligation clearly and explicitly, without any blurring of accountability. One of the major purposes of this Report is to consider how this could be done.

The purposes of Ministerial control

67. Although the obligations to be responsive to the public interest and to operate as efficient undertakings rest with the industries, the fulfilment of these obligations cannot be left to the industries alone. Ministers have responsibilities under both heads. The Chief Secretary to the Treasury argued that the function of Government in relation to the industries is, above all, to see that the economic advantage of the nation as a whole is secured by the individual industries. This meant seeing that the industries are as efficient as possible, and seeing that financial and economic policies are pursued which ensure that a proper balance is maintained between the public and private sectors. It was not the function of Government to manage the industries, but to have regard to the economic welfare and to the 'climate' in which they can best function, or, as the then Minister of Power put it, 'The Minister is in constant involvement with the industry' but 'at the same time preserving (their) managerial functions and responsibilities'.

Securing the public interest 68. Ministers are, to some extent, concerned with using their control over the industries to secure wider public interests. The Chief Secretary expressed one point of view when he claimed that the 'supreme value' of the public sector is to enable the Government to use it as an instrument of overall economic policy. Others might put less emphasis on this purpose, but most Ministers have tried to use their powers to this end.

69. These ends vary greatly, some have already been referred to in paragraph 62, but they have included the broader management of the economy, for example regulating the level of investment in the public sector, ensuring conformity with prices and incomes policies by deferring price increases, and preserving industrial peace by urging a settlement of an industrial dispute. There has frequently been emphasis on securing the provision of socially desirable services such as air services to the Highlands and Islands of Scotland, the supply of electricity to rural areas, the preservation in service of branch railway lines, and assistance for the coal industry. Another conception of the public interest has shown itself in the assumption by Ministers of the responsibilities for formulating long-term policies for the industries, such as the decision to maintain a certain size of railway system. The maintenance

of good employment practices — 'fair wages' for example — may involve the public interest and hence that of Ministers. And finally Ministers may wish to use their powers in response to political or Parliamentary pressures — so long, of course, as they find them in accord with the public interest.

Oversight of efficiency 70. Ministers are also concerned with the industries' obligations to act as efficient commercial bodies. First, they act as the industries' 'bankers' — a role which they have performed explicitly since 1956, and implicitly before then. As such they have much public money at stake in the industries. If an industry is successful it may be able to reduce its borrowing demands or alternatively lower its prices, and either of these results would be welcomed by Ministers. If an industry fails the 'banker' is liable to have to increase his advances, possibly even to cover deficits, and, if the worst comes to the worst, to accept a write-off and lose the interest due to him (the Exchequer is now burdened with £70 million a year of interest charges as a result of write-offs since 1962). As one academic witness, Mr. Coombes, wrote, 'It would be a cause for considerable wonder if a Government did not take a close and continuing interest in the performance of the nationalised industries.'

71. Secondly, Ministers are concerned with efficiency because of its wider relevance to the economy as a whole . . .

. . . . . .

73. The fact that Ministerial responsibility for the efficiency of the industries is at one step removed makes it the more necessary that Ministers should have criteria by which to judge them. They must lay down standards against which performance can be objectively measured, and provide themselves with feed-back for the purpose of making these measurements. These controls relate primarily to pricing and investment . . .

Conclusion 74. As a result of this analysis, starting from the statutes and the obligations which are inherent in them for Ministers and for Boards, the Committee conclude that there are two basic purposes of Ministerial control, namely, first to secure the wider public interest, and secondly to oversee, and if possible ensure, the efficiency of the industries. The Committee have examined the present system of control against the criterion of how well or how badly it makes possible the fulfilment by Ministers of these purposes, and the Committee's recommendations are designed to reduce the factors which inhibit that fulfilment.

The nature of Ministerial control

. . . . . .

Formal or informal control? 82. Control can be formal or informal. Formal controls are primarily those exercised under powers contained in Acts or other legislative instruments. Even if not automatically subject to Parliamentary procedures, they can, of course, be questioned in Parliament and hence made public. Informal controls range from those now well recognised extra-statutory powers, such as control over prices (although Ministers now have a formal status in this field under the prices and incomes legislation) where responsibility is publicly recognised and for which Ministers are accountable to Parliament, to the completely informal, and usually unpublicised, exercise of influence through what has been called the 'lunch-table directive'.

83. Although the industries sometimes complained about its application, most of their witnesses made little criticism of the way control is often exercised informally. On the whole they accepted that this was inevitable . . .

84. The Ministers, not surprisingly, were happy with these informal arrangements. They thought the dangers of the 'lunch-table directive' were exaggerated. Exchanges of information, ideas and pressures were two-way. And in any event informality was inevitable. On this last point they were strongly supported by Professor Hanson, who argued that informality is inevitable since neither the Ministers nor Boards would normally wish to expose their disagreements to public comment, nor could they be compelled to do so, for 'no power on earth apart from actual physical separation and interruption of postal and telephone communications can prevent the Minister from *consulting* with the Board members whom he has appointed and whom he is able to dismiss'. Such consultations would normally end in compromise.

85. . . . . Professor Hanson was so doubtful of the possibilities of enforcing any formal demarcation of responsibilities between Ministers and Boards that he proposed that the statutory requirements should be relaxed to bring them into line with the informal conventions, rather than vice-versa. Ministers should accept a broad responsibility to Parliament for the policies and major activities of their industries.

Parliamentary accountability

86. Whether it is strategic or tactical, formal or informal — and numerous permutations and combinations are possible — all Ministerial control must be seen against the background of the responsibility of Ministers to Parliament. As the Board of Trade evidence put it, 'The Corporations recognise that the President is responsible for answering for them in Parliament on matters of Parliamentary concern, and that he must therefore be well informed on their activities and take a particular interest in their financial results, their reputation and general efficiency'. The industries appeared to recognise and respect this responsibility of Ministers. And the very existence of this Committee reflects the continuing interest of Parliament in the problems, conduct and performance of the industries.

87. . . . . Ministers are responsible to the House, i.e. they may be questioned about, or asked to justify in debate any action they have taken in relation to the industries, whether under statutes or informally, provided, of course — and this is important — that such informal activities have become known to Members. They

may also be asked to exercise their statutory powers or informal powers for which they have clearly accepted responsibility, or asked about their non-exercise. In other words Ministers are liable to account to Parliament for all the actual exercise of their control over the industries, and also for the possible or potential exercise of their formal and better-known informal powers. In addition they may, on some occasions, be required to explain and even defend matters which fall wholly within the responsibilities of the industries themselves. Ministers are not only required to answer for themselves; they may also have to act as advocates for the Boards.

88. One peculiar feature of Parliamentary accountability is that Ministers are responsible to a body which expresses three separate and frequently conflicting interests, namely the interests of the consumers of the goods and services provided by the industries, the interests of taxpayers and the interests of the Board's employees. As Mr. Aubrey Jones pointed out, the public are, through the House of Commons and through Ministers, the proprietors of the undertakings. They are therefore interested in the size of their surpluses or deficits, which have implications for tax requirements. But the public are also consumers and therefore interested in prices, and the lower prices are the lower surpluses are liable to be.

89. These competing pressures are liable to cause considerable difficulties for Ministers . . .

The theoretical demarcation of responsibilities

90. The last matter that must be examined in this analysis of the system of Minis-terial control is the demarcation of responsibilities between the various parties involved. Set out below is the pattern of interlocking responsibilities which the various witnesses claim that it was intended to establish. The reality, as opposed to the intention, will emerge in the course of this Report.

91. The Treasury . . . describe the role of the Government as a whole as, first, to set the parameters within which the industries are to operate (fuel and transport policies, social obligations, etc.), and secondly 'to ensure as far as possible that the industries conduct their economic and financial policies in a manner which provides efficient operation and the most economic use of resources, and in general that they contribute to the needs of the national economy'.

92. 'The sponsoring Departments inevitably have a dual role, being advocates for the industries for which they are responsible and agents of the Government towards these industries.' They are primarily concerned with exercising control 'sector-wise', while taking the broader economic thinking from the central departments. They are in direct contact with the industries. To some extent they must check on the actions and programmes of the industries to satisfy themselves that they conform to the desired ends and standards . . .

93. The Treasury summarised their main functions as follows: 'setting national-ised industry investment into a wider frame'; 'testing individual programmes against the main parameters of the industries' approach' (e.g. demand forecasts, pricing assumptions), but not normally following-up in any detail; providing financial and

economic advice; accepting a special responsibility for looking at the problems of the industries as a whole (this includes co-ordinating policy in relation to the industries on such matters as rating, taxation and forms of accounts); and taking the lead on long-term thinking about such questions as investment criteria, pricing policies and indices for economic performance and productivity. The Treasury also claimed that it was their task to check on the sponsoring departments, particularly regarding investment reviews, and to reconcile differences between departments where necessary. They do not normally deal directly with the industries, but through the sponsoring departments. Thus the Treasury are clearly meant to take a somewhat detached view of the operations of the industries, and to be primarily concerned with economic and financial policies and the broader effects of their implementation.

. . . . . .

97. In brief, as it was baldly put by the Chief Secretary to the Treasury, it is the responsibility of the industry to make sure that it is efficiently run; it is the responsibility of the sponsoring department to make sure that the industry has 'taken pains' before concluding that it is efficient; and it is the responsibility of the Treasury not to provide large sums of money until it is satisfied that it will not be wasted.

. . . . . .

PARLIAMENTARY ACCOUNTABILITY

843. Ministers are accountable to Parliament for all they do in their official capacity and for all that they have power to do. Thus the sponsoring Ministers — and to some extent the Treasury — are accountable to Parliament for their exercise of control over the industries. Moreover, as will be seen, they are liable to have to explain or defend in Parliament the policies, decisions and actions of the industries themselves, including matters over which they, as Ministers, have had no direct control. Inevitably, therefore, Ministers must exercise control over the industries, and look at their activities, with an awareness of this accountability to Parliament always in their minds.

844. The Committee were therefore anxious to consider the full effect of Parliamentary accountability — the opportunities there are to call Ministers to account and the extent to which these opportunities are taken — as well as the views of both Board Chairmen and Ministers on the working of Parliamentary accountability at present.

845. One other general point is worth making. Members of Parliament represent both consumers and taxpayers. As representatives of consumers they are interested in the efficiency of the industries, as it affects prices and quality of service; as representatives of the taxpayers they are interested in the financial performance of the industries and their contribution to furthering the public interest. Thus Parliament provides a reminder to Ministers of their dual responsibilities for the public interest, and for the efficiency of the industries.

The opportunities

. . . . . .

Legislation 847. Periodic public and private legislation is required regarding the nationalised industries. The scope of debate on these occasions will depend on the content of the bills, but borrowing powers bills, which are required to authorise the maximum sums of money that may be borrowed by the industries, give periodic opportunities for wide debates on the industries concerned. Similar opportunities occur from time to time on borrowing powers orders made under such legislation which are also sometimes used to authorise higher limits on borrowing . . . On the whole, the affairs of British Railways and of each of the fuel and power industries have been debatable on some legislative occasion in many years; legislation has presented fewer opportunities for debating the affairs of other industries.

Debates on motions 848. The affairs of the industries may also be debated on substantive motions or by other means on Supply days, including debates on the Reports and Accounts of the Industries or on the Reports of the Select Committee on Nationalised Industries. In most years there have been two or three such debates, although rather fewer in recent years than there were five to ten years ago. To balance the legislative opportunities, perhaps, the choice on these occasions has tended to fall on the transport industries and the Air Corporations. The then Leader of the House thought that such debates were needed if Parliament was to keep a proper check on the relationship of Ministers to the industries. They were most effective, as expressions of Parliamentary criticism, when linked to a current problem.

Adjournment debates 849. One of the best opportunities for raising matters in some detail, without absorbing too much time, are the short adjournment debates at the end of each day's business. Any aspect of the affairs of any industry may be raised on these occasions, and hence Members frequently raised detailed matters for which Ministers are not directly responsible, so obliging the Minister to explain and sometimes defend, on their behalf, the actions of the Boards. In the period 1966 to June, 1967, there were 14 adjournment debates on nationalised industry subjects; all but two of these dealt with British Railways or London Transport matters; nine of them raised local issues.

Parliamentary Questions 850. The most frequent and also the most contentious opportunity for Parliamentary scrutiny, however, is the asking of Parliamentary Questions. The rules of order regarding Questions are discussed and explained in the evidence of the Clerk of the House of Commons and of the Second Clerk Assistant. These rules partly reflect decisions of the House itself, and partly reflect the statutory powers of Ministers, but are largely a recognition of the practices

adopted by Ministers themselves in reply to Questions about the nationalised industries. To put it bluntly, if a Minister had previously shown himself willing to answer
Questions of a certain type, i.e. to accept responsibility, then further Questions of
that type will be in order; if a Minister denies responsibility in a certain area and
refuses to answer, then further Questions in that area would appear to be out of
order. The extent to which Ministers are liable to Parliamentary questioning regarding the affairs of the industries is largely, therefore, governed by their own willingness to answer − at least in regard to matters outside their statutory powers.
Ministers of Transport, for example, had shown an increased willingness to answer
Questions, and this had been reflected in the questions that had been put down to
this Minister.

851. The Committee were glad to learn from the Second Clerk Assistant that
the rules regarding nationalised industries Questions were now generally accepted
by Members. And although many Questions have to be amended to bring them
into order, few questions relating to the industries were nowadays ruled out of
order, and only very rarely do Questions need to be referred to the Speaker for a
decision.

852. The extent to which Members are able to raise even fairly detailed matters
is revealed by a study of the Questions addressed to the Minister of Transport in
Session 1966−67 asking for 'general directions' to be given to one or other of the
Transport Boards. These were produced as examples of one of the means by which
Members are able to ask Questions about the affairs of the industries, namely by
asking the Minister to use his statutory powers to give a Board a general direction in
the public interest on some aspect of their business. Although it is well recognised
that Ministers do not actually use their powers in this way, the statutory power
provides a peg for Questions. The subjects in this sample ranged widely from major
transport policy matters such as railway fares in Scotland, through less specialised
questions such as allegations of indecent advertising by British Railways, to
narrower issues such as the suggestion that some railway compartments might be
reserved for travellers who wish to work in silence.

853. It would appear to the Committee that many of these Questions were seeking to involve Ministers in matters of management, but nevertheless most of these
Questions received substantial answers. Of the 64 Questions listed, 8 were answered
by referring the Questioner back to a previous reply; in 10 cases the Minister said it
was a 'day-to-day' or management matter; and substantial answers, although sometimes pretty brief, were given to 46 Questions.

The Select Committee 854. The last principal opportunity for Parliament to consider the affairs of the nationalised industries is through the work of the Select
Committee on Nationalised Industries. It is not for this Committee to comment on
the value of this work. They hope that their Reports are helpful to the House in
seeking to learn the facts about, and understand the problems of, the nationalised
industries, and also the problems of Ministers in controlling them.

The views of Boards and Ministers

855. Most witnesses were asked for their comments on the working of Parliamentary accountability. The general reaction was that it worked well and that little change was needed . . .

Conclusions

The scope of Parliamentary Questions 856. The present extent of Ministerial accountability undoubtedly − particularly through Parliamentary Questions − involves much work for both Departments and for the industries, and this appears to be mounting. Some details of the latter were given by British Railways. For example, in 1966, 550 Questions were tabled, in both Houses of Parliament, about British Railways; the Board were required to provide information or comment on 246 of these, an increase of 35 per cent over the number dealt with in 1965. In the same year, Members of Parliament addressed over 1,100 letters to the Chairman of the Board. But all this, the Committee believe, is a reasonable price to pay for democracy. Parliament must be able to seek information from those who owe their powers to Parliament.

857. There appear to the Committee, however, to be dangers in advancing still further the opportunities for detailed Parliamentary criticism, such as, for example, the 'freeing' of Questions from all restrictions as was recommended in most interestingly argued evidence by Professor Hanson. In the first place, from Parliament's point of view, in so far as removing the restrictions might lead to many more questions on detailed matters, then Question hour would be subject to even greater pressure than is now experienced. And this might well create less effective scrutiny of Ministers and of the industries' activities, not more. The present rates are a 'useful safety valve', as the Second Clerk Assistant said. (In any event, it is not certain that removing the restrictions would lead to more Questions being asked; it could be that many of the 'general direction' Questions would simply appear in a more direct, specific and less disguised form.)

858. In the second place, and of greater importance, the Committee believe that acceptance of Questions by Ministers on detailed matters that are at present excluded would create a threat to the autonomous management of the industries. The Committee are not much worried about the direct impact on the industries of the questions themselves − they could probably be accepted without greatly disturbing the industries' sense of management responsibility, just as letters direct from Members of Parliament are accepted today. The dangers would rather be in the indirect consequences. Once Ministers become even more involved, through Parliamentary Questions, in the details of management, it would, the Committee suspect, be difficult to avoid a position where the Departments very naturally extended the areas of their interest to other aspects of the Boards' affairs. Once, as

it were, a civil servant has established his rights to enter an industry's private garden by showing a Parliamentary Question as a permit, he would soon become a familiar visitor and could roam around and pick the flowers with or without his permit. The Committee believe that this danger already exists, but that it would be greatly extended if Questions were permitted regularly on local, detailed, or day-to-day matters of management.

859. Some further adjustments of the present rules may be desirable, such as permitting Questions asking for statistics on a regional as well as a national basis, as suggested by the Second Clerk Assistant. But the Committee are anxious not to create the danger of further confusions of responsibilities between Ministers and Boards.

. . . . . .

WHAT HAS GONE WRONG

. . . . . .

871. The central pillars of the system of Government control of the industries are the sponsoring Departments. Whatever the importance of the Treasury — and their influence is enormous and their capacity for innovation has been welcomed — the brunt of the day-to-day supervision of the industries falls to the Departments. They inevitably stand at the centre of the system. And the Committee are of opinion that the underlying weaknesses in the system are mainly to be found in the sponsoring Departments.

872. To be specific. The Committee regret that they heard little from the Ministers or their officials that indicated a readiness to look critically at the system of control in the large, to consider the very purpose of their existence or of their jobs or to look critically at the wider economic aspects of Ministerial control. There were exceptions; some had clearly faced the more awkward questions; but on the whole, all three Departments that gave evidence were more concerned to defend the details of their actions than to question or explain what was the purpose of these actions.

873. Secondly, and this is the fundamental weakness, the Committee have become aware of an underlying confusion touching all the elements in the system, but centring on the sponsoring Departments . . .

874. Not surprisingly, this lack of clarity about purposes and responsibilities has revealed itself in a lack of understanding and in some cases, a breakdown of mutual confidence between Boards and Ministries. Some Board Chairmen, in particular, while ready to voice their complaints to this Committee had not discussed them with their Minister or his officials. And this lack on the part of the boards of confidence in the sponsoring Departments has led some of them to press for more access to the Treasury (so threatening to confuse responsibilities still further), and others to criticise the staffing of the Departments.

875. Lying still deeper than this lack of clarity, this confusion of responsibilities and this breakdown of confidence remains a failure to understand and to work

towards the fulfilment of the basic purposes of Ministerial control in respect of the industries. As set out in paragraph 74, these are first to secure the wider public interest — and secondly, to oversee, and if possible ensure, the efficiency of the industries.

876. The implications of this demarcation, in the opinion of the Committee, were that it was the intention of Parliament that Ministers should be primarily concerned with laying down policies — in particular for the whole of their sectors of the economy — which would guide the operations of the individual industries, and should not intervene in the management of the industries in implementing these policies.

877. The practice has revealed an almost reversed situation. Until fairly recently, Ministers appear, on the whole, to have given the industries very little guidance in regard to either sector policies or economic obligations such as pricing policies or investment criteria; clear policies on some of these matters, including pricing, are still lacking. On the other hand they have become closely involved in many aspects of management, particularly in control of investment in some sectors and also in some aspects of pricing control and control over staff matters.

878. The Committee do not wish to exaggerate. They have picked on the weaknesses to show where the fabric needs strengthening. They are well aware that because of the experience, loyalty, energies and, sometimes, wisdom of many of those involved in the work of the Departments and the industries, the work has gone on, the industries have expanded and developed, and the nation has frequently (although not always) had the benefit of a good service. But they are left with the firm conviction, as it was put by one Chairman of a Board, that 'we have not got yet the proper relationship between the nationalised industries, their sponsoring departments and the Government'.

879. The Committee have made numerous specific recommendations designed to improve this relationship within the present structure of Government. But they now turn to examine the structure of Government itself, as it relates to the problem of Ministerial control.

The case for change

The need for new thinking about institutions 880. The Head of the Government Economic Service said in evidence that he suspected more attention had been paid to economic issues than to organisation issues. The Committee believe this to be true. In recent years there has been much new thinking regarding the economic obligations of the industries, and a new relationship between Ministers and Boards has begun to emerge. The main characteristic of this relationship, as analysed and further advocated by the Committee in this Report, is the development of rationally determined strategic guidance, together with more autonomy for the Boards to interpret and comply with this guidance as efficiently as they can and by whatever means they choose. This relationship has been advocated especially in respect of pricing and investment, which are the main economic regulators of the industries. And the acceptance of this new relationship implies some modification of the respective responsibilities and powers of all the bodies concerned . . .

881. It is impossible, however, to alter the relationship between institutions in such a way as to alter their responsibilities and powers without calling in question whether those institutions are still the right ones for the task.

882. Approaching the issue by another route, the Committee came to the same question. If a basic confusion of purposes and of responsibilities exists, as has been demonstrated, between the industries, the Departments and the Treasury/D.E.A., could it be because different institutions are needed to do the jobs which have become confused?

883. The Committee have welcomed the new economic thinking and have sought to take it a step or two further in some respects. But they believe that the necessary institutional thinking, consequent on the new relationships, has lagged behind — at least among those from the Ministries and industries who gave evidence. The Committee therefore hope to help institutional thinking onwards by a few steps as well. Who should do what? And through what machinery?

The responsibilities of ministers 884. It has already been argued that Ministers have a twin set of responsibilities vis-a-vis the industries. They are, first, to secure the public interest, and secondly, to oversee and to seek to ensure the industries' efficiency. The Committee also recognise that sponsoring Ministers have two allied obligations; on the one hand they are the spokesmen for the interests and wishes of the industries in the Cabinet and in Parliament and on the other they represent the interests and wishes of the Cabinet and Parliament (and through them the general public) to the industries. On the whole, although not completely, a Minister's responsibility for securing the public interest is allied with his role as spokesman for the Government — he tells the industries what they are expected to do; his concern for an industry's efficiency finds expression in his role as spokesman for that industry.

885. The new economic thinking implies some change in the balance of these responsibilities. Securing the public interest is essentially a Ministerial task which cannot be shared with the industries, and for which Ministers must be seen to take full responsibility, including often financial responsibility. Ministers may have to exercise direct, ad hoc and specific controls to secure these interests, in regard to either investment, pricing or services to be provided.

886. The duty to oversee and to seek to ensure the industries' efficiency should be principally exercised by the use of certain economic policies and criteria, which as far as possible should be determined and applied equally to all industries. Therefore, in so far as the industries are operated as commercial bodies, they should be left as free as possible of detailed Ministerial control regarding prices and investment. The Government should not intervene in management.

887. Therefore it will be seen that not only does each of the sponsoring Ministers

bear a double responsibility, but that the nature of their exercising them differs. To combine the two sets of responsibilities in one man is bound to cause confusion in the minds of both Ministries and industries . . .

888. The first purpose, therefore, of the reconstruction of the Departments that the Committee will propose is to separate out these two sets of responsibilities. Until this is done, the Committee are convinced that confusion will continue. They consider that much of the complaint made by witnesses from the industries about the system of Ministerial control stems from a failure on the part of Ministers (and also, sometimes, Boards) to distinguish these responsibilities. In particular, a Minister who has to impose fairly heavy social obligations, perhaps on several industries and even on industries other than those for whom he has sponsorship responsibilities, must find it very hard to limit his concern for more commercial investment to the level that would be appropriate if his only responsibility was the oversight of their efficiency.

The need for concentration and specialisation 889. The second purpose to be secured by reconstruction is quite separate. As has been shown there is a fairly rapid turn round of staff in the nationalised industry divisions of sponsoring Departments; there is little specialisation; and there is little cross-fertilisation of experience and ideas. One object of Departmental re-organisation should be to make better use of the staff of sponsoring Departments.

. . . . . .

A Ministry of Nationalised Industries 892. In the opinion of the Committee the purposes described in the last section could best be achieved by bringing together in the person of one Minister, to be called the Minister of Nationalised Industries, those responsibilities now exercised by the President of the Board of Trade, the Minister of Power, the Secretary of State for Scotland, the Minister of Transport and (after the creation of the Post Office Corporation) the Postmaster General that are chiefly directed at overseeing and seeking to ensure the efficiency of any of the nationalised industries. But only those responsibilities would be so transferred; the other functions of the Ministers would stay with the original Minister or be further re-allocated.

893. The principal responsibilities of the Minister and Ministry of Nationalised Industries would be as follows:

(i) *The appointment (and dismissal) of the members of all the Boards.* While this instrument of control is basic to both 'public interest' and 'efficiency' purposes, the standing of Board Members is the primary expression of the autonomy of the industries; and the power to appoint or dismiss them is essentially associated with concern for the industries' efficiency.

(ii) *Laying down the adopted pricing and investment policies for the industry.* This could be a two-part exercise. In so far as it was a matter of determining a pricing policy, say, appropriate for an industry, the Minister of

Nationalised Industries would deal with the industry direct. But the stated policies could also contain adjustments required by other Ministers for social obligations and other public interest reasons.

(iii) *Agreeing the financial objective that follows from (ii) above.*

(iv) *Reviewing investment programmes and approving investment projects.* Again adjustments might have to be made in programmes, at the request of other Ministers, for social obligations. But it is hoped that, as far as possible, these obligations or services will be 'bought' by the beneficiary Department, and appear on the programme only for information and to enable the aggregate of investment to be reviewed.

(v) *Approving capital structures and borrowing.*

(vi) *Furthering co-ordination and co-operation between industries in the interests of their commercial efficiency.* Co-ordination for other purposes, e.g. fuel policy, would be a matter for other Ministers.

(vii) *General oversight of the structure and organisation of the industries with regard to their efficiency*, including the spread of new management techniques, e.g. critical path analyses, computerisation, and the use of efficiency study units.

(viii) *Undertaking or making arrangements for efficiency studies.*

(ix) *Approving research programmes, training and education programmes, etc.*, in so far as this is thought to be necessary for ensuring efficiency.

(x) *Approving the forms of the Accounts.*

(xi) *Laying annual Reports and Accounts before Parliament.*

(xii) *Accounting to Parliament* for all their own activities and answering on the adjournment debates, etc., on the activities of the industries as commercial bodies. It might be desirable to have separate Ministers of State for the fuel and power, transport and civil aviation sectors. The new Minister would not be expected to attract nearly as many Parliamentary questions as the present sponsoring Ministers in total, first because the present Ministers have other responsibilities, e.g. roads, and secondly because he would not assume their responsibilities for fuel and transport policy, etc.

In addition the Minister of Nationalised Industries would need formal powers to give directions to give effect to Government policies determined by other Ministers . . . But he would not normally exercise powers of direction on his own behalf.

The advantages of a single Ministry 894. One of the strongest arguments in favour of a centralised Ministry of Nationalised Industries is that it would be able to make optimum use of the total staff available for this work. No doubt within the Department they would divide up by sectors, but the allocation of the staff between sectors should be much more flexible than is the case at present between the separate Ministries, and so they could be deployed to the best advantage and the greatest effort could be concentrated on whatever industries at any one time appeared to need such help or attention.

895. The staff of the new Ministry would become experts in the affairs and prob-

lems of nationalised industries, as such, and so further the kind of specialisation desired by the Fulton Committee on the Civil Service. Instead of spending three or four years in the railways division, say of the Ministry of Transport, and then moving, say, to roads or road safety, officials would always be concerned with problems related to nationalised industries so long as they stayed in the Ministry at all . . . As the Permanent Secretary at the Ministry of Power said, 'comparative knowledge of all nationalised industries' is 'almost as important as knowledge of the one they are dealing with at the time'. What better way could there be of achieving this than to have one Ministry?

896. The Committee believe that a single Minister of Nationalised Industries would also develop a more consistent relationship towards all the industries than can the separate Ministers today. This would be reflected in the formulation of common policies and practices for such matters as the salaries and terms of appointment of Board members, and the methods of finding and selecting them. The single Minister would also be better placed than the present separate Ministers to plan the appointment of Board members between industries, for example to appoint someone as a part-time member of more than one Board, and so further the co-ordination of the industries' planning.

897. One of the most important gains would be in the development and promotion of management and control techniques common to the industries. It might be desirable to set up a central development division in the Department with people drawn from work concerned with different industries, which would give particular attention to promoting the use by the industries of sound forecasting techniques and investment appraisal methods, the calculation and application of marginal costs, the further development of pricing policies and the longer-term calculation of financial objectives . . .

898. The new Ministry would undoubtedly be more effective than the present separate Departments in securing the fullest possible co-ordination between the commercial policies of the industries . . .

899. Finally, the new Minister would act as the spokesman for all the industries to the Treasury and in the Cabinet. Unlike the present Ministers he would have to consider the interest of all the industries and not just of those within a particular sector. This should help the balanced planning of the industries' programmes. He would be able to judge the effect on the industries of policies imposed for social or other public interest reasons, to discuss with them how they should be implemented and to put the case for the industries to the Ministers concerned. He would thus look after the interests of all the industries equally, with an equal concern for their efficiency and fortunes.

21 THE GOVERNMENT'S REPLY

Extracts from *The Government's Reply to the Report of the Select Committee on*

Nationalised Industries, 1967–8: Ministerial Control of the Nationalised Industries (Cmnd. 4027, 1969); reprinted by permission of H.M.S.O. This extract gives the Government's reasons for rejecting the Select Committee's main recommendation for a central Ministry of Nationalised Industries; but the acceptance that financially unviable but socially desirable commitments could be specially costed and subsidised was an important step forward.

Introduction The Government welcome this valuable and comprehensive Report, which reviews the developing relationship between Ministers and the Nationalised Industries. They understand the Committee's main thesis to be that Ministers have two quite separate responsibilities giving rise to two distinct functions in this connection. One is their responsibility for the efficiency, in the economic and financial sense, of the industries themselves. The other is their responsibility for the wider public interest.

2. The Government accept that these two responsibilities can be conceptually distinguished. For the reasons given in paragraphs 4–10 below, they do not draw the organisational conclusion which the Committee itself draws from this analysis: that the two responsibilities give rise to separable and distinct functions which would be best exercised by different departments. The Government do however agree with the Committee that these two responsibilities need to be recognised in order to clarify consideration of the objectives of Ministers and of the industries. Many of the remaining recommendations of the Committee are designed to secure this clarification, and the Government accept them accordingly, as explained below.
. . . . . .

A Ministry of Nationalised Industries 4. The Government have given very careful consideration to the closely argued case in the Select Committee's Report (paragraphs 890–930) for a Ministry of Nationalised Industries. They have, however, concluded that the disadvantages of a major change in the machinery of government on these lines would substantially outweigh the advantages.

5. First, while it is true that the requirements of efficiency in one of the industries and the wider public interest (using both terms in the sense in which they were used by the Committee) may sometimes conflict in particular cases, it does not necessarily follow that the decision-making process would be improved if the two interests were the responsibility of different Ministers. There would inevitably be an initial handicap in that decisions now involving one Minister would commonly involve two, informal consultation within a single department necessarily giving way to more formal exchanges between two. And a polarisation of responsibility, under which the Minister responsible for sector policy had no responsibility for efficiency, and the Minister responsible for efficiency no responsibility for the wider national interest, would not of itself be any guarantee that either of these responsibilities would prevail over the other more often than at present. There are of course very many cases in which major conflicts of public interest are resolved within individual departments. This is manifestly true of many large departments,

and the application of a principle that in every case of major conflict of public interest the conflicting aspects must be the responsibility of different Ministers would lead to the break-up of the Ministry of Defence, the Department of Education and Science and a good many others.

6. Secondly, in the Government's view the Select Committee's proposal rests on too ready an assumption about the ease with which the sector responsibility and the efficiency responsibility could be separated into self-contained compartments in practice. For example, the Government regard responsibility for a rational energy policy and responsibility for the investment programmes of the three nationalised fuel industries, as well as for the efficiency of these industries, as inextricably linked. The same would be true of transport policy and investment in railways and roads.

7. In neither energy nor transport is it possible to achieve the best investment result in the national interest simply by attention to the profitability of the investment programme of a single industry. It is essential to have regard to the effect of investment in one industry on the return on investment in others. In having regard to these effects, the responsible department is in fact concerning itself with a national energy or national transport policy. If a Ministry for Nationalised Industries took account of these interactions, both this department and the sector departments would find themselves working on energy or transport policy, with resultant duplication and risk of interdepartmental dispute. If it did not, the sector departments would need to concern themselves still more closely with investment programmes, with the same results.

8. Another implication of separating the sector responsibility and the efficiency responsibility is the division which this would produce between responsibilities for public and private sector undertakings in the same sector. The Committee's proposal assumes a sharp distinction between the type of responsibility exercised in the framework of national energy, transport or civil aviation policy, in relation to the nationalised industries and the sponsorship function in relation to private sector undertakings in the same sector. In practice a lively interest in the performance of, e.g., the privately-owned oil industry, or the private road haulage or civil aviation undertakings, is an important element in sector responsibility; and Government policy in relation to these undertakings may affect substantially their investment and their prices. For this reason the sector department must be concerned with all aspects of the economic health of both public and private undertakings in its sector.

9. Thirdly, the Government are in no doubt that the sub-division of responsibilities in relation to each nationalised industry and the creation of a Ministry of Nationalised Industries at arms length from the sector responsibilities would mean more work and more staff in Government and in the nationalised industries, which would each be concerned with two government departments. Conflicts of public interest now reconciled within a single department would have to be more formally debated between two departments and on such issues both departments might want recourse to the industries and to the central departments. The position of the Chairmen of nationalised industries with two departments could become more difficult

or equivocal. The burden of information, or consultation and of co-ordination would be greater both in Government and in the industries. While there would be two departments instead of one necessarily seeking information from each industry, there would be no single point in Government so well informed as at present about each industry and its relationship to sector policy and the wider national interest. It is true that in exchange there would grow up in the Ministry of Nationalised Industries an expertise in dealing with nationalised industries as such. However, there is already in the Ministry of Power a considerable concentration of such expertise, since the business of the department is mainly with nationalised industries. In the circumstances the Government consider that the exchange which would result from the Select Committee's proposal would not yield a net gain.

10. Fourthly, the Government do not believe that the establishment of a Ministry of Nationalised Industries responsible for the efficiency of those industries, but not for sector policy, would reduce intervention in the management of the industries, as the Select Committee hope and expect. It is not enough to say that the powers and responsibilities of the proposed Minister should be no more than those recommended in the Select Committee's Report. The promotion of efficiency could be held to cover a wide range of existing statutory functions as well as new matters. If Parliament were invited to regard the new Minister as having the general efficiency of the industries as his main responsibility, they would tend to expect him to answer on many aspects of the management of the industries, especially in view of the powers recommended. All the pressures of responsibility would be towards greater intervention.

11. The Government accept that there would be certain advantages in a horizontal organisation, which treated nationalised industry as a function for itself. It is natural and right that the Select Committee on Nationalised Industries should see these advantages very clearly. The Government, however, take the view that these gains would be greatly outweighed by losses if the price were the divorce of industry responsibility from sector responsibility. A department responsible for all nationalised industries and all relevant sectors would be too diverse and too large. If the choice between the two methods of organisation has therefore to be made, the Government consider that organisation by sectors is to be preferred.

The role of departments 12. The Government believe that within the existing pattern of responsibilities the tasks of particular departments require further detailed study. They therefore accept the Committee's recommendation (paragraph 541) that discussions should be held between the Treasury, the D.E.A. and the departments to clarify their respective contributions to the control of investment. Because of the importance of investment as a central feature of Ministerial control over the industries, the Government believe this to be a most important recommendation.

. . . . . .

14. The Committee drew attention to complaints by some industries that they

had insufficient access to the Treasury, and recommend (paragraph 822) that in future, in cases where the final decision rested with the Treasury, industries should have the right to state their case to the Treasury; although the Committee also recognised (paragraph 824) that the Treasury was not a court of appeal against decisions of the responsible departments. Government policies towards the industries are of course finally settled by Ministers collectively, not by officials in individual departments. But the Government agree that it is right for the industries to have opportunities to meet the central economic departments.

15. The Committee suggested (paragraph 664) that, in addition to the present statutory power to issue general directions, and to issue specific directions upon particular subjects specified in the statutes, Ministers should also have a statutory power to issue formal directives upon any specific subject which appears to them to be in the national interest.

16. As the Committee recognised Ministers have in some cases powers to issue specific directions upon particular subjects defined in the statutes. If circumstances arose in future in which it seemed advisable for a Minister to be able to deal with a particular subject by issuing specific formal directions, for which powers did not exist, the Government would seek the necessary powers for the purpose. To this extent, the Government accept the Committee's proposal; but they do not propose to take general powers to issue specific directions on any subject to the nationalised industries. Possession of such wide general powers would, in their view, lead to heavier pressure on Ministers to interfere with the management of the industries than the Committee foresee. It would involve the creation of a new climate in which the industries would be seen to be formally subject to Ministerial control on particular as well as general matters which touched the national interest. This would in the Government's view inevitably lead over the years to a gradual encroachment by Ministers on the management responsibilities of the industries, so undermining their efficiency and reducing their capacity to recruit and keep capable top management.

17. The serious problems which arise in defining an elastic concept such as the national interest would be accentuated if it became possible to issue directions on particular as well as general matters. And the fact that Ministers possessed the power of direction would inevitably require substantial additional staff effort over the whole field in which the power could be exercised — even if in a substantial proportion of such cases it was decided not to exercise the power. This would not, in the Government's view, be a worthwhile use of civil service manpower. The Government therefore prefer that Ministerial relationships with the industries should be developed within the present statutory framework of control. Within this framework practical conventions and usages have evolved which preserve an acceptable degree of autonomy for the industries while at the same time providing the necessary degree of accountability to Parliament.

. . . . . .

Social obligations 34. In paragraph 282, and in greater detail in Chapter XIV of the

Report, the Committee recommended that 'where extra social or wider public interest obligations are imposed on or undertaken by the industries, they should be publicly identified, quantified and appropriately financed by the Ministers concerned'. It will not always be practicable to identify or quantify such obligations precisely. Nor, having done so, would it always be necessary or desirable to make special payments accordingly. Nevertheless, as indicated in paragraph 37 of Cmnd. 3437, where an industry is required to act against its own commercial interests the Government will take responsibility and, where appropriate, make a special payment to the industry or make an adjustment to its financial objectives.

Financial objectives 35. The Committee accepted (paragraph 483) the policy set out in the White Paper, under which financial objectives should become the financial expression of the pricing and investment criteria already laid down. The Government are already working out the consequences of this policy for settling new financial objectives for the gas and electricity industries, and financial objectives for the other industries will fall to be fixed, or revised, from time to time. In this process the views expressed by the Committee in paragraphs 485–498 about the quantification and expression of objectives will be borne in mind. To a considerable extent these views reflect the Government's existing thinking on these subjects as expressed in evidence to the Committee.

36. The Committee recommended (paragraph 496) that objectives should be set for each of the fuel industries as a whole and not for individual Area Boards. So long as the Area Boards enjoy financial autonomy under the statutes, the Minister concerned must formally settle financial objectives with each of them. Where, as in the gas industry and in the electricity industry in England and Wales, there is a Council for the industry, the Minister will seek the advice of the Council before settling the individual objectives.

22 THE MANAGEMENT OF THE PUBLIC ECONOMIC SECTOR

Extracts from Sir Richard Clarke, *New Trends in Government* (Civil Service College Studies 1, 1971); reprinted by permission of H.M.S.O. Here the author examines the conflict between the requirements of managerial efficiency and political accountability and explores newer applications of the public corporation concept.

In this section, I move on from the structure of departments and the organisation of the centre of government to the mechanism by which the State carries out certain functions outside the direct day-to-day responsibility of Ministers and departments.

Nationalised industries

I start with the nationalised industries — the publicly owned industries and services of a commercial character. They are listed in Annex 5 with total assets of nearly £14,000 million in 1969—70, and a total labour force of nearly two million. They comprise coal, electricity, gas, posts and telecommunications, iron and steel, airlines, airports, rail transport, and many other transport organisations. The way in which these industries are run, and their relations with the government, are manifestly of first-class importance to industry and to the whole national economy.

In this country (in marked contrast to most countries in the western world) most of these industries have come into public ownership as a result of government decisions based upon a philosophy of government and in conditions of political controversy. For fifty years, since the Labour Party wrote nationalisation into its constitution in 1918, this has been a continuing live political issue. In many instances the acts of nationalisation were carried through without a political clash, and the earlier ones, indeed, by Conservative governments, Central Electricity Generating Board (1926), BBC (1927), London Passenger Transport Board (1933). But the background of political controversy is always there — in 1970 as strongly as in 1950.

. . . . . .

Frontiers of nationalised industries

. . . It is obvious that a succession of processes of nationalisation, denationalisation and renationalisation (I don't think we have yet experienced a redenationalisation) can be catastrophic for the efficiency of any industry. The political requirements will always be overriding, but the economic cost of such disturbance must be great; and one can legitimately ask that successive governments should try to establish situations in the contested areas which will be tolerable to their opponents, and so get some long-term approach to stability.

. . . . . .

The arguments here are not easy to weigh, and they must have a large political content. It is clearly impracticable, and would not make sense, to try to define a statutory frontier, valid for all time, to be changed only be some parliamentary process. The nationalised industry must be able to adjust itself to technological and market change. On the other hand, private industry competing in these peripheral fields may have legitimate complaint if the nationalised industry, supported by government money and by the profits from the non-competitive parts of its business, is competing too sharply. If the efforts of its top management and its resources of skilled people are diverted to peripheral extensions of the industry's business, this may damage the nationalised industry's effectiveness in carrying out its basic task. A large private business, expanding fast into new fields, can simultaneously abandon others; but the nationalised industry cannot do so. In general, the nationalised industries are too big as management units, rather than too small; and the extension at the periphery may be damaging to the centre.

There is a real problem here, which cannot be sloganised by 'public good, private bad' or vice versa. I am not suggesting here how this should be tackled, though it seems likely that some kind of institutional solution (and possibly mixed public/ private undertakings at the periphery) may be called for. What I am concerned to show is that there is a genuine industrial issue, completely separate from the party-political argument.

Organisation of nationalised industries

Another kind of problem is that of the organisation of the nationalised industry itself. One of the consequences of the public searchlight upon the industries is a continuous interest in government and in Parliament in their organisation, and a readiness to propose changes in all quarters. This attracts much attention to questions of organisation and structure, which are essentially matters for the higher management; and in many of the industries there has been a remarkable series of changes of structure in the last twenty years, each with its Act of Parliament, swinging from centralisation to decentralisation and back again, in accordance with the current fashion in management doctrine. The disturbance costs of this process, in the successive periods of examination, legislation, waiting for the new appointments, and in getting the new organisation under way are heavy.

These periods of uncertainty aggravate two of the inherent weaknesses of nationalised industry – the lack of a clear and simple objective and criterion for policy decisions (like the role of profit in the private sector) and the problem of exercising effective communication and leadership through these huge and inevitably rambling organisations. To overcome these weaknesses calls for continuous and sustained effort by the top management (and co-operation from the department); and this is frustrated beyond repair if the top management itself is paralysed by uncertainty about the future of the organisation.

It is wise to set up the constitution so that change can easily be made within the organisation, and without legislation; and so avoid situations in which there is general acceptance that the organisation needs to be changed (and therefore a lame-duck administration) and there follow years of thought and waiting for the opportunity to legislate – and meanwhile higher management can do nothing. An industry which is growing with the national economy (or faster) will need continuous change and adaptation, and a clear strand of management policy from the centre to do it; if one waits until the structure is top heavy and creaking under its own weight, a revolution is required. In private enterprise the successful firms are those which achieve this continuous transformation. Those who fail are taken over, and somehow in nationalised industry we have to provide for the same processes in a much smoother and more organic manner than is now possible.

The public corporation

Nationalisation in this country has been based upon the concept of the public corporation, applied in the earlier cases in the 1920s and the favoured instrument of the Labour Party's programme of the 1930s, developed by Herbert Morrison. The public corporation was to be an independent body, with the board appointed by the Minister, but free from day-to-day control from the Minister or Parliament; the members chosen on merit and not as representing 'interests'. The statute normally provided for a monopoly, and instructed it to work on business lines, so conducting its affairs that it paid its way taking one year with another. It would raise its finance in the market, like older public boards such as the Port of London Authority, but provision was made for Exchequer guarantee where necessary.

. . . . . .

The emphasis was on an independent corporation, conducting the service efficiently and in the public interest. This was the original strand running through the policy, and broadly enacted in the nationalisation measures carried out by the Labour government of 1945—51. There was no great fear about the profitability of these undertakings. There was an underlying belief that the scope for rationalisation and economies of scale in a national monopoly would be large; that it would be possible to achieve better working relations with the staffs; and that the undertakings would get their finance more cheaply than private companies could. The concepts were founded on profitable public utilities.

Government intervention

But soon another strand began to appear, the possibility provided by public ownership of the nationalised industries, to press them to behave in a way that supported government policy or 'national planning'. This was particularly attractive in the field of wages and prices, but also in the control of investment. When the government were trying to contain the rate of increase of incomes and prices, independent action by the nationalised industries could become highly disruptive, for whatever the constitutional position, everyone thought the nationalised industries were controlled by the government . . .

. . . . . .

The experience of twenty years under both Conservative and Labour governments shows a continuing tendency to seek to exercise control of wages, prices and short-term investment decisions. This is contrary to the original doctrine of the public corporation, and strictly speaking inconsistent with a succession of White Papers by successive governments which sought to develop the original doctrine to sharpen the concept of 'the industry paying its way', and to establish ground rules by which the industries should take their medium and long-term investment decisions and handle their pricing policies.

This conflict of doctrine between the original 'public corporation' concept (as subsequently developed) and the concept of the nationalised industry being an available instrument for government action designed to help in the short-term management of the national economy does appear to be common to Conservative and Labour governments alike. It must, I am afraid, be regarded as a fact of life: the pressures on government to influence the economy with all weapons at their disposal in time of trouble are so clamant that it is hardly reasonable to expect them to refrain from using them. But it is reasonable to try to limit the scope of such interference.

Limits of interference

The efficiency of the nationalised industries, which, given their size and importance to the national economy must be overriding in all but very special circumstances, cannot be sustained if there is continuous interference from Ministers and departments. There will inevitably be interference sometimes; but it is very important to get the circumstances and procedures firmly agreed and established. Some of the problems of relationship between departments and nationalised industries are not dissimilar from the problems discussed earlier of the relations between the centre of Whitehall and the departments: certain points must be identified for control, and outside this there should be no government intervention.

In my judgement, there are four areas that are really important:
(i)   the efficiency of the industry
(ii)   finance and profitability
(iii)   appointments
(iv)   long-term development.

In all of these, it is the industry's system and the ground rules that it has to observe which are crucial. Neither a department nor anybody else can do the industry's work for it; nor in organisations of this size can examination from outside do anything other than check the industry's own system. So this is where to concentrate.

Efficiency. The first step is to discover how the higher management of the industry satisfies itself and measures the efficiency with which the industry works. If the management has an effective system, and reports periodically on what the system shows, there is nothing more that the department can do. The controversial issue is how to define 'efficiency' — the best combination of labour and capital to produce the best service at the lowest cost: if the objective is the cheapest cost, the criteria will be very different from those if the objective were the best service. It is reasonable for the department, representing so to speak both the customers and the shareholders, to approve the parameters. But when the department has laid these down, the operation is the management's. There may be advantage in having a rare but thorough examination from outside. But the relevant point is the internal system.

Finance and profitability. It is now the practice for the department to lay down the average earnings on assets at which the management must aim, and the criteria to be taken into account in taking new investment decisions. When this is done, again, the right course is to leave the management to proceed on this basis. The attempted physical control by the department of the industry's investment, either by fixing an aggregate expenditure figure or by seeking to scrutinise individual projects will be counter-productive: if it does not affect the actual decisions (which will normally be the case) it is a waste of time, and if it does, it is weakening the management's responsibility at the crucial point and so endangering the whole attitude of the industry to finance and the direction of resources.

Appointments. The Minister is responsible for appointing the members of the Board of the industry; and this is probably the Minister's most exacting duty. Ministers of successive governments have been more successful in this over twenty years than could perhaps have been expected; and some of the chairmen of the leading boards have been highly successful. But the proportion of chairmen who came from the industry itself has been lower than would have been the case in private industry over such a period; and the fact that Ministers have so often been compelled to look outside the industry throws some doubt upon the procedures for talent-spotting and career development within some of the industries.

In my opinion, there should be a presumption that the top management posts within each nationalised industry should be filled from within the industry; and that full-time executive appointments should be made from outside only in very special circumstances. But this cannot be acceptable to Ministers unless they can be satisfied with the industries' arrangements for developing the ability and bringing it to the top; and in my view Ministers should insist on being so satisfied.

Again, how little basis there is for judging whether a chairman (or an industry) has been successful or not. One cannot judge simply by the industry's earnings, for these will depend partly on the government background and upon the monopoly situation. Nor are the relations between industry and department a better criterion . . .

Long-term development. The department should periodically consider the industry's corporate plan, and the general pattern of its long-term development (including the extensions of its frontiers). This is the point at which the impact of the industry's plans on other aspects of government policy, e.g. regional policy should be considered — not at tactical moments but when the industry is developing its own strategy.

Wages and prices. On wages, it is impossible for any management to accept the detailed instructions of the government unless the government are in effect willing to take over the wage negotiations themselves, which is the negation of independent management. If there is a national incomes policy, nationalised industry can participate in it on the same basis as private industry. If the government is trying to influence the nationalised industry wage settlements without behaving similarly in the private sector, this is a situation calling for great tact on the government's part. Governments are bound to try to do this from time to time; but such intervention should be rare and quiet, for management becomes impossible if it is not regarded by the labour force as carrying full responsibility for their pay.

Once it is accepted that the attempt to control and prevent nationalised industries' prices from rising to cover costs must necessarily involve an increased burden on the Exchequer, it is likely that governments will press less hard. The experience of twenty years is decisive, as we have seen above, in seeing the end of such a period of attempted direct action on nationalised industry prices as necessitating such a series of price rises that the last stage may well be worse than the first.

Conclusion. These considerations would seem to set out the kind of relationship between the department and its nationalised industry concentrated on a limited number of key elements — which could survive over a considerable period, provided that the government's inevitable preoccupation with the industry's wage settlements and pricing policies were handled with tact by the government and understanding by the industry.

'Hiving off'

The characteristic of the nationalised industries is that they are all producing and selling goods or services on a commercial basis. The operations of some are less sharply commercial than others. Some railway services, kept open on social grounds and receiving a subsidy accordingly are clearly non-commercial. The Atomic Energy Authority has combined wholly commercial operations in the manufacture and sale of fuel elements for nuclear power stations — separated from 1st April 1971 into another organisation — with military R & D paid for by the Ministry of Defence and nuclear civil R & D paid for by the Department of Trade and Industry. But in the normal nationalised industry the work is wholly commercial, and the problem is to create pressures and relationships which will make the behaviour of the industry as responsive to market and cost considerations as is practicable.

There has been much discussion of the desirability and practicability of 'hiving off' certain functions from government and establishing separate agencies of a character similar to nationalised industries to do their work. There are in fact very few truly commercial operations within the field of central government, in which goods or services are being produced and sold as the central purpose of the activity, financed by Votes and staffed by civil servants. There are some commercial institutions, such as the Royal Mint and the Forestry Commission, which are financed by Votes and much closer to government than nationalised industries. It may be sensible to set them up as separate agencies, similar to nationalised industries, for the greater degree of financial freedom of manoeuvre and responsiveness to the market. But there are few of these.

The new Civil Aviation Authority recommended by the Edwards Report is a new type of development, for this would be a regulatory authority, and not a commercial one. It would take over the civil aviation regulatory operations of the Department of Trade and Industry (some conducted hitherto by the department direct and some by separate agencies such as the Air Registration Board and the Air Transport Licensing Board); and the real interest will lie partly in the Authority's ability to develop its whole series of functions effectively together in this new field, and partly in whether it will be able to take the controversial decisions and make them stick, and so relieve ministers of responsibility for them. If it could succeed in doing this successfully, this would be an important and genuine 'hiving off', for it would be reducing the load on the Minister. But if in the end, the decisions have to be defended by the Minister, not very much is gained.

. . . . . .

Management of social expenditures

It is sometimes suggested that the 'public corporation' concept could be adopted in other fields of government activity. The advantages which are claimed for public corporations — more professional management, with greater freedom from government and parliamentary pressure — could apply to social services as well as the nationalised industries.

At one time it used to be suggested that if this were done it would permit increased expenditure on these services. Even as little as ten years ago, it was argued that a National Road Corporation would be able to 'raise loans from the public' and therefore be able to finance a larger programme than was possible in the existing system. Of course, if a National Road Corporation were allowed to charge motorists for the use of the roads, and earned such a large autonomous revenue that it became a commercial organisation, the considerations governing the size of the road programme would be changed very radically. But this course is just as open (or not) to DOE as it would be to a National Road Corporation. The issue is not about the advantage of having a public corporation instead of a government department; it is about whether it would be practicable or acceptable to charge users of the roads on a vastly greater scale than now, and so set up a new economic basis for road-building.

In an 'economy' campaign in the mid-1950s, new legislation was introduced to enable the government to pay grants to local authorities in aid of the cost of servicing loans for water and sewerage projects, instead of giving capital grants to the capital expenditures on these projects. This would reduce the aggregate of government grants to the local authorities in any particular year; and was thought to be an 'economy'. It was sensible policy to bring the arrangements for the government's subsidisation of local authorities' water and sewage works on to the same basis as the subsidies for building schools, technical colleges, police stations, child welfare clinics and so on. But it was not an 'economy' at all. One cannot get 'economies' in public expenditure by switching from one technique of finance to another; and the fact that with the PESC system this is now widely recognised is 100% gain.

Whether a public corporation would be better than a government department for running a social service, assuming that the same resources were available in either case, turns on the weight which is attached to the role of parliamentary questioning (or indeed local authority operation). There is plenty of room for argument whether the right units for running social services are national, regional or local; and at which level the management should be under the control of elected bodies and the criticism of elected representatives.

I would not myself argue that the hospital service or primary and secondary education — to mention two very different services — should be run by public corporations without direct and detailed responsibility to elected representatives. In such services, the requirement of efficiency cannot be regarded as transcending the requirement of contact with the public. Moreover, the expenditures are very large (hospital service £1,250 million, primary and secondary education £1,500 million);

and the priorities are controversial; and I find it difficult to give such responsibility to public corporations. We may need different kinds of organisation for these purposes from what we have now; but I would be reluctant to depart from the idea of direct ministerial control (or regional or local), and close access by elected representatives to such services.

. . . . . .

Public boards and agencies

Another family of public bodies consists of the boards and agencies which are set up to do specific jobs in the economic field, financed from public funds. Within Mintech we had Industrial Reorganisation Corporation, National Research Development Corporation, Shipbuilding Industry Board, Metrication Board, the three Industrial Estates Corporations for England, Scotland and Wales. In each case there was a specific job to be done — to promote the reorganisation and development of industry; to develop and exploit new inventions; to carry out the proposals for the reorganisation of the shipbuilding industry following the Geddes Report of 1966; to guide and co-ordinate the transition to the metric system; to own and let and administer the factories set up by the government in the development areas.

In each case a special body was set up to do the work, with a chairman and a board and a permanent staff (normally drawn from relevant fields), separate from the Minister and the department, and not subject to day-to-day questioning in Parliament. Sometimes the task can be done in the department in the ordinary way; but it is usually easier to bring in outside people both as chairman and board members and for the staff. It is easier to finance such bodies by grants or advances from the departments than within the departmental financial system. So whenever a new and self-contained task arises, requiring more flexibility in recruitment and finance than is customary in departmental work, a Board is usually set up. This is normally an economical and efficient way to proceed but I must list some reservations.

This is a good way to handle tasks of limited and relatively short-term (say, less than five years) duration. Such tasks can be lucidly defined. At the first stage an enthusiast can usually be found to take the lead, and a staff can be recruited for an interesting short-term task. But if the task is going to last for a long time, the problem of continuous recreation of the vitality of the organisation, as the first and second sets of leaders depart, becomes difficult: the problem of careers and permanent employment and pensions for the staff becomes pressing; and the Board tends to turn into a bureaucracy, doing a good job, but too cosy and too prone to take the course with least trouble.

In government departments, this risk of atrophy is met partly by the continuous change engendered by the flow of political life and public events and partly by the fact that these are large organisations and it is possible to keep people lively by moving them about. In private industry, there is the environment of continuous change. In many of the professions, the process of attrition of interest is well known. But the small public board, with a single task and a small staff, is very vulnerable indeed.

Agencies or departments

It is the department's responsibility to guard against this tiredness; and I would advocate a critical review of all such boards after, say, four years and every four years thereafter, to determine whether their work should be drastically reshaped or stopped altogether, or brought back into the department, or merged with that of another body. These are techniques for the short haul and not for the permanent work of government. If there turns out to be a permanent task to be done, of a scale not large enough for a major statutory body with a powerful permanent organisation, it should be done by the department, if necessary with an advisory committee to give it the necessary contact with the specific outside interests involved.

. . . . . .

Departmental strength

There is a long-term consideration here which cannot be ignored. If the new tasks, and particularly those requiring special expertise, are given to new public boards and agencies, the departments' capability to handle them themselves will clearly disappear. The essence of a good department (and particularly of the 'giant' department) is its ability to handle anything that it is required to do. This involves having at the department's disposal a wide range of experience and strong and varied expertise. If the new and testing jobs (by definition involving its most contemporary State-industry relation) are thought to be unsuitable for the department to handle itself, and to acquire the expertise to do so, a time will soon come when the department will be unable to do so and will have no credibility outside when Ministers need it.

Lastly, one of the most formidable tasks of a department is to be able to make proposals to its Minister for men and women to take on the leadership of these public boards and agencies. A great effort is deployed on this, but nobody has yet been able to develop the technique of identifying the promising and available people in industry and elsewhere and to fit them in to the (literally) hundreds of vacancies that the department has to fill. The success of the enterprises, however, turns on the skill with which this is done. Perhaps a more intensive exploitation of the public service itself in all its forms could help.

Conclusion

My conclusion, therefore, is that the allocation of new tasks to public boards and agencies is not necessarily wise, and is positively dangerous if adopted for long-term tasks; and in my opinion we have to pay much more attention to our capability within the public service to carry out new current tasks. I think it is right to set up public corporations to do great permanent tasks, and I would be surprised if there was much dissent from the general line of approach which I have described. But I think it is wrong both on the merits of the job and in the interests of the capability of the public service itself, to treat 'hiving off' as a desirable objective in itself, if one means by this the transfer from departmental management to public corporation or other public board or agency (transfer to the private sector presents different issues). I would myself favour being less eager than we have been in the last decade to set up outside agencies, and in my view we should be increasing our own capability within the service to tackle the current problems of the relationship between industry and the State.

ANNEX 5

Nationalised Industries

	Employ-ees March 1970 ('000)	Average net assets			Annual fixed investment in UK	
		Total (£mn.)	per employee (£'000)	Net income as % of assets	Total (£mn.)	per employee (£'000)
Post Office	420	2,412	5.8	7.4	463	1.1
National Coal Board	376	697	1.9	1.3	73	0.2
Railways Board	275	1,504	5.6	3.7	89	0.3
British Steel Corporation	249	1,168	4.7	2.5	139	0.5
Electricity Council & Boards (inc. Scotland)	216	5,465	25.3	6.3	474	2.2
Gas Council & Boards	120	1,570	13.1	6.5	209	1.7
National Bus Company	80	101	1.3	7.4	13	0.2
London Transport	69	302	4.4	0.2	13	0.2
Airways Corporations	45	365	8.1	13.0	102	2.3
British Transport Docks Board	12	118	9.8	3.6	13	1.1
British Airports Authority	4	69	17.2	13.4	11	2.7
British Waterways Board	3	12	4.0	0.8	1	0.3
Other transport	85	–	–	–	31	0.4
Total	1,954	13,721	7.0	5.8	1,621	0.8

Notes
Average net assets and net income refer to financial years of the industries, as near as possible to 1969–70. Investment is average of three years 1969–70 to 1971–72 estimates. London Transport covers period up to transfer to Greater London Council at 1 January 1970. 'Other Transport' consists of National Freight Company, Scottish Transport Group, and Transport Holding Company. Totals not necessarily the sum of individuals because of different dates etc.

23 GOVERNMENT AND THE PRIVATE SECTOR

Extracts from *The Regeneration of British Industry* (Cmnd. 5710, 1974); reprinted by permission of H.M.S.O. This White Paper reflected the determination of the Labour Government elected in October 1974 to extend the scope of Government intervention in the private sector of the economy, despite a tiny Parliamentary majority.

1. Britain's prosperity and welfare depended on the wealth generated by its industry and all those who work in it. It matters vitally to all of us that British industry should be strong and successful. We need both efficient publicly owned industries, and a vigorous, alert, responsible and profitable private sector, working together with the Government in a framework which brings together the interests of all concerned: those who work in industry, whether in management or on the shop floor, those who own its assets, and those who use its products and depend upon its success.

2. Since the war we have not as a nation been able — for a variety of reasons, social, economic and industrial — fully to harness the resources of skill and ability we should be able to command. We have been falling steadily further behind our competitors. We have not found the self-confidence to bridge that gap; and as it widens, the investment and new industrial relationships that we need if we are to maintain our living standards become progressively more difficult to secure.

3. In 1971, investment for each worker in British manufacturing industry was less than half that in France, Japan or the United States, and well below that in Germany or Italy. In spite of the measures to encourage investment taken since then, it has still lagged behind; indeed, it was significantly less in 1972 and in 1973 than it was in 1970. Moreover, when it comes to making effective use of our manufacturing equipment, we are less successful than most of our competitors. Because there has not been the demand for investment in manufacturing industry here, funds that could have been used to improve and modernise British industry have been deployed elsewhere. In the last ten years the rate of direct investment by British firms overseas has more than trebled.

4. Successive Governments have striven to correct these deficiencies, both by general economic measures and by various forms of assistance to industry. But the attitude of Governments to industry, and indeed of industry to Governments, has been too remote, too much coloured by the concept that the Government's main function towards industry is that of regulation to prevent the activities of industry, or the abuse of its powers, damaging the interests of other sectors of the community. That relationship is no longer enough. Industry and the Government should also be partners in the pursuit of the objectives which spell success for industry and prosperity for this country. This requires a closer, clearer and more positive relationship between Government and industry; and the construction of that better relationship requires the development of new institutions. This White Paper sets out the Government's proposals for achieving these results.

5. The Government's main proposals for extending public ownership were set out in the manifesto on which the Labour Party fought the last General Election, and are now being presented to Parliament and the public in greater detail. They include proposals for community ownership of development land, the establishment of the British National Oil Corporation, the nationalisation of the shipbuilding and aircraft industries, the extension of public ownership in the road haulage and construction industries, and schemes for bringing commercial ports and cargo handling activities under public ownership and control.

6. In pursuit of the more general objectives for the relationship between Government and industry which have already been described, the Government propose in this White Paper the creation of two new instruments: a system of *Planning Agreements* with major firms in key sectors of industry, and a *National Enterprise Board* to provide the means for direct public initiatives in particular key sectors of industry.

7. Planning Agreements will bring about a closer understanding between companies – workforce as well as management – and the Government on the aims to be followed and the plans to be adopted in pursuit of them. They will not only help to ensure that the plans of companies are in harmony with national needs and objectives; they will also provide a securer and more coherent basis than has existed in the past for ensuring that Government financial assistance is deployed where it will be most effectively used. A fuller exchange of information will be an essential ingredient in Planning Agreements; the information which companies provide in this context will be used for this purpose only.

8. The National Enterprise Board will take over the ownership of the shares that the Government now hold in a number of companies. It will be a new source of investment capital for industry, able to provide capital by loan or acquisition of shares – though the general rule will be that, where the Board provides such capital, it should take a proportionate share in the ownership of the firm. It will act as the agent of the Government in the efficient restructuring of industry. It will be able to channel grants to companies in difficulties. In all its activities it will pay close attention to regional development opportunities. For many of its activities the Board will be able to follow the pattern and build on the experience of the former Industrial Reorganisation Corporation.

. . . . . .

PLANNING AGREEMENTS

11. In their application to the private sector Planning Agreements will provide a new and improved framework for co-operation between the Government and leading industrial companies. A Planning Agreement will not be an agreement in the sense of a civil contract enforceable at law. It will, however, be given sufficient recognition by statute to enable the company concerned to rely on assistance promised under it. The Act which gives effect to the new system will also provide reserve powers to require the relevant companies to provide the Government and the workers in the firm with the information needed to formulate and monitor a Planning Agreement.

There will, however, be no statutory requirement upon a company to conclude an Agreement.

12. The heart of this system will be a series of consultations between the Government and companies, leading to an agreement about plans for the following three years; these will be reviewed and rolled forward annually. In the course of these consultations, the Government will assess with the company its needs for assistance to support and reinforce agreed company plans, with special reference to selective assistance for new employment projects in the regions. In particular, if in the course of these discussions it becomes clear that in order to align the company's plans with national needs some financial assistance is required beyond that which would in any case be available to the company by way of capital allowances, regional development aid and regional employment premium, the Government will be ready to provide the kind of discretionary financial assistance by way of grants and loans for which the Industry Act 1972 now provides. They will discuss with the company the scale on which and purposes for which this assistance should be provided, so as to meet the requirements of individual recipients and to further the achievement of national objectives. In order that companies shall have greater certainty in making and carrying out their plans, the Government intend that once an Agreement has been concluded, regional assistance for the projects which it covers will, during the currency of the Agreement, not fall below the rates in force at the time of the Agreement. Moreover these discussions could help to identify requirements for investment funds for consideration by the National Enterprise Board, if necessary by means of joint ventures with the companies. More generally, the intention is that the outcome of discussions with companies will have an important bearing on the formulation of the Government's own plans; in this way the needs of companies and the economy will be better served.

. . . . . .

Companies to be covered

17. The new arrangements will apply to major and strategic firms in key sectors of manufacturing industry, and in selected industries other than manufacturing of particular importance to the economy. Multinational companies will be included only in respect of their British holdings. It will not however be possible to operate Planning Agreements from the very outset so that they cover all the companies that will eventually fall within their scope . . . The Government are determined to see that the benefits of the new arrangements they propose should be secured with the minimum of extra administrative cost for the companies concerned and for the Government service. They will therefore be selective in their initial approach. They will introduce Planning Agreements in selected sectors of particular importance, beginning with companies in sectors which, like the engineering industry, lie at the heart of our export effort.

18. The major nationalised industries and publicly-owned firms will also fall within the scope of the Planning Agreements system, which for them will be admin-

istered through the sponsoring Departments. Their relationship with Government is already very close, and extends beyond the relevant statutes governing the nationalised industries into, for example, the joint scrutiny of their corporate plans. Recent years have seen the introduction of arrangements by which the nationalised industries and major publicly-owned firms submit corporate plans to the Government, and by which Departments monitor their progress at regular intervals against an annual operating plan.

The interests of employees

19. Employees and their representatives will have a major interest in the issues covered by Planning Agreements. The Government intend that the plans to be covered by an Agreement will be drawn up by management in close consultation with trade union representatives from the firm. The framing and updating of Agreements will thus involve a continuing discussion between management and unions and will constitute an important advance in the part to be played by industrial democracy in the planning of company strategy. The Government envisage that union representatives from companies, while not formally parties to Planning Agreements, would also take part where they so wished in consultations on Agreements with the Government.

20. If consultation is to be effective, union representatives must be provided with all the necessary information relevant to the contents of Planning Agreements. The Government will therefore require employers to disclose information of this kind, except where disclosure could seriously prejudice the company's commercial interests or would be contrary to the interests of national security.

. . . . . .

NATIONAL ENTERPRISE BOARD

23. The Government propose to create a new instrument to secure where necessary large-scale sustained investment to offset the effects of the short-term pull of market forces. These new powers of initiative are better exercised through a new agency than dealt with direct by Government, and for this purpose it is proposed to set up a National Enterprise Board (NEB).

24. One of the functions of this new agency will be to build on and enlarge the activities previously discharged by the Industrial Reorganisation Corporation (IRC). It will in addition be an industrial holding company with subsidiary companies in manufacturing industry. A number of existing Government shareholdings in companies will be transferred to the Board immediately on its establishment. Adequate funds will be made available to enable the Board, subject to Governmental and Parliamentary control as set out in paragraphs 38—40, to expand its activities vigorously to discharge the responsibilities set out below:

    a. It will be a new source of investment capital for manufacturing industry; in providing finance it will normally take a corresponding share in the equity capital. In this it will set out to supplement and not to displace the supply of investment from existing financial institutions and from companies' own resources.

b. It will have the former Industrial Reorganisation Corporation's entrepreneurial role in promoting industrial efficiency and profitability by promoting or assisting the reorganisation or development of an industry but, unlike the IRC, the NEB will in general retain the shareholdings it acquires. In discharging these functions it may take financial interests in companies or act in a purely advisory role.

c. It will act as a holding company to control and exercise central management of:

    i.   certain existing Government shareholdings vested in it;

    ii. interests taken into public ownership under powers in the Industry Act 1972, which it is proposed to consolidate and extend;

    iii. new acquisitions under the arrangements described in paragraphs 30–33.

d. It will be a channel through which the Government will assist sound companies which are in short-term financial or managerial difficulties.

e. It will be an instrument through which the Government operate directly to create employment in areas of high unemployment.

f. Government Departments, the nationalised industries and private firms will be able to seek the advice of the NEB on financial and managerial issues.

g. Its main strength in manufacturing will come through the extension of public ownership into profitable manufacturing industry by acquisitions of individual firms in accordance with paragraphs 30–33 below.

h. It will have power to start new ventures and participate in joint ventures with companies in the private sector.

25. The Board will be responsible for securing the efficient management of the companies and assets vested in it. It will compete with companies in the private sector and be expected to operate in accordance with suitable financial objectives. Its guiding financial objective will be to secure an adequate return on that part of the nation's capital for which it is responsible. When the Government require the NEB to depart from this objective on social grounds, the subsidies will be administered by the NEB, and will be separately accounted for. The Board's financial arrangements will have to be carefully worked out to safeguard against uneconomic allocation of the nation's resources.

Industrial democracy

26. The Government envisage a major development of industrial democracy throughout industry in the years ahead. Within that framework, the NEB will play its part in ensuring that enterprises under its control provide for the full involvement of employees in decision-making at all levels.

Provision of investment capital

27. Within the framework of Governmental control outlined below (see paragraph

38), the NEB will have powers to make loans and to take shareholdings in companies where it considers that such action is in the public interest and in particular when in its judgement lack of finance is prejudicing worthwhile industrial development. In deciding which projects to support within its financial allocation, it will be expected to give priority to the promotion of industrial efficiency; to the creation of employment opportunities in assisted areas; to increasing exports or reducing undue dependence on imports; to co-operation with the Offshore Supplies Office in promoting development in the offshore oil supplies industry; and to sponsoring investment that will offset the effect of monopoly.

Restructuring industries

28. In exercising its powers to promote or assist in the reorganisation or development of an industry the Board may take a share in the equity capital of existing companies or take part in the establishment of new enterprises. When it is involved in restructuring programmes, its overriding purpose will be to promote the effectiveness and efficiency of the industry. It will work closely with the Department of Industry which will be able to complement initiatives by the NEB through the use of its powers of selective financial assistance under the Industry Act 1972.

Vesting existing government shareholdings

29. The Government have a number of existing shareholdings in industry. Their acquisition over a large number of years has been in response to a diverse range of policy objectives. Some of these holdings may not be appropriate for vesting in the NEB eg, the holdings in shipbuilding companies or in companies whose activities are largely overseas (the British Petroleum Co. Ltd., Cable and Wireless Ltd. and the Suez Finance Company). It is however intended that the Government shareholdings in the following companies should be vested in the NEB:
    Rolls-Royce (1971) Ltd.
    International Computers (Holdings) Ltd.
    George Kent Ltd.
    Nuclear Enterprises Ltd.
    Dunford and Elliott Ltd.
    Kearney and Trecker Marwin Ltd.
    Norton Villiers Triumph Ltd.

Future acquisitions

30. The NEB will be the instrument by which the Government ensure that the nation's resources are deployed to the benefit of all, by extending public ownership into profitable manufacturing industry in accordance with the policies defined in paragraphs 31–33 below.
    31. Acquisitions by, or on behalf of, the NEB may take place in a number of

ways. The intention is that all holdings in companies, whether 100 per cent or in part, should be acquired by agreement. Where part holdings in companies may be acquired in future in return for assistance from the Government under the Industry Act 1972 they will normally be held by the NEB. The Board may also acquire part holdings in companies through joint ventures or through its participation in a reorganisation. But to act decisively in its role of creating employment and creating new industrial capacity, the Board will need a number of companies where it holds 100 per cent of the equity capital, in order to avoid conflict between its objectives and the interests of private shareholders. The Government consider that suitable criteria for the acquisition of a company should include the following: danger of its passing into unacceptable foreign control; and stimulation of competition in a sector where that is weak.

32. Although the NEB will be principally concerned with profitable companies, it may on occasion be called on to take over an ailing company which is in danger of collapse but needs to be maintained and restored to a sound economic basis for reasons of regional employment or industrial policy. This responsibility of the NEB will be distinct from its other functions, and it will be separated in such a way from them that the NEB will be compensated specifically for this rescue activity, to ensure that its overall financial discipline and viability are not undermined. The Board may also be asked to act in support of financial measures by the Secretary of State for Industry to assist a company in temporary difficulty, for example by providing managerial reinforcement.

33. Together with the separate proposals in paragraph 5, the preceding paragraphs represent the whole of the Government's policy towards public ownership for the next Parliament. If in any case compulsory acquisition proved to be necessary, this would normally be authorised by a specific Act of Parliament. If unforeseeable developments of compelling urgency were to arise – for example, the imminent failure or loss to unacceptable foreign control of an important company in a key sector of manufacturing industry – the Government would bring the issue before Parliament, and any action would require specific parliamentary approval. Compulsory acquisitions would be subject to prompt and fair compensation to existing shareholders.

. . . . . .

Financial arrangements

36. The National Enterprise Board will be funded by the Government and the Secretary of State for Industry will be empowered, with the approval of the Treasury, to make funds available by way of loans or in the form of public dividend capital. This is capital which does not bear a fixed rate of interest, but on which a public corporation is expected to pay a dividend similar to dividends on equity shares in private companies. Since the NEB will be competing with the private sector and is intended primarily to operate within profitable sectors of manufacturing industry,

it is appropriate that a part of its funds should have the character of equity rather than of fixed interest finance.

37. As envisaged in paragraph 27 the Board will be a source of finance for the companies in which it holds shares, and for any new public enterprise which it establishes. The NEB's internal financial relationships with its subsidiary companies will be for it to settle with them. The NEB will be given financial obligations which reflect its duty of securing the efficient management in the public interest of the companies vested in it. Detailed financial guidelines for this purpose will be prescribed by the Government.

Relations with the Government

38. Within the framework of its constitution and the funds made available to it, the NEB will be free to exercise its commercial judgement in carrying out the functions described in paragraph 24 above. It will however require the prior agreement of the Government before it takes a controlling interest in any enterprise or a minority interest exceeding £5 million. There will also be occasions when the Government will wish to influence the activities of the Board and its constituent companies in the national interest. The Government will therefore need a power to give general and specific directions to the Board. The Government will not however interfere in detailed issues of day-to-day management. Directions to the NEB will have to be given in writing by the Government and will be published in due course in the Board's annual report.

Parliamentary control

39. The NEB will be set up under a new Industry Bill which will consolidate and develop existing legislation to promote national industrial expansion. The Board will be accountable for its actions to the Government who, in turn, will be fully accountable to Parliament for the funds which it makes available to the Board. In addition, the Board will produce an annual report and accounts which will be laid before Parliament and its activities, like those of any other major public sector body, will come under review by the appropriate Parliamentary Committee.

40. The Government already have powers under Sections 7 and 8 of the Industry Act 1972 to provide financial assistance to a company by taking share capital. These powers of agreed share purchase will be widened and made permanent. The Government propose that parliamentary control of this extended power should be on the lines of Section 8 of the Industry Act, ie expenditure on a single acquisition in excess of £5 million should be authorised by Resolution of the House of Commons under main legislation which provides the means by which this is to be done.

Scotland, Wales and Northern Ireland

41. The Government have announced their intention to introduce legislation setting

up in Scotland a Scottish Development Agency, responsible to the Secretary of State, which will be given a substantial measure of responsibility for the promotion of industrial and economic development.

42. The Government consider that the most effective assistance and support for the modernisation and growth of Scottish industry will be achieved by giving the Scottish Development Agency executive responsibilities over a wide field. It has therefore been decided that appropriate functions of the NEB should be carried out in Scotland by the Scottish Development Agency, and that the Agency should be fully associated with the Board in consideration of matters of relevance to employment and economic growth in Scotland. Similar arrangements will be made for Wales, on the basis envisaged in the Secretary of State for Energy's Report of Parliament of 11 July 1974 about United Kingdom off-shore oil and gas policy. Industrial development in Northern Ireland is a transferred matter under the Northern Ireland constitution, and the relationship between the NEB and the Northern Irish authorities is under consideration.

24 THE CONSUMER INTEREST

Extracts from *National Consumers' Agency* (Cmnd. 5726, 1974); reprinted by permission of H.M.S.O. This White Paper resulted in the establishment of a non-statutory body, the National Consumers' Council, with Dr Michael Young as the first Chairman.

4. It is at the national level that many experienced in consumer affairs have long considered that there is a gap in the spectrum of bodies which represent the consumer. This gap was widened by the disappearance of the Consumer Council, which operated in two main ways. One of those was by making information available to consumers. This is now one of the functions of the Director General of Fair Trading. The second main role of the Consumer Council was as a partisan body to promote action for furthering and safeguarding consumers' interests. This gap cannot suitably be filled by the Director General whose role in respect of monopolies, mergers, restrictive practices and consumer credit precludes him from acting exclusively in the interest of consumers. Existing consumer bodies have played a most valuable role on behalf of the consumer, doing much to make the consumer voice heard, and consumer interests have greatly benefited by their efforts. But there remains a lack of any independent national consumer body sufficiently representative and influential to ensure that those who take decisions which will affect the consumer can have a balanced and authoritative view before them.

Establishment of the Agency

5. The Government proposes to fill this gap by the establishment of a National Consumers' Agency financed by the Government. Those concerned in the pro-

duction of goods and services are extensively involved with Government in the national counsels through the TUC and the CBI. The role of the consumer in economic activity is as important as that of the producer, and the Government considers that the consumer ought through the new Agency to have a similar opportunity to be heard.

6. Workpeople and management have each formed their own self-financed unions and associations because there is a direct and obvious need for them to bargain collectively, and they gain direct benefits from doing so. The benefits which will be gained from the consumer voice being heard properly will be shared by all. Indeed it is the inarticulate and disadvantaged who most need a body to speak for them and ensure that they are protected, and it is they whose needs have least been met by the consumer activities of the last decade. The Government believes that the new body proposed will be in a position to insist that the interests of all consumers, including the least articulate, should be taken into account.

Functions and appointment of the Agency

7. The functions the Government envisages for the Agency are:
(*a*) to make representations of the consumer view to central and local government, to the Director General of Fair Trading, to industry, and to any other quarter where the consumer voice ought to be heeded. This will include making representations on the law and on proposed legislation; on advertising standards and methods; on the adequacy and availability of consumer advice services; on consumer interests during the remaining stages of metrication; and on the availability of facilities for testing product safety and suitability;
(*b*) to be available to be consulted by those who seek a consumer view on policies and proposals. In particular, the Agency will consider and report on the consumer interest in matters referred to it by the Government;
(*c*) to represent the consumer on appropriate Government and other bodies, and within the framework of international organisations such as the European Community;
(*d*) to review the present arrangements for consumer representation in the nationalised industries as part of the Government's policy of enabling the nationalised industries to be more responsive to the consumer's needs.
Existing consumer bodies will of course be able to make representations direct to the Government as at present, if they wish, and the Government will continue to consult them directly where appropriate.

8. The Agency will be a non-statutory body, with a Chairman and members appointed by the Secretary of State for Prices and Consumer Protection. This will in no way prejudice its independence and freedom to criticise the Government. To operate effectively the Agency's membership will need to be limited. Part of the membership will be appointed in a representative capacity. The main consumer and women's bodies will be invited to submit short lists of nominees from which the

Secretary of State will make appointments. The remainder of the members will be appointed by the Secretary of State in an individual capacity. There will be special arrangements for Scotland and Wales; the membership of the Agency from each country, together with additional members, will form national committees with separate offices. There will be corresponding arrangements for Northern Ireland recognising the responsibilities of the Northern Ireland authorities in this field under the Northern Ireland Constitution Act 1973.

Nationalised industry consumer councils

9. When the nationalised industry consumer councils were set up by the national-isation statutes for the coal, gas, electricity, and surface transport industries, and for the Post Office, they were an important innovation in the consumer's interest. Now that a separate Department of Prices and Consumer Protection has been created, the Government has decided that certain statutory functions in respect of these councils should be transferred to that Department. Accordingly, once the National Consumers' Agency has been established, appointments to the councils will be made by the Secretary of State for Prices and Consumer Protection, with the advice of the Agency or its appropriate national committee, and after consul-tation with the Minister responsible for the industry. Members of the Scottish electricity consultative councils will continue to be appointed by the Secretary of State for Scotland, with the advice of the Agency's Scottish committee. References to the councils will be made jointly by the Minister responsible for the industry and the Secretary of State for Prices and Consumer Protection, who will both receive the council's representations and reports. Any consequent directions to the industry would be given by the Minister responsible for the industry, after consulting the Secretary of State for Prices and Consumer Protection about the decision. The Government will be able to seek the advice of the Agency in exercising its functions in relation to these councils. The Government will also in due course introduce legislation so that all the councils are financed directly by the Government.

Operation of the Agency

10. The establishment of the National Consumers' Agency will not affect in any way the position and responsibilities of the Director General of Fair Trading under the Fair Trading Act 1973. Likewise unaffected will be the operation of the Con-sumer Protection Advisory Committee, whose function is to advise on consumer trade practices referred to it which may adversely affect the economic interests of consumers and on remedies the Director General may propose under Part II of the Fair Trading Act.

11. The National Consumers' Agency will concern itself closely with the adequacy and availability of assistance for consumers with individual problems. It will not itself handle individual consumer complaints and cases; these will continue

to be dealt with by the existing range of agencies — consumer advice centres, trading standards departments of local authorities, Citizens' Advice Bureaux, nationalised industry consumer and consultative councils and others.

12. Central and local government are expanding their services to consumers, and the new Agency will be available to advise them on these, and on the many problems individuals face in the provision of public sector services. It has been an important role of consumer organisations in the past to promote adequate arrangements for consumer representation in these areas. Where there are bodies already established for this purpose, the Agency will naturally wish to work in consultation and co-operation with them, and not in competition. It is not intended that the setting up of the Agency will in any way affect the responsibilities of local authorities, or derogate from the customary consultations with local government through the local authority associations. Nor is it the intention that the Agency will supersede or duplicate the work of bodies with an existing responsibility for looking after consumer interests in specific areas such as the health service, the nationalised industries or broadcasting. The Agency's role in all these fields will primarily be one of ensuring that adequate mechanisms exist for expressing the consumer voice, and of drawing attention to matters of concern to consumers.

. . . . . .

Section V
The changing Civil Service

'It is an inevitable defect, that bureaucrats will care more for routine than results.'
(W. Bagehot, *The English Constitution*, 1867)

The Civil Service has conceivably received more attention, but suffered less change, than any other area of government in the past thirty years. There has been no lack of recognition that the permanent bureaucracy is a powerful force at the heart of the British political system; indeed, many critics attribute Britain's post-war economic difficulties to the inadequacy of the bureaucracy. Although the convention of ministerial responsibility assumes that there is a clear distinction between policy and administration which finds institutional reflection in the differentiated roles of Minister and Official (25, 26, 34), it is clear beyond doubt that in practice the complex nature of the policymaking process produces a closer identity between Ministers and Civil Servants than the constitutional formulations indicate (28). The primacy of technical information can give the civil servant real political power (27), leaving to the Minister the more restricted function, as Sir William Harcourt put it, of telling the civil servant what the public won't stand. It was the acknowledgement of the power, and therefore the importance, of the Civil Service which stimulated so much public concern in the early 1960s, and the consequent Fulton inquiry. The evidence to the Committee, whether official or external to the Civil Service (28, 29), overwhelmingly accepted the existence of defects and the need for remedies, though official opinion was upset by Fulton's basic criticism of the Civil Service as a body of generalist amateurs owing more to nineteenth- than twentieth-century conceptions of government (30). Although this strong condemnation made a significant public impact, Fulton's bite scarcely matched its bark, and the Report's many proposals were based on essentially moderate and gradualist principles of reform. An elaborate machinery set up by the Civil Service to review and implement Fulton has produced changes of form rather than substance (31). But the separation of the responsibility for the Civil Service from other Treasury functions was an important change, and new Civil Service attitudes to management, the handling of personnel, and training, are substantial gains from this period of scrutiny (31, 32, 33). Organisational changes are also likely to have an impact on the future operation of the civil service, and the requirements laid upon civil servants (35), but there has been little response to suggestions for the reformulation of the conventional role of the civil servant in more public and accountable terms, though such a reform would correspond to the logic of the continued accretion of political power to officials.

173

Other appropriate references are **1, 5, 13, 14, 16, 17, 19, 20, 22, 37, 38, 39, 40, 41, 44, 49** and **57**.

25 MINISTERS AND CIVIL SERVANTS

Extracts from Herbert Morrison, *Government and Parliament* (3rd edn., Oxford University Press, 1964); reprinted by permission of the publisher. Herbert Morrison was a senior Cabinet Minister in the war-time Cabinet and in the post-war Labour administration. The final quotation from Sir David Maxwell Fyfe is still regarded as defining the operation of the principle of individual Ministerial responsibility, but subsequent developments, notably the Vehicle and General Affair in 1972 (Chapman, 1973), have produced considerable confusion about the practical application of the principle.

To the general public the relationship between Ministers and civil servants is something of a mystery. Some people, for example, may think that a Minister is too much dominated by his civil servants . . . This allegation is understandable when it is made by an ordinary citizen or a Member of Parliament who has sought unsuccessfully to get some departmental decision changed. But it is untrue as a generalization though it can be true in particular cases. Anyway, it would not be easy to be sure unless one had the chance of seeing the Minister and his civil servants in action together. Indeed, it is my general experience that if the Minister in charge knows what he wants and is intelligent in going about it, he can command the understanding co-operation and support of his civil servants. The kind of Minister who is most tiring to the officers of a Department is the Minister who does not know his own mind and cannot make it up. If the policy of a Department is hazy, vacillating, and ineffective, it is, after all, the responsibility of the Minister; it is quite as likely to be his fault as that of his civil servants.
. . . . . .

The Permanent Secretary of a Department is its chief civil servant. He is responsible to the Minister not only for the organization and efficiency of the Department, but also for the advice given to the Minister by the Department through the whole range of its duties, even though some of the advice reaches the Minister direct from lower down the line . . . On many matters Under-Secretaries and Assistant Secretaries will do business direct with the Minister, but proposals of importance always come to the Minister through either the Deputy Secretary or the Permanent Secretary or both . . .

The Permanent Secretary of an important Department carries great responsibilities, materially greater than the chief officer of any local authority, not excluding the London County Council. He has to wrestle with high and difficult matters of policy which continually arise in the course of administration. He is not and should not be a politician, but he should know enough about politics and politicians to be on his guard against blunders and indiscretions, although it is the

Minister rather than the Permanent Secretary who is paid for his political experience and understanding of the public.

. . . . . .

The Minister and his advisers

In considering departmental problems or policy it is necessary for there to be frequent meetings between the Minister and his advisers. Sometimes it will be the Permanent Secretary alone or an individual civil servant lower down the line or the Private Secretary; but often the issue will be of such a character that it will be necessary for the Minister to have a gathering of quite a number of his civil servants, especially when more than one branch of the Department is involved, together with the Parliamentary Secretary. It is well to encourage at such meetings not only the presence of the civil servants below the top flight, but to encourage them to speak their mind even though they may not entirely agree with their superiors. This is good training and it enables them the better to get that understanding of the mind of the Minister which is very desirable in the interests of good administration . . .

The relationship between the Minister and the civil servants should be — and usually is — that of colleagues working together in a team, co-operative partners seeking to advance the public interest and the efficiency of the Department. The Minister should not be an isolated autocrat, giving orders without hearing or considering arguments for alternative courses; nor, on the other hand, should the civil servants be able to treat him as a mere cipher. The partnership should be alive and virile, rival ideas and opinions should be fairly considered, and the relationship of all should be one of mutual respect — on the understanding, of course, that the Minister's decision is final and must be loyally and helpfully carried out, and that he requires efficient and energetic service.

The senior civil servants will confer freely with the Minister (unless, as rarely happens, he is unwilling to listen), and to the best of their ability place the facts before him and give such advice as they think right and proper. To discourage honest official advice — whether in national or local government — is both foolish and harmful. Advisers who are mere yes-men playing up to the Minister in the hope of advancement are just as dangerous as are obstinate and obstructive no-men. Both types are bad. Both sides to an argument should be heard and considered. At the end of the discussion it is for the Minister to come to such conclusions and give such directions as he thinks appropriate. It is then the duty of the civil servants to carry out the ministerial decision, doing their best to ensure the success of the Minister's policy, whether they have advised its adoption or not.

. . . Somebody must be held responsible to Parliament and the public. It has to be the Minister, for it is he, and neither Parliament nor the public, who has official control over his civil servants. One of the fundamentals of our system of government is that some Minister of the Crown is responsible to Parliament, and through Parliament to the public, for every act of the Executive. This is a corner-stone of our system of parliamentary government. There may, however, be an occasion on which so serious a mistake has been made that the Minister must explain the circumstances and processes which resulted in the mistake, particularly if it involves an issue of civil liberty or individual rights. Now and again the House demands to know the name of the officer responsible for the occurrence. The proper answer of the Minister is that if the House wants anybody's head it must be his head as the responsible Minister, and that it must leave him to deal with the officer concerned in the Department.

There is a circumstance in which I think a considerable degree of frankness is warranted. If a Minister has given a specific order within the Department on a matter of public interest and his instructions have not been carried out, if he is challenged in Parliament and if he is so minded, he has a perfect right to reveal the facts and to assure the House that he has taken suitable action. Even so he must still take the responsibility. It is, I think, legitimate in such a case that disregard of an instruction should be made known, even if it involves some humiliation for the officer concerned and his colleagues knowing that he was the one who disobeyed; for the Civil Service should at all times know that the lawful orders of Ministers must be carried out . . .

. . . . . .

One of the most significant results of the Crichel Down case was the fact that it caused a reconsideration, if not a redefinition of the relations of the civil servant with his Minister and with the public. When Sir Andrew Clark, at the request of the Minister of Agriculture, held his seven-day public inquiry into the procedure adopted concerning the disposal of land at Crichel Down, individual civil servants had to give evidence in public. The six volumes of evidence and a great deal of correspondence were available to Members in the House of Commons library, and the whole affair was widely reported in the newspapers. This was a radical departure from the normal practice, whereby the actions of individual civil servants are kept anonymous. The resulting publicity led to a strong feeling of dissatisfaction with the way the case had been conducted, and this was increased when on the day Sir Andrew Clark's report was published, Sir Thomas Dugdale announced in the House of Commons that no further action was to be taken, as the inquiry had achieved its main purpose since no trace of bribery or corruption had been found. Because of all these criticisms the Crichel Down case was debated on the Adjournment on 20 July 1954, and in the course of the debate Sir Thomas Dugdale announced his resignation. This was accepted, although the resignations of his two Parliamentary Secretaries were withdrawn at the request of the Prime Minister.

In the course of the debate the then Home Secretary, Sir David Maxwell Fyfe, now Lord Kilmuir, stated certain views on the constitutional relationship between Ministers and civil servants with which I find myself in general agreement. His observations on that occasion are worth printing in full (the references to the right honourable Gentleman are to myself):

'The position of the civil servant is that he is wholly and directly responsible to his Minister. It is worth stating again that he holds his office 'at pleasure' and can be dismissed at any time by the Minister; and that power is none the less real because it is seldom used. The only exception relates to a small number of senior posts, like permanent secretary, deputy secretary, and principal financial officer, where, since 1920, it has been necessary for the Minister to consult the Prime Minister, as he does on appointment.

I would like to put the different categories where different considerations apply. I am in agreement with the right hon. Gentleman who has just spoken. In the case where there is an explicit order by a Minister, the Minister must protect the civil servant who has carried out his order. Equally, where the civil servant acts properly in accordance with the policy laid down by the Minister, the Minister must protect and defend him.

I come to the third category, which is different. Again, as I understand the right hon. Gentleman, he agrees with me on this. Where an official makes a mistake, or causes some delay, but not on an important issue of policy and not where a claim to individual rights is seriously involved, the Minister acknowledges the mistake, and he accepts the responsibility, although he is not personally involved. He states that he will take corrective action in the Department. I agree with the right hon. Gentleman, that he would not, in these circumstances, expose the official to public criticism. I think that is important, and I hope that the right hon. Gentleman will agree with me that it should come from both sides of the House that we are agreed on this important aspect of public affairs.

But when one comes to the fourth category, where action has been taken by a civil servant of which the Minister disapproves and has no prior knowledge, and the conduct of the official is reprehensible, then there is no obligation on the part of the Minister to endorse what he believes to be wrong, or to defend what are clearly shown to be errors of his officers. The Minister is not bound to approve of action of which he did not know, or of which he disapproves. But, of course, he remains constitutionally responsible to Parliament for the fact that something has gone wrong, and he alone can tell Parliament what has occurred and render an account of his stewardship.

The fact that a Minister has to do that does not affect his power to control and discipline his staff. One could sum it up by saying that it is part of a Minister's responsibility to Parliament to take necessary action to secure efficiency and the proper discharge of the duties of his Department. On that, only the Minister can decide what is right and just to do, and he alone can hear all sides, including the defence.'

26 WHO ARE THE POLICY-MAKERS?

Extracts (a) and (b) are from 'Who are the Policymakers?' in *Public Administration*, Autumn 1965, Vol. 43 reprinted by permission of the Editor and authors. This article was the report of a Conference held under the auspices of the Royal Institute of Public Administration. Extract (a) is by Lord Boyle, a former Conservative Minister of Education; and extract (b) is by Sir Edward Playfair, a former senior civil servant. Extract (c) by Sir Charles Cunningham, also a former senior official, is from the article 'Policymaking' in *Public Administration*, Autumn 1966, Vol. 44. Reprinted by permission of the editor and author.

(a)

Now for the work of officials. Obviously this can be put in terms of the old Bagehot phrase about the Crown — the right to advise, to encourage, to warn, and to be consulted. Officials with their experience can do a number of extremely important things. They can warn Ministers of criticisms to which a policy will render him liable — I think this is a very important function. They can point out to Ministers the snags they may not have thought of. I suspect that new Ministers may have to be reminded rather often — rather painfully — about the fact that money does act, rather more often than is realized, as a restraint on what can be done, and that whichever party is in power there are certain situations in which getting more money is not easy. One of these is when the Estimates have been finalized and the time has not yet arrived when one can start thinking about Supplementary Estimates. Officials obviously have to do all those things. There is also the point that, with their long experience, officials can encourage or can warn on the merits of some proposed policy. However definitely a policy may have been laid down in an election manifesto, a Permanent Secretary always has a right to send to the Minister a minute saying in effect: 'Before you go ahead with this I think I ought just to put on record the following points' May I say here that of course practically every Minister knows quite well that the real life of ministerial power is not quite like drafting an election manifesto. He knows there is a very considerable difference when as a Minister he becomes responsible for what is done. I do not think it takes many Ministers very long to make what is the most important discovery one ever makes in politics; this is that the most important distinction in our whole national political system is the distinction between the Government and the non-Government. This is the absolutely crucial difference — whether one is part of the Government or is not. As soon as one becomes a member of the Government one has to measure one's words and actions and think in terms of reality, in a way that one does not have to do when the executive machine is not at one's disposal.

This is a rough statement of the relationship between Ministers and officials but of course there is much more one can say about it than that. For instance, on a great many issues Ministers will naturally ask officials for their views, and this will include views on a number of matters which involve political or value judgements. It is impossible to discuss a large number of subjects in the office without officials saying things or putting things on paper which imply value judgements and even political judgements. By 'political judgements' I mean statements which imply preference on the writer's part about the sort of society he would like to live in or the sort of political developments he would like to see, rather than others. I think it is fair to say that in all departments Ministers will have a relationship with their senior advisers, with the heads of branches, and with Under Secretaries, in which no-one feels 'estopped' from expressing their views freely. I personally feel that it is particularly important — in a department that is not too big — for Ministers to be on those terms not only with the Permanent Secretary and the Deputy but with the Under Secretaries as well. They are the officials who work at the point where policy and administration fuse. They are both responsible for policy within their branches and in touch with day to day administration; they are particularly key people.

. . . . . .

I think this is really saying that Ministers need all the expertise they can get, and that if discussions on policy matters between Ministers and officials are to be fruitful each side has got to do its work. These discussions work much better if both sides are pulling equally and Ministers are not just receptive to whatever views are put before them. I have not known many cases where I felt that officials were putting unfair pressure on Ministers. I have known a few where fairly senior officials have kept the Minister in the dark, or have tended to keep him in the dark, about the fact that there was quite a lot of debate further down the line; and I think any wise Minister — any Minister, that is, who really wants to know about the full range of possibilities — should always be careful to keep his ears open not just for what is being said by the very top people, but for what is being said rather farther down the line as well. This is where, without any disloyalty or any impropriety, the work of the Minister's Private Office is extremely important. The Minister ought to be on the sort of terms with his Private Office that results in the Minister gaining a pretty good idea of what extra questions he might be asking, what little bit of extra probing he might be doing, so that he learns of any ferment going on within the department, not all of which might otherwise reach his ears.

(b)

First of all I should like to ignore those Ministers who leave everything to their civil servants and just read out their briefs. One can safely ignore them because that kind of Minister does not last very long. Nor, as Boyle has said, does the civil servant like it. Successful administration depends on constant interaction and a lot of feedback between Minister and civil servant . . . I should also like to ignore — with a shudder — the case where a Minister gets together in a huddle with a few of his colleagues and does not consult the machine at all. That usually means that they do not want to hear the facts or advice which might be given to them: disaster often follows. So, in the words of Dante, 'let us not speak of them but look and pass on.'

It is the normal case which interests us, where Ministers and civil servants genuinely work together. Before getting on to how this works I would like to touch on one or two particular points. One is perhaps not necessary to make to this audience — that we are loyal by upbringing. One can see it in the very peculiar psychological reaction of the ordinary civil servant when there is a matter in dispute between two Ministries. Great passion can be worked up — we get our Ministers involved (they may even have started it) — we feel desperately about it. Then finally, after tremendous manoeuvres and lobbying it goes to the Cabinet and a decision is made. Instantly, all passion is spent; there is no looking back; one gets ahead with the job . . .

The job of the Permanent Secretary is one of high responsibility — and, first of all, of very high managerial responsibility, which is something most Permanent Secretaries do not have nearly enough opportunity for exercising, because they are so busy acting as personal advisers to the Minister. A good Permanent Secretary must be available to his Minister at all times if so required. The Minister will usually want to consult the Permanent Secretary on anything of importance that comes his way — even in those cases such as the Defence Departments which I have mentioned where the Minister has other and independent advisers. Now what does this involve? I think the outside world very seldom realizes that if this job is done honestly and well it involves total subordination. After all it is the Minister who in the end has to take nearly all the raps. From this point of view the permanent civil servants are in a pretty good position . . . But I come back to the point which I regard as vital in all this — that the Minister in the end has to go to the House and to the Cabinet unaccompanied. The civil servant is not there . . .

The second point is the well-known and universal civil service axiom — that the civil servant must present the alternatives but he must come down on one side or the other; otherwise the Minister is left floating. The Minister must be presented with a definite proposal; he may or may not agree with it, but it concentrates the civil servant's mind and his own; it shows for one thing that the proposal has been thought about seriously.

When dealing with the normal kind of Minister of which I am talking, I would be sending in to him a number of files on all kinds of questions, some of them quite small matters, some of them quite big, some a particular aspect of something very big. I am now talking about the daily routine; for the really big issues there would be a lot of sitting round the table, discussion and so forth. I would go in daily and the Minister would go through my pile of files; normally he would agree with them but every so often he would come to one and say: 'No, I do not agree with this at all — I want to phrase it quite differently' or 'I don't want to take this line' or 'I want to do the opposite'. Human instinct on those occasions makes one want to stand up for the views one has expressed, particularly as one has tried to express them fairly definitely; but I always regarded it as my duty to support the Minister and not to supplant him. It was my job to give him every help — because his burden was so heavy that he should be spared all unnecessary disputes. Therefore on those occasions I turned my tongue three times round in my mouth and said to myself: 'Does it matter a damn how this is decided?'. If it did then I would say so and argue my case; and, as the Minister knew me to be a man who did not waste arguments, he would always pay attention. I am not concerned with which way the matter was eventually decided, but only with the fact that he would pay attention. But in nine cases out of ten it was a matter of presentation. In others his view depended on his relations with his fellow Ministers, or the matter was trivial and all that mattered was that something should be decided. In those cases, which were the majority, I

would not argue but would accept the Minister's view, preferably giving him credit
for having seen something which had escaped me, so as to make him feel happy.
. . . . . .

. . . On balance, of course, the Civil Service is a conservative influence; they have
got to keep the machine going; they have got to consider whether the new may not
be more upsetting than the old. They are growingly — to an extent that is hardly
realized — the guardians of some form of public interest. The Minister must be the
judge of the possible in the light of all that comes to him through his fellow Members of Parliament and others. But do not forget that Ministers are all men interested
in power and they will tend, whatever their party, to what I might call intervention-
ist solutions. It is the job of the civil servant to say not: 'The voter won't stand this'
but: 'This is going to bear hard on such and such a class of person and you must
remember these people' . . .

When a Minister has been sufficiently long in office, and particularly when a
Government has been sufficiently long in power and Ministers have circulated a bit,
there is one great danger that arises out of their interaction with the Civil Service.
The symbiosis between Ministers and civil servants becomes too close: Ministers
become identified with departmental interests; the necessary and wise distinction
between the two begins to disappear and this is a phenomenon which I think one
finds whatever the government . . .

There is no simple answer to the question how decisions are made. In the last
resort it is a Minister who makes them, because at the crucial point he goes off
without the civil servant to the Cabinet and to Parliament. The civil servant is
absent and powerless at the point of major decision. But the formation of policy is
a joint effort — the result of constant discussion. The good civil servant subordinates
himself totally to the Minister's decision but speaks out frankly when and only
when advice and criticism is helpful or necessary; the good Minister listens with care
to all the advice and criticism which he gets and then makes up his own mind . . .

(c)

Policy in the sense of the deliberate determination of what should be done or aimed
at may be shaped in a variety of ways. It may be determined politically. The
Minister may take office with a policy already settled — with an objective which his
Government has an electoral mandate to attain. All the civil servant can then do is
to make sure that all the implications and foreseeable consequences of the policy
are put impartially before the Minister, so that he may take the final decision — or
ask the Cabinet to do so — with his eyes open. He cannot — and he must not —
contest the wisdom of the policy. If, for example, it has been decided politically to
nationalize the comic postcard industry, it is legitimate to raise the question
whether the structure of the postcard industry, as a whole, is such that this section
of it can be hived off without injury to productivity and the economy. It is legitimate to point out that nationalization may involve the Minister not only in the
production of comic postcards but in determining the standards of taste to be

observed in their design. And, of course, it is legitimate to examine the form of organization best suited for running the nationalized concern ...

Secondly, policy very often results from the examination of a problem of current concern by a Royal Commission or departmental committee. The origins of such inquiries are very diverse. They may arise out of Parliamentary or public controversy — like the Royal Commission on the Press. They may arise from a general appreciation that some branch of the law is out of date and ought to be reviewed — like the Committee on Sunday Observance. They may arise from some individual case which has raised doubts about the way in which such cases have hitherto been handled — like the Royal Commission on the Police. Inquiries of this sort are much maligned. They are represented as a device for putting off the evil day; and there is a belief, which recent practice has not wholly dispelled, that a pigeon hole awaits the egg which they will eventually lay. But on the whole, this tried method of investigation has proved its value. It ensures that the problem is examined by a body which almost always reflects a broad range of experience and opinion. They look at it in the light of evidence. And their report, when received, enables opinion to be tested against a background of informed analysis before final decisions are taken.

And, thirdly, policy may of course evolve in the ordinary course of administration. Experience of handling individual cases, contact and discussion with local authority and other interests, representations received, Press and Parliamentary comment, realization of changing social and economic conditions, reports from inspectors in touch with local administration — all these things, and many others, may make it clear that past policy must be modified or new policy must be devised. The department carries out a study of the problem and its possible solutions and submits the matter, after any necessary consultations, to the Minister for his consideration and decision.

Ministerial—Departmental relationship First, they all inevitably involve the ministerial/departmental relationship, and this is something which perhaps we accept too readily as natural and satisfactory. It is characteristic of this country that no attempt, so far as I know, has been made to define the relationship with any precision, or to indoctrinate either of the parties to it in the way in which it ought to work. In spite of this, it has normally worked extremely well. But with the multiplying functions of government, the expanded and constant relationship of both central and local government with the individual citizen who is increasingly and properly conscious of his rights, the incessant and highly critical attention of the various media of opinion, the essential unity of Minister and department could easily come to be questioned. The two, in theory and in fact, are and ought to be indistinguishable. The department is the instrument of the Minister; it helps him to shape policy and to execute it. But the responsibility for policy is his and his alone — subject of course to the overriding authority of the Cabinet and of Parliament.

It is only when this essential unity of Minister and department has a practical manifestation in the day-to-day work of the department that sound policy is likely to be shaped. The wise Minister realizes that his department has a wealth of know-ledge and experience to put at his disposal, just as the wise department relies on the Minister not only for the final decision, which must be his, but for the political direction which must often govern its thinking. A department is, of course, strictly a-political; but it does not work — or it ought not to work — in a political vacuum. It must advise a Minister on a matter of policy in a realistic way; and realism means that account must be taken of political as well as other realities. If the machine is to work efficiently and effectively, there must be a relationship of complete confidence and frankness between the Minister and his senior advisers; and they, in turn, must ensure that their colleagues generally are aware of the main trends of the Minister's political thinking, and of the directions in which, as the political head of the depart-ment, he wants policy to develop.

It is no less important that the department should have an understanding of the Minister's general attitude and habit of mind. If discussion leading to policy decisions is to be fruitful it must be conducted as far as possible in a common language. It is up to the department to present to its Minister its assessment of the factors he must take into account in a way which ensures that they are fully under-stood. So it must form a judgement of his background of knowledge of a matter submitted for his decision as well as of his general approach to policy-making. Some Ministers are not content unless a case presented to them sets out not only the facts which have to be taken into account but every step in the argument leading to the conclusion reached. Others prefer a concise and cogent statement of the grounds which lead the department to make a particular recommendation. With the press of business which a Minister has to deal with in these days of intense govern-mental activity, the latter course is usually preferred; and the civil servant who fears that by adopting it some relevant consideration may be overlooked can comfortably salve his conscience by putting the detail into an appendix.

This necessity of understanding the Minister's general attitude to things is one reason why I personally regard administration as an art and not a science. It involves the almost intuitive adjustment of techniques to the personality of the individual Minister.

. . . . . .

Communication The execution of policy, like its shaping, involves continuously the ministerial/departmental relationship. The bulk of the practical work of day-to-day administration must be done without reference to the Minister. But he is responsible. He is answerable to Parliament. He is attacked in the Press. He is now satirised by young men and women on the stage and on television. So we must be sure that what we do in the Minister's name is indeed in accordance with the policy he has adopted or endorsed. For he may well have to defend it — and if necessary us.

This poses many questions. But where there is a proper understanding between a Minister and his senior officers the problem is again essentially one of communi-cation. It is necessary that at all levels at which decisions — however unimportant — are taken, there should be a proper understanding of what the Minister's policy is, and of the limits within which decisions may safely be taken without prior reference to him. Here, I am sure, is something which demands urgent examination and reflection. How do you ensure that the officer in contact with the public, the executive or junior administrative officer dealing with individual cases, really understands the background of his Minister's political attitudes, his Parliamentary difficulties, the shifting trends of public opinion, the current emphasis of policy, in the light of which he should be acting? Some of it you can write down in instructions and memoranda of guidance. But much of it, for obvious reasons, can only be communicated personally.

. . . . . .

There is a reverse side to this coin. In the practical work of administration the officer must not only understand the mind and policy of his Minister; he must also try to put himself in the shoes of his client, whoever he may be. The citizen who believes that his rights have in some respect been denied him is unlikely to be convinced by a letter saying that his obedient servant, the writer, is directed by the Minister to refer him to paragraph 5 of the Seventh Schedule to such and such an Act which, as read with the relevant amending provisions of two other statutes, makes it clear that no one of sound mind could suppose he had any rights at all. All that sort of thing achieves is an angry citizen and a bad name for the Minister and the department. Can we do more to teach public servants not only to give a prompt and honest answer, but first of all to see the matter from the other fellow's point of view and then try to explain to him, in a way he will understand, why the decision which is probably going to be such a disappointment to him is in fact inevitable? . . .

27 AN OUTSIDE VIEW OF BRITISH BUREAUCRACY

Extracts from *Educational Planning in Britain* (an Organisation for Economic Co-operation and Development report, extracts from which were published in the *Times Higher Education Supplement*, 9 May 1975); reprinted with permission.

Further attention must be given to a particular characteristic of the planning process in the United Kingdom which invites and yet transcends the term 'paradox'. This is the role played by the Civil Service.

The permanent officials of the DES in the tradition of British civil servants, are non-political in their function. In no country, it is safe to say, does the Civil Service govern itself more closely by a code of loyalty to whatever government is in power. The protections in the British system against the Civil Service's being captured by a political party go very far.

In the DES, an incoming Secretary of State normally makes no appointments from the outside, though the Secretary of State in the present Labour Government has appointed an economist as a special adviser. Perhaps in no other democracy are ministers' powers of appointment so strictly limited.

To the Civil Service's own code of professional neutrality there are thus added stringent safeguards against political patronage. This means that the expression of politically-oriented points of view in the daily work of the ministries is exceptional. Nor do the political parties intrude in the service's selection procedures or internal communications. By means of these practices and traditions, the British nation has been served by a continuing stream of knowledgeable and experienced officials with a strong tradition for discipline, fidelity and morale, and chosen for their individual merits, not their political allegiances.

But there has been a by-product. A permanent officialdom possessing such external protections and internal disciplines, becomes a power in its own right. A British department composed of professional civil servants who have watched the ministers come and go, is an entity that only an extremely foolish or powerful politician will persistently challenge or ignore.

The prestige, acquaintanceships, and natural authority of leading civil servants give them a standing in the civil forum often superior to that of their *de jure* political superiors. They are, in the continental phrase, notables, whose opinions must be given special weight, whether or not votes in the next election will be affected.

There has also to be taken into account the momentum of thought and action within a department composed of career officials who have long known one another, who have the same training and prospects, and who work within a common tradition and point of view. An essential part of their ethos is to serve their 'political masters'. They interpret this as imposing upon them the obligation to remain at all times sensitive to the changing realities of political pressures and to endeavour to identify in all situations a social consensus as to the priority issues towards which policy planning could be directed.

Accordingly, it is a simplification to describe the planning process in the DES as a purely technical affair in which resources are canvassed and strategic alternatives weighed, but decisions about ends and goals are neatly partitioned off, and left to the politicians, the electorate and the civil consensus. It is equally simplification, of course, to say that planning is entirely the Civil Service's doing.

For example, the White Paper under scrutiny in this examination bears the impress of the views on priorities, for example, nursery education and basic schooling, held by the Secretary of State under whom it was written. It further bears the impress of long-accepted goals in the United Kingdom such as the raising of the school-leaving age to 16 — something the British of all political complexions have contemplated since the second world war, and which was in fact envisaged in the Education Act of 1944.

Written under a Conservative minister it received initial criticism by the Labour Party as a statement of overall educational policy; none the less this does not appear to conflict with the decision of the Labour Government to implement the main proposals contained in it. The immediate instrument of continuity was the permanent officialdom of the Department of Education and Science.

The inertial power of historically enshrined goals and the power of bureaucracies to guide the policies of their political masters are facts of life in all democracies, and in non-democracies as well. The phenomenon of Civil Service predominance in educational planning is in fact partly attributable to the circumstance that the civil servants in the DES remain within the confines set for them by the law and their professional code. Their influence, like that of respected scholars or judges, derives from their justified reputation for neutrality and professional integrity. It might be said of them that they become powers by seeking not to be powers. But this does not make the role they play in planning any the less decisive. They do not make the plan in answer to their own beliefs and desires alone. But neither do they make it simply as passive respondents to the political process or the general will of the community.

28 FULTON: EVIDENCE FROM CIVIL SERVANTS

Extracts from *The Civil Service, Vol. 5 (2). Evidence to the Committee: Opinions and Proposals* (Cmnd. 3638, 1968); reprinted by permission of H.M.S.O. Extract (a) is from a memorandum by a group of members of the First Division Association, the 'trade union' of the former Administrative Class; extract (b) is from the formal evidence of the First Division Association. It is interesting to see that the views expressed by, and on behalf of, the senior levels of the Civil Service are notably more progressive than post-Fulton Civil Service practices.

(a)

Pressures and constraints

4. The part played by the Civil Service, particularly the Administrative Class, in helping to form and execute government policy has been subject to criticism from outside the Civil Service on what appear to be three main grounds:
   (*a*) amateurism both in outlook and in use of techniques;
   (*b*) absence of creative ideas;
   (*c*) lack of success generally . . .
   5. Those who make the criticisms and suggest remedies should, however, be aware of the forces which shape the Civil Service. We are not impressed with the argument, often heard, that the basic principles can be taken for granted, that everybody knows what the Civil Service is expected to do, and all we want are some reforms which will make it do the job better. On the contrary, the requirements are often confused and confusing.
   6. A few examples will show what we mean:
   (*a*) Senior Civil Servants are expected to think about the broadest areas of
          policy — and at the same time are answerable both to the Minister and to
          Parliament for the execution of the most detailed items.
   (*b*) We are expected by Ministers at times to accept general lines of policy with-

out hesitation and at other times to argue fearlessly against a course that we think inadvisable.

(c) The Civil Service is expected to produce results within the political time-scale — which varies from five years at the most to a matter of months or even days — and yet is blamed for shortness of sight; we are expected to be loyal to the Government of the day and yet not to be unprepared when a new one takes over.

(d) We must be 'non-political' in our advice — and yet are expected to initiate and develop policies in major fields of vital interest to the public.

(e) We are criticised for being inexpert and 'out of touch' but frequently prevented from carrying out consultation with those outside the Civil Service who are 'in touch' by the need to avoid either embarrassment of the Minister or the disclosure of official information.

(f) We are criticised for bad public relations, but discouraged from contact with the media of publicity.

7. What lies behind these apparent contradictions?

(a) *Ministers* place two major demands on Civil Servants. First, they require them to devise and operate the machinery for carrying out the policies to which the Government of the day is committed. Second, they expect to be warned of the pitfalls in these and other policy fields, and to be forearmed with developments of their policies devised to meet continually changing situations. At the same time, Ministers expect Civil Servants not to play an independent role in developing and executing policies in ways which might prejudice the Government's freedom of political action.

(b) *The public* expects the Civil Service to provide the element of stability and continuity which must survive changes of Government and policies. It also expects efficiency in the sense of a loyal, expeditious and well-managed response to political direction; and it demands impartiality and fairness in the application of agreed policies to individual cases. It increasingly requires Civil Servants to provide the backing for — and conceivably to participate in — the full public explanation of policies and the justification of their detailed execution.

8. Clearly these various roles expected of the Civil Service (and the constraints they imply) can pull in different, often opposite directions. Furthermore, the emphasis has shifted with time. For instance, it has for many years been the practice to defend the Administrative Class by saying that, since the reforms of the last century, it has been incorrupt, impartial, intelligent and free from nepotism. The 19th-century reforms have, however, to some extent been overtaken by events. For example, the traditional recruitment system concentrated on testing purely academic ability on the assumption that people with the best education then recognised should be able to enter the Service for a life-long career, and should have incentives to do so; now, however, the whole of society, and the Government's role, are much more complex and there are new professions, special skills, and changed educational

requirements which the Service has to comprehend and adapt itself to. A more fundamental point is that the concept of impartiality has shifted so that, although it still applies in many fields, this traditional virtue might be regarded as leading to lack of involvement in pressing social and economic problems: this helps to explain the accusations of apathy, obscurantism and lack of creative ideas. But those who now criticise the Civil Service as obsolete and unimaginative must ask themselves how far they are ready to risk sacrificing any of the traditional virtues in order to attain new qualities of administration − this could lead to abuse and public outcry.

Criteria of success

9. In looking for reforms one must be sure what one is trying to achieve. Ideally one requires a simple objective criterion to test the performance of the government machine. But so wide is the range of governmental aims, and such is the difficulty of quantifying progress against some of them, that no adequate criterion can be found. We would therefore suggest that the efficiency of the government machine should be judged by its performance in each stage of the process of making and applying policies, in quantifiable terms if that is appropriate, but otherwise by more general criteria.

10. The main stages of the governmental process seem to be four:
   (*a*) formulating objectives and taking strategic decisions;
   (*b*) collecting and analysing information in ways that are relevant both to individual policies and overall objectives;
   (*c*) executing policies;
   (*d*) providing feedback mechanisms to ensure that the Executive can learn and adapt itself to new situations, so that either objectives or methods of achieving them can be adjusted if they become incompatible.

. . . . . .

There must be a readiness to make changes to improve efficiency at all four stages. But the process must be viewed as a whole so that, for example, superficial improvements in execution are not achieved at the expense of feedback or the formulation of clear objectives.

11. The Civil Service plays a part in all these stages of decision-taking. Some people seem to think that Ministers, subject to Parliament, determine all policy and that Civil Servants are required only to carry it out. Others take an opposite view that the Civil Service makes the running and that Ministers become rubber-stamps. The truth seems to be that the programmes and doctrine of political parties (and, indeed, the pre-existing views of individual ministers) cover a narrow field compared with the total range of problems with which a Government in office has to deal. Civil Servants cannot escape offering policy advice on a wide range of undetermined issues and, as the permanent part of the Administration, they have a duty to advise on policy going beyond the framework of existing party doctrine and beyond the term of office of a Government. Moreover, even where Ministers have stated the strategic aims, the very process of considering the means of achieving

them raises issues which tend to modify them, and which only a continuous dialogue can resolve.

. . . . . .

Formulating objectives and taking strategic decisions

17. Setting policy objectives − taking the strategic decisions − is the key Ministerial role, and we consider here what Civil Servants can do to help Ministers make rational and informed choices. Imprecise or unrealistic objectives will result in muddled or misdirected policies . . .

18. The scope for party political influences to determine the definition of strategy is wide. Civil Servants can, however, help in many ways. First, they can identify and quantify needs − they can discover and verify facts and attitudes and formulate the concepts on the basis of which Ministers can themselves decide on objectives in the political sense. Secondly, they can bring into the open the implicit assumptions about objectives which lie behind all proposals or actions − when this is done the objectives may be found to be invalid or mutually conflicting. Third, the Civil Service can help Ministers to rank objectives in an order of priority when they cannot all be pursued simultaneously; or it may be possible to bring objectives and policies in several fields within a wider framework. Finally, the Civil Service can highlight objectives which are unrealistic, and which, if maintained, will only give rise to cynicism.

. . . . . .

. . . In the British context, if there is a problem of communication between Ministers and officials on the basic subject-matter of departmental policy, the appointment of special expert advisers could help towards a solution. So far as the secretariat function, however, is concerned (perhaps one of the things the traditional Civil Service is best at), the introduction of extra political cogs in the machine would not necessarily make it work better. We do not object to this idea on doctrinal grounds (though, depending on the proposals, there could be serious implications for the Civil Service) . . . We think, however, that a more fundamental solution to the problem of Ministerial time for involvement in policy work is called for.

22. The load could, for instance, be lightened not only by devolution of executive functions, as is discussed under the heading 'Execution of policy', but also by reducing the boundaries of Ministerial responsibilities through re-allocation where they overlap with those of other Ministers or public authorities. More formal delegation of some executive responsibilities to junior Ministers is also possible. Furthermore, the better mechanisms discussed under the heading of 'Feedback' would reduce the load by enabling the emergence of potentially political problems to be recognised before they became 'alive'.

(b)

3. The doctrine on the need for anonymity is vague, and practice varies not only

from Department to Department but also from subject to subject and from situation to situation. Such formal doctrine as there is goes back to the Masterman Report, which was primarily concerned with the political neutrality of the Civil Service, and with limitations that must be imposed on the exercise by civil servants of the ordinary political rights of the citizen. In practice, since all the affairs of Government are political to the extent that they are open to political challenge, civil servants tend to be inhibited from participation in public or semi-public discussions on matters of policy within their purview. However, we think it is important to draw the distinction between overt commitment to a political party, and participation by civil servants in public discussions of the subjects with which they deal. The Masterman Report was concerned almost exclusively with the former. We are primarily concerned here, however, with the latter, and consider that some changes in practice are desirable.

4. Already — but to a limited extent — civil servants are identified publicly with their responsibilities. Thus:

(i)   senior civil servants give oral evidence to the Public Accounts Committee, the Estimates Committee and the Select Committee on Nationalised Industries; they are excused from answering questions on matters of policy, but this does not, in practice, exclude very much;

(ii) some civil servants — and especially members of the professional grades — read papers, make speeches, or otherwise take part in public discussion, on such occasions as formal enquiries, local government committee meetings, or professional gatherings; their views appear in professional publications, and (in a limited way because the issues are seldom of sufficiently general interest) in the national press, on the radio or even on television;

and (iii) as a matter of everyday routine, civil servants consult particular sections of outside opinion about the evolution and application of policy. For this purpose, a number of Departments have consultative committees on particular subjects. These consultations are usually confidential. Informal contacts with interested individuals (including academics) are quite common. The machinery of the Economic Development Committees and the Regional Development Committees was set up to provide opportunities for exchanges of this kind.

5. In our view these contacts are insufficient and can give an impression outside the Service that civil servants are not fully in touch with public opinion. But in practice 'public' is different for each subject and for most matters it does not mean the electorate as a whole but quite a small section of it. The people to whom the civil servant may profitably address himself are those who want to know more about the subject in general or want to know in some detail how particular aspects of a policy affect them. They may also want the opportunity to feed back to the Government machine some of the problems that policies raise for them. It is entirely right that there should be greater communication of this sort. We think that public policy would be better conceived and better understood if civil servants were prepared and encouraged to participate in discussions of this kind.

6. There are two other advantages that would stem from civil servants participating more openly in discussions on questions of policy. The first is the effect on recruitment: there is some evidence that the anonymity of the Civil Service is a deterrent to some recruits. The second advantage comes from the fact that civil servants constitute a significantly large section of informed opinion in this country: they have a useful contribution to make to informed debate.

7. Of course, a policy of greater openness has its risks:

(i)   there is the risk of starting rumour: if civil servants take part in discussions on a particular proposal then it may be taken to indicate future Government intentions;

(ii)   there is the risk that individual civil servants will be regarded as supporting or opposing particular policies, or measures, and their views may be thought to be at variance with those of their Minister (or a successor Minister);

(iii)   the civil servant may imply that he dissents from settled policy, whereas in no public exchange would it be permissible for this to happen.

All these could be embarrassing to Ministers as well as to officials.

8. We think, however, that these risks are acceptable, both in general and as they affect the interests of our members. We do not envisage our members participating in the more artificial confrontations of television journalism, or in an exchange where objectivity is at a discount. Moreover, a civil servant who participates in open exchanges would be foolish to commit himself to outright support of a proposed policy and the rejection of all its alternatives; it is usually possible to discuss policies and their implications intelligently and informedly without plumping for one course to the exclusion of all others. We think that, for the rest, the more generally that open participation in these exchanges is accepted and practised, then the less significance will be read into this participation in itself and the less importance will be attached to the occasional embarrassment. In some areas of policy there may even now be little room for development in these directions, and in a few there are special problems of security. But in most areas we think the emphasis should be on taking and creating opportunities for informed discussion, rather than on avoiding it, and that this change of attitude would make a valuable and substantial difference to the quality of the work of the Service.

9. We see open exchanges as being particularly valuable in the exploration of long-term policy options, in the explanation of settled policy, and in discussion of its application. The risks of embarrassment are greatest when policy is in the later stages of formation at or near Ministerial level. At this stage it would rarely be opportune for officials to take part in the more open type of discussion. But the more professional or academic the forum in which the discussion is held, the smaller the risk of subsequent embarrassment, and, in general, the greater the value of the discussion to all participants. As a rather obvious working rule it could be said that the less appropriate the occasion is for officials to speak then the more appropriate it may be for Ministers to do so.

29 FULTON: REPORT OF THE MANAGEMENT CONSULTANCY GROUP

Extracts from *The Civil Service, Vol. 2. Evidence to the Committee: Report of a Management and Consultancy Group* (Cmnd. 3638, 1968); reprinted by permission of H.M.S.O. This evidence clearly influenced the Committee's final Report, and puts an emphasis on management which is reflected in post-Fulton changes.

303. Management, as we understand it, consists of the formulation and operation of the policy of the enterprise. This can be seen as a continuum ranging from first line supervision through a hierarchy of line managers to the board of directors. At each level assets — whether human, financial or material — have to be deployed in the manner best calculated to achieve particular objectives which contribute to the overall policy objectives formulated by the board. From our experience, this definition is also applicable to most of the work of the Civil Service. However, such an all-embracing definition is not sufficient for our purpose in this report. This is because there is an added 'political' dimension to the work of the Civil Servant which manifests itself in public accountability and ultimate political direction. Within this context, the functions of the Civil Service may be analysed in many ways, but we have found it convenient to distinguish four aspects which make up the total management task of the Civil Service.

    (a) formulation of policy under political direction,
    (b) creating the 'machinery' for implementation of policy,
    (c) operation of the administrative machine,
    (d) accountability to Parliament and the Public.

Normally, we use the term 'management' to cover all of these aspects but where necessary we distinguish between them.

. . . . . .

    305. As we have mentioned earlier, a unique feature of the work of the Civil Service is the involvement of so many of its officers with the community at large. Whether he be a Clerical Officer helping a pensioner to fill in a claim form or an Engineer concerned with the line and design of a Motorway, a Civil Servant has to make even small decisions in the light of their effect on the lives of his fellow-citizens. His fellow-citizens have come to expect of him the utmost impartiality and scrupulous care for their rights, concern for their views, the most careful stewardship of public money and property and, at the same time, have little toleration for delay or vacillation. In addition, a number of watchdogs of the community, both official and self-appointed, frequently call him or his superiors to account on matters large and small. We have seen the closeness of this scrutiny, and its effects, across the whole range from the enquiries of the Public Accounts Committee to Parliamentary questions and letters from M.P.s and members of the public.

    306. Subjection to scrutiny of this intensity and randomness means that not only does the individual officer have to show great care, even caution, in arriving at

equitable decisions but that the Civil Service has had to develop organisational and procedural forms — e.g. the division of responsibility for expenditure, complicated cross-checking routines, the maintenance of detailed records — which, on the face of it, are cumbersome when compared with those of industry. Industry, after all, exists to risk capital in the expectation of a return; the Civil Service is expected by the public to organise its work to maximise equity and minimise the risk of error.

307. This emphasis on equity also affects the way the Service manages its own staff. As we have described in our section on Establishment work, it particularly shows itself in the procedures for promoting and deploying staff. These procedures, reinforced by the operation of the Whitley machinery, limit the freedom of the Civil Service manager to organise his manpower assets as he sees fit.

. . . . . .

309. Unlike an industrial organisation, a Department of State has written terms of reference — the legislation and regulations it operates — within which to work. Some pieces of legislation are more explicit than others, but the fact remains that for many Civil Servants the task is to produce rulings on cases according to legislation, regulations or precedent rather than to show the initiative and entrepreneurial verve so highly prized in industry.

310. In addition to administering the great volume of accumulated legislation, Departments also exist to implement the current policies of Ministers. Ministers change frequently and, not infrequently a change of Minister is accompanied by a radical change in important aspects of a Department's activities. Civil Servants, particularly senior ones, have to be able to adapt to, even identify themselves with, totally new policy goals at very short notice without allowing the machine to falter. Senior managers in industry rarely have to contend with changes of similar order and frequency.

. . . . . .

313. Big economic and social issues inevitably involve more than one Department and we noted the extent to which interdepartmental discussions were necessary before policy decisions could be taken. This produces a complex system of inter-departmental co-operation and consultation, largely by means of committees, with the consequent lengthening of the decision-making process.

314. Management in industry generally has control over the implementation of its policy decisions. Policies developed in Government Departments are frequently implemented in detail by autonomous or semi-autonomous bodies such as local authorities and nationalised industries. Departments are therefore often in a position of partial responsibility and limited power. The results of this are that a Civil Servant frequently has to persuade rather than direct and that ultimate implementation of policy decisions can be slow and piecemeal. This dispersal of executive responsibility can inhibit the return flow to the Department of information on which the success of policy can be judged and future policies can be based.

315. It is noticeable, compared with big companies, that the long-term planning role of top management is given far less emphasis than dealing with day to day matters, many of them relatively trivial. In big firms, the evaluation of different

courses of action based on research is a major concern of top management. In the Civil Service, top management is largely pre-occupied with reacting to such immediate pressures as Ministers' cases, Parliamentary debates and questions, reports of Parliamentary Committees and deputations.

316. Despite these important differences in the environment in which Civil Servants operate, in our experience, management in the Civil Service nevertheless has much in common with management in industry. Both are concerned with the formulation of policy and its implementation. Though most of the Civil Service cannot qualify its performance in terms of the financial return on resources, both it and industry are concerned with meeting objectives at the lowest possible cost. They are both concerned with making the best use of the scarce resources of skilled manpower for which they compete. Increasingly, the decisions of commercial and industrial managers have to take account of their impact not only upon the market but upon the community at large.

. . . . . .

The managerial style of the service

. . . . . .

Management and class 321. In essence, the Civil Service class system is based on the idea that distinctions can be drawn between the detailed management of day-to-day operations (allocated to the Executive Class); the provision of 'specialist' or 'professional' advice (the duty of the specialist classes) and policy making and financial control (laid to the Administrative Class). Generally, though not universally, entry to each class is governed by a particular level of academic qualifications. Again generally, an officer enters the class for which he has been predestined by his educational attainments and is expected to progress in that class by moving up a ladder of salary grades mainly according to length of service.

322. In earlier sections we have discussed the working of the class system and have demonstrated that it is a major obstacle to efficient management in the Civil Service. In modern conditions, it prevents the flexible deployment of talent by artificially restricting individuals to a defined range of tasks historically deemed appropriate to their class. Thus it confines scientists, professionals and other specialists such as accountants to particular roles and assumes that management skills are not transferable from specialist to administrative areas. The maze of classes frequently results in artificial distinctions between officers engaged on identical or closely comparable tasks. Moreover, administering a Service which contains well over one thousand different classes, each with its own salary and career structure, is bound to be a task of infinite complexity.

323. Within this class system, the role of the Administrative Class is of particular managerial significance. Not only does the formal definition of the duties of this class give it the dominant position in management but this is reinforced by its control over Establishment and financial matters. In organisational terms, financial

responsibility rests with the Accounting Officer (i.e. the Permanent Secretary) who, as we have seen, normally delegates this authority to members of his own class. By the exercise of this financial responsibility, ultimate control decisions are the preserve of the Administrative Class and, as we have discussed elsewhere, this concept has profound effects on the organisation of Departments and the allocation of duties between classes.

324. Despite the dominant position of the Administrative Class, we found that its members did not visualise their managerial task as embracing all four of the elements at (a) to (d) of paragraph 303. Their primary interest is in being advisers on policy matters to people above them rather than in managing the administrative machine below them. The process of selection, training and movement from job to job is designed to produce generalist administrators familiar with the processes of policy making, Ministerial cases and correspondence and the system of financial control. It does not, however, equip them to handle the total managerial task nor to develop the specialist knowledge or techniques required by Departments for their particular policies and activities. Yet as Departments have grown, sometimes to the size of whole industries, so the management task in all four aspects has increased in importance until today it demands professional management of the highest order.

325. One noticeable result of the present system, which is designed to train a small élite in the processes of policy making and public accountability and then promotes them into positions of substantial managerial authority, is that the top management of the Service arrives in post largely unprepared for the full managerial role. An A.P. spends most of his first five years in having 'a first go' at writing policy briefs and dealing with Ministerial correspondence; he becomes a Principal and is then almost always used in a small 'policy' group; he becomes an Assistant Secretary (around the age of 40) in charge of several score of staff, an Under Secretary in charge of several hundred and at higher levels he may be responsible for many thousands. His formative years as an A.P. and Principal give little experience of supervision and of the practical human relations involved in motivating people to get things done. Nor does he acquire any first hand knowledge of managerial techniques which can have important implications for top management: e.g. data processing. The emphasis on the formulation of policy and on the processes of public accountability throughout the Administrator's early career means that the other aspects of management, in our view no less important, are thought of as a lower order of activity to be left mainly to members of the Executive Class. We met several examples of the lack of interest of Administrators in the executive/clerical groups nominally under their control: the Assistant Secretary who visited a group of over 360 staff only once a year at the time of the Christmas party is one of them.

326. In the sections of this report on the Administrative and Executive Classes we have dealt at length with the disadvantages of management by generalist. A particular disadvantage is the way that rotation between jobs prevents the development of knowledge in depth of the subjects being dealt with. The usual practice in industry, in which men are recruited for, and trained in, a particular function of the

enterprise over a number of years and then assume the more general responsibilities of higher management should, in our view, be applied in the Civil Service so as to supply the professionalism in depth which we believe essential at these levels.

Organisation 327. Although the detailed organisation of Departments varies considerably, the traditional Whitehall Department is organised into divisions each responsible for a block of work defined by, for example, legislative or policy responsibility (e.g. Distribution of Industry Division, Gas Division), or geographical area. In addition Departments usually have two functional divisions: Finance and Establishments, which fulfil the Treasury role of control over expenditure. Divisions are normally further divided into branches.

328. Within Divisions, the Service frequently organises separately policy and legislative work, executive/clerical casework, and specialist advice. The policy and legislative work, which includes high level casework, Parliamentary and Ministerial matters and drafting legislation, is allocated to branches staffed by Administrators and supporting Executives. The general run of day-to-day casework is then handled by separate branches headed by Executives, while specialist advice is provided by branches manned by specialist officers . . .

. . . . . .

330. An outsider is struck by the tall, thin pyramidal form of organisation generally adopted by the Service. In a Whitehall Department there are at least nine organisational levels (from C.A. to Permanent Secretary), several more than there would be in a typical industrial situation, and spans of control (i.e. the number of subordinates reporting directly to a superior) are very narrow, averaging only 2 to 3, except in some large executive/clerical groups. In industry, this type of organisational structure indicates a situation in which authority is very sparingly delegated and supervision is close.

331. There are a number of obvious factors which have contributed to the adoption of this tall narrow structure:

(a) the drafting procedures in policy areas, in which an officer at one level has a 'first go' at a paper, the next does a draft, the next amends and approves or submits the finished article to his superior (e.g. H.E.O.–Principal–Assistant Secretary);

(b) the meticulous checking and double-checking in all financial matters: we came across one estimating routine that ran through five levels (E.O.–S.C.E.O.) of preparation and scrutiny (the more levels, the greater insurance against error);

(c) the frequent rotation of Administrative and Executive staff in many areas requires cover in depth to provide continuity;

(d) it is conventionally accepted that the organisational structure must reflect the grading structure of the classes concerned . . .

(e) the concentration of ultimate authority on financial and other matters in the hands of one person – the Permanent Secretary.

It will be seen that these factors are themselves the product of one or other of the following: the strength of centralised financial control, the emphasis on the need to minimise error and the convention that work must be organised to accommodate as many as possible of the grades in the class hierarchies.

. . . . . .

333. In specialist areas, organisation structure often takes a looser, more organic form, with less emphasis on the pyramidal hierarchy and more on the formation of teams for particular projects. We met such groups in areas of scientific research and development, architectural design, and civil engineering. We saw these arrangements at their most developed in scientific research and development where *ad hoc* project teams had been formed using members of several different classes and where there was no rigid emphasis on allocating the work according to the classes or grades of the team members.

334. In some respects, lines of authority and responsibility in Departments are exceptionally clear. An officer knows who his superior and his subordinates are: their relationships are usually clearly understood. He knows which piece of legislation he is operating and can refer to it and the precedents that have been built up around it. On the other hand, in the course of our investigation we have often found it difficult in many of them to locate the precise responsibility of individuals. Individual responsibility often seems to disappear into the committee decision, or the consensus view at senior levels . . .

Line management in the Civil Service 335. The unique constraints upon the line manager in the Civil Service are fundamental to any consideration of its managerial style. As we have noted in our section on Establishments work he cannot hire or dismiss, he cannot reward merit by any form of payment, he cannot promote, he cannot reprimand formally, he cannot even stop the annual increment of an unsatisfactory subordinate. It is therefore extremely difficult for a manager in the Service to motivate his staff except by example and verbal encouragement or criticism. The only action that a manager in the Service can take to ensure that the system recognises the strengths or weaknesses of a subordinate is in marking the subordinate's annual confidential report form and we have noted that there are powerful conventions which discourage exceptionally good or bad markings and that the tendency is to enter 'good' for all but very exceptional cases. In addition, it is widely felt that promotion boards take less notice of annual report markings than of a man's showing before the board.

336. The emphasis upon equity and fair chances for all deprives the line manager of what in industry is his main motivational tool. On the face of it, there is little encouragement for his subordinates to do anything other than avoid mistakes or inaction so serious as to call for an adverse annual report. It is surprising that such a system has called forth the dedication, conscientiousness and enthusiasm that we so often saw. We frequently saw work that, in our view, merited the special recognition that is precluded by the present system . . .

. . . . . .

338. The centralised financial arrangements by which the Treasury ultimately

exercises control over the expenditure of Departments are more marked than in the generality of industrial situations. Although there are financial delegations to Departments, it is noticeable that the Treasury interest in expenditure extends in practice to raising questions concerning the details of departmental policy even on technical issues. The line manager in the Service concerned with expenditure is therefore often conscious of, and subject to, a greater degree of central management control over his decisions and activities, from outside his Department, than is usual with his industrial counterpart. This control can take the form of the manager having to defend his decisions or proposals and to be questioned on possible alternatives.

339. This must result in managers exercising great caution in considering any issue with financial implications; the pros and cons of different courses of action have to be meticulously recorded and at length; and proposals are often referred to higher levels of departmental management in order to ensure support for the manager's view. Subsequently, there may be considerable debate with the Treasury, usually via the Department's Finance Division. All this slows down the decision-making process and makes it difficult to pin down individual responsibilities; it also means that primarily technical decisions are open to lay criticism at points further and further removed from the place where action has to be taken and therefore have to be justified at length by a dialogue in highly simplified non-technical terms. The superimposition of the requirements of public accountability and the resultant scrutiny by the Comptroller and Auditor General and the Public Accounts Committee intensify this caution.

Management techniques 340. As we have discussed earlier, the man in charge of any division or branch is not immediately responsible for the size of the group or its composition. It follows that he is not responsible for its cost and indeed the system of annual vote accounting emphasises this situation since it is not designed to provide total cost figures for the particular divisions or branches of a Department. In most cases, the Establishment and Finance Divisions of Departments are concerned with monitoring expenditure against the global votes; the control over staff costs, which are the main item of expenditure in many administrative divisions, is left to Establishment Divisions. The Civil Service manager therefore has a passive role in the key task of controlling the costs of his own staff.

341. Management control techniques in the Civil Service are mainly based on the requirements of public accountability and most of the emphasis has been on control systems designed to prevent error. More positive concepts of management control — setting standards of performance for individuals or groups, expressing these in terms of budgets, ratios, indices of efficiency or jobs to be done by a certain time and monitoring achievement against them — has made very little headway in the Service . . .

. . . . . .

343. In general, we were struck by the contrast between the development in

some areas of advanced techniques of considerable sophistication and the virtual isolation of other parts of the Service from current debates on management concepts and techniques. In these latter areas, the lack of awareness of modern management methods seemed to spring in part from the generalist philosophy and its associated lack of recognition of the value of expertise . . .

Possible lines of reform

344. We now put forward, for the Committee's consideration, possible major lines of reform and development of the Service based on our analysis of the evidence we have gathered and our knowledge of industry and commerce.

The class system 345. We believe that we have seen a sufficient variety of Civil Service work to come to the conclusion that the present class system hinders the adaptability of the Service to new tasks; prevents the best use of the talents of individuals and causes frustration; leads to the creation of cumbersome organisational forms and frequently prevents the entry into line management of officers who are fitted to it.

346. We are therefore persuaded that all interests would be best served by the abolition of the present class system and the creation of a classless uniformly graded Service. Clearly, a number of pay grades would be required to provide a ladder in which each rung corresponds to a level of responsibility and job content. It therefore follows that a system is required which would permit across-the-Service comparison and ranking of the content of jobs: i.e. a system in which a scientific job in a research establishment, a high level casework job in an administrative division, an engineering job and a line management job in an executive/clerical establishment can all be analysed and ranked in the same terms. This system can be provided by job evaluation techniques.

347. In our view the job evaluation techniques most appropriate for this purpose are those whereby the content and requirements of any job are analysed into factors or attributes, such as the education and experience required to do it, the number and level of staff controlled, the level of responsibility in terms of financial expenditure or effect on policy, the discretionary content of the work, the analytical, managerial and innovative characteristics required of the incumbent. These factors are then enumerated to give a quantitative measure of the content of the job. Jobs can then be grouped into grades and pay scales or ranges can be applied to each grade, taking appropriate outside comparisons into account.
. . . . . .

354. The advantages of a common grading system are manifold. It would permit the flexible use of members of the present-day classes. It would permit the integration of officers with various backgrounds of education, training and skill into the organisation structure most appropriate to the job in hand. Many more officers would have open to them a ladder up which they could rise on merit, regardless of

their entry qualifications, knowing that the top jobs are not the preserve of people with different academic qualifications. Properly trained specialists would have access to managerial positions right to the top of Departments.

355. Necessary adjuncts to such a reform are, of course, the recognition of the prime importance of performance on the job as a qualification for promotion to a job in the next superior grade, the recognition of the value of specialist and managerial experience as the background for promotion to top management and the provision of training and experience in the processes of public accountability for all those who are likely to reach higher management positions.

The recognition of merit 356. We pointed out earlier that the manager in the Civil Service has very little discretion in encouraging and rewarding his staff. We are, however, very well aware of the advantages of the present system. The security of tenure and very remoteness of reward obviates the worst aspects of jockeying for position that can be a feature of some outside organisations. There are no excesses of favouritism and nepotism, and this prevents the promotion of the wholly incompetent. A Civil Servant is guaranteed by the system a measure of independence and security from the prejudices of his superiors. Competition between managers, which in its worst forms militates against their co-operation is rarely seen in the Service and this makes not only for a pleasant working atmosphere, but contributes to the efficient conduct of public business.

357. Nevertheless, in our view, the Service would benefit from a system in which there was scope to reward excellence in performance or to reward the acquisition of further skills or formal qualifications. All increments should be based on a review of the officer's performance in the past year. Unsatisfactory performance should be marked by the withholding or reduction of an increment, while exceptional merit could receive, say, a double increment. In the case of young entrants, while special merit may be rewarded, automatic increments would be appropriate while they are settling into the Service. We would also see an advantage to the Service if an officer who acquired an external degree, diploma or other qualification relevant to the work of his Department were rewarded at the time of qualification. We are aware that the merit awards suggested above open the Service to the risk of favouritism but in our view the incentive effect would outweigh this disadvantage.

. . . . . .

359. We also consider that there should be a change of emphasis in promotion procedures so that more weight is given to performance on the job as assessed by an officer's superiors and rather less to seniority and to performance before a promotion board . . .

A new managerial style 360. We consider that there is considerable scope, both within Departments and for the Service as a whole, for a group of inter-related management research programmes aimed at:

(a) defining the objectives and priorities for areas of the organisation;

(b) devising new organisational forms related not to classes but to the task in hand;

(c) increasing the use of management controls;

(d) delegating responsibility clearly to individuals;

(e) measuring managerial effectiveness.

361. The first step in instituting such programmes is, in management consultancy terms, a management appraisal or review to decide on the current objectives of the organisation and systematically to analyse them so as to establish the key functions, their place in the organisation, their staffing and the associated arrangement of levels and individual posts and the optimum form of supporting structure that they should receive.

362. Such an analysis might well show scope for new organisational forms. The rigid hierarchical form which is customary in executive/clerical areas may generally be the most appropriate for routine clerical work and the lower levels of casework involving the application of clear rules and precedents. In the course of our assignment, however, we formed the opinion that there were situations in which looser groupings and 'flatter' structures might be adopted, where levels could be omitted and where greater delegation and schemes to enlarge the content of individual jobs might encourage the more effective use of staff.

363. We can also see scope for experiments in new upper management structures which a classless Service would facilitate:

(a) The increasing importance, and policy implications, of such specialisations as data processing, operational research and management accounting might indicate the need for their direct representation at the higher levels of management.

(b) There seems to us to be a need for the clearer definition and separation of functions at the highest management levels. For example, the management of existing policies including public accountability for them might be separated organisationally from the forward planning role concerned with research into, and evaluation of, new policy options. In addition, it may well be that other functions such as internal management consultancy services and management training and development should be separately organised at these levels.

Such experiments in organisational forms might ensure that the administrative implications of policy options both for the Service itself and for the public generally are adequately considered and costed by specialised groups freed from day-to-day management responsibility before decisions are taken.

364. We see a particular need for the formation of high level departmental units concerned with strategic planning. Such units would be engaged on preparing 'scenarios' of the department's situation in future years, identifying the likely policy needs and the associated demands for resources. On this basis the allocation of resources can be planned and can be adjusted to meet changing situations, programmes of work can be initiated and objectives set for the various parts of the organisation.

. . . . . .

374. The development of a new managerial style is, we believe, essential for the Civil Service of the future. It depends upon a management that is constantly appraising and criticising its own efforts and seeking to apply new techniques and organisational forms appropriate to the evolving tasks of the Service. This implies the need for an awareness by management of developments outside the Service coupled with a highly professional internal management consultancy service. Great emphasis should be given to the development of managerial skills in staff at all levels and of all specialisms. The development of such skills would be aided by the evolution of organisations in which more scope is given to managerial initiative, with proper safeguards; in which this initiative is encouraged and rewarded; in which suitable controls are devised so as to permit management by objective; in which there is as clear a delegation of authority and responsibility as possible and in which management is judged according to its skill in achieving the objectives for which it is responsible. In the system we envisage, great attention should be devoted to the early identification and encouragement of managerial skill and promotion should be rapid for those, whatever their entry point and their academic qualifications, who show evidence of possessing it.

Top management 375. This change of style must be initiated by, and reflected at, the top levels of management. We feel it appropriate to conclude by referring to the type of professional managers whom we see as required for the top management of Departments in the future. First, we believe that they should be drawn from a wider range of education and experience than at present; all entrants to the Service should have a real chance of reaching top management. Secondly, that they should have a deep knowledge of at least one function of a Department gained over a number of years. Thirdly, that they should have successfully held managerial responsibility at lower levels in the Department prior to being trained for the general management and policy role of the top manager. Fourthly that, in common with other staff, whatever academic qualifications they have on entry to the Service should be broadly appropriate to the work of the Department and the greatest possible encouragement should be given to acquiring relevant post-entry qualifications.

376. We have defined the total management task in the Civil Service as comprising the formulation of policy under political direction; implementation of policy; operation of the administrative machine and accountability to Parliament and the Public. This calls for the highest level of professionalism.

30 FULTON: THE BASIC CRITIQUE

Extracts from *The Civil Service, Vol. 1. Report of the Committee 1966–68* (The Fulton Report, Cmnd. 3638, 1968); reprinted by permission of H.M.S.O.

1. The Home Civil Service today is still fundamentally the product of the nineteenth-

century philosophy of the Northcote—Trevelyan Report. The tasks it faces are those of the second half of the twentieth century. This is what we have found; it is what we seek to remedy.

2. The foundations were laid by Northcote and Trevelyan in their report of 1854. Northcote and Trevelyan were much influenced by Macaulay whose Committee reported in the same year on the reform of the India Service . . .

3. These reports condemned the nepotism, the incompetence and other defects of the system inherited from the eighteenth century. Both proposed the introduction of competitive entry examinations. The Macaulay Report extolled the merits of the young men from Oxford and Cambridge who had read nothing but subjects unrelated to their future careers. The Northcote—Trevelyan Report pointed to the possible advantages of reading newer, more relevant subjects, such as geography or political economy, rather than the classics. But as the two services grew, this difference between the two reports seems to have been lost. There emerged the tradition of the 'all-rounder' as he has been called by his champions, or 'amateur' as he has been called by his critics.

. . . . . .

7. Meanwhile, the role of government has greatly changed. Its traditional regulatory functions have multiplied in size and greatly broadened in scope. It has taken on vast new responsibilities. It is expected to achieve such general economic aims as full employment, a satisfactory rate of growth, stable prices and a healthy balance of payments. Through these and other policies (e.g. public purchasing, investment grants, financial regulators) it profoundly influences the output, costs and profitability of industry generally in both the home and overseas markets. Through nationalisation it more directly controls a number of basic industries. It has responsibilities for the location of industry and for town and country planning. It engages in research and development both for civil and military purposes. It provides comprehensive social services and is now expected to promote the fullest possible development of individual human potential. All these changes have made for a massive growth in public expenditure. Public spending means public control. A century ago the tasks of government were mainly passive and regulatory. Now they amount to a much more active and positive engagement in our affairs.

8. Technological progress and the vast amount of new knowledge have made a major impact on these tasks and on the process of taking decisions; the change goes on. Siting a new airport, buying military supplies, striking the right balance between coal, gas, oil and nuclear-powered electricity in a new energy policy — all these problems compel civil servants to use new techniques of analysis, management and co-ordination which are beyond those not specially trained in them.

9. The increase in the positive activities of government has not been solely an extension of the powers and functions of the State in an era of technological change. There has also been a complex intermingling of the public and private sectors. This has led to a proliferation of para-state organisations: public corporations, nationalised industries, negotiating bodies with varying degrees of public and private participation, public participation in private enterprises, voluntary bodies financed

from public funds. Between the operations of the public and the private sectors there is often no clear boundary. Central and local government stand in a similarly intricate relationship; central government is generally held responsible for services that it partly or mainly finances but local authorities actually provide. As the tasks of government have grown and become more complex, so the need to consult and co-ordinate has grown as well.

10. The time it takes to reach a decision and carry it out has often lengthened. This is partly because of technological advance and the resulting complexity e.g. of defence equipment. Another reason is that the public and Parliament demand greater foresight and order in, for example, the development of land, the transport system and other resources, than they did in the past.

11. Governments also work more and more in an international setting. The improvement in communications and the greater interdependence of nations enlarges the difficulties as well as the opportunities of government.

12. To meet these new tasks of government the modern Civil Service must be able to handle the social, economic, scientific and technical problems of our time, in an international setting. Because the solutions to complex problems need long preparation, the Service must be far-sighted; from its accumulated knowledge and experience, it must show initiative in working out what are the needs of the future and how they might be met. A special responsibility now rests upon the Civil Service because one Parliament or even one Government often cannot see the process through.

13. At the same time, the Civil Service works under political direction and under the obligation of political accountability. This is the setting in which the daily work of many civil servants is carried out; thus they need to have a lively awareness of the political implications of what they are doing or advising. The Civil Service has also to be flexible enough to serve governments of any political complexion – whether they are committed to extend or in certain respects to reduce the role of the State. Throughout, it has to remember that it exists to serve the whole community, and that imaginative humanity sometimes matters more than tidy efficiency and administrative uniformity.

14. In our view the structure and practices of the Service have not kept up with the changing tasks. The defects we have found can nearly all be attributed to this. We have found no instance where reform has run ahead too rapidly. So, today, the Service is in need of fundamental change. It is inadequate in six main respects for the most efficient discharge of the present and prospective responsibilities of government.

15. First, the Service is still essentially based on the philosophy of the amateur (or 'generalist' or 'all-rounder'). This is most evident in the Administrative Class which holds the dominant position in the Service. The ideal administrator is still too often seen as the gifted layman who, moving frequently from job to job within the Service, can take a practical view of any problem, irrespective of its subject-matter, in the light of his knowledge and experience of the government machine. Today, as the report of our Management Consultancy Group illustrates, this concept

has most damaging consequences. It cannot make for the efficient despatch of public business when key men rarely stay in one job longer than two or three years before being moved to some other post, often in a very different area of government activity. A similar cult of the generalist is found in that part of the Executive Class that works in support of the Administrative Class and also even in some of the specialist classes. The cult is obsolete at all levels and in all parts of the Service.

16. Secondly, the present system of classes in the Service seriously impedes its work. The Service is divided into classes both horizontally (between higher and lower in the same broad area of work) and vertically (between different skills, professions or disciplines). There are 47 general classes whose members work in most government departments and over 1,400 departmental classes. Each civil servant is recruited to a particular class; his membership of that class determines his prospects (most classes have their own career structures) and the range of jobs on which he may be employed. It is true that there is some subsequent movement between classes; but such rigid and prolific compartmentalism in the Service leads to the setting up of cumbersome organisational forms, seriously hampers the Service in adapting itself to new tasks, prevents the best use of individual talent, contributes to the inequality of promotion prospects, causes frustration and resentment, and impedes the entry into wider management of those well fitted for it.

17. Thirdly, many scientists, engineers and members of other specialist classes get neither the full responsibilities and corresponding authority, nor the opportunities they ought to have. Too often they are organised in a separate hierarchy, while the policy and financial aspects of the work are reserved to a parallel group of 'generalist' administrators; and their access to higher management and policy-making is restricted. Partly this is because many of them are equipped only to practise their own specialism; a body of men with the qualities of the French *poly-technicien* – skilled in his craft, but skilled, too, as an administrator – has so far not been developed in Britain. In the new Civil Service a wider and more important role must be opened up for specialists trained and equipped for it.

18. Fourthly, too few civil servants are skilled managers. Since the major managerial role in the Service is specifically allocated to members of the Administrative Class it follows that this criticism applies particularly to them. Few members of the class actually see themselves as managers, i.e. as responsible for organisation, directing staff, planning the progress of work, setting standards of attainment and measuring results, reviewing procedures and quantifying different courses of action. One reason for this is that they are not adequately trained in management. Another is that much of their work is not managerial in this sense; so they tend to think of themselves as advisers on policy to people above them, rather than as managers of the administrative machine below them. Scientists and other specialists are also open to criticism here: not enough have been trained in management, particularly in personnel management, project management, accounting and control.

19. Fifthly, there is not enough contact between the Service and the rest of the community. There is not enough awareness of how the world outside Whitehall works, how government policies will affect it, and the new ideas and methods which

are developing in the universities, in business and in other walks of life. Partly this is a consequence of a career service. Since we expect most civil servants to spend their entire working lives in the Service, we can hardly wonder if they have little direct and systematic experience of the daily life and thought of other people. Another element in this is the social and educational composition of the Civil Service; the Social Survey of the Service which we commissioned suggests that direct recruitment to the Administrative Class since the war has not produced the widening of its social and educational base that might have been expected. The public interest must suffer from any exclusiveness or isolation which hinders a full understanding of contemporary problems or unduly restricts the free flow of men, knowledge and ideas between the Service and the outside world.

20. Finally, we have serious criticisms of personnel management. Career-planning covers too small a section of the Service — mainly the Administrative Class — and is not sufficiently purposive or properly conceived; civil servants are moved too frequently between unrelated jobs, often with scant regard to personal preference or aptitude. Nor is there enough encouragement and reward for individual initiative and objectively measured performance; for many civil servants, especially in the lower grades, promotion depends too much on seniority.

21. For these and other defects the central management of the Service, the Treasury, must accept its share of responsibility. It is unfortunate that there was not a major reform in the post-war years when the government took on so many new tasks and the Service had been loosened by war-time temporary recruitment and improvisation. There was then a great opportunity to preserve and adapt to peace-time conditions the flexibility which war had imposed. For a number of reasons, not all of them internal to the Service, this opportunity was not taken. In the 1950s the old ways reasserted themselves. The nature of the task was changing and the Service was left behind. Only recently has any attempt been made to introduce significant reforms. Despite the recent improvement in its management services the Treasury has failed to keep the Service up to date.

. . . . . .

24. One basic guiding principle should in our view govern the future development of the Civil Service. It applies to any organisation and is simple to the point of banality, but the root of much of our criticism is that it has not been observed. The principle is: look at the job first. The Civil Service must continuously review the tasks it is called upon to perform and the possible ways in which it might perform them; it should then think out what new skills and kinds of men are needed, and how these men can be found, trained and deployed. The Service must avoid a static view of a new ideal man and structure which in its turn could become as much of an obstacle to change as the present inheritance.

25. We have sought to devise a form of management for the Civil Service that will ensure that it is better run and able to generate its own self-criticism and forward drive. One of the main troubles of the Service has been that, in achieving immunity from political intervention, a system was evolved which until recently

was virtually immune from outside pressures for change. Since it was not immune from inside resistance to change, inertia was perhaps predictable.

31 POST-FULTON DEVELOPMENTS

The implementation of the main Fulton proposals is summarised in progress reports by the National Whitley Council (a body representative of the whole Civil Service, both as employers and as employees). Extract (a) from *Developments on Fulton* (1969) describes the establishment of a new Civil Service Department to take over from the Treasury the responsibility for the management of the Civil Service. Extract (b) from *Fulton: A Framework for the Future* (1970) deals with the rationalisation of internal structures. Extract (c) from *Fulton: The Reshaping of the Civil Service* (1971) describes the arrangements for the merger of the old administrative and executive classes into a new, unified grading structure.

(a)

THE CIVIL SERVICE DEPARTMENT

Establishment of the Department

7. On the day of publication of the Report, the Prime Minister announced that the Government accepted the proposal to establish a new Civil Service Department, covering broadly the Civil Service Commission and the responsibilities of the Pay and Management Divisions of the Treasury.

8. The Civil Service Department came into formal existence on 1st November, 1968. The functions of the Civil Service Commission under the Civil Service Order in Council were unaffected, but a Transfer of Functions Order . . . transferred to the Minister for the Civil Service (the Prime Minister) the formal functions previously exercised by the Treasury on the following matters:

(a) the organisation and conduct of the Civil Service and Civil Service pay and conditions of service;

(b) the approval of competition regulations;

(c) certain other statutory functions in relation to pay, superannuation etc. in the public sector; and vis-a-vis other public bodies.

11. These changes meet the general recommendations of the Report that 'the expanded and unified central management of the Service should be made the responsibility of a new department created specifically for the purpose' (Recommendation 117) and that 'central management should have the appropriate degree of ultimate authority in those questions that affect the interests of the Service as a whole' (Recommendation 116) . . .

12. The Lord Privy Seal (Lord Shackleton) has been appointed by the Prime

Minister to assist him in the day-to-day operation of the Department. This is in line with the suggestion made in the Report (Recommendation 123). The Lord Privy Seal normally answers Questions, and otherwise speaks for the Department, in the House of Lords. Responsibility for answering Questions in the House of Commons is shared between the Prime Minister and the Paymaster General (Mrs. Judith Hart). The Paymaster General also on occasion speaks for the Department in debates in the House of Commons.

13. The official head of the Civil Service Department (Sir William Armstrong) remains Official Head of the Home Civil Service, as proposed in the Report (Recommendation 121).

14. The creation of the Civil Service Department represents more than a simple transfer of functions. By separating the management of the Civil Service from the Treasury and bringing it directly under the Prime Minister, the Government have established it as a central function in its own right, which will have its own independent standing and develop its own outlook and professional skill. Without detracting from the role hitherto played by the Treasury, or from the essential parts that will continue to fall to other Departments and to the National Staff Side, the establishment of the new Department marks the importance of the programme of change and development that is now needed.

Functions of the Department

15. The functions of the Civil Service Department (including the Civil Service Commission) can be broadly classified as follows:

(a) Personnel Management — policy and central arrangements for selection and recruitment, the selection process itself, training, promotion, personnel management, posting and general career management of civil servants, including problems of staff wastage together with welfare, security and retirement policy; responsibility for advising on 'top level' appointments;

(b) the development and dissemination of administrative and managerial techniques; general oversight of departmental organisation, inter-departmental arrangements and the machinery of government, the working environment of civil servants and the provision of central services, including O. and M., computers and operational research;

(c) the supervision of departmental administrative expenditure generally and departmental manpower requirements in terms of both numbers and grading;

(d) the control of rates of pay, procedures for reimbursing expenses incurred in the public service, and allowances in the Civil Service, and of its structure in terms of grades and occupational groupings; the co-ordination of Government policy in relation to pay etc. in the public services generally, including the approval of salaries, allowances etc. for the members and staff of non-departmental bodies;

(e) the development and execution of policy on Civil Service superannuation; co-ordination of pension arrangements throughout the public sector.

. . . . . .

Civil Service Commission

18. As has been noted, and in accordance with Recommendation 117 of the Report, the Civil Service Commission has been integrated with the Department, and the Commissioners and their staff have become members of the Department. The aims, advocated in the Report, are the closer association of recruitment and selection and the other aspects of management. Their achievement will be helped by the First Civil Service Commissioner having been made at the same time a Deputy Secretary in the Department. Under him, the Commission is responsible for recruitment policy as well as actual recruitment. A new post of Second Civil Service Commissioner has been set up to assist the First Commissioner/Deputy Secretary in his dual role.

19. At the same time, the Report recommended that the selection of recruits should be independent of any form of Ministerial control. This recommendation has been accepted and the arrangements whereby the Civil Service Commissioners derive their independence from the Civil Service Order in Council 1956, and are appointed by Order in Council, will be retained to ensure their continuing independence.

. . . . . .

RECRUITMENT

. . . . . .

26. The Prime Minister announced in the House of Commons debate on the Fulton Report that the Government had rejected the majority recommendation for 'preference for relevance', i.e. that the selection of graduate entrants to administrative work should be deliberately weighted in favour of those whose university studies had been in subjects thought closely relevant to Civil Service work (Recommendation 24). This proposal was rejected for three main reasons: there seems to be no evidence to support the majority view on the Committee that the study of certain subjects at university is a reliable guide to whether a person has a practical interest in contemporary problems; it would be difficult, it not impossible, to define 'relevant' courses in a way that would be fair and acceptable to the universities; and, given the competitive nature of the market for able graduates, a bias in favour of certain academic disciplines would be more likely to reduce than to increase the number of acceptable candidates. The Government's rejection of relevant academic studies as a qualification for entry does not mean, however, that they have rejected the more general Fulton recommendation that the Civil Service should select people with the *potential* for developing the kinds of quality and expertise which are relevant to Civil Service work; only that they have rejected formal academic relevance as an important factor in the recruitment of trainee administrators. The Prime Minister explained in the debate that ' . . . we are aiming,

with this emphasis on the individual, to seek out and identify not a group of widely varying students with the same relevant academic qualifications, but a wide range of entrants, each of whom, by his personal qualities, academic or otherwise, is a "relevant" man or woman' (21st November, Col. 1554). Once the 'relevant' man or woman has been recruited, the Civil Service will give the necessary training after entry . . .

(b)

OUR APPROACH TO THE FULTON OBJECTIVES

6. The Prime Minister announced the Government's policy on the day the Fulton Report was published in the following terms:

'Thirdly, the Government accept the abolition of classes within the Civil Service and will enter immediately into consultations with the Staff Associations with a view to carrying out the thorough-going study proposed by the Committee, so that a practicable system can be prepared for the implementation of the unified grading structure in accordance with the timetable proposed by the Committee.'

The Committee's proposal, with which the thorough-going study announced by the Prime Minister is concerned, was that 'the present multitude of classes and their separate career structures should be replaced by a classless, uniformly graded structure' (recommendation 102); the timetable which they envisaged for its study and implementation was 3 to 5 years.

. . . . . .

'OCCUPATIONAL GROUPS'

29. The Fulton Committee criticised three main aspects of Civil Service structure:

(a) the complexity of the structure, and the multiplicity of classes with separate grading and pay;
(b) the barriers between the classes which made it unnecessarily difficult to develop and make the best use of people;
(c) in the Administrative and Executive Classes, inadequate specialisation which led to a lack of knowledge in depth.

It is generally accepted that there was some substance in these criticisms.

30. To deal with them, Fulton recommended a unified grading and pay structure covering the whole of the non-industrial Civil Service, within which there should be a series of 'occupational groups' for the purposes of recruitment, training and career management. It is clear from paragraphs 223/225 of the Report that the Committee saw these groups as serving some of the uses that classes serve today. For example, new entrants should be recruited to groups and trained as members of them; the groups should develop their own career patterns and career prospects. At the same time, the Committee plainly intended that the groups should be free from the

rigidities which they saw in the class structure, and in particular that there should be no artificial obstacles to movement between groups.

. . . . . .

32. . . . [I] t will take a long time to determine whether the completely unified structure recommended by Fulton is practicable. Meanwhile, however, we agree that the present multiplicity of separate grading and pay structures is undesirable. We believe that much can be done quite quickly to simplify and rationalise it.

33. We noted . . . that one of the main issues to be solved in the introduction of unified grading was the difficulty of preserving responsiveness to shifts in the rates of pay in the outside market. We shall not know for some time how and down to what level in the Service this problem can be solved. Meanwhile we think it essential to preserve the principle, established by Priestley and endorsed by Fulton, of 'fair comparison with the current remuneration of outside staffs employed on broadly comparable work'. For the time being, therefore, we shall continue to require a system in which the need for sectional grading and pay is one of the criteria on which groups are formed. Many classes, however, both General Service and Departmental, are already linked for these purposes with other General Service Classes. We therefore see considerable scope for progress over the next year or two by assimilating classes into larger grading and pay structures. Pending the completion of the study of a unified grading structure, the objective will be to move towards the smallest number of such structures that is consistent with the principle of fair comparison with outside pay as it is understood today. For ease of reference, we refer to these grading and pay structures as *'categories'*.

34. We also need however to form groups which will constitute the right kind of units for the purposes of recruitment and career management. Here a different set of considerations has to be taken into account . . . For ease of reference we call these units for recruitment and management *'occupational groups'*. Within them, it may be possible to identify a number of distinct specialisations . . .

35. Some groups will be quite small. It will however be undesirable to multiply their number beyond what is strictly necessary. In particular, we see no need to insist that all members of a group should be interchangeable. Lawyers, for example, specialise in different kinds of legal work, and scientists belong to different disciplines. But they need not on that account be sub-divided into separation occupational groups.

36. We thus have two main bases for grouping: on the one hand, grading and pay; on the other, recruitment and management. If these requirements were identical, the task of forming occupational groups would be simple and could be very quickly carried through. But they are not.

. . . . . .

39. In all this, at lower levels as well as at higher, it will be of the first importance that the formation of categories and groups should not give rise to the rigidities which Fulton rightly criticised in the class system. In particular, there must be much greater freedom of movement between categories and groups than

there is between classes. The joint statement on the timing of interim changes laid down the principle. We repeat it here:

> 'Meanwhile, it is an essential concomitant of the mergers discussed in this paper that there should also be free lateral movement: it is no part of our purpose to set up new structures in which the jobs are the exclusive preserve of the members of the groups that constitute them. Within procedures to be worked out, management should be free to move individuals between different groups, different classes (while they still exist) and the different structures which will emerge from the interim changes discussed in this paper, in the interests of the Service and its work; in particular it should be able when appropriate to select individuals without directly relevant qualifications or experience for jobs in new fields in order to widen their experience and test and develop their potential'.

. . . . . .

The grouping of scientists and technologists

42. As we said in the joint statement on interim changes, the present division between the Scientific Classes and the Works Group and its supporting classes is by no means obviously right. The essence of the problem is that while these classes differ in function (though there is a significant overlap in some areas), they both contain a large number of staff with a similar specialist education. There is thus a degree of cross-classification between classes, eg. engineers are included in the Scientific Officer Class, the Works Group and a number of variant classes. At the same time, the Works Group is not itself homogeneous: there are significant departmental variants and related classes to be considered and there are supporting classes which between them cover a very wide area. We think that we should examine the practicability of bringing all these classes together into a single grading and pay structure.

44. As well as taking decisions on whether there should be one or more categories for grading and pay purposes in this area, and what groups are needed for recruitment and management purposes, we shall also be examining what other General Service and Departmental Classes can be incorporated in the larger categories and, again, how they should be grouped.

. . . . . .

Administrative specialisation 47. We referred in paragraph 29 to the Fulton Committee's criticism of inadequate specialisation among administrators (ie. in the Administrative and Executive Classes; we use 'administrator' in the same sense). Briefly, the Committee found that many administrators lacked the fully developed professionalism that their work demands, because they failed to develop adequate knowledge in depth. This was attributed to the 'cult of the generalist' — Fulton's term for the view that administrators are almost wholly interchangeable — and to the practice of moving them both too often and between jobs which provided no continuity of subject-matter. To remedy this, the Fulton Report recommended that administrators should be divided into two broad groups, the economic/financial and the social. The Committee regarded this as a starting-point and proposed that the Service should develop and refine further grouping on this basis.

48. A survey of administrative work has been conducted accordingly. Its aim was to see what kinds of groups administrative jobs fell into, and whether those groupings could be used for the purpose of a new system of training and career management which could supply the element of continuity and knowledge in depth which Fulton felt was lacking.

49. There is an obvious link between this study and the subject of occupational groups. The depth and rigour of the specialisation which the work demands varies from one part of the Service to another. The Fulton Committee described their two groups of administrators as occupational groups (recommendation 106); at the same time they emphasised that specialisation should not be narrowly conceived, and should mainly take place in the early years of the administrator's career (paragraph 42). We therefore have to consider, and one of the aims of the survey was to throw light on, the question whether and how far greater specialisation should be given a structural framework: should administrators engaged on different kinds of work be managed in distinct occupational groups in much the same way as lawyers or doctors?

50. The survey, which was planned in close consultation with the National Staff Side and the Associations chiefly concerned, was mainly based on a questionnaire sent to over 2,000 individual civil servants in the grades concerned in major Departments, of whom 1923 responded. Their replies were checked by their Heads of Divisions, and by Establishment Officers who then analysed and commented upon them. The Civil Service Department then conducted a statistical analysis of the data and comments, and drew the threads together into a report which is now being studied by the Official and Staff Sides.

51. A number of broad conclusions emerged from the survey:

(a) There is scope for a greater degree of specialisation.

(b) It need not necessarily start right at the beginning of an officer's career, since a number of unrelated postings will often be needed to discover his aptitudes, preferences and performance; and those likely to go above Principal/CEO level will need to broaden their experience as they climb the ladder.

(c) Although many of the jobs surveyed fall broadly into one of the two groups proposed by Fulton, this two-fold classification is not one that could be put to practical use on a Service-wide basis.

(d) The more natural area for specialisation would seem to be the field covered by the officer's Department. This would not on its own, however, represent any appreciable advance on the position as it is today.

(e) It will however be practicable to divide many departmental fields into *sub-fields* or areas of activity based on common subject-matter, within which a policy of related postings would provide the framework for a coherent form of career development.

(f) At the same time, as Fulton suggested (paragraph 56), there are a number of *functions*, such as computer work, management services, purchasing, accounts work and staff management, which also provide some basis for specialisation. Not all of them offer a satisfactory career structure within Departments, and more work needs to be done in order to see whether and how far they can be regarded as specialisations crossing departmental boundaries, and what would be the implications of this for management and for the staff concerned . . .

(g) Specialisation by function should supplement specialisation by departmental sub-field, but neither should be exclusive. There must be enough flexibility to give people from time to time experience of other kinds of work.

52. The results of the survey have thus laid the foundations for decisions which we are confident will go a long way to meet the Fulton Committee's objectives. The survey has shown that increased specialisation is practicable and we agree that it should help to achieve greater efficiency in administrative work. Our objective is to provide guide-lines for improved career management, which will enable the administrator to stay longer in each post (which would be a major step towards achieving greater efficiency in its own right) and to be moved between jobs in such a way that he builds up a body of related knowledge and experience which he can bring to bear on his successive tasks . . .

. . . . . .

84. We consider our *objectives* to be so important as to justify restatement. The overall objective must be to enable the work of the service to be done as efficiently as possible. Our approach to this is based firmly on the Fulton principle 'look at the job first', on which all the surveys discussed in this report have been based. Within this approach, our objectives are to eliminate the obstacles to the flexible deployment of the human resources on which the Service depends, and to provide those at present in the Service and those who join it in future with the fullest possible opportunity to develop their talents. In particular, it is essential that there is clearly seen to be an 'open road to the top'. All the proposals in this report are directed to these ends.

85. We intend to concentrate over the next year on five main things. They are:

(a) to establish unified grading in the first place at the higher levels of the Service, where the greatest benefits may be expected from lateral flexibility of movement;

(b) beneath this, to rationalise and simplify the structure, where possible quickly on an interim basis, by the creation of continuous grading structures in which class barriers are removed between higher and lower classes; to include other classes with affinities in their work, grading and pay in these structures; and to provide freedom of movement within and between these structures;

(c) to construct a rational set of occupational groups for recruitment and management purposes, and to develop agreed principles and practices for the management of staff in these groups;

(d) to expand training so as to provide full opportunity for staff to develop their abilities;

(e) to extend and improve personnel management and career development.

(c)

MERGER OF THE ADMINISTRATIVE, EXECUTIVE AND CLERICAL CLASSES

The Official and Staff Sides of the Civil Service National Whitley Council have reached agreement on the following arrangements for the setting up, with effect from 1 January 1971, of an Administration Group formed by the merging of grades from the Administrative, Executive and Clerical Classes.

Aims of the merger

2. The aim of the merger is to enable the work of the Service to be done more effectively. This means removing such barriers as remain to the use of staff in the posts for which they are best suited. It also means ensuring that the way to the higher levels of the Service is open, and is seen to be open, to the most able people, no matter by what method they entered.

Structure of the merged Group

3. The grades in the Administration Group will be as follows:

Assistant Secretary
Senior Principal
Principal
Senior Executive Officer
Higher Executive Officer (A)   Higher Executive Officer
Administration Trainee   Executive Officer/Higher Clerical Officer
Clerical Officer
Clerical Assistant

4. The new grade of Assistant Secretary will cover all posts at present graded Assistant Secretary and Principal Executive Officer, and officers serving in those grades will be absorbed into the new grade. The new grade of Senior Principal will cover all posts formerly graded Senior Chief Executive Officer, and all officers serving in that grade will be absorbed into the new grade. The new grade of Principal will cover all posts formerly garded Principal and Chief Executive Officer; and officers serving in those grades will be absorbed into the new grade. Posts at present graded Senior Executive Officer, Higher Executive Officer, Executive Officer, Higher Clerical Officer, Clerical Officer and Clerical Assistant will be covered by the similarly named new grades and those serving in them will be absorbed into the new grades.

Two new grades to develop staff for faster advancement to Principal

5. With the introduction of the new grades of Administration Trainee and Higher Executive Officer (A) the grade of Assistant Principal will be abolished . . . Entry to

the AT grade will be open, by competition on equal terms through the Civil Service Selection Board and Final Selection Board, to those already in the Service who are eligible under rules agreed between the Official and Staff Sides, and also to graduates from outside the Service. The initial aim will be to find some 250/300 successful candidates each year for entry to this grade, the members of which will be given special training and the chance to be considered for faster advancement to Principal. At most 175 of these will be recruited from outside the Service; the remaining places will be reserved for internal candidates (in fact all internal candidates who reach the required standard will be accepted for the new grade and recruitment from outside the Service will, if necessary, be reduced in the following year to allow for this). Former EOs serving in the AT grade will remain eligible for departmental promotion to HEO. If they are so promoted they will be appointed to HEO posts under normal departmental arrangements and will be paid on the HEO scale. They will, however, continue to be treated as ATs and will be reported on as such for selection purposes (see paragraph 6 below).

6. The best ATs (about one-third of the total) will be selected for promotion to HEO(A) between 2 and 4 years after becoming ATs. Departments' recommendations for promotion to HEO(A) will be subject to confirmation by the Central Probation Board, by an extension of its probation functions. ATs will be selected for HEO(A) with a view to their later promotion direct to Principal, in competition with SEOs; they should normally achieve that promotion after 2 to 3 years in the HEO(A) grade. In the event of any HEO(A) not being found suitable for promotion direct to Principal, he will be moved to the HEO grade.

7. Those ATs who are not selected for HEO(A) can normally expect to be considered for promotion to HEO, through departmental procedures which will include the 'special merit' arrangement referred to in paragraph 15 below; if they are already HEOs they will continue in that grade. Those ATs who do not secure promotion to HEO by the end of the 4-year maximum period of training will be moved to the EO grade.

. . . . . .

Management of the merged Group

10. The merged Assistant Secretary and Principal grades will each be managed as a unitary whole. Postings in these and the Senior Principal grades will be made according to the ability and experience of individuals and in the light of their interests and those of the department, irrespective of whether the person or post concerned was previously regarded as an Administrative Class or Executive Class officer or job. Promotion from the combined Principal grade will be either to Senior Principal or (in competition with Senior Principals) to the combined Assistant Secretary grade. It is not the intention that all those promoted from Principal should pass through the Senior Principal grade to Assistant Secretary; those considered suitable will be promoted direct to Assistant Secretary. This 'grade-skipping' feature will operate at all levels within the Group except in relation to promotion from EO to SEO.

. . . . . .

Principles of career development in the Administration Group

64. The Survey on Administrative Specialisation made in 1969 showed that there was scope for a greater degree of specialisation among administrators (i.e., members of the former Administrative and Executive Classes) but that the greater professionalism that the Fulton Committee recommended required more than moves of administrators between jobs related to each other. The growth of this professionalism was seen to call for a new programme of career development, its main elements being:

(a) The placing of all staff in jobs appropriate to their qualifications, experience, and aptitudes, taking into account so far as possible any preferences they may themselves express.

(b) Appraisal of their current performance and assessment of their potential for advancement.

(c) Provision of training to improve performance in their present jobs and prepare them for future jobs.

(d) Movement from one job to another at suitable intervals in a way which not only employs them effectively and enables them to build on their previous knowledge but also develops their potential for the future.

(e) Promotion of those meriting it at the point most appropriate to their development and the needs of the Service.

. . . . . .

Administrative career development — policies and procedures

67. The primary aim must be to relate the potential of administrators and the quality of their performance more closely to the ways in which they are moved and trained. Methods of achieving this aim would include the following:

Regular review of the desirability (or otherwise) of a move. Particular attention in the early stages of an administrator's career, aimed at giving him a sound knowledge of the work and the structure of the Department and at deciding where his potential and abilities will take him.

Thereafter a more positive approach, as the potential and abilities of each individual become clear, to his career development in the sense of closely related movement and training.

For those who show promise of advancing several grades higher, postings across the sub-fields and functional specialisms in their Departments and where appropriate outside them so that they develop breadth, as well as depth, of experience.

For those administrators whose potential is less clear, more time to acquire depth of knowledge in areas of work suited to their aptitudes and postings more closely related to the sub-field or functional specialism to which they are suited.

Consideration of a change of posting when an administrator has become stale in a job or particular area of work, or when he asks for such a change.

32 CIVIL SERVANTS AND CHANGE

Extracts from *Civil Servants and Change: Report of the Wider Issues Review Team* (Civil Service Department, 1975); reprinted by permission of H.M.S.O. This report is interesting because it is an unusual official acknowledgement of the psychological pressures upon civil servants in the modern state.

7. About sixty per cent of non-industrial civil servants are employed in four departments, namely:
— the Ministry of Defence (130,000);
— the Department of Health and Social Security (85,000);
— the Inland Revenue (72,000);
— the Department of the Environment (including the Property Services Agency) (43,000)
Nine other departments employ another thirty per cent of non-industrial civil servants. The remaining 50,000 belong to over fifty smaller departments.
. . . . . .
9. Many civil servants are entirely engaged in local or regional case work — whether collecting income tax, placing people in employment, or administering social security benefits . . . Although some people tend to identify the Civil Service with Whitehall, in fact less than a fifth — about 92,000 — work in the headquarters of departments in inner London; 58,000 other civil servants work in the rest of London and 70 per cent of the Service works elsewhere . . .
10. The cartoon stereotype of a non-industrial civil servant shows a middle-aged man with a bowler hat, but in fact although men outnumber women by 3 : 2 overall, two thirds of the staff in the clerical grades are women. And there are few staff in the middle of their working lives.
— over a third are of an age to have started work before the end of World War 2;
— another third were born after the War;
— but the middle generation — those now between thirty and fifty years old, who might be expected to account for half the service, in fact account for less than a third.
All departments have this marked scarcity of people of the middle generation. But in some the younger generation predominates — for instance in the Department of Health and Social Security nearly half the staff are under thirty years of age; while in others the older generation predominates; nearly half the staff of the Ministry of Defence are over fifty . . .
11. The factual account of the Civil Service today indicates that it is much more widely dispersed through the country, much more involved in local rather than national affairs, and much more diverse in the work it does than is generally sup-

posed — even by many civil servants. It is also, and will increasingly be, a young service. And socially it is much more representative of the working population than it may seem if you look down Whitehall.

The changing character of the Service

12. The facts and figures we have given, if compared with those of ten or twenty years ago, show that the Service has changed in several respects over the years. However, the main changes are only hinted at in the statistics, for it is the character and atmosphere of the Service that has changed most markedly:

   — Older civil servants joined when recruitment was highly competitive; before the war some schools would inscribe on the honours-board the name of a boy who was accepted into the Civil Service as an executive officer; he had joined a small elite by open competition— in one year for example fourteen eligible candidates were turned away for each one who was accepted. But other jobs have become attractive and more widely available to those who meet the Service's recruitment standards, and today the very much larger numbers of executive officer entrants do not regard the Civil Service or themselves as very special.
   — Over the years, the Civil Service has become increasingly a regional and local service and many, particularly in the lower grades, never move away from the area in which they were recruited; they retain their regional roots, and do not naturally associate themselves with the business of government in London.
   — Today a large proportion of the staff in the Civil Service were born and brought up in the post-war world and naturally their values, assumptions and attitudes have been shaped by the existence of the welfare state and the security it provides, by the changes in our educational system which encourage a more questioning outlook, by the wider horizons of the television age and the greater awareness of what is happening in the outside world.
   — The pay of office workers, outside the Civil Service as well as in it, compares less well with that of people in industrial or other manual employment. The earnings of a clerk or a technician have not increased in real value by any-thing like as much as those of a man who works at an assembly line or on a building site. This has also lowered the social standing of civil servants.
   — Seeing the material success of organised labour in industry, the Civil Service staff associations — like those of some white collar workers in other public services — have tended more to resemble other trade unions; for example, industrial action was unheard of in the non-industrial Civil Service ten years ago.

For all these reasons, the Civil Service has changed in character. In many parts of it, the majority do not have traditional white collar attitudes, and do not aspire to them.

13. Furthermore, the Civil Service has had a pretty unsettling time in the last ten years or so:

— Successive governments have tended more and more to adjust and change their predecessors' policies — and even their own. Sometimes the alterations are radical; they are always required quickly; and too often they are soon reversed. And a change in the system of taxation or social security can alter the everyday work of tens of thousands of civil servants.

— Departments have been created, merged and abolished . . . These changes undermine valuable traditions and old loyalties. The consequent institution of new working procedures and the assimilation of new people cut across on-going efforts to improve a department's performance and they distract central and line management from what they see as their proper work.

— From time to time, staff shortages, higher turnover or the operation of man-power ceilings have made it more difficult to staff offices as the work requires, and to provide enough experienced staff to do it properly. The first major industrial action in the non-industrial Civil Service was due to undermanning.

— Successive governments have brought in incomes policies which civil servants feel have hit them first, and often hardest, of the working population.

— Other economic and social policies have had their effects: reductions in public expenditure have included cuts in the amounts spent on the upkeep and improvement of public buildings; as a result, in many places accommodation is now the most serious issue of all, apart from pay. Decisions to move Civil Service jobs from London and relocate them in the regions have had more regard to the needs of importing areas than to the efficiency of the Service, or the options which the staff have expressed through their associations in formal consultations.

Civil servants are there, of course, to serve the requirements of the public and the country, as laid down by Ministers and Parliament. They know they must be adaptable. They know the Service, like other organisations, must comply with the overriding requirements of government policies. Some of the changes have enabled (or will enable) the Civil Service to provide better what Ministers, Parliament and the public want. Some, too, have brought new opportunities to civil servants: thus the changes in personnel management systems and mergers of the Civil Service classes have given wider opportunities for civil servants to exercise their talents and to progress.

14. For all that, civil servants feel that they have been mucked about a lot in the last five or ten years. So there is an atmosphere of sourness in many parts of the Service, and we have found it at every level . . .

. . . . . .

Personnel development and careers

31. In a longer perspective the individual's job with his department is worthwhile if he has opportunities to widen his experience and to advance according to his abilities; these opportunities balance the needs of the department itself. The Fulton

Report of 1968 accordingly placed high priority on personnel management; it recommended that more resources be devoted to the career management of all civil servants; and that all should have the opportunity to progress as far and as fast as their talents and appropriate training and experience could take them.

32. Much has been started since then:

— between 1968 and 1975 there will have been a thirty per cent increase in the number of staff providing personnel services;

— a unified pay-and-grading structure has been introduced at the top of the Service; and changes have been made in the structure of Civil Service classes, the science group, the professional and technology category, so as to remove some of the artificial barriers to advancement;

— a system of job appraisal reviews has been devised and these are being progressively introduced to enable the individual regularly to discuss with his reporting officer his performance in his job, and how he can improve;

— a system of career interviews is being instituted so that at intervals personnel managers discuss the individual's experience, training needs and range;

— in the administration group serving staff now have the opportunity of accelerated advancement through the Administration Trainee scheme;

— since 1972 some young professional and scientific staff have had the chance to take part in a scheme which gives a couple of years wider administrative or managerial experience, and so helps them in their subsequent careers;

— many departments have devised career development schemes as a framework for individual career planning;

— seniority fields (governing eligibility for promotion) have been standardised and shortened;

— the effort devoted to training by departments has been substantially increased and the Civil Service College opened in 1970 has developed and expanded central training. A major review of Civil Service training has recently been undertaken to consider whether the division between central and departmental training adequately reflects the needs of the Service and whether these needs are properly met.

These and other developments provide departments and the Service as a whole with a very complete set of systems for assuring the individual of opportunities and assuring the department itself of a steady supply of talent.

. . . . . .

The adaptability of the Service

61. It is only realistic to acknowledge that, by tradition or of necessity, the Civil Service has some characteristics which can hamper its efforts to solve its managerial problems:

— first, **size**: the Service itself is large, and its managerial units can be large: a Department of Health and Social Security region may comprise 6,000 individuals; and there are many units of over 1,000 staff on a single site. Managerial structures and units often share a location with others that are managerially separate: all this handicaps orderly and effective communications;

— **Resources** — both of manpower and of finance — are centrally controlled both within departments and for the Service as a whole; this can hold back an immediate and flexible approach to problems as they arise; and resource allocations from the centre will not always fit the local sense of priorities;

— the Civil Service is committed to **equity** and **consistency** both in its treatment of the public, and in the treatment of its staff. It is answerable for every decision to what are often distant headquarters, and ultimately through Ministers to Parliament; this leads to detailed control over administrative practice, and tends to reduce the amount of local discretion as well as restricting its use;

— in **organising** its **work**, the service seeks to avoid any waste of staff or other resources by assigning particular areas of work to specialised — and often centralised — units; this can give rise to narrow jobs; although it concentrates expertise, it can also tend to accumulate the problems to an extent which makes them more intractable;

— the **staff relations** of the Civil Service are conducted, as regards most groups of staff, at three levels — the national, the departmental and the local, and for some at a regional level too. Too many issues are unresolved locally and go on to higher levels with consequent delay in their settlement, and broadening in their scope;

— the **security** of tenure which civil servants enjoy can lead to a toleration of mediocrity;

— the increasing **scope** of government work, and the widening range of government objectives, make conflicts of direction both more frequent and more difficult. These require resolution at relatively high levels, and so draw non-routine decisions away from workaday levels.

We recognise that many of these characteristics of the Service are an integral part of its traditional strength and virtues. It and individual departments are the size they are because successive governments and Parliament have entrusted whole ranges of required activity to a properly constituted public service. The Service must be under the proper control of Parliament and Ministers, both as to the use of resources, and as to the quality of its work. And elsewhere in this report we have emphasized the value of job security and of lively staff relations at all levels, not for their own sake, but as necessary features of a public service organisation in the modern world. Taken together, these characteristics have made the Service one whose efficiency and fairness stand up well to any detailed scrutiny. They cannot lightly be discarded, especially because to do so would subject to a radically new course of treatment a Service which has undergone much strain and surgery in recent years.

Ministers

63. Constitutionally civil servants are servants of the Crown but for all practical

purposes Ministers are their ultimate employers. Some of the present troubles of the Civil Service can fairly be attributed to decisions which successive governments have taken (cf paragraph 13). The resources that governments can devote to the Civil Service are not unlimited; but as many Ministers have recognised that sets a limit to what they can expect of their departments. If they want to help the Civil Service out of its present difficulties and help to keep it out of difficulty in future:
- they can, in the words of the Prime Minister, avoid discriminating against the public service in the application of their economic and social policies;
- they should, in a desire to get things done, and quickly, still duly consider what it is possible for their staff to do and to do properly.

If Ministers adhere to these principles, and in other ways regard their staff as any other large employer would, they will help to ensure that the Civil Service is the effective instrument they require to carry through their policies.

33 CIVIL SERVICE TRAINING

Extracts from *Civil Service Training* (Report by R. N. Heaton and Sir Leslie Williams, Civil Service Department, 1974); reprinted by permission of H.M.S.O. This extract focusses on the Civil Service College, established in response to a main Fulton recommendation.

THE PAST FOUR YEARS

5.1. In Appendix I we outline the emergence of the concept of a college for the Civil Service from the first hazy concept of a staff college . . . to the large scale and broad based institution recommended by the Fulton Committee. That recommendation was instantly accepted by the Government. The first Principal was appointed at the end of June 1969 and the College formally inaugurated a year later.

5.2. It could be regarded as premature, and even unreasonable, when the College has been in existence for no more than four years to ask whether it has lived up to, or shown promise of fulfilling, the expectations of its founders. Even so there are few people who would claim that it has yet done so . . . considered as a whole, the College has not won the complete confidence of the Civil Service. Its research effort is slight; and, although there are welcome signs of a change, it has not, hitherto, been the forum to which one would instinctively turn either for the discussion of important Civil Service problems or for the promotion of a greater understanding between civil servants and the outside world.

5.3. The fact that the College has not made a more impressive beginning is due to a number of factors, not all of which have been within its control. In the first place, the College, unlike the justly esteemed Ecole Nationale d'Administration, is not an elitist institution. If it had been, it might have found it easier both to establish its repute with some of its more demanding critics and to fulfil the research and promotional roles proposed for it. On the contrary, it was proposed by the Fulton Committee, and accepted by two successive Governments, that it should be a large scale and broad-based institution. As such, it has been expected to provide a very widely assorted range of courses, more varied, probably, than those of any comparable institution in this country and of such a divergent nature as to generate not a little ambiguity, and even some inner-contradictions, in its role. All this for a very large and constantly changing body of trainees of very widely varying abilities, experience and degrees of commitment and enthusiasm. It is as though the same institution were expected to combine the roles of All Souls and an adult education centre, with some elements of technical education and teacher training thrown in for good measure. At the same time the views of departments about what they think the College should do (as distinct from their criticisms of what it has been attempting to do) have not, insofar as they have been expressed at all, been noticeably constructive. The Staff Associations and the National Staff Side have made clear their desire for a greater 'relevance' in College courses and their determination that it should not be a Higher Civil Service College.

. . . . . .

5.5. The criticisms that are still voiced about the work of the College are to some extent based on a misunderstanding of what it is seeking to do and do not always take account of the changes that have and are still being made. Nevertheless, when every allowance is made for this and also for what is said in the immediately preceding paragraphs, these criticisms — the lack of clarity in the College's objectives, the poor quality of much of the teaching, the over-academic nature of some of the courses, their lack of coherence, the confused lines of responsibility in the organisation of the College, and more generally, the lack of involvement in the life and work of the Civil Service — seem too widely and persistently voiced for us to dismiss them as of no account.

. . . . . .

THE COLLEGE'S REMIT

5.7. We do not see the College as another business school, or a polytechnic, or a University institution. Its basic task, through the courses it provides is, in the words of the Principal, 'to contribute to improved efficiency in the Civil Service' and, in particular, as we would add, to help improve the management capabilities of the Service, in its more specialised areas as well as in its more generalised activities. Like the universities and other places of advanced learning it should maintain its academic integrity and set high standards but it should remember that its task is different from a university in that all it does must have a practical purpose in view. It must, therefore, develop its own ethos and on that basis establish its position and repute, both with the Civil Service and with the outside world. Its main contribution will be in management education for the Service. At the same time, in association with departments, it could make a significant contribution to the development of training for all levels of the Service.

5.8. On the basis of experience so far we believe that this calls for some changes – changes in the College's organisation . . . and changes also in the College's approach to its task. The problem to be solved is that of achieving the right balance between what is desirable on academic grounds and what is considered by the Civil Service and by the trainees to be 'relevant' to their needs.

5.9. We believe that, possibly because of its inherited responsibility for ATs and HEOs(a) the College's approach in its general courses has been biased too much towards the developmental side, with, as a consequence, an over-emphasis on the subjects which it is thought a civil servant in the course of his career 'ought' ideally to know something about. But circumstances are changing continually and, even though some needs persist, not all that is now thought to be needed will necessarily be so regarded ten years or more ahead. The criterion which we believe should be adopted is 'What will a civil servant need to know to be an effective operator in the posts he is likely to occupy in the period of time for which his career can be realistically forecast and planned'.

5.10. We also believe that there should be a greater emphasis at the College on training measures designed to develop the practical management capabilities needed for the jobs the Civil Service has to perform. A great deal can be learned from the private sector but there is also a great deal of substance in the statement that 'it is not enough to take management and organisational theory as they have been developed in the private sector, substitute "department" for "company" in all appropriate places in the text books and swallow the medicine as prescribed'. The government's business differs from that in the private sector and needs to be managed in other ways. And just as the Service must develop its own systems, methods and organisational structures to enable it to do the very varied and constantly varying jobs it is given, so should the training the College provides be related to the practical needs of the Service.

5.11. There are two consequences, whose importance is enhanced by the fact that within the Civil Service 'management' covers such a very great variety of activities. The first is that, in our view, it is essential that there should be continuing arrangements for the College to extend and keep up to date its knowledge of the management needs of the Civil Service and to consider in consultation with departmental representatives how those needs can best be met by training. The proposals we make later for strengthening the contacts between the College and departments and also what we have to say about the College's research function all have this purpose.

5.12. The second is that it will, we think, be necessary to reconsider the decision, taken when the College was founded, not to appoint a senior officer with specific responsibility for management studies and training. This decision, as the Principal explains in his Report for 1972/73, was taken in the belief that an approach to the teaching of management through individual subjects would produce 'a better understanding of the uses and limitations of management techniques'. As a result, the Principal says:

'Some management techniques are discussed under the heading of Operational

Research, our economists take an interest in costing, management accountancy, a subject for which we employ a professional adviser as outside consultant, and the appraisal of capital investment projects, and we have a large team of people teaching personnel management, among whom are included specialists in organisation theory and social psychologists with an interest in the study of motivation and morale'.

5.13. We believe that a more positive and more concentrated approach would be achieved by the appointment of a Director with responsibility for management training programmes and studies. This would be a key post and to attract a person of sufficiently high quality and with the requisite expertise its grading may well have to be higher than that of existing Director posts.

5.14. There are two other points we wish to make about management training:

(1) Training in personnel management is likely to be of increasing importance for the Civil Service in the future. It is arguably the most crucial management system, which must be effective if a department is to do its job properly and which must, therefore, be related to the job (or jobs) the department is there to do.

(2) The development of sound industrial relations training and the drawing together of experience in this field is another area in which the College could make a greater contribution. The possibility of involving in face to face discussion those engaged on both sides of industry as well as those with experience of staff relations in the Civil Service should be considered as an alternative to the 'statutory' Whitley lecture.

. . . . . .

ORGANISATION

5.19. When the College was in the process of being set up it was proposed by the Principal, and accepted by CSD, that the College should have a faculty based organisation, with Directors of Studies responsible for the academic input in each of the main fields of teaching and research within the College (namely Economics, Statistics, Personnel Management, Social Administration and Public Administration) and, in parallel, Directors of Programmes, drawn from the Civil Service at Assistant Secretary level, responsible for the organisation of the courses. This organisation has since been modified to the extent that in certain instances (eg economics) the roles of Director of Studies and Director of Programmes have been combined.

5.20. The Principal has informed us that he is now reviewing the organisation as a whole. We welcome this initiative. From all that we have learned, it seems to us that the diarchical form of organisation, which appears to be unique, has serious defects. From Assistant Secretary level downwards the lines of responsibility are confused; individual members of the staff on both 'sides' are unclear as to their precise role and responsibilities; and tensions are generated that are not always creative. There is, too, a tendency for tasks that are not of immediate concern to fall between the two sides, with the consequence that either they are not done at all or they are tackled on an ad hoc basis. But the most serious weakness of all, which is particularly noticeable in the multi-disciplinary courses, such as those for the ATs and HEOs(a), is that the present form or organisation encourages the 'carve-up' approach which leads to each faculty contending for what it considers to be its right share of the 'cake'. This, as well as generating a certain inflexibility in the composition of the courses, makes for the lack of coherence in them to which we have already referred.

5.21. It would be presumptuous of us, even if we had the necessary knowledge and experience, to attempt to usurp the Principal's responsibilities and to say how the College should be organised. We do, however, suggest that in his review of the College's organisation the Principal should consider a form of organisation in which the responsibility for a particular programme or group of related programmes is placed on a single individual, who would head a mixed team of academics and civil servants. To complement the work of these teams, but in no sense forming a parallel organisation, the teachers of particular subjects (or closely related subjects) could be constituted into specialist panels. These panels could consider among themselves the academic input to the different programmes, in the light of the requirements specified by the teams responsible for these programmes.

. . . . . .

5.24. There are two other points we wish to make with regard to the teams:
(1) co-ordination of their work could be a specific responsibility of the Deputy Principal, who could have periodic meetings with the team leaders;
(2) there is no need for all the team leader posts to be graded alike. It could be that the load on the teams will vary.

5.25. Whatever form of organisation is eventually adopted, suitable provision will have to be made for:
(1) counselling, which is particularly necessary in the case of the younger trainees; and
(2) considering and taking action on the views expressed by trainees and others about current courses.

. . . . . .

STAFFING

5.29. The College is staffed by a mixture of civil servants, who are seconded from their departments for a period of two or three years, and of people recruited from the universities and other educational establishments. The aim has been to secure some 70–75% of the College's teaching input from its own staff. (The actual figure is nearer 50%, though if STW were excluded the figure would be substantially lower.) This has been justified on the grounds that the employment of occasional lecturers 'involves staff of relatively high seniority in a good deal of relatively un-productive administrative work', whereas the employment by the College of its own specialist teaching staff is more economical and enables those recruited to become attuned to the special needs of its trainees and to acquire some degree of expertise in teaching them.

5.30. The difficulty of recruiting sufficient staff of sufficiently high quality has been a recurrent theme in the College's Annual Reports. Several reasons have been advanced for this — in the case of academics, the College's practice of not offering contracts of more than five years' duration and, as a consequence, its inability to provide suitable career opportunities for them; in the case of civil servants, manpower restraints, the shortage of good Principals, and the reluctance of departments to release staff for a tour of duty in the College.

5.31. To these considerations, if we are to be candid, we must add others. To the good academic the opportunity of a restricted period of service in the College is not sufficiently attractive to induce him to move out of the mainstream of academic employment into what he, as likely as not, regards as a backwater. The College has an, as yet, undistinguished record in the field of research; and there is also the somewhat daunting prospect of work which necessarily has a large repetitive element and which cannot, for the most part, be taken to a satisfactory depth. So far as civil servants are concerned, departments have, in addition to meeting their own needs, to cope, as best they can, with other demands for staff. We can well understand that Permanent Secretaries and Establishment Officers look less favourably on a period of service in the College for their better Assistant Secretaries and Principals than on a tour of duty in the Cabinet Office or the Treasury or, indeed, CSD. Much the same considerations are likely to actuate the bright young men. If they were seconded to the College they would probably see themselves as conscripts rather than as enthusiastic volunteers. What can be done to break this vicious circle?

5.32. So far as academics are concerned, their engagement for a limited period has been justified on the grounds that the advantages of security of tenure do not outweigh the disadvantages of the stagnation which could result if there was an insufficient turnover of staff to ensure an adequate supply of new ideas and fresh approaches. We do not underestimate the importance of those considerations and we gladly acknowledge that the College's staff includes men and women who are very able teachers, enthusiastic and brimful of good ideas. But the standard generally is too low. If it is to be raised to a sufficiently high level, we believe that more should be done to enable the College to retain those academics who have proved their worth in the College and also to attract men and women who have proved their worth elsewhere.

5.33. We therefore make the following recommendations:

(1) (a) The 'five year rule' should be modified to the extent that it should normally be possible for a lecturer of proved worth to have his contract renewed for at lease a second period of service.

(b) As a corollary of the foregoing a member of the academic-staff who is employed on a contract basis should be told not later than eighteen months before his contract is due to expire what are the prospects of its being renewed . . .

(2) There should be a number of posts at Senior Lecturer level which should be filled either by promotion from within the College's ranks or by appointment from outside.

(3) In addition, the College should introduce an individual merit promotion scheme for advancement from the grade of Lecturer to Senior Lecturer of those who have made an especially valuable contribution to the work of the College.

(4) Academics who have served for an appropriate period, say five years, on the College's staff should, if they are suitably qualified and so inclined, be given every encouragement to enter the mainstream of the Civil Service.

5.34. We are also disposed to think that, notwithstanding the financial advantage and the administrative convenience of the College's employing its own specialist teaching staff, the ratio of College employed staff to staff engaged from the outside, whether on a recurrent or occasional basis, should be less than the 70–75/30–25 currently proposed. We are in no position to recommend a precise figure but we think it should be in the region of 60/40 or, possibly, 65/35.

5.35. Civil servants have a vitally important contribution to make to the success of the College . . . If it could be seen that the successful completion of a two or three year period of service in the College is followed by promotion, without the interposition of another period of 'normal' work, that would do a great deal to overcome the present lack of enthusiasm to be considered for such service.
. . . . . .

RESEARCH

5.38. The importance of research has been a recurrent theme in the findings of those bodies which have deliberated upon the need for a Civil Service College. The Fulton Committee said that the College would be uniquely placed to conduct research into problems of administration and the machinery of government. The combination of its teaching and research functions should, they considered, assist the College to become a 'focus for the discussion of many of the most important problems facing the Civil Service as a whole'. The Committee also suggested that the departmental Planning Units they proposed (though this particular recommendation was not accepted by the Government) should commission from the College research into 'problems of present and future policy' on which they needed assistance.

5.39. Three additional reasons have been advanced for encouraging research – its value in attracting high quality staff, the relief it affords from the tedium of a job with a repetitive element, and the benefit to the College's reputation from the publication of significant and well conducted researches.

5.40. It was for these reasons that when the applicability to the College of the Rothschild concept of the customer/contractor relationship was considered within CSD, it was accepted that the College should be free to carry out research sponsored by itself, though it was also suggested that there should be arrangements for CSD to intervene exceptionally.

. . . . . .

5.43. We appreciate the view that the best research is often done where the inquiring spirit 'bloweth where it listeth'. Even so we take the view that, especially in the still formative period of the College's life, there are good grounds for giving a more specific orientation to the College's research function. This, we consider, should, for the time being, be directed to the problems of management in government and to the processes of administration. Later, the College might undertake project work of the kind that is being developed by the Manchester Business School. In conjunction with the other proposals we have made for developing the College's knowledge of management in government, this concentration of the College's research effort should help it to establish a position of special authority in this area of training. Departments could then look with increasing confidence to the College to expand upon their own contributions to the improvement of managerial performance.

5.44. In any case the College's research function should be complementary to its basic responsibility for promoting study and training for management in government. Some of those we have spoken with seem to conceive of its becoming a wide-ranging 'Institute of Government Studies' which, among other things, would provide an easy means of access to departmental papers. In our opinion such a development would be neither practicable nor desirable.

THE ADVISORY COUNCIL

5.45. The Fulton Committee recommended that the College should be under the general direction of CSD but should have its own governing body. They did not explain how an institution under the general direction of one body was to be 'governed' by another with no financial responsibility, or what the functions of the two bodies should be. CSD cut the knot by setting up an advisory council, constituted according to the Fulton Committee's recipe and with the Head of the Civil Service as chairman. It had been stated at the time the post of Principal was advertised that he would be responsible to the Head of the Civil Service 'for the standards of work and teaching at all three centres'.

5.46. It appears to have been the practice hitherto for the Advisory Council to meet once a year, in the afternoon after lunching together, to discuss, in such time as has been permitted by the members' other preoccupations, the limited number of topics referred to it. Of these the most substantial has been the draft of the Principal's Report for the preceding year, which has been taken as the basis of a general discussion. For practical purposes the Council has been able to do little more than 'take note'. In these circumstances it is hardly surprising that the question has been raised, within the ranks of Council members as well as elsewhere, whether, in the way the Council has been permitted to function so far, its members, all very busy people with heavy responsibilities, are spending their time in a worthwhile way. The question can also be asked whether the Council serves any useful purpose at all.

5.47. We are not impressed by the argument that the Council provides the Principal with useful contacts. He should be able to develop these contacts without the interposition of a formally constituted intermediary. To our minds the only case for the continuance of the Advisory Council rests on the grounds that it can help to preserve, as far as is desirable, the academic freedom of the College and, even though the possibility may be remote, could come to the protection of the College, if CSD's 'direction' should ever become oppressive. Its members, especially those with experience of teaching and educational administration, and of the outside world, can also, we are sure, give valuable advice to the Principal, if they are given effective opportunities to do so. But if the Council is to continue in being, it is, in our opinion, essential that it should be used properly and allowed to consider policy issues and proposals at the formative stage. That there are such issues we have no doubt. Examples are the College's staffing policy, including the concept of joint College/university appointments, the changes in the AT/HEO(A) courses, the scope of the College's research, the nature of the training required to meet the Service's management needs, and, perhaps, even this Report.

CONTACTS WITH DEPARTMENTS

5.48. We consider the College's contacts with departments need to be strengthened. At present there are formal arrangements for consultation with Establishment Officers, organised through CSD, and whenever important changes in existing courses or new courses are proposed it is the practice for these to be discussed between members of the College staff and representatives from departments. In addition, there are informal contacts at various levels between members of the College staff and departments.

5.49. We have come to the conclusion that these arrangements are not sufficiently extensive, do not go sufficiently deep and do not rest on a sufficiently firm basis. CSD in the nature of its role operates some way behind the 'front line'; Establishment Officers (and in particular Establishment Officers Meetings (EOM) have many other things to consider besides training, while schemes of work devised by central committees and working parties inevitably are cast in fairly general terms. There is still a need for more detailed planning and co-ordination and also for continuing contact with departments. For these purposes the present informal contacts with departments seem to us to depend too much on the initiative of the individual member of the College's staff and on his having had, or taken, an opportunity to establish, contacts with a particular officer or officers in a department. And civil servants seconded to the College tend to look first to their parent departments.

5.50. We, therefore, propose that there should be established a Liaison Committee whose basic purpose would be to serve as a forum for the interchange between the College and departments of views on matters of joint concern and to develop the liaison between them. This Committee, which need not, we think, meet more than three or four times a year, should be under the chairmanship of a Permanent Secretary, if possible, one of those on the Advisory Council (assuming that the body is kept in being) together with the Principal and about eight other members drawn from the College's staff and from departments. Membership should also be offered to the National Staff Side. The departmental members should not be restricted to Establishment Officers but should include one or two 'line managers' of Under Secretary rank. They should be appointed on a personal basis (and not allowed to send 'deputies') and for a fixed term, so that membership can be rotated among departments but not in such a way as to create a presumption that every department should 'have its turn'. The objective should be to secure the best men for the job. The Secretariat should be provided by CSD.

5.51. It should be open to the Liaison Committee to constitute advisory panels to review the courses of instruction in particular subjects or particular programmes. In addition to members from the College and from departments these panels might also include members from the outside world or other academic institutions who have current experience of the work to be reviewed.

5.52. We also propose that individual members of the College's staff should be given formal responsibility for liaison with particular departments and getting to know as much as they can about the work of those departments and their training needs. In the case of the smallest departments one such liaison officer should be sufficient, but more than one may be needed for the medium sized departments and certainly will be for the 'jumbo' departments. In the allocation of responsibilities for this work among the College staff account should be taken of their personal inclinations and of any ties they may already have formed.

5.53. It will also be necessary for departments to make appropriate 'inter-face' arrangements. Whether or not the central focal point for liaison between the College and a department is located in the latter's Establishment Division or Training Branch those designated as contacts with the College's liaison officers should not be drawn exclusively from those sources.

5.54. All this may seem a formidable administrative apparatus with which to burden the College but in our view measures of this kind are needed if contact between the College and departments is to be developed to the extent we consider essential. It will, of course, be necessary for teaching, research, liaison and other work to be taken into account in determining the College's establishment.

. . . . . .

TRAINING MATERIAL

5.58. The co-operation of departments will also be needed for the procurement of suitable training material. This subject was considered by a Treasury Working Party, established under the chairmanship of Mr P R Rogers (as he then was) in November 1967 'to advise on the preparation of material for the training of civil servants in the machinery and practice of government'. They found that there were large gaps in the material which was readily available on the internal structure and organisation of government departments and they recommended that in assembling training material priority should be given to comparative studies in departmental organisation, and to studies in the motivation and morale of civil servants. At the same time they recognised that case studies of actual decisions would be needed in studying administrative procedures and structures, and that suitable examples should be prepared as soon as possible.

5.59. For reasons which will be apparent from other parts of this Report we attach more importance to the preparation of case studies. The more up to date they are the more meaningful they are likely to be. We recognise that their preparation could impose a burden on departments and that if researchers or case study writers from outside were to be employed there could be questions about their access to papers covered by the thirty year rule and about the publication of their findings.

5.60. These are matters which we think should be further considered by the Liaison Committee . . .

COURSES FOR ATs' AND HEOs(A)

5.61. ATs and HEOs(a) are a delightfully fresh and stimulating body of young men and women. Nevertheless there were times during the course of our review when we were disposed to think that their needs receive a disproportionate amount of attention, to the detriment of the no less pressing needs of others, less highly favoured. We had expected too, that, since the courses for ATs/HEOs(A) had recently been revised, we should need to pay little, if any, attention to them. Nevertheless in the light of what we heard and observed and because the views of ATs/HEOs(A) are apt to colour the views of their colleagues, and even more senior officers in their departments, about the work of the College as a whole, we concluded that we could not ignore the subject. It is not without significance that when we discussed with senior officers the work of the College it was the training of ATs and HEOs(A) to which they tended to refer first.

5.62. The views of the ATs/HEOs(A) about the training they receive are sometimes confused and immature but sometimes, also, shrewd and penetrating, always expressed frankly and, in some instances, in 'positively vitriolic' terms. They are, too, the only civil servants (apart from juveniles on day release courses) whose education is continued compulsorily. It is understandable if they want to be freed from 'the slavish drudgery of schools' and feel, like the young Melbourne that 'it is only the poor spirited or the morbidly conscientious who can go on doing lessons, in the flush of their first appearance in the world as mature young men'.

5.63. We sensed that there is a general feeling among the AT/HEOs that even the three ten-week courses are too long — they are longer than the normal university term; there is too much straight lecturing, not always of a very high quality, and not enough work on problems and case studies; some elements of the courses have little practical application — a criticism particularly directed at the sociological component — and the courses as a whole, through being based too much on watertight academic disciplines, lack coherence. There is also a feeling that insufficient account is taken of an individual AT's existing knowledge of one or other of the subjects covered in the course.

APPENDIX I: THE ORIGINS OF THE CIVIL SERVICE COLLEGE

1. The origins of the Civil Service College may be traced back at least to the Sixteenth Report of the Select Committee on National Expenditure for the Session 1941–42. That Committee had been impressed by the need for post entry training in the Civil Service and recommended the creation of a Civil Service Staff College. Their report led directly to the appointment of the Assheton Committee 'to examine the general question of the training of civil servants, including the question whether a staff college should be established'.

2. The Assheton Committee in its Report, published in May 1944, made a number of recommendations which profoundly influenced the development of training in the Civil Service. These included a recommendation that the Civil Service should have its own central organisation for training Administrative cadets, which 'might also serve a number of purposes connected with background training and be a centre for bringing together administrators from the Service and from outside to discuss common problems'. The Committee did not favour the idea of a National Administrative College, to be set up in co-operation with industry and commerce, primarily because of the difficulty of finding a firm foundation on which could be based a method of teaching administration common to both business and the Civil Service but also because it was thought that 'such an institution would end by becoming a commercial college concerned with office methods'. The Committee also rejected the idea of sending Administrative cadets on courses specially arranged by the universities because they thought that the universities' 'remoteness from the actual process of administration would narrowly limit their usefulness'.

3. The move to establish a central training centre received further impetus from the Report, in 1961, of the Plowden Committee on the Control of Public Expenditure, which stressed the importance of training as a tool of management, and also from the report of the Morton Committee which had been set up within the Treasury to consider what subjects should be covered in an extended course for Assistant Principals. The Morton Committee did not consider the case for a Civil Service Staff College but it did propose that the new course for Assistant Principals should be provided at a specially constituted centre and be given by a mixed group of civil servants, academics and others, eg from industry. At the same time a study group set up in the Economic Section of the Treasury made a report recommending a course in economics and statistics of about 13 weeks for administrators in 'economic' departments.

4. The two latter reports formed the basis for the establishment of the CAS. The Director (an Assistant Secretary) had been appointed in April 1963 and the Centre opened in December 1963. The essential features of the Centre were that it was limited to Assistant Principals, who were recruited in comparatively small numbers (about 50 a year), and was based on the concept of a small nucleus of civil servants with knowledge of the academic disciplines thought relevant – these were altered or re-arranged in the light of experience – working in partnership with academic teachers on secondment and with contributions from a much greater number of

academics, business-men, management consultants, and on occasions, Ministers and MPs. The role of the civil servants was to assess the relevance of the actual concepts to the work of the Service and to obtain for use on the courses material about current problems to which the concepts and techniques might be relevant. Where problems of government were studied, civil servants directly responsible for the particular issues took sessions.

5. At the same time there was a growing feeling, on the one hand, that not enough was being done for the Executive and Professional grades and, on the other, that the provision of management training was inadequate. This led to the establishment by:

(1) The JCT, in June 1963, of a working party under the chairmanship of Mr S P Osmond of the Treasury to review the general question of Civil Service training in the light of developments since the Assheton Committee had reported, 'including the question whether a central staff college should be established'.

(2) The Chancellor of the Exchequer, in November 1965, of a working party, also under the chairmanship of Mr Osmond, to consider 'the training needs for middle and higher management . . . taking account of the long term future of the Centre for Administrative Studies, and the desirability or otherwise of setting up a Civil Service Staff College'.

6. The high cost of establishing a Staff College led the first working party, whose report was submitted in September 1964, to conclude that an extension of short intensive courses for middle grades of all classes might constitute a better use of resources. They did, however, consider that 'the value of a centre for new thought and doctrine, and for the research on which valid doctrine can be based, may, in time, be found by means of the extension and development of the recently founded Centre for Administrative Studies'.

7. The second Working Party's recommendations were made available in the first instance to the Committee which had been set up in February 1966 under the chairmanship of Lord Fulton to enquire into the structure, recruitment and management, including training, of the Civil Service. Before proceeding to the recommendations on training which that Committee made it is worth noting that the Working Party's criticisms of the existing arrangements were directed to the two main points that:

(1) Neither the longer CAS courses nor the shorter departmental courses were of sufficient length to cover in the required depth the full range of subjects relevant to management training in the public service.

(2) Selection for the longer courses was determined solely by method of entry to the Service — the courses at CAS being limited to Assistant Principals.

8. The Working Party considered that there was enough common ground between the requirements of departments to justify arrangements being made for central management training, that this was the best way of ensuring its provision at a high standard and as economically as possible, and that this training should be planned and directed by a single Civil Service organisation operating in two centres, a non-residential London centre developed out of the CAS and a residential centre out of, but with good communications to, London. Such an organisation, the Working

Party concluded, 'though perhaps under another name, will give the Civil Service a Staff College, which many have advocated over twenty or twenty-five years'. They thought that another name might be needed because the college would be fulfilling a different role from that of a conventional staff college and 'a title emphasising its management training responsibilities would be preferable'.

9. The Fulton Committee's recommendations on training were a natural development both of their own thinking about the wider issues referred to them and of the trend of thought about Civil Service training in the preceding decades. They recommended the creation of a Civil Service College, with three main functions:

(1) The provision of major training courses in administration and management.

(2) A wider range of shorter training courses, in both general management and vocational subjects, designed for all levels of staff and particularly for the more junior.

(3) Research into problems of administration and those of machinery of government — with a view to the College's becoming 'a focus for the discussion of many of the most important problems facing the Civil Service as a whole'.

10. The major courses, including residential courses, should, it was considered, be concentrated in 'a single establishment large enough to be the natural centre of training and research within the Service'. The shorter courses for the larger student body should be provided in London within easy reach of Whitehall and the main range of Government offices.

11. The Committee also recommended that:

(4) the courses provided by the College should not be restricted to civil servants. They considered that the College would have 'an important part to play in laying the foundations for a greater understanding between civil servants and the outside world'.

(5) The College should give advice and guidance to departments about the running of their own training courses.

12. The Government's acceptance of a number of the Fulton Committee's recommendations, including the creation of a Civil Service College, was announced in the House by the Prime Minister (Mr Wilson) on 26 June 1968.

34 CIVIL SERVANTS AND POLITICS

Extracts from *Britain 1974: An official handbook* (H.M.S.O., 1975); reprinted by permission of H.M.S.O. This extract sets out the formal restrictions on the partisan political activities of civil servants.

Political and private activities

The position and functions of a civil servant remain the same whichever political party is in power; and it is his duty to serve the government of the day irrespective of his own political opinion. The extent to which he is free, as a private individual, to participate in political activities varies according to grade. For this purpose civil servants are divided into three groups: those who are completely free to engage in all kinds of national and local political activities (although if they intend standing for Parliament, they must resign their appointment before nomination day on the understanding that if not elected they will be reinstated in their previous capacity within a week of the declaration of the election result); those who are free, subject to the acceptance of the need for discretion and with the permission of the department, to take part in most activities except parliamentary candidature; and those who are debarred from national political activities though they may seek permission to take part in local government political activities. In the non-industrial Civil Service, the completely free groups are members of the minor classes such as cleaners and messengers. The intermediate group includes mainly members of the clerical and typing grades and the granting of permission by the department depends, broadly, on the nature of the work done. The remainder are not allowed to take part in national political activities. Permission is usually granted to members of all groups to engage in local political activities to the maximum extent consistent with the reputation of the Civil Service for political impartiality and the avoidance of any conflict with official duties. Where permission is granted, it is subject to a code of discretion and to the obligation to notify the department of election or co-option to a local council.

All civil servants enjoy the right to register their private political opinions on appropriate occasions, for instance, at general or local authority elections. They may also engage in such private activities as they wish, provided that these do not in any way conflict with their official duties, nor with the provisions of the Official Secrets Acts 1911 and 1920, and the Prevention of Corruption Act 1906. However, since a civil servant must not use his official position to further his private interests, he is subject to certain restrictions in commerce and business: for instance, he may not hold private interests in public contracts and he may not use official information in writing, broadcasting or lecturing without the approval of his department.

Security

The political views of civil servants are not as a general rule a matter of official concern, but there are some civil service duties in which secrecy is so vitally important to State security that the Government does not feel itself justified in employing anyone to carry them out whose reliability is in doubt. For this reason no one who is known to be a member of, or actively associated or in sympathy with, the Communist Party or with Fascist organisations, or is liable to be a security risk in any other respect, is employed in connection with secret work.

Each government department is responsible for its own internal security, and the Security Service, which operates independently under a Director-General who is responsible for its efficiency to the Home Secretary, deals with national security. In addition, there is a Security Commission which, if requested by the Prime Minister in consultation with the Leader of the Opposition, may investigate and report on breaches of security in the public service and, in certain circumstances, advise whether any change in security arrangements is necessary or desirable.

35 THE CIVIL SERVICE AND CHANGING GOVERNMENT

Extracts from Sir Richard Clarke, *New Trends in Government* (Civil Service College Studies 1, 1971); reprinted by permission of H.M.S.O. This extract explores the implications for the Civil Service of post-Fulton developments.

. . . One of the most important questions about 'giant' departments is the ability of the civil service to breed people who can run them with the necessary combination of management ability, ability to handle policy and objectives and resource allocation over a wide field, and the ability to hold the confidence of Ministers and be the interface between them and the department. Here in the long term is where the success of the concept of 'giant' departments is at stake; and this presents something of a challenge.

. . . [I]f the Cabinet is to spend more time on policy and objectives and priorities, and less time on technical detail (whether diplomatic or economic or military or social), more of the detailed decision-making will have to be done by departmental Ministers and their departments; and the departmental Ministers themselves will require to delegate more within their departments. We should ignore the old saw about Ministers being concerned with policy and officials with administration. It is officials' business to advise their Ministers on policy; and he would be a poor Minister who did not concern himself with the administration of his department, for this is what makes policy effective.

One might see the total work of a department as a spectrum, at one end of which is the formulation of objectives and priorities (which is the responsibility of the Minister) and at the other end what might be called the permanent foundation of the administrative structure (which is normally left to the Permanent Secretary). Near one end of the spectrum, in the decisions how to carry out the Minister's objectives, the officials will be heavily involved: near the other end, in the determination of senior appointments or the working system of the department it would be unwise for the Minister not to be involved. These relations are never black and white; and they reflect the personalities and interests of individual Ministers and officials, with a tacit recognition of fields of prime responsibility.

But if the Cabinet is to devote more systematic effort to the objectives and priorities (and to their exposition to the public) then it is likely that the spectrum will shift a little, and the responsibilities of top officials will tend to grow. It is this kind of consideration, coupled with the work of the giant departments, that led me to say that the civil service would need to be equipped for more authority and responsibility over a wider field. The job of 'civil servant' will not become easier and will call at all levels for people at least as good as now.

. . . . . .

Senior Policy and Management Group

It is probably true that the people of Under-Secretary (or equivalent) grade and above, who constitute what Fulton called a 'Senior Policy and Management Group' (SPMG) are a more homogeneous group than most of the service. They will now be completely unified on an all-service basis, without distinction of academic background, or department, or generalist or specialist experience — the new open structure of the civil service at the top. They will become more homogeneous as the new organisation develops. There were 657 in the first quarter of 1970 — administrators 400; economists and statisticians 31; legal 58; medical 16; scientific 67; engineers, architects and other works group 44; others 41. There are perhaps five times as many who are poised upon the various ladders leading to these posts, and, of course, some will succeed and some fail.

These are the people who are in positions of direct responsibility to Ministers for conducting the State's business and running the government machine. They are responsible for advising Ministers in all kinds of matters with an immense variety of expertise; they manage the departments and a diversity of institutions. They do different kinds of work. Some are concerned primarily with general policy and continuous advice to Ministers; some with technical work and advice — scientific, legal, economic; some with management; and some with all three. But with few exceptions they share the common strand of direct personal responsibility to their Ministers. None of these can shrug his shoulders and say that it isn't really his business: and this is really what makes them one group.

Fulton: three years later

It was towards this group (and particularly the administrators in it) that most of the criticism in the Fulton Report was directed. Three years after Fulton, I do not intend to return to old controversies; but some points have emerged from my own experience and seem important after the intensive discussions since then.

I think most senior civil servants were bound to take some umbrage at Chapter I and this view was strongly expressed in Parliament. The last three years have shown on the contrary, however, that there was very little in the actual proposals to cause any difficulty to even the most traditionally-minded civil servant of the old Administrative Class. Some were already under way; some were unexceptionable in principle but very difficult in practice — so difficult as to be doubtfully cost-effective: some provided valuable support for new ideas. Apart from a few points which were clearly not doctrinally fundamental, the proposals have been worked forward without encountering any serious civil service difficulty except what is inevitable in the hard grind of turning ideas into realities; and the successive reports of the Joint Committee of the National Whitley Council show impressive progress. There is a certain paradox here; but I will not try to unravel it.

Most people who are familiar with the present situation in the service would, I think, agree that the criticism in Fulton three years ago for insufficient attention to management now looks somewhat threadbare. Maybe Fulton has helped to make it so. It may be true that as late as the 1950s, policy ranked well above management in most Permanent Secretaries' priorities. One could, however, make an impressive list of advances in management techniques in the 1940s and 1950s, beginning with O & M and continuing with automatic data processing, in which the civil service was well to the fore nation-wide; and certainly the emphasis on management in the Plowden Report in 1961, which resulted from two years' dialogue between the Committee and the Permanent Secretaries, fell on receptive ears.

The setting-up in 1962 of the management side of the Treasury under a separate Joint Permanent Secretary and Head of the Civil Service, Sir Laurence Helsby, and Helsby's own contribution in this field gave a further push. This has been carried on by the Civil Service Department; and all this has made a great change over a decade. In my opinion it is certainly not possible now to criticise the higher civil service for insufficient attention to management. Indeed, the pendulum may be swinging too far this way; it is too easy to forget that the forging of the instrument is important, but deciding what the instrument does is crucial.

Amateurs and professionals

Three years later, one certainly would not expect to find support for criticism of 'amateurism' in the higher civil service, for the demand in every walk of life for 'generalists' and 'all-rounders' — people who have broad enough backgrounds and interests to relate together a host of different subjects and to handle many different kinds of things simultaneously — is becoming continuously more insistent. It does not follow from this that the right way to train such people is by starting them off as 'generalists' at the age of 23 and giving them a 'butterfly' experience tasting one flower after another. But this idea is outside my own experience in the service. In 21 years in the Treasury, I had basically four jobs, for nine, two, four and six years respectively. In five years as head of a department, as I said earlier, one of my main objectives has been to keep people in the same jobs for as long as four years if we could. In a rapidly changing civil service — and industry has just the same problem — this is not at all easy to do, though it pays off every time when one can do it.

It is my own opinion, indeed, as one who came into the service relatively late in life, and with experience at Permanent Secretary level both in the Treasury and in charge of quite substantial departments, that the leading characteristic of the service is not its 'amateurism' but its highly developed 'professionalism'. This is not a professionalism in education or agriculture or defence or whatever the subject may be, though the people in the departments are not in my experience noticeably worse informed about their subjects than the people with whom they have to deal, although often more reluctant to express an opinion (again a matter of professionalism, for a civil servant must not allow himself to get out of step with his Minister).

It is a professionalism in government, beginning at the age of 23 and continuing for a lifetime. The proof of the reality of this professionalism is that a man can move more efficiently from a top job in one department to a top job in another, than to move from his job in the department to a job outside the service in the same field. I use the word 'efficiently' quite deliberately. He is better equipped, by his professional life and training, to do the civil service job in a different field than to do a non-civil service job in the same field.

This professionalism has its limitations and weaknesses, just as other professions have theirs. I think it is unfortunate that the remorseless pressure of work and the need to maintain discretion and disinterestedness tend to keep senior civil servants somewhat aloof from the rest of the community — one sees similar characteristics in judges. I think the nature of the work requires and develops a sharp critical faculty, and may indeed overdevelop it, though when the opportunity calls for constructive work, no one likes it better. We all know how our professional political impartiality can lead too readily to a tacit acceptance of whatever Ministers may want; although the criticism that one hears is often the exact opposite!

If I were looking at the problems of the future of the higher echelons of the civil service, indeed, I would devote more thought to what could be done to diminish the problems arising from our particular professionalism, rather than to seek to create a more thoroughgoing professionalism.

36 CIVIL SERVICE STATISTICS

Extracts (a), (b) and (c) are from *Civil Service Statistics 1974* (H.M.S.O., 1975); and extract (d) is from *Civil Servants and Change: Report of the Wider Issues Review Team* (Civil Service Department, 1974). All extracts are reprinted by permission of H.M.S.O.

(a)

Civil Service staff in post at 1.1.1973 and 1.1.1974

	Numbers (000's)	
Departments (by Ministerial responsibilities)	1.1.1973	1.1.1974
Agriculture, Fisheries & Food	15.7	15.5
Cabinet Office	0.6	0.6
Chancellor of the Exchequer	111.1	111.0
Treasury	1.1	1.0
Customs & Excise	22.6	24.8
Inland Revenue	70.8	69.4
Department for National Savings	13.9	13.4
Small departments	2.7	2.5
Education and Science	4.3	4.0
Employment (including Office of Manpower Economics)	34.4	33.8
Environment	74.7	73.9
Department of the Environment excluding PSA	47.2	44.8
Property Services Agency (PSA)	22.7	24.6
Ordnance Survey	4.7	4.6
Foreign and Commonwealth	12.8	12.4
Foreign and Commonwealth Office	10.4	10.2
Overseas Development Administration	2.3	2.2
Home Office	28.5	28.3
Lord Chancellor	15.0	15.2
Lord Chancellor's Department & Courts Service	9.3	9.3
Land Registry	4.8	5.0

Notes
1 The Ministerial responsibilities are those of the government in office at 1st January 1974 and have since been changed.
2 In January 1974 the Department of Energy was created and in March the Department of Trade and Industry was divided into the Department of Industry (with responsibility for Posts and Telecommunications added), the Department of Trade and the Department of Prices and Consumer Protection.

Departments (by Ministerial responsibilities)	Numbers (000's)	
	1.1.1973	1.1.1974
Public Trustee Office	0.5	0.5
Public Record Office	0.3	0.3
Lord Privy Seal	11.9	13.4
Civil Service Department	3.3	5.0
Central Office of Information	1.3	1.2
Her Majesty's Stationery Office	7.4	7.2
Northern Ireland	0.1	0.2
Posts and Telecommunications	0.5	0.5
Scotland	11.2	11.5
Scottish Office	9.6	9.7
Scottish Courts Administration	0.5	0.7
Small departments	1.0	1.1
Social Services	79.1	83.6
Department of Health & Social Services	76.5	80.9
Office of Population Censuses & Surveys	2.6	2.7
Trade & Industry	20.4	20.4
Department of Trade and Industry	18.8	18.7
Export Credits Guarantee Department	1.7	1.6
Wales	1.0	1.1
Other civil departments not included above	1.3	1.3
All civil departments	422.4	426.5
Defence	270.2	267.9
Total for civil departments and defence	692.7	694.4
Males	463.6	456.5
Females	229.1	237.9

3 As figures are rounded independently, there may be some slight discrepancies between the sums of constituent items and the totals.

4 The statistics relate to all industrial and non-industrial staff and include established and unestablished staff but exclude casual or seasonal staff. Part-time staff are counted as half-units

(b)

Staff in principal groups and classes of non-industrial Civil Service as at 1.1.1974

Numbers

Group, class or grade	Men			Women			All staff		
	Whole time	Part time	Total	Whole time	Part time	Total	Whole time	Part time	Total
Open Structure (Under Secretary and above in Home Civil Service)	793	–	793	24	–	24	817	–	817
Administrative (Diplomatic Service)	1,101	–	1,101	43	–	43	1,144	–	1,144
General Category	111,193	179	111,282½	123,251	2,632	124,567	234,444	2,811	235,849½
Administration Group:	109,691	176	109,779	122,839	2,627	124,152½	232,530	2,803	233,931½
Assistant Secretary	1,083	2	1,084	53	2	54	1,136	4	1,138
Senior Principal	514	–	514	16	–	16	530	–	530
Principal	3,528	12	3,534	285	9	289½	3,813	21	3,823½
Senior Executive Officer	5,782	–	5,782	509	–	509	6,291	–	6,291
Higher Executive Officer (A)	134	–	134	46	–	46	180	–	180
Higher Executive Officer	13,730	1	13,730½	2,253	6	2,256	15,983	7	15,986½
Administration Trainee	300	–	300	147	–	147	447	–	447
Executive Officer	32,341	4	32,334	13,680	6	13,683	46,021	10	46,026
Clerical Officer	38,238	103	38,289½	54,382	782	54,773	92,620	885	93,062½
Clerical Assistant	14,041	54	14,068	51,468	1,822	52,379	65,509	1,876	66,447

Economist Group	228	2	229	23	1	23½	251	3	252½
Information Officer Group	953	1	953½	323	4	325	1,276	5	1,278½
Statistician Group	321	–	321	66	–	66	387	–	387
Departmental Executive grades	30,424	129	30,488½	5,816	16	5,824	36,240	145	36,312½
Customs and Excise	3,740	–	3,740	6	–	6	3,746	–	3,746
Department of Employment	5,962	–	5,962	1,996	3	1,997½	7,958	3	7,959½
Diplomatic Service	1,395	–	1,395	294	–	294	1,689	–	1,689
Home Office:									
Immigration Service	1,222	–	1,222	35	–	35	1,257	–	1,257
Prison Governors	522	1	522½	34	–	34	556	1	566½
Inland Revenue:									
Collection Service	1,339	–	1,339	277	–	277	1,616	–	1,616
Chief Inspector's Branch	4,836	58	4,865	416	6	419	5,252	64	5,284
Tax Officers (Higher Grade)	6,625	–	6,625	2,405	5	2,407½	9,030	5	9,032½
Other branches	423	4	425	90	–	90	513	4	515
Others	4,360	66	4,393	263	2	264	4,621	68	4,655
Departmental Clerical grades	19,554	21	19,564½	26,785	575	27,072½	46,339	596	46,637
Department of Employment	7,063	18	7,072	11,417	502	11,668	18,480	520	18,740
Diplomatic Service	589	–	589	193	–	193	782	–	782
Inland Revenue:									
Collection Service	2,261	1	2,261½	3,312	14	3,319	5,573	15	5,580½
Valuation Service	2,360	2	2,361	1,194	1	1,194½	3,554	3	3,555½
Tax Officers	6,587	–	6,587	10,523	56	10,551	17,110	56	17,138
Others	694	–	694	146	2	147	840	2	841

(c)

Civil Service manpower by main departments at 1 January 1974

Trade & Industry 18,500

Agriculture, Fisheries & Food 15,000

National Savings 13,500

Foreign & Commonwealth Office 12,500

Other civil departments 60,500

Customs & Excise 25,000

Home Office 28,000

Employment 34,000

Environment 69,500

Inland Revenue 69,500

Health & Social Security 81,000

Defence 268,000

(d)

Categories of staff (Number of non-industrial staff in post by category at 1 July 1974)

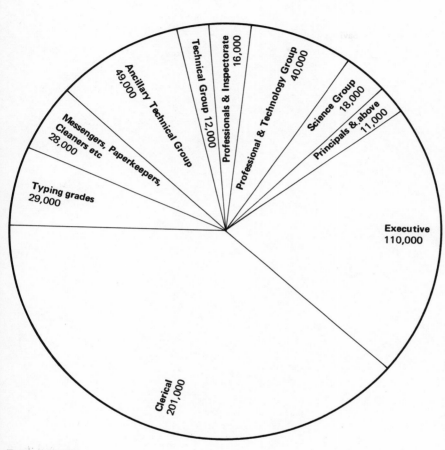

Total: 514,000

Section VI
The control of government

'The object of Government is security against wrong. Most civilised governments tolerably secure their subjects against wrong from each other. But to secure them, by laws, against wrong from the Government itself, is a problem of a far more different sort.'

(Sir James Mackintosh, 1818)

A central concern of democratic societies has been to restrict the powers (and the opportunities of abuse of powers) of those who control the executive area of government. The very activity of framing constitutions is rooted in this concern. Constitution-builders devote much attention both to the institutional arrangement of executive, legislative, and judicial powers in forms which allow one power to act in restraint of another, and to the construction of protections for the individual against the unrestrained claims of the state. Neither of these constitutional safeguards is fully available to the British citizen. There is a diffusion rather than a separation of powers; even though the legislature is intended to check the executive, the operation of party government considerably weakens this restraint. For the same reason, the individual cannot expect much help through political channels. These tendencies are exacerbated by the obsessive secrecy of British government. It is difficult even for Parliament to obtain information about the intentions and actions of the executive, let alone the ordinary citizen. This aspect of British government has attracted critical attention in recent years, but the response of government to this challenge has been minimal (37). Secrecy in government is partly a matter of attitudes: civil servants and Ministers simply find secret government more convenient, less embarrassing, than open government. More sinister is the statutory underpinning of this habit by Sections 1 and 2 of the Official Secrets Act 1911, breaches of which constitute a criminal offence. Concern over the use of these provisions led to an official inquiry in 1972; the Committee's report recommended the repeal of Section 2 and its replacement by a less restrictive Official Information Act, which would not attract criminal proceedings, and Government announced their acceptance of these proposals (38). The extreme sensitivity of the executive showed itself in the case of the Crossman Diaries. The government regarded these diaries as in breach of the existing law (as well as conventions) governing the disclosure of information by former Ministers, but the attempt to restrain publication was unsuccessful. Government decided not to pursue this case any further, but set up a Committee of Privy Counsellors to consider the implications of the publication of Ministerial memoirs, and quickly accepted recommendations which endorsed the arguments against over-informative disclosures by ex-Ministers (39).

The weakness of the convention of Ministerial responsibility has focussed attention on the lack of effective means of redress against the manifold routine acts and decisions of civil servants. The existing Parliamentary instruments, particularly Question Time, have proved ineffective in this area. A useful device employed elsewhere, notably in Denmark and Sweden, is the 'Ombudsman', an independent official who may investigate complaints by citizens against the State administration. The British version, introduced in 1967, is tied to Parliament in line with the convention of Ministerial responsibility. It is therefore as strong or as weak as Parliament in the face of the executive, and both its powers and effect have been correspondingly modest **(40)**, though the original exclusions from the Parliamentary Commissioner's jurisdiction have been partly corrected by the creation of similar Commissions for the Health Service **(41)** and in relation to local government in England, Wales and Scotland. A further cause for criticism is that the first two Commissioners, Sir Edmund Compton and Sir Alan Marre, were former civil servants and arguably insufficiently detached from their brief.

The ordinary citizen can, of course, look to the law itself for protection; a deep-rooted legal tradition and the professional neutrality (despite individual lapses) of the judiciary underwrite the strength of law as a safeguard against the exercise by the state of arbitrary power. Unfortunately, the legal instruments available to the citizen who wishes to challenge the State are clumsy, and legal procedure is daunting by its complexity, its proneness to delay, and its potential cost **(43)**. The comparative advantages of specially constituted tribunals and inquiries in the administrative process are cheapness and accessibility. The extensive growth of such bodies in line with heavy legislative programmes in the post-war period generated a special enquiry (the Franks Committee) which resulted in some useful reforms **(42)**. The system is still marked by inconsistencies of practice and uncertainties of purpose **(44)**, but it is a system nonetheless which offers individuals opportunities to dispute bureaucratic decisions at little cost or risk to themselves.

The concentration in this section upon the administrative rather than the political impact of the State upon the individual is a measure of the extent to which the political freedoms of the individual are relatively well established. But this situation is a function partly of political stability; where there is instability, as in Northern Ireland, basic freedoms quickly come into conflict with the necessities of the state **(45)**, and it is possible that the problem of the political rights of the individual in conflict with the state will become more of an issue in the future than it is at present.

Other appropriate references are **1, 2, 3, 24, 46** and **47**.

37 GOVERNMENT INFORMATION

Extracts from *Information and the Public Interest* (Cmnd. 4089, 1969); reprinted by permission of H.M.S.O. This White Paper reports on the results of an internal inquiry, stimulated by the Fulton Report, into the possibilities of more open government; the defensive tone of the paper demonstrates the conservativeness of the official approach to this issue.

Introduction

The Fulton Committee, in their Report on the Civil Service (Cmnd. 3638), welcomed the trend in recent years towards wider and more open consultation in the Government's administrative processes, and hoped that the trend would continue. They recognised that 'there must always be an element of secrecy (not simply on grounds of national security) in administration and policy', but suggested that some of the secrecy maintained hitherto was unnecessary and that there should be an enquiry into possible ways of getting rid of it (paragraphs 277—280).

2. The Government decided to carry out this enquiry on a wide interdepartmental basis, studying comprehensively both the existing trend and its possible further development. The aim has been not to lay down hard and fast rules for the future on what should be published and what withheld, but rather to find ways of reinforcing the increasingly liberal attitude of the last few years.

3. The enquiry showed that the trend had been expressed in two main forms. The first was an increase in the amount of factual information now being disclosed; the second a much greater readiness to publish forecasts and other considerations involved in policy decisions . . .

Forecasts and other material related to policy decisions

4. Perhaps the most striking development has been the growth in the practice of publishing forecasts and other considerations involved in policy decisions. Although Governments have often in the past consulted those most closely concerned, especially before initiating legislation, this wider consultation is a new practice with great potential benefit for the future. Some of it has developed in the last year, and was therefore not available in time for assessment in the Fulton Report; but it fully accords with the Committee's recommendations.

5. One key example is the provision of much more information in relation to the Budget. In the Financial Statement accompanying the Budget of March 1968, the Chancellor published for the first time the details of the economic assessment for the ensuing 15 months in the light of the measures contained in the Budget. Taking this process further, the Financial Statement published with the 1969 Budget was restyled *Financial Statement and Budget Report*, and offered in addition to a forecast of the economic outlook to mid-1970 a reconciliation between the previous year's forecast and the actual return. The Statement also contained for the first time an analysis of the means by which the United Kingdom's external deficit had been financed over the previous five years.

6. A similar development has been taking place in the provision of forward-looking assessments of public expenditure. The White Paper of January 1968 included a functional analysis looking two years ahead. The White Paper of

February 1969 confirmed the assessments for 1968—69 and 1969—70 and included figures for 1970—71. Still more far-reaching proposals were put forward by the Treasury in April of this year in a Green Paper — a form of publication introduced by this Government to set out for public discussion major Ministerial proposals while they are still at the formative stage. This new Green Paper — *Public Expenditure: A New Presentation* — proposes among other things that the Government should undertake to publish each autumn information on public expenditure programmes for the current and ensuing two years, together with projections of the public sector's receipts (at existing rates of central government taxation) presented so as to provide other relevant information and guidance on the underlying issues. There would also be outline projections of public expenditure for two further years. These proposals have been submitted to the Select Committee on Procedure.

. . . . . .

9. In other fields too the Government has explained much more fully and widely than before the grounds on which future policy is based. Examples are the Green Papers on the regional employment premium, the reorganisation of the health service, speed limits and highways strategy, and the recently published report from the Department of Employment and Productivity on the implications of a national minimum wage — the most recent of a series of surveys of problems in the employment field.

. . . . . .

14. It does not follow, of course, that public consultation on tentative proposals is invariably the right course. It may result in slower decisions and slower action when prompt action is essential. Sometimes, too, conflicting views and conflicting interests are already well known. In such cases a prolonged period of consultation will merely impose delay without any compensating advantages. Each individual case has to be considered on its merits. But the guiding principle which the Government have adopted is that the prior publication of information about the considerations involved in policy matters should form a continuing part of the decision making process whenever reasonably possible.

. . . . . .

Discussions within Government

26. The Fulton Committee said that at the formative stages of policy-making both civil servants and Ministers should be able to discuss and disagree among themselves about possible courses of action without feeling that their individual views must become a matter of public knowledge. The Committee thought that it was difficult to see how on any other basis there could be mutual trust between colleagues and proper critical discussion of different hypotheses.

27. The Government agree with this view. If discussions at the formative stage of policy-making within government could not remain confidential, not only would the basis of trust between Ministers, and between Ministers and civil servants, be

undermined but the collective responsibility which is a cardinal feature of our system of government could hardly continue. Any proposal to reject the Fulton Committee's view on this point would therefore raise major constitutional issues.

Civil servants and the public

28. The Fulton Committee did suggest, however, that civil servants should be able to go further than now in explaining what their departments are doing, at any rate so far as concerns managing existing policies and implementing legislation. At the same time they pointed out that they did not 'underestimate the risks involved in such a change' and that it would be best 'left to develop gradually and pragmatically' (paragraphs 283–284).

29. It has in fact long been the practice for civil servants to explain the work of their departments, and also to describe Government policy, to House of Commons Select Committees, to bodies representative of particular sections of the community and to individual firms or members of the public. In many cases what they have had to say has been subsequently published. The information officers of Government departments are particularly concerned with explaining Government policy, and where necessary Government organisation, to the public as their full time work. In addition, senior civil servants concerned with implementing and advising on policy have increasingly taken part in interviews with the press and on radio and television, and have spoken at public conferences and other meetings. Particularly in those departments which have local offices, it is also common practice for officers to accept invitations to describe at meetings of local organisations particular policies and procedures and the main reasons for them. This trend is likely to continue. The names and appointments of particular officials working in different branches of Government departments, corresponding to the main divisions of policy, are readily ascertainable from published works of reference.

30. It will, of course, be necessary to ensure that further developments on these lines are encouraged in such a way as not to prejudice the confidential basis of the relationship between Ministers and their officials. The risk must be avoided of officials becoming personally identified with a particular line of advice on a particular issue of policy or exposed to pressure to discuss in what respects their advice has not been accepted by Ministers. It is clearly right that officials should not be drawn into expressing personal views on policy matters which could be represented as in conflict with those of their Ministers, or as reflecting any political bias. The main responsibility for explaining policy to Parliament and the public must continue to rest with Ministers. For this reason the Government agree with the view of the Fulton Committee that the increased participation of civil servants in the task of explaining the work and organisation of the Government to the public should be allowed to develop 'gradually and pragmatically', but they are in no doubt that this development should be encouraged.

38 OFFICIAL SECRETS

Extracts from *The Franks Report on Sections 1 and 2 of the Official Secrets Acts* (Cmnd. 5104, 1972); reprinted by permission of H.M.S.O. Section 2 has particular implications for the freedom of the press, and this Committee was appointed after a controversial criminal prosecution. The Government accepted the main recommendations set out below.

Government secrecy and democratic control 1. The Official Secrets Acts have been in existence in this country for only eighty years. Section 2 of the Official Secrets Act 1911, which is our concern, has been in force for sixty-one years. But from the earliest times governments of all types have been anxious to preserve secrecy for matters affecting the safety or tactical advantage of the State. It is, however, the concern of democratic governments to see that information is widely diffused, for this enables citizens to play a part in controlling their common affairs. There is an inevitable tension between the democratic requirement of openness, and the continuing need to keep some matters secret.

2. This tension has been increasing in recent years. In part this is because the dangers to the State have changed in character and become more complex, and have come to seem internal as well as external. The processes of government have become more sophisticated; the activities of a government increasingly affect all the affairs of the citizen. Its economic manoeuvres have come to be considered no less vital to the basis of the life of the community than the movement of its troops. Many new advances in science have both peace-time and military applications. Rapid changes in society, and the increased influence of centralised institutions, further complicate the issue. More and more information about the private affairs of citizens comes into the possession of the Government: there is a feeling that the Government should safeguard the confidences of the citizen almost as strictly as it guards information of use to an enemy.

3. Such developments have increased the pull towards secrecy. They have at the same time made more obvious the need to improve the effectiveness of democratic control. This must mean more information to enable citizens to make rational decisions about matters which affect so much of their lives. Progress in education and in technology has increased the possibility of circulating information on a wide scale and in considerable detail. It has also increased the possibility of effective propaganda, centrally controlled. Those concerned with the mass media of communications in Britain have felt the need not just for more openness in government but for a loosening of control of information at all levels in the machinery of government. Only thus, they have argued, could they play a developing part in the operation of a modern democracy. We are faced, therefore, with an increased area in which considerations of secrecy may arise, and at the same time with an increased need for the diffusion of information together with the technical capacity to supply this need.

. . . . . .

General issues underlying our work 11. We have so far indicated these wider issues in the most general terms. But they can be more simply expressed. Even a democratic government requires a measure of secrecy for some of its functions, as a means whereby it can better carry out its duties on behalf of the people. Among the primary tasks of government are the defence of the nation from external threats, the maintenance of relations with the rest of the world and the preservation of law and order. Defence against external attack would be severely prejudiced if potential enemies had access, directly or indirectly, to the details of our plans and weapons. It would be impossible to negotiate with other countries if all discussion, however delicate, was conducted completely in the open. Some measures for the prevention or detection of crime would be ineffective if they were known to criminals. Some of the internal processes of government should be conducted in confidence if they are to result in effective policies. The presentation of clear issues to Parliament and to the electorate depends upon Ministers and administrators being able, in some instances and at some stages, to argue out all possibilities with complete frankness and free from the temptation to strike public attitudes.

12. A totalitarian government finds it easy to maintain secrecy. It does not come into the open until it chooses to declare its settled intentions and demand support for them. A democratic government, however, though it must compete with these other types of organisation, has a task which is complicated by its obligations to the people. It needs the trust of the governed. It cannot use the plea of secrecy to hide from the people its basic aims. On the contrary it must explain these aims: it must provide the justification for them and give the facts both for and against a selected course of action. Nor must such information be provided only at one level and through one means of communication. A government which pursues secret aims, or which operates in greater secrecy than the effective conduct of its proper functions requires, or which turns information services into propaganda agencies, will lose the trust of the people. It will be countered by ill-informed and destructive criticism. Its critics will try to break down all barriers erected to preserve secrecy, and they will disclose all that they can, by whatever means, discover. As a result matters will be revealed when they ought to remain secret in the interests of the nation.

13. The means of preserving secrecy in any operation are various. The need for keeping some discussions confidential is felt in private undertakings and in business as it is in public affairs. Not all discussions can be carried on at noon in the market place any more than at midnight in a debating chamber. The discipline of a service, the penalty of dismissal, may often be enough to maintain the confidence of private concerns. But the affairs of government are of a different order of difficulty and importance from those of ordinary business. They affect the whole community, for good or ill, and special measures are needed both to inform the public and to protect the public against damaging breaches of trust in a dangerous world. There is, therefore, a justification for using the criminal law as well as professional discipline to protect secrets of the State.

14. Our direct concern is the part which the criminal law should play in the protection of official information. In this context we have had to consider how the demands of Parliamentary democracy for the fullest information and for efficiency in operation can be reconciled. The present law, contained in section 2, is notable for its extreme width and for the considerable uncertainty attaching to its interpretation and enforcement. It does not carry public confidence. We propose its replacement by provisions reduced in scope and less uncertain in operation. We believe that these provisions provide the necessary minimum of criminal law required for the security of the nation and the safety of the people, and for the constructive operation of our democracy in the conditions which obtain today.

The main features of Section 2

16. Although we have been concerned with only one section of one Act of Parliament, this section has extensive ramifications. Section 2 is short, but it is in very wide terms and it is highly condensed. It covers a great deal of ground, and it creates a considerable number of different offences. According to one calculation over 2,000 differently worded charges can be brought under it. It is obscurely drafted, and to this day legal doubts remain on some important points of interpretation. The section forms an integral part of the Official Secrets Acts 1911–1939, and its relationship with section 1 of the 1911 Act is of particular importance. The starting point in any examination of section 2 is to understand it. The text of sections 1 and 2 is set out in full in Appendix I, which also explains their meaning and summarises related provisions of the Official Secrets Acts.

Section 2 is a catch-all 17. The main offence which section 2 creates is the unauthorised communication of official information (including documents) by a Crown servant. The leading characteristic of this offence is its catch-all quality. It catches all official documents and information. It makes no distinctions of kind, and no distinctions of degree. All information which a Crown servant learns in the course of his duty is 'official' for the purposes of section 2, whatever its nature, whatever its importance, whatever its original source. A blanket is thrown over everything; nothing escapes. The section catches all Crown servants as well as all official information. Again, it makes no distinctions according to the nature or importance of a Crown servant's duties. All are covered. Every Minister of the Crown, every civil servant, every member of the Armed Forces, every police officer, performs his duties subject to section 2.

The dispensation from the catch-all: authorisation 18. Nevertheless governments regularly reveal a great deal of official information. These disclosures do not contravene section 2. A Crown servant who discloses official information commits an offence under the section only if the information is disclosed to someone 'other than a person to whom he is authorised to communicate it, or a person to whom it is in the interest of the State his duty to communicate it'. The Act does not explain

the meaning of the quoted words. We found that they were commonly supposed, by persons outside the Government, to imply a fairly formal process of express authorisation. Actual practice within the Government rests heavily on a doctrine of implied authorisation, flowing from the nature of each Crown servant's job. In the words of the Home Office, 'the communication of official information is proper if such communication can be fairly regarded as part of the job of the officer concerned'. Ministers are, in effect, self-authorising. They decide for themselves what to reveal. Senior civil servants exercise a considerable degree of personal judgement in deciding what disclosures of official information they may properly make, and to whom. More junior civil servants, and those whose duties do not involve contact with members of the public, may have a very limited discretion, or none at all.
. . . . . .

The deterrent effect of section 2 26. The evidence which we received reflected widely differing general views on section 2. But witnesses from both the Government and the news media shared the view that the effect of the section was not to be judged by the number of unauthorised disclosures actually resulting in prosecution. A number of Government witnesses said to us that section 2 had a widespread deterrent effect in preventing improper disclosures by Crown servants. The news media said to us that the section frequently deterred or prevented Crown servants from disclosing information of public interest which, in their view, should have been disclosed. Section 2 is rarely activated in the court room, but is seen by many as having a pervasive influence on the work and the behaviour of hundreds of thousands of people.
. . . . . .

Constitutional factors
56. The way in which our constitution works determines both the degree of openness in government and the role and behaviour of the Civil Service. In this country Ministers take decisions and lay down policy. Ministers are held responsible for their decisions and are accountable to Parliament for them. It is the function of Ministers to explain and defend their decisions and their policies and to decide what official information shall be revealed. The function of the Civil Service is to advise Ministers, and to carry out their decisions and their policies. Owing to the wide range of governmental functions today, and the sheer size of the Government machine, senior civil servants in practice take many decisions within the ambit of broad Ministerial policies, and have a substantial role in explaining official policies and disclosing official information. Senior civil servants also engage in consultations, soundings and discussions, both formal and informal, to enable them to formulate advice to Ministers. In doing so they inevitably give information and views as well as receiving them. Junior civil servants are more circumscribed, but those whose work involves contact with the public may also have a function of explaining policy and giving information.
57. There is no direct connection between these constitutional arrangements and

section 2. The section does not fetter Ministers in any way in deciding what to disclose and what to withhold. Their decisions are influenced mainly by the normal operation of the system of Parliamentary government, by the attentions of the media and by public pressures of all kinds. Senior civil servants who disclose official information do so on behalf of Ministers, and in accordance with their express or implied wishes. Junior civil servants act in accordance with their instructions.

Civil Service sanctions 58. Section 2 provides one sanction to ensure that civil servants do not make unauthorised disclosures. This sanction is rarely invoked. Other sanctions, formal and informal, are of greater practical consequence. The informal sanction lies in the fact that a civil servant who is regarded as unreliable, or who tends to overstep the mark and to talk too freely, will not enjoy such a satisfactory career as colleagues with better judgement and greater discretion. He may fail to obtain promotion, or he may be given less important and attractive jobs . . .
. . . . . .

Recruitment, vetting and training 60. The Government does not rely entirely on sanctions after entry to ensure the reliability and discretion of Crown servants. Its recruitment procedures are designed to ensure fitness for appointment in these as well as in other respects. Those whose work involves regular access to sensitive information receive appropriate training and instructions. There are also vetting procedures to check further the suitability of those with access to particularly sensitive information.

Security classifications and privacy markings 61. In addition to the restraints upon unauthorised disclosure which we have mentioned, the Government uses various systems of marks to identify official information which requires special protection. *Security classification* is the most important and most widely known of these systems. We found that some witnesses were uncertain about the significance of security classification, and its relationship to section 2. As the law now stands, there is no connection between them. Security classification is a purely administrative system, unrelated to the criminal law. The classification of a document determines the precautions to be taken in handling it. The higher the classification, the more stringent the physical precautions required (e.g. locking up in safes), and the more restrictive the rules about who may have access to the document. Classification does not determine the sanctions taken for unauthorised disclosure.

62. There are four levels of classification, and the criterion for awarding a classification is the degree of damage that would be caused by the unauthorised disclosure of the information in question. The four classifications, and the criteria for awarding them are:

TOP SECRET	Exceptionally grave damage to the nation
SECRET	Serious injury to the interests of the nation
CONFIDENTIAL	Prejudicial to the interests of the nation

RESTRICTED   Undesirable in the interests of the nation

The 'interests of the nation' are interpreted broadly, and are not confined to questions of national security in the military sense.

......

'D' Notices 65. There is another administrative system for protecting certain official information, the 'D' Notice system. Unlike the various means of protection mentioned earlier in this Chapter, 'D' Notices are addressed to the news media, not to Crown servants. The 'D' Notice system is entirely voluntary and has no legal authority. A 'D' Notice may be issued only on the authority of the Defence, Press and Broadcasting Committee, which is composed of officials from Government Departments concerned with defence and national security and representatives of the press and broadcasting organisations. The Notices are addressed to editors of newspapers, to those concerned in broadcasting, and to others concerned with publications on defence and related subjects. Their purpose is to advise editors that the Government regards certain categories of information, which the Notices usually but not always define in general terms, as being secret for reasons of national security, and to ask editors to refrain from publishing such information. An editor who is in doubt can contact the Secretary of the Committee for advice. There is no direct relationship between this system and the Official Secrets Acts, and nothing in the 'D' Notice system relieves an editor of his responsibilities under the Acts.

......

100. . . . A proper balance between openness and secrecy requires a reformed law, in place of the present section. Our first major proposal is that section 2 should be repealed, and replaced by narrower and more specific provisions.

......

102. . . . The distinction between espionage and leakage − that is, between those who intend to help an enemy and those who disclose information with no such intention − is important. This distinction should be reflected in the structure of the law. It has been obscured by the inclusion of section 2 in the Official Secrets Acts. This is one reason for the dislike of the section which emerges in much of the evidence.

103. A new statute separate from the Official Secrets Acts, with a new title free of the emotive overtones of the existing title, is therefore necessary if the new provisions which we propose are to command public confidence. These provisions will fit together naturally in a separate statute. There is no technical reason why they should form part of the Official Secrets Acts; they can still be used in cases where the evidence does not justify a charge under section 1 although the circumstances are close to espionage. Our second major proposal is that the new provisions which we recommend, in replacement of section 2, should form a separate statute, to be known as the Official Information Act.

......

190. We propose that the Official Information Act should apply to Cabinet documents, that is, documents submitted for the consideration of the Cabinet and

documents recording the proceedings or conclusions of the Cabinet, irrespective of subject matter. 'Cabinet' for this purpose includes committees of the Cabinet the members of which are Ministers. Cabinet documents to which the Act applies should be marked in a manner prescribed by the Secretary of the Cabinet. The Act should provide that the communication of a Cabinet document means either the transmission of that document or a substantial part of it, or the communication of information about the document by other means which enable another person to reproduce the document or a substantial part of it in verbatim or virtually verbatim form.

. . . . . .

The general effect of our proposals

275. Our main conclusion is that the present law is unsatisfactory, and that it should be changed so that criminal sanctions are retained only to protect what is of real importance.

276. Section 2 of the Official Secrets Act 1911 should be repealed, and replaced by a new statute, called the Official Information Act, which should apply only to official information which

- a. is classified information relating to defence or internal security, or to foreign relations, or to the currency or to the reserves, the unauthorised disclosure of which would cause serious injury to the interests of the nation; *or*
- b. is likely to assist criminal activities or to impede law enforcement; *or*
- c. is a Cabinet document; *or*
- d. has been entrusted to the Government by a private individual or concern.

The Act should contain safeguards relating to the classification of information of the kinds mentioned in a. above.

277. It should be an offence under the Official Information Act

- a. for a Crown servant to communicate information to which the Act applies, contrary to his official duty;
- b. for a Government contractor or a person entrusted with official information in confidence to communicate information of one of the kinds in paragraph 276 a., b. and c., otherwise than for the purposes of the contract or for which it was entrusted;
- c. for any person to communicate information of one of the kinds in paragraph 276 a., b. and c., which he knows, or has reasonable ground to believe, has reached him as the result of a contravention of the Official Information Act;
- d. to communicate or use official information of any kind for purposes of private gain.

Prosecutions should require the consent of the Attorney General in the case of information of the kinds mentioned in paragraph 276 a., c. and d., and of the Director of Public Prosecutions in the case of b. and of private gain.

39 MINISTERIAL MEMOIRS

Extracts from the *Report of the Committee of Privy Councillors on Ministerial Memoirs* (Cmnd. 6386, 1976); reprinted by permission of H.M.S.O. This Committee was appointed following the case of the Crossman Diaries (the Lord Chief Justice's judgement is summarised in paragraph 64 below); and the Government have announced acceptance of the Committee's recommendation that a voluntary code of conduct should govern future practice. All Ministers will be informed of the new arrangements and will be invited to sign the appropriate declaration.

38. The conventions that have come to govern the position of the ex-Minister can only be understood against the background of the obligations that he acquired during his period of office. So understood, they are essentially concessions made to him rather than restrictions imposed upon him. Here in effect is somebody who has come into possession of a body of information, comprising facts, attitudes and opinions, which have been entrusted to him by virtue of his office under the Crown and for no other immediate purpose at any rate than that he should make use of it in discharging that office. Now he is out of it. What use is he to be free to make of that accumulated stock?

39. It is not enough to say that his lips are sealed now because he was governed then by the Ministerial convention of collective responsibility. That period is over, and so is the particular obligation of conduct that goes with it. Nor is it enough, in our view, to say that all his information and experience originate in the relation of confidence that he owes to the State or his fellow servants and therefore he has no liberty to say anything at his own discretion and must remain at the mercy of the Crown for permission to open his lips. The origin of his material will always be a potent consideration: but time itself, as we know, erodes the force of such principles, and he is entitled to call time to his aid in support of his freedom.

40. It is not only the mere impact of time, however, that is to be allowed for in his case. There is a public interest at stake in the dissemination of that kind of informed experience of the affairs of government that an ex-Minister is peculiarly equipped to supply. And that interest extends to ensuring so far as possible that the experience revealed is neither out of date nor stale. There is also another type of public interest involved in securing that a man who has held public office in the service of his country and has been exposed accordingly to controversy and criticism as to his discharge of it should be enabled to offer to the public a reasoned and documented account of his stewardship at the end of the day.

41. These are valid considerations to be set against each other, and they suggest that the ex-Minister's memoirs occupy an area in which compromises of principle are called for on each side.

. . . . . .

45. Within the limits of the general conception that the author is free to use his

Ministerial experience for the purpose of giving an account of his own work and not for the purpose of discussing or criticising the policies and opinions of other Ministers who have been his colleagues, we identify certain separate categories of subject that call for restriction. We will mention and discuss them in what follows.

46. First, the author must not reveal anything that contravenes the requirements of national security operative at the time of his proposed publication. We do not anticipate serious debate about this . . .

. . . . . .

49. The third category of restriction has as its text the phrase 'information the publication of which would be destructive of the confidential relationships . . . which may subsist between Minister and Minister, Ministers and their advisers, and between either and outside bodies or private persons'. The idea is very comprehensive, it involves the exercise of a much more subjective type of assessment than that required for the two preceding categories, and its application to any given set of circumstances calls for what is essentially editorial judgement. For this reason alone it does not break down easily into any set of more precise rules. It is a general principle and everything depends on its interpretation.

50. . . . We asked ourselves very seriously the question whether, with all the pressure of the day in favour of openness of government and public participation in the formation of public policies, the principle itself which enjoins confidentiality in all that goes to the internal formulation of Government policy ought to be regarded as an outmoded and undesirable restriction. We always came round to the same answer. It is necessary and it ought to be observed.

51. The argument in its favour is quite simple and does not gain by elaboration. We have indicated it before. Those who are to act together in pursuance of a policy agreed in common do require and expect the observance of confidence as to what they say to each other; and unless they can be assured of the maintenance of that confidence they will not speak easily or frankly among themselves. Opinions, perhaps unpopular, perhaps embarrassing, will be muted or suppressed if they are known to be liable to future disclosure at the whim of some retired colleague. Business which should be discussed by the whole body will tend to be settled by two or three in a corner. Given our system of Cabinet and Parliamentary government, the interests of the State will suffer if policy cannot be formed on a basis of mutual confidence . . .

. . . . . .

53. So much for Minister and Minister. But the relation between a Minister and his advisers in the Civil or other Services is just as clearly one of inherent confidence. Indeed the case of the departmental adviser is stronger than any other since it is his professional duty to tender his advice when so required, and in our view it is critically important that he should be free to do so in the assurance that the confidence that he has given will be respected. He should be entitled to think that his advice will be confined to the departmental purpose that called it forth and will not be treated as available for general publication and comment by the Minister to whom it was offered. We accept the validity of the description of an adviser's task

which Lord Bridges offered to the House of Lords after his retirement:

'He has to analyse the position and set out all the courses, and not cover up any uncomfortable facts. That is a job which has to be done fearlessly and frankly, and if it is going to be done as it ought to be done, the people concerned must have confidence that their advice will not be disclosed prematurely. That, of course, is the basis of the whole confidential relationship between civil servants and Ministers, and likewise between Ministers and the Cabinet.'

. . . . . .

56. We are able to extract from the considerations as to confidentiality that we have now laid out three working rules as to the reticence due from an ex-Minister. We will phrase them as follows:

(a) In dealing with the experience that he has acquired by virtue of his official position, he should not reveal the opinions or attitudes of colleagues as to the Government business with which they have been concerned. That belongs to their stewardship, not to his. He may, on the other hand, describe and account for his own.

(b) He should not reveal the advice given to him by individuals whose duty it has been to tender him their advice or opinions in confidence. If he wishes to mention the burden or weight of such advice, it must be done without attributing individual attitudes to identifiable persons. Again, he will need to exercise a continuing discretion in any references that he makes to communications received by him in confidence from outside members of the public.

(c) He should not make public assessments or criticisms, favourable or unfavourable, of those who have served under him or those whose competence or suitability for particular posts he has had to measure as part of his official duties.

. . . . . .

64. There are three considerations arising from this Judgement's exposition of the law which we will set out briefly below, because they seem to us to be critical for the purposes of our own inquiry.

(a) The common law does extend so far as to be capable of prohibiting an ex-Minister or his inheritors from publishing in his memoirs information which he has received in confidence by virtue of his office. He is not merely under 'a gentleman's agreement to refrain from publication'. But to enable a Court of law to intervene the threatened disclosure must be 'improper'; and this description is evidently intended to describe some more particular combination of circumstances than the bare fact that the Crown's permission has not been obtained or that the material to be used is itself an account of some proceedings of the Cabinet or one of its Committees.

(b) The impropriety of disclosure which the Court needs to find in order to justify its intervention must be proved before it by evidence in each case. With regard to 'public secrets' there cannot be 'a single rule governing the publication of such a variety of matters'. While the basic confidentiality of

Cabinet proceedings or discussions itself creates secrets the necessity of protecting which a Court can recognise, the restriction imposed must not go beyond the 'strict requirement of public need' on the facts of the case before it. The Judge indeed may hold that there are 'other facets of the public interest contradictory of and more compelling than' the maintenance of the inviolability of Cabinet confidence. An example suggested is the importance of maintaining freedom of speech. While the disclosure of individual opinions expressed by Ministers in the course of Cabinet discussions does involve the sort of breach of confidence which a Court of law has the power to restrain, the Judge must be satisfied by demonstration that the confidentiality continues at the time when he is asked to give relief. In the case of Volume 1 of the Crossman Diaries, which was the subject of the recent litigation, the Lord Chief Justice, after reading the book, refused to hold that the material disclosed after what has become a gap of some ten years retained a sufficient element of confidentiality to call for legal remedy.

(*c*) The categories of information described as (1) advice given by senior Civil Servants to their Ministers and (2) observations made by Ministers on the capacity of individual senior Civil Servants and their suitability for specific appointments do not, it seems, qualify for legal protection from disclosure on the ground of any intrinsic confidentiality. The Judgement does not enter in any detail into the considerations which are thought to distinguish material of this kind from other forms of confidential discussion belonging to the internal processes of government and we are left in uncertainty how far to treat the Court's refusal of relief as based on general principles or on a mere allowance for the time factor involved in the particular case.

65. If we ask ourselves whether the established principles of law, as now expounded, provide a system which can protect and enforce those rules of reticence that we regard as called for when ex-Ministers compose their memoirs of Ministerial life, we are bound to say that we do not think that they do. There are three main objections to reliance on the protection offered. First, what an intending author needs when he sets to work is the availability of some short code of working rules for his guidance which he can count upon to be treated as equally applicable to his own case and those of other intending authors, both before and after him. The Crossman case does not seem to have laid down any set of rules of this nature, since the essence of the decision appears to be that there are no fixed principles of legal enforceability and that each case presented to the Court must be decided on its merits according to the facts that appear in evidence during the course of the case . . .

66. Secondly, it is the Judge who tries the case who is installed as the authority to decide on his own responsibility the weight and urgency of the claims of 'continuing confidentiality'. Such a decision is bound to be extremely hazardous in any but the most obvious circumstances: but the reasons that persuade us that confidentiality is a value that it is important to maintain in this special field of government relations do not lead us to think that a Judge is likely to be so equipped as to

make him the best arbiter of the issues involved. The relevant considerations are political and administrative, and if enforcement is to be looked for at all they must either be applied according to a general received rule, such as an arbitrary time limit, or according to the opinions of persons whose experience has made them more intimately familiar with the field.

67. Lastly it seems to us a substantial defect in the legal conspectus that it does not appear to be able to envisage confidences of or about Civil Servants as ranking for protection on the same basis as confidential exchanges between Ministers themselves.

68. Since therefore the law as it stands does not address itself either precisely enough or fully enough to achieving the outcome that we favour, ought we to recommend the introduction of legislation to lay down as a statutory duty the observance of principles to govern the conduct of the ex-Minister memorialist? This, to us, is the point at which the ways divide. Either, if Parliament so decides, a set of legal obligations must be designed to cover the subject fully: or, while it must not be forgotten that neither the criminal law nor the common law can be wholly excluded from consideration, the true emphasis for the future must lie in acceptance that the rules to be observed are voluntary obligations, known in advance and dependent for their observance upon no more than the decency and honour of those concerned.

. . . It is to be remembered that in all we are speaking of the occasional and limited activities of a small number of persons; and those persons men or women who *ex hypothesi* have held high office under the Crown and responsible positions in public life. They should be able, surely, to conduct themselves properly and recognise their obligations without the creation of statutory offences or statutory penalties. To be driven to suggest otherwise would be to acknowledge a sad decline in the prestige of modern government.

. . . . . .

70. We must now describe what arrangements we think are needed to secure observance of the principles that we have recommended. If a statutory code is not to be resorted to and if litigation at common law does not offer itself as a satisfactory instrument for general guidance, it becomes important to try to devise some working procedure that will be both widely understood and easy to operate . . .

71. The first thing seems to be therefore that every Minister on taking office should have his attention drawn explicitly to the obligations with regard to the future that he is assuming by virtue of that office . . . We should like to see a system instituted, if the principles of our Report commend themselves, under which each Minister would be furnished at the start with a separate memorandum abstracting the substance of this Report and asked to sign a declaration similar to that which he signs with reference to the Official Secrets Acts.

. . . . . .

73. We recommend that . . . every ex-Minister who wishes to make public an account bearing on his Ministerial life should make it his business to let the Secretary of the Cabinet see in advance the full text of what he proposes to say.

. . . . . .

78. . . . . the Cabinet Secretary will have several duties to perform when he receives the text of a proposed publication. We will divide them into two sections, since the implications of the two are not the same and they call for rather different procedures.

79. On the one hand there is the need for clearance in respect of national security and the preservation of international relations. For this he will submit the text to the Government Department or, very possibly, Departments concerned for scrutiny and advice. If objections are raised under either head he will transmit them to the author. Since departmental advisers on such subjects are sometimes disposed to take a line that is over-cautious or unnecessarily rigid, we envisage the Cabinet Secretary as acting as mediator in any controversy that follows as to what should or should not be said. He is entitled to feel that he has the more central position and can claim a more objective standpoint. Nevertheless, if in the end the objection stands, it is in our opinion the positive duty of the author to give way to it (see Part II, paragraphs 47 and 48). These are not matters upon which in the last resort he is at liberty to set his judgment against the official view. It may be that an unabated sense of dissatisfaction will lead him to ask for the issue to be referred to the decision of the Prime Minister himself. If so, he should, we think, have this right of reference, and he should be heard. But that should be the end. The Prime Minister's decision should be accepted as final.

80. On the other hand lie those various considerations that we have discussed and formulated under the category of 'Confidential Relationships' in Part II (see paragraphs 49—57). The problem how these relationships are to be respected in the writing of memoirs is, as we have said, very much one of judgment: it involves questions of identification and degree, how much or how little is to be said and how far specifically or only in general. Judging by past experience, many ex-Ministers value the views of the Cabinet Secretary on their handling of these matters. In any event we think that he should offer them, whether or not directly invited. Given goodwill and a readiness to make adjustments it may well be possible for both points of view to be reconciled, since a measure of flexibility is called for in this sort of debate. But this is not a range of subject upon which we feel justified in recommending that it should be the duty of the author in the last resort to give way to the view of the Cabinet Secretary or of the Prime Minister, if the issue reaches the latter. In so many cases the right balance is a matter of degree upon which two opposing views may fairly be held. On all these questions we think that the author must take upon his own shoulders the responsibility for deciding what he is going to say and how he is going to express himself . . .

. . . . . .

The time factor

82. The more we have had to consider the various problems raised by 'secrecy' considerations, the more clearly it has been borne in upon us that the time factor is the critical element. There may be some things that have come to the ex-Minister's

knowledge that should never be recorded in any measurable period of time. Even they probably depend upon questions of personal taste or discretion. But, generally speaking, what we are talking about are the underlying constituents of public affairs, knowledge of which is of value to the accumulating stock of historical, social and political information. At some point of time the secrets of one period must become the common learning of another. How then to find any working rule for the ex-Minister author which will do justice to the proper claims of governmental and administrative life on the one side and to the demands of genuine historical inquiry on the other?

83. Reviewing the various categories of restriction that we have recommended, we see that the time factor has not the same significance for all of them . . .

84. . . . the problem is fundamentally different for those issues which we have classed as Confidential Relationships. Essentially they do not depend upon the special circumstances of individual cases; they arise from the general assurance or expectation of confidentiality which is owed to the efficient conduct of Government business. The 'secrecy' which it enjoins has no need to be permanent in order to be effective; and we are led to the conclusion that a fixed time limit, at the expiry of which the restrictions proposed under this heading of Confidential Relationships will be lifted, is the only satisfactory way of reconciling the interests of the State, the needs of the author, and the demands of the interested public.

85. Any such time limit must necessarily be arbitrary and general. It does not admit of any reasoned process of measurement. We take into account the desirability of a man who thinks that he has something important to say being able to give his account publicly during his own lifetime. We think it advantageous too that what he has to say should be said during the probable lifetime of others who may be involved in his account. These considerations persuade us that a period of 30 years analogous to the present moratorium on the availability of public records is altogether too long for the purpose. Nor do we think a period of that length is needed to satisfy the basic requirements of confidentiality. Controversies die down and issues become stale. What we propose for the time limit is a period of 15 years . . .

40 THE PARLIAMENTARY COMMISSIONER FOR ADMINISTRATION

Extract (a) is from *The Parliamentary Commissioner for Administration* (Cmnd. 2767, 1965); extract (b) is from *The Parliamentary Commissioner for Administration: Annual Report for 1968* (H.C. 129, 1969); extract (c) is from Sir E. Compton 'The Administrative Performance of Government' in *Public Administration*, Spring 1970, vol. 48; extracts (a) and (b) are reprinted by permission of H.M.S.O., extract (c) by permission of the Editor and author. The first extract is from the White Paper setting out the proposals which were given statutory form in the Parliamentary Commissioner Act, 1967. They are generally regarded as having been stimulated by the Whyatt Report (*The Citizen and the Administration: The Redress of Grievances*, Stevens, 1961), whose proposals were rejected by the Conservative administration in November 1962, but taken up by the Labour administration of 1964. The powers of the so-called 'Ombudsman' are modest, and extract (b) indicates attempts by the Select Committee on the Parliamentary Commissioner for Administration to broaden the Commissioner's frame of reference. Extract (c) provides an early assessment of the new institution by the first Commissioner, Sir Edmund Compton.

(a)

2. The interests of the citizen who is affected by a decision of central Government are already safeguarded in a number of ways. He may have an opportunity of putting his case at an inquiry held before administrative action is taken. He may have a right of appeal to a tribunal against a decision. He may have a remedy before the courts.

3. But these arrangements cannot cover every instance where a private person feels that he is suffering injustice as a result of faulty administration on the part of a Government Department.

The citizen and Parliament

4. . . . In Britain, Parliament is the place for ventilating the grievances of the citizen — by history, tradition and past and present practice. It is one of the functions of the elected Member of Parliament to try to secure that his constituents do not suffer injustice at the hand of the Government. The procedures of Parliamentary Questions, Adjournment Debates and Debates on Supply have developed for this purpose under the British pattern of Parliamentary government; and Members are continually taking up constituents' complaints in correspondence with Ministers, and bringing citizens' grievances, great or small, to Parliament, where Ministers individually and Her Majesty's Government collectively are accountable. We do not want to create any new institution which would erode the functions of Members of Parliament in this respect, nor to replace remedies which the British Constitution already provides. Our proposal is to develop those remedies still further. We shall give Members of Parliament a better instrument which they can use to protect the citizen, namely, the services of a Parliamentary Commissioner for Administration.

5. Under our proposals, the Parliamentary Commissioner will be an independent officer, whose status and powers will be conferred by statute. He will be appointed by the Crown; his salary and pension will be a charge on the Consolidated Fund; and he will be secure from dismissal, except by parliamentary motion. He will report to Parliament each year, and otherwise as occasion requires.

Functions of the Parliamentary Commissioner

6. The Commissioner will act only at the instance of a Member of the House of

Commons, as the elected representative body in Parliament, and on a complaint of personal injustice suffered by the complainant. It will be for the Member to decide whether the complaint appears to be one appropriate for reference to the Commission. A complainant will not be restricted to approaching the Member for his own constituency; Members will doubtless establish their own conventions for ensuring that the constituency Member is kept in touch when another Member takes up a case. Most complaints will come from private individuals, but companies or other corporate bodies — other than those under publicly elected or appointed authority — will not be excluded.

. . . . . .

Central Government administration to be covered

7. Except for some exclusions which are explained later in this Paper, the field for the Commissioner will be the whole range of relationships between the private person and the central Government. We propose to list in the statute the bodies to be subject to investigation by the Commissioner in matters within his scope. The proposed list is as follows:

Ministry of Agriculture, Fisheries and Food
Ministry of Aviation
Office of the Chancellor of the Duchy of Lancaster
Civil Service Commission
Colonial Office
Commonwealth Relations Office
Customs and Excise
Ministry of Defence
Department of Economic Affairs
Department of Education and Science
Export Credits Guarantee Department
Foreign Office
General Register Office
General Registry Office, Scotland
Ministry of Health
Home Office
Ministry of Housing and Local Government
Central Office of Information
Inland Revenue
Ministry of Labour
Ministry of Land and Natural Resources
Land Registry
Lord Chancellor's Department
Office of the Lord Privy Seal
National Assistance Board
National Debt Office

Ordnance Survey
Ministry of Overseas Development
Paymaster General's Office
Ministry of Pensions and National Insurance
Ministry of Power
Ministry of Public Building and Works
Public Record Office
Public Trustee
Department of Registers of Scotland
Registry of Friendly Societies
Royal Mint
Scottish Office:
    Department of Agriculture and Fisheries for Scotland
    Scottish Development Department
    Scottish Education Department
    Scottish Home and Health Department
Scottish Record Office
H.M. Stationery Office
Ministry of Technology
Board of Trade
Ministry of Transport
Treasury
Treasury Solicitor's Department
Office of the Minister without Portfolio
Welsh Office.
. . . The list will need to be amended from time to time as the structure of the
government machinery itself is changed, and we shall seek power to do this by sub-
ordinate instrument.

Exclusions

8. The exclusions which we propose to make from the Commissioner's field of
investigation are those where there are dominant considerations of national or
public interest — namely, the exercise of powers to preserve the safety of the State;
matters which Ministers certify as affecting relations with other countries; matters
relating to the administration of colonial territories; and the exercise of powers in
relation to investigating crime or determining whether a matter shall go to the
courts. The Commissioner will not normally pursue matters which are within the
competence of the courts; he will have discretion to act if he thinks that the
remedy open in the courts is not one which the complainant could reasonably be
expected to use, but this will not affect anyone's right of access to the courts. He
will not pursue issues already covered by tribunals or other quasi-judicial bodies, or
by the Council on Tribunals and its Scottish Committee — of both of which he
himself will be an ex officio member. Nor will he look into the exercise of the

Prerogative of Mercy or into the exercise of the personal authority of the Sovereign in conferring honours and privileges, or into appointments by the Crown or by Ministers. He will be excluded from investigating actions of Departments in personnel matters, including orders and discipline in the Armed Forces. Finally, purely commercial relationships of Departments with customers or suppliers will not come within his purview.

Procedure

9. We intend the Commissioner's procedure to be as informal as possible, subject to the requirement that if he takes up a case he must give to the person against whom the complaint lies the opportunity to comment on it. He will be empowered to decide whether the parties can be legally represented, but legal representation will be the exception, not the rule. Legal aid will not be available. The Commissioner will be able to call for oral or written evidence; and he will have power to compel production of documents, including departments' minutes, but excluding Cabinet or Cabinet Committee documents. He will have power to take evidence on oath, although we would expect this power to be used infrequently . . .

10. The Commissioner will have discretion to refuse to pursue a case where he thinks there are insufficient grounds for the complaint or where he does not regard it as within his scope. He will not normally pursue a case where the matter complained of had been known to the complainant more than twelve months previously but he will have discretion to do so.

11. The Commissioner will be concerned with faults in administration. It will not be for him to criticise policy, or to examine a decision on the exercise of discretionary powers, unless it appears to him that the decision has been affected by a fault in administration. If he finds nothing wrong, he will inform the Member of Parliament who has approached him. If he finds that there is justifiable cause for complaint and the Department responds to his invitation to put it right, he will inform the Member. So far as the Commissioner is concerned, this will be the end of the matter, save for a possible reference to the case in his annual report of Parliament. If the Department does not act to the Commissioner's satisfaction, it will be open to him to report his conclusion to Parliament *ad hoc*.

12. It will be for Parliament to decide what arrangements to make to receive and act upon reports from the Commissioner. This will not be a matter for legislation. It may well be found convenient to establish a Select Committee to take these reports in the first instance. This Committee would have the usual powers of a Select Committee to summon witnesses (including Ministers) and to take evidence and report to Parliament.

13. It will be for Parliament, with the help of this Committee (if one is appointed), to consider what action should be taken on the reports of the Commissioner — whether the annual report, or reports *ad hoc*. The Commissioner in his annual report may comment on defects in the system which have come to his notice as a result of investigating individual complaints.

14. We do not intend that a reference to the Commissioner should automatically hold up action on the case by the Government; sometimes this might be contrary to the public interest. Ministers will have discretion to proceed with a case even where it is being examined by the Commissioner. They will also have discretion to prevent disclosure of information by the Commissioner where the safety of the State or the public interest makes it necessary to do so.

15. The fact that we are proposing this scheme does not mean that we think that the administration of Government departments is open to serious criticism or that injustices are frequently suffered by individual citizens. Far from it. We are in no doubt that the tradition of integrity and impartiality in our public administration is being fully maintained. But our proposal should increase confidence in that administration — by enabling complaints about administrative action to be fully and impartially investigated, so that, if a grievance is justified, it may be remedied, or, if it is unjustified, this may be demonstrated. It should also result, as has proved to be the case in other countries, in the further improvement of administrative standards and efficiency.

(b)

Conduct of investigations

16. **Maladministration: Discretionary Decisions.** The Select Committee, in their Second Report, Session 1967–68 (H.C. 350), encouraged me to extend the scope of my investigations so as to consider not merely the quality of the procedures attending a decision taken in the exercise of a discretion vested in the department concerned but also the quality of the decision itself. In my First Report, Session 1968–69 (H.C. 9), I said I was acting on the Committee's recommendations. The effect of this new practice has so far been slight, and I report as a fact that I have not yet come across any decision which, after full investigation, has seemed to me so bad as to indicate bias or perversity on the part of the person who took it.

17. **Maladministration: Departmental Rules.** The Select Committee also considered it proper for me to enquire whether, given the harsh effect of the departmental rule, the department had taken action to review the rule. It has always been open to me to draw attention in my individual reports to Members to rules which, although applied without maladministration, seemed to me to bear hardly on the complainant . . . Having reviewed my practice in the light of the Select Committee's Report I now feel entitled, before deciding the terms of my report to the Member who has referred such a complaint, to enquire whether the department have reviewed the rule in the light of the hardship sustained by the complainant. But I should point out that the decision whether or not the rule should be changed will rest with the department and not with me. I enquire whether the department have reviewed the rule, and I consider whether that review has been conducted without maladministration. But provided there had been no maladministration in the review, Section 12(3) of the Act would prevent me from questioning a decision of

the department to maintain the rule. And as the Select Committee recognised, there might be grounds of public need which in the judgement of the department over-rode the hardship to the individual whose complaint had been referred to me . . .

(c)

After two years of work as Parliamentary Commissioner, I think it is fair to point to three . . . items on each side of the balance sheet.

On the credit side, the first item naturally consists of cases of maladministration detected and put right. The second item consists of the complaints fully disposed of, in the sense that till I came there was only the department's word for it: now the Commissioner will have investigated independently and reported either that the complaint was justified or that it was not, but final in either case. The third credit item really confirms the 1965 White Paper's hope that the Parliamentary Com-missioner's presence has a tonic effect on the quality of government administration. I said 'the quality', so that it is not a measurable effect. But I have seen evidence of its working and I am confident that it will grow as the Office makes itself felt by its investigations and the results of its casework become known. So much for the credit side. Now for the debits.

The first is the extent to which this new Office adds to the coefficient of friction in government. My Office has, at present, investigating and other staff of fifty-nine. But their work occupies the time of many more civil servants in Whitehall. I would not presume to calculate the workload generated in the civil service by me. I hope this is a price worth paying to raise the standard of public administration and to remedy individual injustices. But I think it part of the Parliamentary Commissioner's duty to bear in mind in all his operations that this price *is* being paid, and paid by the public and the taxpayer. An investigation by me *may* result in the satisfaction of a citizen's grievance: whatever the outcome, it *must* result in an increase in the staff of the department concerned, or longer time taken over the work that the department does for the public.

The second debit item is the risk that my presence will make departments less forthcoming and helpful in the work they do for the public. Departments, particu-larly the Social Service departments with local offices throughout the country, are frequently helping members of the public with advice given outside the limits of their statutory obligations. The risk is that if I report adversely when they have given wrong advice, they will play for safety and not give advice at all.

The third item to be added to the debit side is not, I think, due only to the Parliamentary Commissioner, but is inherent in the system of ministerial responsi-bility. It will be said that the risk that the Minister may be brought to account must work against delegation, must work against the taking of responsibility down the line. When I was a new entrant into the public service, at least one old stager's advice to me was 'when in doubt, report to higher authority'. During my career I, like others in the civil service, have often heard the Minister complain, 'Why wasn't I told?', and seldom 'Why are you bothering me with this?' Here I must confess that the working of my Office may add to the pressure against delegation. The principal officers of the Ministry of Housing and Local Government and of the Civil Service Department have said as much in their evidence to the Select Committee on the Parliamentary Commissioner: and the evidence of such authorities must indeed be attended to.

. . . . . .

. . . [M]inisterial responsibility and delegation of authority in government administration are not incompatible. It is evident enough that ministerial responsibility must generate pressures against delegation. But these are pressures that can be counteracted, and it might be said that the successful combination of ministerial responsibility and delegation of authority is the most rewarding, as well as the most difficult, thing to bring off in public administration. I am glad to say that I know of several departments where this compatibility is achieved. I shall not be invidious by naming them: the success of such arrangements depends upon the determination and example of the Ministers and senior officials concerned, and both are liable to change. If I am pressed on the ingredients of success, I would list them like this. First, clearly expressed rules of delegation. Second, encouragement to staff down the line to use their delegated authority, with a clear indication that they will not be penalized for mistaken action. Finally — and this is the hard part — judicious support from higher authority for mistaken action. I say 'judicious' because neither Ministers nor senior civil servants for that matter, can undertake to give unconditional support to the man on the spot. What they can do, having delegated authority to that man and finding his decision challenged in Parliament or elsewhere, is to say 'I would have decided differently', but to say it to themselves. If the decision was his to take, and wasn't thoroughly bad — wrong-headed, perverse, corrupt or otherwise indefensible — then I believe the Minister or the senior civil servant should have the strength of character to defend the subordinate's decision as one that he was authorized to take and which in his judgement was the right decision. This analysis may well need improving, and I hope it will be improved. I have had to make it for myself. For Parliament has recently set me the task of identifying the 'bad decision' — that is, a complaint against a departmental decision which is claimed to be so bad as to be infected by maladministration. My problem is to reach my finding in such a case without substituting my judgement for that of the official whose decision is in question. I hope that my approach to the problem is the same as I suggest for the Minister, for I believe that our objects are the same; not to undermine the proper delegation of authority, while not attempting to defend the indefensible.

41 THE HEALTH SERVICE COMMISSIONER

Extracts from *First Report of the Health Service Commissioner* (H.C. 161, 1974); reprinted by permission of H.M.S.O. The Parliamentary Commissioner's jurisdiction does not extend either to local government or to the National Health Service, both of which now have their own 'Ombudsmen'. This extract describes the working arrangements for the Health Service Commissioner established under the National Health Service Reorganisation Act, 1973, and applied to Scotland under the National Health Service (Scotland) Act, 1972. The offices of Parliamentary Commissioner and Health Service Commissioner are held jointly by the same person. The Health Service Commission arrangements show one major improvement on the Parliamentary Commissioner: the power to receive complaints direct from the public. It is worth noting that the first incumbent, Sir Alan Marre, was formerly Second Permanent Secretary in the Department of Health and Social Security, a factor which in one case led to accusations of bias.

Background

7. When announcing, on 22 February 1972, the Government's decision to create the office of Health Service Commissioner, the Secretary of State for Social Services said:

'The Government have decided that there should be a Health Service Commissioner as part of the arrangements for dealing with complaints in the National Health Service. Although the great majority of complaints are satisfactorily dealt with by health authorities, there are some that the citizen should be able to refer to an entirely independent person if he remains dissatisfied with the action taken by the Health Service authority. A Commissioner would serve this independent function and would reinforce the rights of those who use the Health Service, without detracting from the responsibilities of the Health Service authorities or reflecting on the value of the work done by the staff of the service.'

8. The new offices were, therefore, seen as a supplement to, and a reinforcement of, the existing complaints procedures . . .

Procedure

12. In these initial stages, I have felt it right to keep the procedure for handling complaints referred to me flexible and fairly informal. There are, broadly, two stages. During the first I have to establish the substance of the complaint. This is not always easy. It may be embodied in a long, diffuse letter, and may raise a number of different issues. I have to satisfy myself that it has been referred to the appropriate authority and adequate time allowed for a reply. And I have also to decide whether all or any part of it is excluded from my jurisdiction on any one of a number of grounds. During this stage I may have to consider whether to exercise any discretion I have, for example whether to waive the time limit prescribed by the Act.

. . . . . .

13. The second stage applies when I have decided to carry out an investigation. It starts with the preparation of a statement concisely setting out the complaint. In accordance with the terms of the Act I send this to the authority or authorities

concerned for comment. Once I have these, I decide on the form the investigation is to take. It generally involves examination of minutes, correspondence or other papers, and often interviews with the complainant and officers of the authority or authorities. I take care also to ensure that any individual who may be criticised is given the opportunity to comment. Once I have all the information I require I prepare and issue my report. Copies of this are sent to the complainant, anyone named in the complaint, the authority concerned and such other authorities as are, under the Acts, entitled to receive copies.

Medical advice

14. The first procedural stage, described in the previous section, may, in a particular case, require me to consider whether the actions of a doctor in diagnosing a patient's illness or giving him treatment could be said to have arisen solely from the exercise of his clinical judgement; if so, the complaint, or that part of the complaint, would lie outside my jurisdiction.

15. Although I foresaw that, in most cases, I would have no problem in reaching a conclusion on this point, it seemed to me that it would be helpful for me to have medical advice available for cases in which I was doubtful. At my request the Presidents of the English Royal Colleges in conjunction with the Chairman of the Council of the British Medical Association, and the Presidents of the Scottish Royal Colleges in conjunction with the Chairman of the Scottish Council of the Association, have been good enough to provide me with the names of, respectively, ten doctors for England and Wales, and three doctors for Scotland, to any one of whom I might turn when the occasion arose . . .

Relationship with Office of the Parliamentary Commissioner for Administration

16. My appointment as Health Service Commissioner for the three countries, while continuing to hold the office of Parliamentary Commissioner for Administration, has meant that I have been able to apply to the new appointments the experience of conducting investigations that I have had in the earlier appointment. It has also made possible the close integration, and economical use, of staff employed on the different sides of my work.

17. This has proved of particular value in what I may call 'overlapping complaints', that is, complaints against the actions of both a central Department responsible for health services and a health service authority over a related series of events.
. . . . . .

Jurisdiction

General 19. The Acts define my responsibilities as Health Service Commissioner. These are to investigate complaints from complainants who allege that they have sustained injustice or hardship as a result of:

(*a*) a failure in a service provided by a health service authority;

(*b*) a failure of a health service authority to provide a service which it was its duty to provide;

(*c*) any other action taken by or on behalf of a health service authority which involved maladministration.

21. Complaints must be submitted by the person who is actually aggrieved. But if he cannot act for himself (or has died), it may be made on his behalf by a suitable person or organisation. Complainants from whom I have accepted complaints have included not only the aggrieved person (or a close relative) but also on occasion a solicitor instructed to act for him. Sometimes the complaint has come from an organisation which I have looked upon as representing, collectively, the views of particular individuals who were aggrieved. And equally where a Member of Parliament or a local Councillor has, on behalf and at the request of an aggrieved person or group of persons, forwarded a complaint, I have considered myself entitled to accept it as validly submitted.

22. From 1 April 1974 Community Health Councils (Local Health Councils in Scotland) may play a similar role. These Councils are new bodies set up under the Acts to represent the local community's interests in the health service to managements. And while it is, as I understand, not part of their responsibility to investigate individual complaints, they will be able to give advice on how and where to lodge a complaint and act as 'patient's friend'. I will accept from them in that capacity a complaint forwarded at the request and on behalf of a patient or other individual against a service in which the Council are interested, where the complaint has not been resolved locally to the complainant's satisfaction.

23. A complaint can be referred to me if in the opinion of the complainant it has not been satisfactorily dealt with by the health service authority. Exceptionally I may accept a complaint which has not first been referred to the health service authority if it is made by a member of the authority's staff on behalf of a patient who cannot act for himself.

24. As paragraph 19 shows, my concern must be essentially with administrative failures which affect patients, their relatives and friends: these would include, for example, bad communications (which may take the form of inaccurate or inadequate information or advice); delays in admission from the waiting list or in obtaining outpatient appointments; inadequate facilities or unsuitable accommodation; or failure to deal soon enough or properly with an aggrieved person's representations or complaints.

25. The Acts however specifically preclude me from investigating action taken in connection with the diagnosis of a patient's illness or his care or treatment if in my opinion it was taken solely in the exercise of clinical judgment. Similarly I cannot investigate the actions of family practitioners in pursuance of their Health Service contracts, or the actions of Executive Councils (in future Family Practitioner Committees or Health Boards), in inquiring into complaints against such practitioners. Nor am I permitted normally to carry out investigations where there is an already established procedure open to the complainant, such as recourse to the courts or

appeal to a tribunal, or (in Scotland) where the Mental Welfare Commission has jurisdiction.

26. Personnel matters are also outside my jurisdiction, though I would not regard this as necessarily preventing me, in the course of an investigation of a complaint submitted by a member of an authority's staff, from looking into an allegation that the submission of the complaint had led to victimisation.

27. The Acts prescribe, as the normal time limit within which a complaint must be made if I am to investigate it, a period of one year from the time when the matter complained about came to notice; but I can waive this time limit at my discretion if I consider it reasonable to do so.

. . . . . .

Cases not taken up . . . I have had to reject a considerable proportion of complaints as falling outside my jurisdiction. (In this respect the position is similar to my experience as Parliamentary Commissioner for Administration and that of Ombudsmen in most countries.)

29. The main grounds of rejection are that they concern the actions of persons (such as family practitioners) or bodies (such as local authorities) who are not subject to my jurisdiction; or that I have concluded that the actions complained of were taken solely in the exercise of clinical judgment. I have also rejected a significant number because they were submitted outside the normal time limit of one year and I did not consider it reasonable to waive the limit; a good many of these related to complaints arising from events which took place a very long time ago.

30. A considerable proportion of other complaints I have not been able to entertain at the time they were made because they had not previously been submitted to the health service authority. I have sometimes found it necessary to get in touch myself with the authority to establish whether this was so; and on occasion this has of itself resulted in getting the matter put right. In other cases I have advised the complainant himself to approach the authority, and to bring his complaint to me again if he is dissatisfied with the outcome; and some have already done so.

42 ADMINISTRATIVE TRIBUNALS AND INQUIRIES

Extracts from *Report of the Committee on Administrative Tribunals and Inquiries* (The Franks Report, Cmnd. 218, 1957); reprinted by permission of H.M.S.O. This Committee was appointed to review the operation of the numerous *ad hoc* administrative tribunals and inquiries which had grown steadily over the years. The principal recommendation for a standing Council on Tribunals was given effect by the Tribunals and Inquiries Act, 1958 (extended by the Tribunals and Inquiries Act, 1966). The recommendation that chairmen of tribunals should be appointed by the Lord Chancellor has not been acted upon, and the recommendation that all members of tribunals should be similarly appointed has only been partly implemented.

Disputes between the individual and authority

7. How do disputes between the individual and authority arise in this country at the present time? In general the starting point is the enactment of legislation by Parliament. Many statutes apply detailed schemes to the whole or to large classes of the community (for example national insurance) or lay on a Minister and other authorities a general duty to provide a service (for example education or health). Such legislation is rarely sufficient in itself to achieve all its objects, and a series of decisions by administrative bodies, such as Government Departments and local authorities, is often required. For example, in a national insurance scheme decisions have to be given on claims to benefit, and in providing an educational service decisions have to be taken on the siting of new schools. Many of these decisions affect the rights of individual citizens, who may then object.

8. Once objection has been raised, a further decision becomes inevitable. This further decision is of a different kind: whether to confirm, cancel or vary the original decision. In reaching it account must be taken not only of the original decision but also of the objection.

The resolution of these disputes

10. But over most of the field of public administration no formal procedure is provided for objecting or deciding on objections . . . Of course the aggrieved individual can always complain to the appropriate administrative authority, to his Member of Parliament, to a representative organisation or to the press. But there is no formal procedure on which he can insist.

11. There are therefore two broad distinctions to be made among these further decisions which we have been discussing. The first is between those decisions which follow a statutory procedure and those which do not. The second distinction is within the group of decisions subject to a statutory procedure. Some of these decisions are taken in the ordinary courts and some are taken by tribunals or by Ministers after a special procedure.

12. These two distinctions are essential for understanding our terms of reference. We are not instructed to consider those many cases in which no formal procedure has been prescribed. Nor are we instructed to consider decisions made in the ordinary courts. What we are instructed to consider are the cases in which the decision on objections, the further decision as we have called it, is taken by a tribunal or by a Minister after a special procedure has been followed.

. . . . . .

20. It is noteworthy that Parliament, having decided that the decisions with which we are concerned should not be remitted to the ordinary courts, should also have decided that they should not be left to be reached in the normal course of administration. Parliament has considered it essential to lay down special procedures for them.

Openness, fairness and impartiality

23. . . . . [I] t is clear that there are certain general and closely linked characteristics which should mark these special procedures. We call these characteristics openness, fairness and impartiality.

24. Here we need only give brief examples of their application. Take openness. If these procedures were wholly secret, the basis of confidence and acceptability would be lacking. Next take fairness. If the objector were not allowed to state his case, there would be nothing to stop oppression. Thirdly, there is impartiality. How can the citizen be satisfied unless he feels that those who decide his case come to their decision with open minds?

25. To assert that openness, fairness and impartiality are essential characteristics of our subject-matter is not to say that they must be present in the same way and to the same extent in all its parts. Difference in the nature of the issue for adjudication may give good reason for difference in the degree to which the three general characteristics should be developed and applied. Again, the method by which a Minister arrives at a decision after a hearing or enquiry cannot be the same as that by which a tribunal arrives at a decision. This difference is brought out later in the Report. For the moment it is sufficient to point out that when Parliament sets up a tribunal to decide cases, the adjudication is placed outside the Department concerned. The members of the tribunal are neutral and impartial in relation to the policy of the Minister, except in so far as that policy is contained in the rules which the tribunal has been set up to apply. But the Minister, deciding in the cases under the second part of our terms of reference, is committed to a policy which he has been charged by Parliament to carry out. In this sense he is not, and cannot be, impartial.

The allocation of decisions to tribunals and Ministers

. . . . . .

31. Starting with the facts, we observe that the methods of adjudication by tribunals are in general not the same as those of adjudication by Ministers. All or nearly all tribunals apply rules. No ministerial decision of the kind denoted by the second part of our terms of reference is reached in this way. Many matters remitted to tribunals and Ministers appear to have, as it were, a natural affinity with one or other method of adjudication. Sometimes the policy of the legislation can be embodied in a system of detailed regulations. Particular decisions cannot, single case by single case, alter the Minister's policy. Where this is so, it is natural to entrust the decisions to a tribunal, if not to the courts. On the other hand it is sometimes desirable to preserve flexibility of decision in the pursuance of public policy. Then a wise expediency is the proper basis of right adjudication, and the decision must be left with a Minister.

. . . . . .

33. We shall therefore respect this factual difference between tribunals and

Ministers and deal separately with the two parts of the subject. When considering tribunals we shall see how far the three characteristics of openness, fairness and impartiality can be developed and applied in general and how far their development and application must be adapted to the circumstances of particular tribunals. We shall then proceed to the decisions of Ministers after a hearing or enquiry and consider how far the difference in method of adjudication requires a different development and application of the three characteristics.

35. . . . The continuing extension of governmental activity and responsibility for the general well-being of the community has greatly multiplied the occasions on which an individual may be at issue with the administration or with another citizen or body, as to his rights, and the post-war years have seen a substantial growth in the importance and activities of tribunals. In some cases new policies or regulatory legislation have meant new tribunals, for example those established under the Agriculture Act, 1947, and under the Rent Acts. In other cases an earlier system has been adapted to wider purposes: for example, the local tribunals under the National Insurance Act, 1946, are the successors of the Courts of Referees. In other cases tribunals now perform functions previously carried out by the courts . . .

36. Tribunals today vary widely in constitution, function and procedure. Appointments of chairmen and members are usually made by the Minister responsible for the legislation under which they operate, but some are made by the Crown and some by the Lord Chancellor, even though he may have no direct responsibility for the subject-matter of their work. Most tribunals deal with cases in which an individual citizen is at issue with a Government Department or other public body concerning his rights or obligations under a statutory scheme. But a few (for example Rent Tribunals) are concerned with disputes between citizens. Still others (for example Licensing Authorities for Public Service and Goods Vehicles) have regulatory functions and are therefore just as much administrative bodies as they are adjudicating tribunals. Some tribunals, like the courts, have a detailed code of procedure, with testimony on oath and strict rules of evidence. Most have a simple procedure, usually without the oath and sometimes with a ban on legal representation. Finally, there are differences regarding appeals. Sometimes there is no appeal, and further redress can only be had by seeking a court order to set aside the decision. But in most cases there is an appeal — either to an appellate tribunal, a Minister or the courts.

37. Reflection on the general social and economic changes of recent decades convinces us that tribunals as a system for adjudication have come to stay. The tendency for issues arising from legislative schemes to be referred to special tribunals is likely to grow rather than to diminish . . .

The choice between tribunals and courts of law

38. We agree with the Donoughmore Committee that tribunals have certain characteristics which often give them advantages over the courts. These are cheapness, accessibility, freedom from technicality, expedition and expert knowledge of their

particular subject. It is no doubt because of these advantages that Parliament, once it has decided that certain decisions ought not to be made by normal executive or departmental processes, often entrusts them to tribunals rather than to the ordinary courts. But as a matter of general principle we are firmly of the opinion that a decision should be entrusted to a court rather than to a tribunal in the absence of special considerations which make a tribunal more suitable.

39. Moreover, if all decisions arising from new legislation were automatically vested in the ordinary courts the judiciary would by now have been grossly over-burdened . . .

Tribunals as machinery for adjudication

40. Tribunals are not ordinary courts, but neither are they appendages of Government Departments. Much of the official evidence, including that of the Joint Permanent Secretary to the Treasury, appeared to reflect the view that tribunals should properly be regarded as part of the machinery of administration, for which the Government must retain a close and continuing responsibility. Thus, for example, tribunals in the social service field would be regarded as adjuncts to the administration of the services themselves. We do not accept this view. We consider that tribunals should properly be regarded as machinery provided by Parliament for adjudication rather than as part of the machinery of administration. The essential point is that in all these cases Parliament has deliberately provided for a decision outside and independent of the Department concerned . . .

The application of the principles of openness, fairness and impartiality

41. We have already expressed our belief, in Part I, that Parliament in deciding that certain decisions should be reached only after a special procedure must have intended that they should manifest three basic characteristics: openness, fairness and impartiality. The choice of a tribunal rather than a Minister as the deciding authority is itself a considerable step towards the realisation of these objectives, particularly the third. But in some cases the statutory provisions and the regulations thereunder fall short of what is required to secure these objectives . . .

42. In the field of tribunals openness appears to us to require the publicity of proceedings and knowledge of the essential reasoning underlying the decisions; fairness to require the adoption of a clear procedure which enables parties to know their rights, to present their case fully and to know the case which they have to meet; and impartiality to require the freedom of tribunals from the influence, real or apparent, of Departments concerned with the subject-matter of their decisions.

The proposed Councils on Tribunals

43. These general statements give expression, in the field of tribunals, to that fair

play for the citizen which it is both the citizen's right to expect and the duty of good administration to provide. We shall now attempt to work out in some detail the proper application of these principles. Our most important recommendation in this Part of the Report is that two standing councils, one for England and Wales and one for Scotland, should be set up to keep the constitution and working of tribunals under continuous review. We suggest that the Council for England and Wales should be called the Lord Chancellor's Council on Tribunals and be appointed by and report to the Lord Chancellor. The Scottish Council should, we suggest, be appointed by and report to the Secretary of State for Scotland. In succeeding Chapters we recommend that certain specific functions relating to the constitution and procedure of tribunals should be entrusted to the Councils.

. . . . . .

The appointment of chairmen and members

45. We have already said that it is important to secure the independence of the personnel of tribunals from the Departments concerned with the subject-matter of their decisions. This is particularly so when a Government Department is a frequent party to proceedings before a tribunal. We wish to make it clear that we have received no significant evidence that any influence is in fact exerted upon members of tribunals by Government Departments. But present practice can give no guarantee for the future. It appears to us undesirable in principle that the appointment of so many chairmen and members of tribunals should rest solely with the Ministers concerned, and we have received some evidence that this method of appointment can lead to misunderstanding.

46. A substantial volume of the evidence has advocated the appointment of all chairmen and members of tribunals by the Lord Chancellor. There is no doubt that such a change would serve to stress the independence of tribunals; it might also, by reason of the esteem in which the office of Lord Chancellor is held, enhance their status. The change would not involve any new principle, since the Lord Chancellor is already responsible for the appointment not only of a number of chairmen of tribunals but in some cases for the appointment of members also.

. . . . . .

48. We appreciate the force of the contention that all appointments to tribunals should be made by the Lord Chancellor so as to demonstrate clearly the intention that tribunals should be wholly independent of departmental influence. But we feel that the best practical course would be for the responsibility of the Lord Chancellor for such appointments not to be extended beyond the chairmen, though we consider that he should retain his present responsibility for appointing members of certain tribunals and that there may be scope for extending this responsibility to a few other tribunals.

49. Although we are unable to recommend that all members of tribunals should be appointed by the Lord Chancellor we are satisfied that their appointment should

not rest with the Ministers concerned with the subject-matter of the adjudications. In order to enhance the independence of tribunals, both in appearance and fact, we consider that the Council on Tribunals should make these appointments . . .

. . . . . .

52. Our recommendations concerning the appointment of members of tribunals are intended to apply also to appointments to the panels from which the members of some tribunals are selected as required. In such cases the selection should be carried out not by the Minister or the clerk of the tribunal, as is usually now the case, but by the chairman of the tribunal.

. . . . . .

The qualifications of chairmen and members

55. There has been substantial agreement among witnesses that at any rate the majority of chairmen of tribunals should have legal qualifications. We attach great importance to the quality of chairmanship. Objectivity in the treatment of cases and the proper sifting of facts are most often best secured by having a legally qualified chairman, though we recognise that suitable chairmen can be drawn from fields other than the law. We therefore recommend that chairmen of tribunals should ordinarily have legal qualifications but that the appointment of persons without legal qualifications should not be ruled out when they are particularly suitable.

. . . . . .

Clerks

59. The practice whereby the majority of clerks of tribunals are provided by the Government Departments concerned from their local and regional staffs seems partly to be responsible for the feeling in the minds of some people that tribunals are dependent upon and influenced by those Departments. Not only for this reason but also because there would appear to be advantages in improving the general quality of tribunal clerks we have considered the possibility of establishing under the Lord Chancellor's Department a central corps of clerks from which a service could be provided for all tribunals.

60. Though this idea has many attractions we have, after careful consideration, rejected it. It would have the advantage of further enhancing the independence of tribunals, and it would be more appropriate for independent clerks to advise and help applicants than for departmental clerks to do so. The main objection is that it is difficult to see how any reasonable prospects of a career could be held out to the members of such a general service . . .

. . . . . .

SUPERVISION OF TRIBUNALS

The need for supervision

127. We have already recommended, in Chapter 4, the establishment of two Councils on Tribunals. We believe that this offers the only satisfactory means of solving many of the difficulties about tribunals both now and in the future. These difficulties are not met by review at an interval of about 25 years by *ad hoc* committees like ourselves or the Donoughmore Committee, which in the nature of the case must inevitably concentrate their attention upon general principles. In this Chapter we set out the reasons which have led us to this proposal and the constitution and functions which we recommend for the Councils.

128. Perhaps the most striking feature of tribunals is their variety, not only of function but also of procedure and constitution. It is no doubt right that bodies established to adjudicate on particular classes of case should be specially designed to fulfil their particular functions and should therefore vary widely in character. But the wide variations in procedure and constitution which now exist are much more the result of *ad hoc* decisions, political circumstance and historical accident than of the application of general and consistent principles. We think that there should be a standing body, the advice of which would be sought whenever it was proposed to establish a new type of tribunal and which would also keep under review the constitution and procedure of existing tribunals.

. . . . . .

Councils on Tribunals

130. We consider that if a standing body of this kind is to be effective it should for the most part be advisory in nature and its advice should be given to a Minister or Ministers. The Joint Permanent Secretary to the Treasury expressed the view that such a body should report to the Prime Minister, on the ground that tribunals were properly to be regarded as part of the machinery of administration and that reports on such questions should be submitted to the Prime Minister because of his general responsibility for the machinery of government. If such a body were responsible to the head of the Government, its reports would acquire additional prestige, and it may therefore seem surprising that we have not been able to accept this suggestion. Our reason for recommending otherwise is that, as we have already explained, we cannot accept the view that tribunals are part and parcel of the ordinary machinery of administration. We consider that they are properly to be thought of as independent organs of adjudication. Therefore we think that it would be more appropriate for the standing body for England and Wales to be appointed by and report to the Lord Chancellor. It should be named the Lord Chancellor's Council on Tribunals.

131. The Lord Chancellor would, as a result of his responsibility for the Council and the somewhat wider responsibilities for appointment to tribunals which we

have suggested should in future be vested in him, come to exercise a supervision over the proper functioning of tribunals as a whole. We recommend that the Lord Chancellor should be responsible for the statutory action to give effect to the Council's recommendations . . .

132. It would, we think, be necessary to have a separate Council for Scotland, appointed by and reporting to the Secretary of State for Scotland. The Chairman of the Scottish Council should sit as an additional member of the Lord Chancellor's Council, and reports by the Scottish Council relating to tribunals established on a basis common to Great Britain should be referred by the Secretary of State to the Lord Chancellor. The Secretary of State should, however, retain sole responsibility for action on purely Scottish matters.

133. We have already recommended that the Councils should be responsible for the appointment of members of tribunals and should exercise certain other functions in relation to the constitution and procedure of tribunals. The main function of the two Councils should be to suggest how the general principles of constitution, organisation and procedure enunciated in this Report should be applied in detail to the various tribunals. In discharging this function they should first decide the application of these principles to all existing tribunals; thereafter they should keep tribunals under review and advise on the constitution, organisation and procedure of any proposed new type of tribunal. We recommend that any proposal to establish a new tribunal should be referred to the Councils for their advice before steps are taken to establish the tribunal. The Councils should have power to take evidence from witnesses both inside and outside the public service, and their reports should be published. All their functions should be statutory.

134. Finally, we turn to the composition of the Councils. We think that in each case there will be advantage in a fairly small body, of nine or ten persons, composed partly of lay members and partly of members with legal experience and qualifications, the lay members being in a majority. We think that the chairmen should be persons who have attained distinction in public life, but we do not think that they need be lawyers. They will doubtless be called upon to devote more of their time to the work than will the members of the Councils, and we therefore think that it would be right to offer them a salary. Some members of the Councils should have experience of agriculture and industry. It is also desirable that the experience of voluntary organisations in the social service field and that of senior retired members of the public service should be available to the Councils. It would be valuable if a place were found amongst the legal members for an academic authority on administrative law or administration . . .

CONCLUSION

. . . . . .

405. We wish to emphasise that, whatever our recommendations under either part of our terms of reference may be, nothing can make up for a wrong approach to administrative activity by the administration's servants. We believe that less

public resentment would be aroused against administrative action if all officials were trained in the principle that the individual has the right to enjoy his property without interference from the administration, unless the interference is unmistakably justified in the public interest. For example, the attitude of an owner or occupier may well turn on whether he receives reasonable and courteous notice of a proposal to inspect the land.

406. We regard both tribunals and administrative procedures as essential to our society. But we hope that we have equally indicated our view that the administration should not use these methods of adjudication as convenient alternatives to the courts of law. We wish to emphasise that in deciding by whom adjudications involving the administration and the individual citizen should be carried out preference should be given to the ordinary courts of law rather than to a tribunal unless there are demonstrably special reasons which make a tribunal more appropriate, namely the need for cheapness, accessibility, freedom from technicality, expedition and expert knowledge of a particular subject. Similarly, preference should be given to a tribunal rather than to a Minister, and this requires that every effort should be made to express policy in the form of regulations capable of being administered by an independent tribunal. We recognise, however, that this may not always be possible and that in these cases the adjudication must be made by a Minister.

407. Where, in the light of these considerations, it is justifiable to establish a tribunal or to entrust adjudicating functions to a Minister we are convinced that an ultimate control in regard to matters of law should be exercised by the traditional courts. We are not satisfied that a sufficient case has been made out for the establishment of a separate administrative court to hear appeals from tribunals or ministerial adjudications.

43 A CRITIQUE OF ADMINISTRATIVE LAW

Extracts from Appendix to *Remedies in Administrative Law* (Law Commission Working Paper No. 13, 1971); reprinted by permission of H.M.S.O. This extract, drawn from a 1969 White Paper, summarises the defectiveness of the remedies available to the aggrieved citizen in the ordinary courts. The Law Commission, a review body which has done much valuable work, had recommended in 1969 (Cmnd. 4059) that there should be a Royal Commission on this problem. In the 1971 Working Paper, the Law Commission proposed that the prerogative orders should be replaced by a single new procedure of 'application for review' by the High Court. Neither suggestion has yet been adopted.

5. Four main lines of criticism of our administrative law have at this stage been brought to the attention of the Commission.

6. First, there appears to be a widely held feeling that the remedies available in the courts for the review and control of administrative action are in urgent need of rationalisation. The procedural complexities and anomalies which face the litigant

who seeks an order of certiorari, prohibition or mandamus have long been the subject of criticism, whilst the circumstances in which injunctions and declarations are obtainable would also appear to call for review. The law of judicial control, it has been argued, is at present at the mercy of a formulary system of remedies. The technicalities and uncertainties, which mainly for historical reasons are a feature of the judicial control of public authorities under our legal system contrast sharply with the simplicity with which administrative proceedings may be started in other systems, e.g. that of France.

7. Secondly, it has been suggested that in our system of pre-decision safeguards our concern for a judicial quality in inquiries and similar procedures, exemplified by the recommendations of the Franks Committee (1957 Cmnd. 218) may perhaps have created a tendency to concentrate upon 'procedural due process', i.e. the propriety of the procedure, whilst giving insufficient attention to 'substantive due process', i.e. the quality of the decision reached. This is not to underrate the contribution to British public administration of the standards of 'openness, fairness and impartiality' strengthened by the provisions contained in and made under the Tribunals and Inquiries Acts 1958 and 1966 and overseen by the Council on Tribunals, in particular those aspects of 'openness' which require policies to be explained and reasons for decisions to be given. Nor is there any lack of awareness of the need to review and simplify the pre-decision and decision making procedures, as evidenced by the recent White Paper on Town and Country Planning (1967 Cmnd. 3333). But it has been suggested by some, including distinguished administrators, that pre-decision safeguards which not infrequently impose great delays upon activities of social importance often fail to secure in practice any comparable benefit in the shape of an effective control over the administration. In particular, the control by our courts in relation to the issues of fact involved in administrative decisions has been compared unfavourably with that which applies in certain other systems. In this connection it has been suggested that the remedies available under the American Administrative Procedure Act in cases of administrative actions unsupported by substantial evidence might involve an elaboration of the records of our administrative agencies which might not be desirable on other grounds. Nevertheless this is an aspect of judicial control which may call for examination.

8. Thirdly, the opinion has been expressed that whilst the existence of administrative law as a separate topic has come to be recognised, we still lack a sufficiently developed and coherent body of legal principles in this field. Views on this matter vary considerably. It has been suggested that we need a body of law which, inter alia, makes the remedy for damages more widely available where administrative acts are found to be unlawful, and which recognises in the fields of contract and tort that the administration as a party is different from a private party and, as in a number of other countries, provides special rules of public law accordingly. It has also been suggested that there is a need to re-define for the purposes of public law many of the concepts of private law, e.g. negligence, including negligent misstatement, malice, fraud etc.

9. Fourthly, the view is held by some that in dealing with administrative matters

our judges are sometimes unable to get near enough to the administrative decision and that one reason for this may be their lack of expertise in the administrative field. It is said that in the case of the French Conseil d'Etat, for example, the high degree of administrative expertise possessed by its judges has been one of the important factors which have given to the working of that Court the qualities which have been so widely admired. It is recognised that our system of judicial control has great effectiveness where it operates, and that it would be inappropriate to attempt to reproduce in this country features of the French and other systems produced by historical factors which have no counterpart in this country. But suggestions for reform have been made, ranging from the creation within the Privy Council of a specialized administrative court, the personnel of which would possess both judicial and administrative experience of a high order, to less radical suggestions for a greater degree of specialization within the existing framework of the High Court.

44 TRIBUNALS AT WORK

Extracts from Ruth Lister, *Justice for the Claimant* (Research Series 4, Child Poverty Action Group, 1974); reprinted by permission of C.P.A.G. This extract from a research study of supplementary benefit appeals tribunals suggests that in practice tribunals operate in ways which do not meet the requirements set out in the Franks Report (see extract **42**).

The central conclusion of this report must be that the three essential conditions cited by the Franks Committee of openness, fairness and impartiality, are not being adequately met in the supplementary benefit appeal tribunals covered by the study. The Franks Committee interpreted these three conditions in the following terms:
  'openness appears to us to require the publicity of proceedings and knowledge of the essential reasoning underlying the decisions; fairness to require the adoption of a clear procedure which enables parties to know their rights, to present their case fully and to know the case they have to meet; and impartiality to require the freedom of tribunals from the influence, real or apparent, of Departments concerned with the subject matter of their decisions.'
  It is important to note that this conclusion is based primarily not on the views of appellants and their representatives but on evidence of the attitudes and know-ledge of those who actually sit on the tribunals. It is the more damning as a result.
  Openness. The question of the openness of the tribunal was not looked at in any great detail. However, two points of relevance did emerge. The first of these was the problem of non-attendance. This was a problem of which members were themselves very aware. The non-attendance of appellants clearly has a very damaging effect on their chances of success and research is needed to find out why so many appellants do not attend. There are no doubt a number of factors involved and some of these will be a function of the openness of the tribunal. The importance of attending the tribunal is not stressed sufficiently in the official form sent to appellants and if, like

the majority, the appellant does not have any help or advice before the hearing, nervousness might deter him from attending . . .

The other point relates to what Franks termed 'knowledge of the essential reasoning underlying the decisions'. From the evidence that CPAG has, it is unlikely that many appellants ever acquire such knowledge despite the fact that SB tribunals are now required to furnish written reasons for their decisions, for it is a rare statement of reasons that actually explains on what grounds the decision was arrived at. The comments of some of the chairmen suggested that their duty to provide reasons to the appellant is not taken very seriously and that they tend to represent an *ex post facto* justification of the decision (sometimes worded with the help of the clerk) rather than the 'essential reasoning' behind it. Furthermore, greater care tends to be taken in justifying a decision to the Commission than to the appellant.

Fairness. There is no clear procedure in SB tribunals that enables appellants 'to know their rights'. Within the framework of very broad regulations, each chairman decides on the procedure to be adopted and, from the comments of members, they appear to vary considerably in the trouble they take to explain this procedure to the appellant. Great emphasis was placed by both chairmen and members on the importance of the hearings being informal, but while it may be desirable to preserve an informal atmosphere, observations and the comments of some members suggest that this informality can jeopardise the fairness of the proceedings. Appellants were not always able to present their case fully and it appeared to be not uncommon for the tribunal to interrupt the appellant with questions which were in any case of doubtful relevance to the appeal itself. Some members were also critical of the leeway given to the presenting officer to intervene in the proceedings when he wished. The fairness of the procedure was brought into question in particular in cases where the appeal was against a decision to withdraw benefit. The tribunals tended to accept totally inadequate evidence from the Commission as justification of its decisions. This meant, in effect, that the appellant was being treated as 'guilty' until able to prove him or herself 'innocent'. A further problem of evidence arising from the lack of any established rules of procedure, mentioned by members of CPAG who have acted as representatives, is its variable treatment. Complaints have been made that documentary evidence produced by appellants has been refused yet hearsay evidence presented by the Commission has been accepted as admissible.

The third aspect of the fairness of the proceedings referred to by Franks, that appellants should know the case they have to meet, involves more than just the procedure adopted by the chairman. Only a minority of appellants is represented and of those who are it is usually by a friend or relative. Statistics show a strong relation between representation and success and this can largely be accounted for by the fact that the majority of appellants, unversed in social security law and the techniques of presenting a case, do not understand the case they have to meet. They have to argue their case against an experienced presenting officer and, given that a number of the tribunal members complained that *they* could not understand the various schedules, regulations and policy decisions quoted at them by the officer, it is unlikely that many appellants will understand them. The case papers sent to the appellant before the hearing are not very full and no attempt is made to explain, in simplified terms, the provisions of the Act. Ignorant of the law and of the Commission's rules which underlie the decision, he is in no position to present an effective counter-argument. Furthermore, lack of help and advice at the point of making the appeal means that the appellant does not know how to word it and this can have important consequences for the appeal's success, particularly if the appellant does not attend. The tribunals can make a decision only on the basis of the actual subject of the appeal; and on the whole, they appeared to interpret rather narrowly what could be considered to be within their scope. Thus an appellant who appeals because he simply cannot manage might lose the appeal for want of being able to specify the conditions under which he might be able to get more. On the other hand, it appeared that appellants who did know their rights could be penalised because they were suspected of 'pulling a fast one' by some members.

Impartiality. The Franks Committee elaborated further on their interpretation of impartiality: 'When Parliament sets up a tribunal to decide cases, the adjudication is placed outside the Department concerned. The members of the tribunal are neutral and impartial in relation to the policy of the Minister, except insofar as that policy is contained in the rules which the tribunal had been set up to apply.' This is not a description of the reality of SB tribunals at the present time. That many of those sitting on the tribunals in the London area are not impartial, as defined by the Franks Committee, is the most serious finding of the study. Commentators have tried to draw attention to various threats to the tribunals' independence but the full nature of the problem has not yet been fully comprehended. Some tribunals are not making independent decisions. They are functioning merely as appendages of the Supplementary Benefits Commission.

A number of factors, contributing towards the tribunals' lack of impartiality have been pinpointed by the study. One of the points that emerged was that, in terms of age and social class among other things, the membership was unrepresentative of the groups appearing before them and of the community as a whole. They had little first hand knowledge of the problems faced by those living on benefit and appeared to be appointed more for their experience of committees than for any knowledge of the subject involved. The attitudes they expressed towards the appellants are probably shared by many in the social groups to which they belong. The prevalent ideology, though not subscribed to by all the respondents, was reminiscent of the old poor law; appellants were categorised according to whether they were considered 'deserving' or 'undeserving', 'genuine' or 'fiddling'. Pensioners tended to be considered 'deserving'; the unemployed, and particularly the young unemployed, 'undeserving'.

Clearly there is scope for extending membership to those from the same social groups as the appellants. But the point that needs to be made here is that while no decision is going to be totally value free, the values of the tribunal members should not be the main criteria according to which the decision is made. From the members' own responses their decisions appeared to be very much the product of their values. Indeed, this is a corollary of their general image of the tribunal as a kind of social work case committee rather than as an adjudicating body. The members lacked any form of training for their role. The law was seen as largely irrelevant and decisions were made on the merits of the appellant rather than of the appellant's case. Such an approach places the appellant at the mercy of the subjective whims of paternalism, thereby denying him the possession of any rights.

A further consequence of the general image held of the tribunal was that members relied on the presenting officer and clerk as impartial sources of information and advice on the law. Because they did not comprehend the distinction between the law and the administration's interpretation of it, they failed to see that this advice was often based not on the law itself but on the policy of the Commission by which they are not bound. Those who did understand the distinction were, nevertheless, often reluctant to be seen to be going against Commission policy. Thus, instead of being based upon an independent scrutiny of the facts in relation to the law, the decisions were often made purely within the framework of the interpretation of the law held by one of the parties to the dispute. The chairmen appeared to dominate the decision-making and members sympathetic to the appellants were impotent for want of a firm knowledge of their powers within the law. It was ironical that many of these were anxious to 'keep the law out of it', not realising that it was their own ignorance of the law that prevented them from being effective in their desire to help the appellants.

. . . . . .

RECOMMENDATIONS

Membership

Appointments. It was recommended by the Franks Committee that responsibility for the appointment of chairmen and members should be withdrawn completely from the Minister of the Department involved and be placed with the Lord Chancellor's Department and Council on Tribunals respectively. Although the Lord Chancellor now nominates a panel of chairmen, the basic control over selection still lies with the DHSS. This is one of the threats to the tribunals' independence raised by a number of authorities on administrative law and their fears are given support by the fact that in the present study 20 respondents considered themselves responsible to the Department. It is important that any threat to the tribunals' independence is removed and thus it is time that the recommendations of the Franks Committee were implemented, though with the modification that responsibility for the appointment of members should also rest with the Lord Chancellor.

Even more important is that emphasis should be placed on widening the scope of the membership to make it more representative of the groups appealing. The net needs to be extended beyond the usual 'stage army' of committee men to take in more young people, women, and black people. A positive attempt should, in particular, be made to involve claimants and ex-claimants who would bring to the tribunal first-hand understanding of the problems faced by claimants. One possibility would be to advertise vacancies on the tribunal and appoint an independent selection board. Another would be to give a statutory right to certain groups such as trade unions, immigrant organisations and claimants groups to submit nominees.

Legally Qualified Chairmen. Some of the main arguments for and against the exclusion of chairmen without legal qualifications have been examined. In the interests of fair procedure, impartial decision-making and the provision of adequate reasons for decisions, there is a strong case to be made for a policy of appointing only legally qualified chairmen ...

Training. Great emphasis has been placed by the Franks Committee and others on the importance of the quality of the personnel of tribunals and of their having an expert knowledge of their subject. It was clear from the study that the majority of respondents did not have anything like an expert knowledge of the supplementary benefit legislation and thus were severely handicapped in their effectiveness. The sheer ignorance of some of the members was startling. It is thus recommended, and the majority of members were themselves in favour of this, that all those appointed to sit on the tribunal should have some form of training. This would cover principles of fair procedure and information about the administration of supplementary benefits but would concentrate mainly on the legislation and the tribunal's powers within it. It should also include some information on the social and economic conditions of claimants. Any training would have to be undertaken by an independent body, for otherwise the members would simply be being trained in Commission policy. The tribunals (and the appellants too) should have access to the relevant sections of the confidential codes in which this policy is set out in detail, but on the explicit understanding that they are in no way bound by them. The evidence suggests that the ignorance of the tribunal members is one of the main causes of their failure to make independent decisions. The provision of training is thus put forward as one of the most crucial recommendations of this report.

The Hearings

Rules of Procedure. A basic set of rules of procedure needs to be established by statutory instrument to ensure that adequate standards are maintained throughout the country. There is no reason why these should interfere with the informality cherished by those who sit on the tribunals but they should ensure that this informality does not prevent the appellant from getting a full and fair hearing. The appellant should be provided with the rules, set out in layman's terms, in advance of the hearing. Chairmen and members would also be provided with them in similar form to the guide at present issued to the chairmen and members of National Insurance tribunals. The rules should establish the following:
(a) the right of both sides to state their initial case without interruption;
(b) the degree of proof required of the Commission in specific types of cases;
(c) the absolute right to call witnesses and present documentary evidence;
(d) the relative weight of hearsay and first-hand evidence and the inadmissibility of anonymous allegations;

(e) the exclusion of all interested parties from the deliberation;

(f) the duty to furnish a clear, typewritten record of the proceedings as is done in National Insurance tribunals;

(g) the form in which the reasons for the tribunal's decisions are to be set out. This should be a statement which related to the relevant statutes the facts and arguments presented;

(h) the rights of appellants who do not attend the hearing.

Representation. If the hearings are to be fair in substance as well as in form, it is important that representation is made available to all appellants who want it. As a first step legal aid should be extended to tribunals, but it must be stressed that this is only a first step and does not represent the ultimate solution which the claims of some of its advocates suggest. If legal aid is to make any real impact, the legal profession must respond to the challenge and broaden its horizons. Tribunal representation should not become the sole province of lawyers, however, and the challenge must also be accepted by social workers and CAB workers. A national representation service is required based possibly on the existing CAB network supplemented by local law centres, though this would have to be extended if the service were to be geographically comprehensive. This service would not only provide representatives but would give advice and help with the drafting of the appeal. A duty should be placed on the local social security office to inform all appellants of the availability of this service . . .

. . . . . .

The Clerk. One of the most urgent questions facing the supplementary benefit appeals system is the role of the clerk. It is not a new problem; it was the subject of much of the Franks Committee's questioning of witnesses and has been raised by many people since. Yet no attempt has been made to resolve the issue. The appointment of legally qualified chairmen and the training of members should do much to reduce the tribunal's reliance upon the clerk for advice, but it is still important that an independent tribunal should be served by independent staff. The best way to achieve this would be to establish a central, independent corps of clerks under the Lord Chancellor's office which would be interchangeable between tribunals and which could also, possibly, be linked to the courts in order to provide a satisfactory career structure. As in magistrates' courts, the clerk would not automatically retire with the tribunal but would be available for consultation. The deployment of the clerks within the supplementary benefit appeals system could be one of the responsibilities of the president.

The Right of Further Appeal. There is no justification for the present state of affairs by which the supplementary benefit appeals system is virtually alone in not offering the dissatisfied appellant a further right of appeal, either to a second tier appeal body or to the courts on a point of law. The only option available is the highly complex and lengthy process of applying for a prerogative order from the High Court to quash the original decision. The evidence presented of the quality of the tribunals' decision-making lends support to the argument for a second-tier appeal body, staffed by experienced lawyers. If desired, limitations could be placed on access to the body, for instance by excluding questions of fact except, possibly, where the decision was not unanimous. Alternatively, the SB appeals system could be brought within the jurisdiction of the National Insurance Commissioner. The implications of a second-tier appeal body go beyond the provision of a further right of appeal; it should do much to improve the quality of the tribunals' decision-making through the introduction of case law and the injection of a greater sense of responsibility into the tribunals. It is, therefore, the most important of the recommendations made.

If it is accepted that tribunals form part of the machinery of justice in this country and are not merely adjuncts of the administration, then they must be accorded the importance due to a judicial body. Supplementary benefit tribunals play a crucial role in the administration of justice for poor people; their decisions affect an appellant's very livelihood. It is thus inconceivable that they can continue to be run in the amateurish way that they are at present. Claimants of supplementary benefit have a right to a fair and impartial means of appeal against the decisions of the Commission. Until reforms on the lines of those recommended above are made, the present supplementary benefit appeals system will not guarantee this right.

45 CIVIL LIBERTIES IN NORTHERN IRELAND

Extracts from *Report of the Gardiner Committee on Terrorism and Subversion in Northern Ireland* (Cmnd. 5487, 1975); reprinted by permission of H.M.S.O. The report was followed by new arrangements for the review of cases of detention (the Northern Ireland Emergency Provisions Amendment Act, 1975) and the appointment of a Standing Advisory Commission on Human Rights. Detention was progressively phased out and ended in December 1975 (though detention powers remain in force), and the Advisory Committee has embarked on a major study of the proposal for a Bill of Rights for Northern Ireland. But terrorism continues unabated, and makes inevitable continued derogations from human rights in Northern Ireland.

Civil liberties and human rights

15. Our terms of reference require us to consider the problem of terrorism and subversion outlined above with due consideration for the preservation of civil liberties and human rights. We have been set the difficult task of maintaining a double perspective; for, while there are policies which contribute to the maintenance of order at the expense of individual freedom, the maintenance without restriction of that freedom may involve a heavy toll in death and destruction. Some of those who have given evidence to us have argued that such features of the present emergency provisions as the use of the Army in aid of the civil power, detention without trial, arrest on suspicion and trial without jury are so inherently objectionable that they must be abolished on the grounds that they constitute a basic violation of human

rights. We are unable to accept this argument. While the liberty of the subject is a human right to be preserved under all possible conditions, it is not, and cannot be, an absolute right, because one man may use his liberty to take away the liberty of another and must be restrained from doing so. Where freedoms conflict, the state has a duty to protect those in need of protection.

16. The European Convention for the Protection of Human Rights and Fundamental Freedoms 1950 sets out in Article 5 the general right of liberty and security of persons; but Article 17 specifically negates the right 'to engage in any activity or perform any act aimed at the destruction of any of the rights and freedoms set forth herein'. Article 15 gives any High Contracting Party the right to derogate from its obligations under Article 5 'in time of war or any other public emergency to the extent strictly required by the exigencies of the situation'. The United Kingdom ratified the European Convention in 1951, and has given due notice of derogation necessary to deal with terrorism in Northern Ireland. The 1973 Act is therefore not in breach of international agreement.

17. The suspension of normal legal safeguards for the liberty of the subject may sometimes be essential, in a society faced by terrorism, to counter greater evils. But if continued for any period of time it exacts a social cost from the community; and the price may have to be paid over several generations. It is one of the aims of terrorists to evoke from the authorities an over-reaction to the violence for which the terrorists are responsible, with the consequence that the authorities lose the support of those who would otherwise be on the side of government.

18. In the present situation there are neighbourhoods in Northern Ireland where natural social motivation is being deployed against lawful authority rather than in support of it. Any good society is compounded of a network of natural affection and loyalties; yet we have seen and heard of situations in which normal human responses such as family affection, love of home, neighbourliness, loyalty to friends and patriotism are daily invoked to strengthen terrorist activity.

19. The imposition of order may be successful in the short term; but in the long term, peace and stability can only come from that consensus which is the basis of law. The tragedy of Northern Ireland is that crime has become confused with politically motivated acts. The common criminal can flourish in a situation where there is a convenient political motive to cover anti-social acts; and the development of a 'prisoner-of-war' mentality among prisoners with social approval and the hope of an amnesty, lends tacit support to violence and dishonesty.

20. We acknowledge the need for firm and decisive action on the part of the security forces; but violence has in the past provoked a violent response. The adoption of methods of interrogation 'in depth', which involved forms of ill-treatment that are described in the Compton Report (Cmnd 4823), did not last for long. Following the Report of the Parker Committee in 1972 (Cmnd 4901) these methods were declared unlawful and were stopped by the British Government; but the resentment caused was intense, widespread and persistent.

21. The continued existence of emergency powers should be limited both in scope and duration. Though there are times when they are necessary for the preser-

vation of human life, they can, if prolonged, damage the fabric of the community, and they do not provide lasting solutions. A solution to the problems of Northern Ireland should be worked out in political terms, and must include further measures to promote social justice between classes and communities. Much has been done to improve social conditions in recent years, but much remains to be done. Though these matters, strictly speaking, lie outside our terms of reference, we should like to see a number of developments: the implementation of the recommendations of the van Straubenzee Report on Discrimination in the Private Sector of Employment (now eighteen months old); further improvements in housing; and a new and more positive approach to community relations. Consideration should be given to the enactment of a Bill of Rights . . .

. . . . . .

148. After long and anxious consideration, we are of the opinion that detention cannot remain as a long-term policy. In the short term, it may be an effective means of containing violence, but the prolonged effects of the use of detention are ultimately inimical to community life, fan a widespread sense of grievance and injustice, and obstruct those elements in Northern Ireland society which could lead to reconciliation. Detention can only be tolerated in a democratic society in the most extreme circumstances; it must be used with the utmost restraint and retained only as long as it is strictly necessary. We would like to be able to recommend that the time has come to abolish detention; but the present level of violence, the risks of increased violence, and the difficulty of predicting events even a few months ahead make it impossible for us to put forward a precise recommendation on the timing.

The devolution of government: Scotland and Wales

'You will never get the . . . separate concerns of the different parts of this United Kingdom treated either with adequate time or with adequate knowledge and sympathy until you have the wisdom and the courage to hand them over to the representatives whom alone they immediately affect.'   (Asquith, 1912)

Dissatisfaction with British government has been most marked in the remoter regions with their own historical traditions. The modest upsurge of nationalist feelings in Scotland and Wales, underlined by Nationalist by-election victories in both areas, stimulated the appointment of a Royal Commission on the Constitution, in 1969, with terms of reference in part 'to examine the present functions of the central legislature and government in relation to the several countries, nations, and regions of the United Kingdom . . . and whether any changes are desirable . . . in present constitutional and economic relationships'. The Commission was united on the need for change, but fragmented in support of a number of alternative schemes (46, 47, 48). It therefore seemed possible that no action would result, but Nationalist electoral successes in 1970 and 1974 left them with considerable bargaining power in relation to the Government's tiny Parliamentary majority. The Government came down firmly in favour of a qualified version of the Majority Report (49), proposing a scheme of fairly comprehensive legislative devolution to Scotland, and an elected assembly with much more limited legislative powers for Wales (only six of the Commission's thirteen members had supported legislative devolution for Wales). The proposals do not go as far as the Nationalists would have wished: Whitehall will still have Secretaries of State for Scotland and Wales, the composition of Westminster will be unaffected by the new assemblies, Whitehall retains powers of intervention in relation to the Scottish executive, and although finance will be allocated on a block grant basis, and may be supplemented by additional local government taxation, Whitehall and Westminster will remain responsible for decisions about the distribution of national resources between Scotland, Wales, and the English regions. The Government specifically rejected the idea that off-shore oil should be Scottish property: 'such a proposal . . . would mean the break-up of the United Kingdom'.

Since the Government has no reliable majority in the Commons, the legislation to give effect to these proposals may have a rough passage, but the sensitivity of both major parties to nationalist feeling is likely to ensure implementation. Meanwhile, it is possible that pressure will grow for a degree of devolution to the English regions, and this belief underlay the interesting proposals in the Kilbrandon Memorandum of Dissent (47, 48).

The proposals for Scotland and Wales contain interesting constitutional innovations, as yet only imprecisely formulated. In Scotland, the Scottish Assembly will
have 'a highly developed system of committees to advise the Executive and investigate what it is doing': these committees will correspond to each main devolved subject, and will also act as pre-legislation committees. The Assembly will be unicameral
and will sit for a fixed term of four years. A Chief Executive and Executive Members will be responsible to the Assembly, but need not be Assembly members,
though they would still then sit in the Assembly, lacking only the power to vote.
There will also be Executive Assistants, who will be 'political in character, but will
not be members of the Executive nor require Assembly approval'.

In Wales, in essence, the Assembly will act as a controlling executive in relation
to devolved subjects, and as both legislature and executive in relation to delegated
legislation over the field of devolved subjects: in short, the Assembly will be responsible in these areas for 'anything that does not require new primary legislation'.
Organisation of the Assembly will be on the basis of standing committees for each
main subject, each subject being the primary responsibility of an Executive Member
(who would be one of the Assembly members). There would be a co-ordinating
Executive Committee 'to draw business together, to ensure that cohesive proposals
are presented to the Assembly . . . to act for the Assembly as a whole on major
issues . . . [and] to settle the allocation of resources between the services administered by the subject committees . . . ' The Executive Committee will be composed
of at least 75% of the Executive Members, and up to 25% other Assembly members.
The chairman will be the Chief Executive, appointed by the Assembly.

It is more difficult to see the implications of the Welsh proposals for political
organisation inside the Assembly than it is for Scotland. For both areas, many
details remain to be settled, but the operation of these new Assemblies will be of
great constitutional interest, and could conceivably influence future developments
in British parliamentary and executive arrangements.

46 THE KILBRANDON MAJORITY REPORT

Extracts from *The Royal Commission on the Constitution, 1969–73, Vol. I, Report*
(The Kilbrandon Report, Cmnd. 5460, 1973); reprinted by permission of H.M.S.O.
These extracts are taken from the Kilbrandon Majority Report; they identify the
defects to be remedied and explain the arguments for and against the solution of
legislative devolution advocated by the Majority Report.

THE DEFECTS TO BE REMEDIED

. . . . . .

Centralisation

1096. The main complaint under this heading is that too much government activity is centred on London, which as a result has too dominating an influence on the life of the country. This centralisation of the ever increasing volume of government business is said to impose such strains on both Westminster and Whitehall that congestion and delay are caused and the quality of the decisions taken is adversely affected. Provincial leaders believe that more decisions should be taken in the regions by people living and working there and possessing a greater knowledge of the regions' needs and interests. They want, probably more than anything else, a fair share of public money for their regions and some means of ensuring that regional as well as national priorities are taken into account in deciding how it is spent. It is argued that the dispersal of government power to provincial capitals would provide opportunities for using political talents which are now wasted, and would help to attract other centres of power, in the commercial, industrial and cultural fields.

1097. Our enquiries suggest that as a counter to over-centralisation a majority of people would probably favour a moderate degree of devolution. But the precise nature of devolution is not well understood, and few people have thought out its implications. It is not, for example, generally appreciated that it could lead to variations in standards between different regions; and whether people in fact want varying standards or uniform standards is by no means clear.

The weakening of democracy

1098. Under this heading a number of specific complaints are made about the working of the machinery of Parliament. They relate to the powers of the Prime Minister, the government and the party whips, and to the role of the backbench Member of Parliament. The right to vote for a Parliamentary candidate every five years or so is said to be no longer an adequate expression of the democratic will. And the drift towards government by nominated bodies is regarded as having gone too far.

1099. More generally, it is felt that government has developed a momentum of its own which seems to leave the people out of account. It is thought to be remote from them, insufficiently sensitive to their views and feelings and too much carried on behind closed doors, and to have enlarged its activities at the expense of individual freedom without providing adequate machinery for appeals and for the redress of grievances and without giving the people effective guidance on how to deal with the multitude of government organisations. In relation to these complaints, most people feel that government should do more to keep in touch with them and take their views into account. A significant minority of people, perhaps as many as a quarter, also feel that they are qualified to participate in government in a more direct way, though there is no clear evidence that they would do so if given the opportunity.

National feeling

1100. In both Scotland and Wales we have found that, while only small minorities favour complete independence, there are larger numbers of people who wish their distinctive national identities to be recognised in the system of government in some way falling short of political separation.

1101. In these two countries the centralisation of politics and government in London is resented more than it is in England. The present extent of administrative devolution to the Scottish and Welsh Offices is not generally recognised; but even among people who are well informed about the activities of those offices and know that, largely through their endeavours, Scotland and Wales have fared better than most regions of England in the *per capita* allocation of public expenditure and in other ways, there is criticism that the present system does not permit the best use to be made of the funds provided and encourage the development of distinctive and coherent Scottish and Welsh policies. A particular complaint is that economic policies designed for the United Kingdom as a whole have been inappropriate for Scotland and Wales. In Scotland another complaint is that Scots law is not sufficiently understood in London or catered for in United Kingdom legislation. There is a substantial feeling also that the Scottish Office should be subject to closer democratic supervision. To some extent there is a similar feeling in Wales about the Welsh Office, though pro-democratic sentiment there tends to be more often directed against the *ad hoc* appointed bodies.

Our general assessment

1102. These, very briefly, are the complaints that are made. Having regard to both their nature and their strength, the general impression we have formed is that, while the people of Great Britain as a whole cannot be said to be seriously dissatisfied with their system of government, they have less attachment to it than in the past and there are some substantial and persistent causes of discontent which may contain the seeds of more serious trouble. We think that devolution could do much to reduce the discontent. It would counter over-centralisation and, to a lesser extent, strengthen democracy. It would be a response to national feeling in Scotland and Wales . . .

Constitutional principles

. . . . . .

1104. We believe that the essential political and economic unity of the United Kingdom should be preserved. Subject to that, diversity should be recognised. New arrangements should be such as will be regarded as a natural development out of what has gone before. They should have regard to cost and workability, and be likely to prove acceptable and produce the results desired. In the fluid conditions of the present day, with a good deal of change going on at home and with entry into the European Communities, there is much to be said for reforms which can readily be adapted to suit changing circumstances. Flexibility is desirable, too, in the actual working of any new system. Government as a whole, irrespective of the form of its institutions, should be democratic and human, should pay due regard to the preservation of the liberty of the individual and should wherever possible be carried out in the open.

OUR APPROACH TO DEVOLUTION

The limits of devolution

1105. To remove the causes of discontent, particularly those arising under the heading of centralisation, most people look to the transfer of power to a level of government in the regions (a term which, for convenience, we have used throughout this Report to apply to Scotland and Wales as well as to the regions of England, while recognising that the separate national identities of Scotland and Wales put them into a different category and that in Scotland the term is at present used in a quite different sense to denote the top tier of local authorities). It was primarily for the purpose of examining the possibilities of such a transfer of power that we were appointed.

1106. In the application of our general principles we have . . . rejected both separatism, which would involve the breaking up of the United Kingdom into a number of separate independent states with sovereignty in all matters, and federalism, which would involve the creation of states within the United Kingdom sharing sovereignty with the centre. We have concentrated for the most part on forms of devolution, that is on arrangements which would provide for the exercise of government powers at the regional level while preserving to the central authorities full sovereignty and ultimate power in all matters. Having examined all the possibilities, we now have to decide whether the adoption of any particular form of devolution, or of any combination of forms of devolution, would be desirable in the interests of the prosperity and good government of the people of England, Scotland and Wales.

The case for and against uniformity

1107. One important matter we have had to consider is the extent to which systems of government may be permitted to differ from one part of the United Kingdom to another. One of the main objects of devolution is to allow policies to be formulated and applied in such a way as to meet differing regional requirements. But can recognition of the diversity of the United Kingdom and of the need to have some policies determined or applied regionally extend to the adoption of substantially different systems of government? Or does the preservation of political and economic unity impose limitations in this respect?

1108. We are not agreed on this. Two of us, believing that all citizens of the United Kingdom should enjoy equality of political rights and obligations, think that all should have the same relationship with government in an institutional sense. They should have equal opportunity to participate in their own government. The political unity of the United Kingdom depends upon this principle of equality of rights and treatment. On this view, if a representative assembly is established in one region all other regions should have similar assemblies, with a range of functions which is comparable if not identical. Rights conferred on one component of the United Kingdom cannot be denied to another. If it is thought to be in the interest of good government under the Crown to have an elected assembly in Scotland or in Wales, it should not be denied to the regions of England. The grant of a measure of self-government to Scotland or Wales alone, with nothing comparable in the English regions, would produce a situation of intolerable anomaly and injustice. If Scotland and Wales continued to have representation at Westminster (as we unanimously recommend) Scottish and Welsh citizens would enjoy two votes — one for a representative in their national assembly and one for a representative in the United Kingdom Parliament — to the Englishman's one, and the Scottish and Welsh assemblies would enjoy complete autonomy in the domestic functions devolved to them, while the English would be denied a similar autonomy in purely English affairs, which would continue to be determined by a Parliament including a large number of Scottish and Welsh Members. The very measure, therefore, which conferred the good of domestic autonomy upon Scotland and Wales would automatically deny the same good to England. This could lead, and would be likely to lead in some cases, to decisions being arrived at in domestic English affairs which did not command an English majority. In the view of the two of us who take the minority view, this is unacceptable, and would be unacceptable to the English people.

1109. The rest of us do not take this view, and consider that neither on grounds of principle nor for any practical reason is it necessary for the same system of government to be applied to all parts of the country. The equality of democratic rights which is a necessary consequence of political unity is seen as relating to the opportunity to vote for those responsible for operating government at the levels where power in fact resides, and not to the number of levels of government provided. There are already wide differences. Northern Ireland, under the new as well as the old constitution, has a form of legislative devolution. Scotland and Wales have administrative devolution, with the two Secretaries of State possessing extensive but not identical powers. The English regions have a far less developed form of administrative devolution, with some central government powers being exercised by regional officials and, from time to time in the past, by Ministers charged with special responsibilities for particular regions. Northern Ireland, Scotland, Wales and England, and sometimes even the separate regions of England, have thus been treated in accordance with their individual needs. These have differed in the past and may be expected to differ in the future.

1110. The system of government that is best for one part of the country will not necessarily be best for another. An important factor in deciding what is best for a particular region is the degree of support that the various possible systems are likely to command there. Popular feeling differs greatly in the different parts of the United Kingdom, and in a country which depends on the contented membership of disparate groups provision is needed to satisfy the sense of community of each group. There is very little evidence of a demand for representative assemblies in the regions of England comparable to the demand for Scottish and Welsh assemblies, and probably few people in England would consider that they had ground for complaint if assemblies were to be established in Scotland and Wales. If such assemblies were considered to be in the best interests of Scotland and Wales there would be no ground either for refusing them because there was no similar requirement in the regions of England or for establishing them in England simply to match what was being done in Scotland and Wales. If assemblies were to be established in Scotland and Wales and this later led to a demand for similar assemblies in some or all of the English regions, that would be the time to consider establishing them. But that, in the view of the majority of us, is not so likely a consequence that it ought to be anticipated by laying down a uniform system of government at the outset.

1111. If different systems of government are to coexist, they must be compatible in the sense that any practical problems arising out of their interaction must be capable of solution. We have, for example, noted the thorny problem of the representation of Scotland and Wales at Westminster if they alone were to have legislative assemblies of their own; the difficulties are not, however, in the view of most of us so great as to make legislative devolution to Scotland and Wales impracticable unless it is extended to England.

. . . . . .

1115. It will be helpful to indicate here in general terms, for each of the three countries, the schemes which have some measure of support. For Scotland there are three schemes, one based on the devolution to a directly elected assembly of full powers in prescribed subjects, including the power to determine policy and to make laws (legislative devolution), a second based on the devolution to a directly elected assembly of responsibility for subordinate policy making and administration (executive devolution), and a third involving the establishment of a directly elected assembly or council with advisory and deliberative functions and some powers in relation to Scottish legislation introduced in the United Kingdom Parliament. For Wales there are the same three schemes, though in the case of the third without functions in relation to legislation. For the English regions there is support first for executive devolution, secondly for a scheme of regional councils, part indirectly elected by local authorities and part nominated by the central government, with advisory and co-ordinating functions, and thirdly for maximum devolution to local authorities together with a system of regional committees consisting entirely of representatives of local authorities and directed towards narrower functions.

. . . . . .

The case for legislative devolution

1149. Those of us who favour legislative devolution for both Scotland and Wales do so mainly for the following reasons:

(a) The conferment of wide powers of government on the assemblies would do much to counter the physical remoteness from government which is felt in Scotland and Wales.

(*b*) It would provide in each country a new focus of political interest and power which would have a revitalising effect on Scottish and Welsh life, encouraging able persons, now attracted to wider prospects outside Scotland and Wales, to remain and work there.

(*c*) If it is agreed that Scottish and Welsh assemblies should be something more than advisory bodies, the transfer to them of full responsibility for policy and legislation on prescribed matters is the only realistic course to adopt. Any more restricted transfer of power would leave the assemblies at all times at the mercy of the centralising tendencies of government.

(*d*) Only in this way can it be made clear where democratic responsibilities lie. In the transferred matters the assemblies would have full power and responsibility, and this would add greatly to their authority and prestige.

(*e*) The Scots and Welsh would not be likely to agree to forgo the advantages which the present Secretary of State system confers for anything less.

1150. In the case of Scotland the existence of the separate system of Scottish law is an added argument for legislative devolution. It produces a requirement for a considerable volume of separate Scottish legislation. Though in many instances the policies embodied in the legislation do not differ greatly from those for England and Wales, separate Bills or parts of Bills may be required and take up a good deal of Parliamentary time. Whether influenced by political considerations, or with a view to saving Parliamentary time, the government sometimes includes Scottish provisions in a general Bill when Scottish interests would be better served by having a separate Bill. The Scottish assembly would have more time than Parliament now has to devote to Scottish legislation, and would probably by its membership, which could be expected to include a number of Scottish lawyers, be better equipped to deal with it. Moreover, some Scottish legislation differs in substance from that for England and Wales, and there is probably scope for greater differences. Scotland would benefit from having more of its domestic policies designed to meet its special interests.

1151. Wales, on the other hand, has no separate system of law, hardly any separate legislation and a geographically less well defined border. Two of us who favour legislative devolution for Scotland regard these and other differences between Scotland and Wales, and the strong desirability of retaining a Secretary of State for Wales, as sufficing to preclude its extension to Wales.

1152. The others among us who favour legislative devolution consider that the arguments in paragraph 1150 amply justify its application to Wales as well as to Scotland. While Wales has no separate legal system, it is a distinctive community with its own needs and interests and with a culture and language to preserve and foster, and there is scope for a substantial volume of separate legislation devised by the Welsh people to meet those special needs. Those of us who take this view believe that a generous measure of devolution, in recognition of the national identity of Wales and as a counter to the growing scale of government and spread of uniformity, would be more likely to strengthen than to weaken the unity of the United Kingdom.

1153. The main arguments against legislative devolution, seen by those of us who do not support it for either Scotland or Wales, are as follows:

(a) The scope for the adoption of distinctive policies consistent with the maintenance of political and economic unity is not large, and is likely to be progressively diminished by the increasing restriction on freedom of action imposed by membership of the European Communities. It would be misleading, and make for bad relations between Parliament and a Scottish or Welsh assembly, to purport to confer on the assembly wide legislative powers which were not capable of being extensively used in an independent way.

In the view of the supporters of legislative devolution the possibilities for independent action would still be substantial. Other member countries have regional problems, and there is no reason to think that Community legislation will not leave enough scope for regional differences. Even if the assembly were to make little use of its legislative powers to adopt distinctive policies, the fact that in the transferred subjects it exercised all powers of decision would be of immense value.

(b) The assembly might sometimes use its powers to adopt policies which, while not unreasonable in themselves, would be incompatible with policies adopted in other parts of the United Kingdom; and the risk of the adoption of incompatible policies, or of policies which were inconsistent with the maintenance of political and economic unity, would be particularly acute in a situation, such as would be likely to obtain in both Scotland and Wales, in which one political party dominated the assembly for long periods.

The supporters of legislative devolution consider that the assemblies could be relied upon to use their powers responsibly for the benefit of their people and with due regard to the interests of other parts of the United Kingdom and of the United Kingdom as a whole; and that this would be so even if, as is by no means certain, the assemblies were to remain for long periods under the control of a single political party. In the last resort, as a safeguard against abuse of the devolved powers, the paramount powers of the United Kingdom Parliament and Government would be available.

(c) Some of the objections to federalism apply also to legislative devolution. Power would be fragmented and there would be an element of rigidity in the relationship between the United Kingdom and Scottish and Welsh authorities which might sometimes be a hindrance to good government. Although the paramount power of Parliament in all matters would be retained, as it would not under a federal constitution, the power would not in practice be capable of being exercised against the wishes of the Scottish or Welsh authorities save in the most exceptional circumstances.

The supporters of legislative devolution, however, consider that this rigidity would be a source of strength in protecting the assemblies from what would otherwise be an inevitable whittling away of their powers through the centralising tendencies of government. At the same time the retention of

Parliamentary sovereignty would permit some flexibility and facilitate the adjustments in the constitutional relationship that would no doubt from time to time be found desirable.

(*d*) Legislative devolution is quite unsuitable for the regions of England, and no scheme of representation at Westminster can be devised which would satisfactorily reflect the fact that Parliament would be legislating for England on matters for which in Scotland and Wales it had transferred legislative responsibility to Scottish and Welsh assemblies. Even if the representation of Scotland and Wales were reduced to parity with England, a serious injustice would be done to the people of England.

The supporters of legislative devolution do not consider that the English people would in fact have any feeling of injustice, or that the admitted difficulty about representation should be allowed to stand in the way of a desirable measure of devolution.

47 THE DISSENTING MINORITY REPORT

Extracts from *The Royal Commission on the Constitution, 1969–73, Vol. 2 Memorandum of Dissent by Lord Crowther-Hunt and Professor A. T. Peacock* (Cmnd. 5460, I, 1973); reprinted by permission of H.M.S.O. These extracts explain the reasons for the Dissenting Memorandum and set out the report's diagnosis of the defects to be remedied. Though this is not significantly at variance with the Majority Report's diagnosis, the Dissenting Memorandum lays more emphasis on the widespread sense of disillusion with government revealed by the Commission's research (see **Part I**) and draws quite different conclusions (see **48** for the two alternative schemes).

1. We regret having to present a separate Memorandum of Dissent. However, it gradually became clear that we were at variance with our colleagues on so many points that no other course was possible.

   2. The extent of our disagreement with the majority can be summarised as follows:

(*a*) We have interpreted our terms of reference as meaning that we should consider what changes might be necessary in our system of government as a whole if it is to meet the needs and aspirations of the people. Our colleagues have concentrated almost exclusively on the single question of devolution – though the word was not in fact used in our terms of reference; and they make no specific recommendation on any other issue.

(*b*) The majority report, we believe, has the effect of magnifying the extent of the social and cultural differences between Scotland, Wales and England. This is partly because of the way it handles in the historical section the concept of 'nationhood' – with Scotland and Wales thus appearing as separate nations with distinctive values and ways of life 'struggling to be free'. In contrast there is no matching study of the more homogeneous contemporary pattern of social and cultural values and behaviour which characterise all the different parts of the United Kingdom. This imbalance, we believe, has led many of our colleagues into recommending more extreme 'solutions' for Scotland and Wales than the evidence actually warrants.

(c) Our colleagues do not give an analytical assessment of the validity or otherwise of the particular complaints about our system of government which were made to us. They summarise these complaints under such headings as 'centralisation' and 'the weakening of democracy'. But nowhere do they say whether in their view the complaints about over-centralisation or about the 'weakening of democracy' are in fact justified. They conclude simply that 'while the people of Great Britain as a whole cannot be said to be seriously dissatisfied with their system of government, they have less attachment to it than in the past, and there are some substantial and persistent causes of discontent which may contain the seeds of more serious trouble'. But unless we determine which complaints are justified and which not, we cannot, in our view, make well-founded recommendations for change.

(d) The principles and criteria adopted by our colleagues as a background to their recommendations are stated so generally as to have no precise implications. Thus they point in no particular direction; they can justify radical change or the maintenance of the status quo. We have sought to bring out the full implications of the principles and criteria we have adopted.

(e) We believe that our colleagues have seriously underestimated the likely consequences of United Kingdom membership of the Common Market. We consider that over the years this will have a major impact on the working of our main institutions of government; we have, accordingly, sought to take account of this in our recommendations.

(f) No single group of our colleagues is presenting a comprehensive scheme for the United Kingdom as a whole which will achieve what we consider must be the three essential objectives of any changes in our system of government:

  (i)   to provide equality of political rights for people in all parts of the United Kingdom;

  (ii) to reduce the present excessive burdens on Whitehall and Westminster;

  (iii) to provide full opportunities for democratic decision-making by people in all parts of the United Kingdom at all levels of government;

  (iv) to provide adequate machinery for the redress of individual grievances.

(g) We cannot accept the scheme of legislative devolution for Scotland and Wales recommended in the majority report. This scheme (akin to the old Stormont system of government) would devolve to Scottish and Welsh Parliaments and Governments 'sovereign' or 'autonomous' powers in a wide range of subjects — with the Westminster Parliament normally precluded from legislating for Scotland and Wales in these matters. We oppose this because

  (i)   we believe it makes no sense today to seek to move 'sovereignty' down-

wards when in more and more subjects it is actually moving upwards —
to Brussels;

(ii) it would be giving to the people of Scotland and Wales significant
additional political rights which would be denied to the people in the
different regions of England (all of which have larger populations than
Scotland and Wales and a range of problems no less special to themselves). This would be the more unacceptable in that some of the
English regions would be providing, perhaps for Scotland, and certainly
for Wales, substantial economic and financial support while being
denied the same degree of self-government;

(iii) we cannot believe it is right or acceptable that the Westminster Parliament should be precluded from legislating for Scotland and Wales in a
wide range of subjects (including education, housing and health) while
at the same time, about 100 Scottish and Welsh M.P.s at Westminster
would have a full share in legislating in these same matters for England
alone;

(iv) the scheme at best would not result in any significant reduction in the
burdens on Whitehall and Westminster; and, indeed, it is all too likely
in our view to increase those burdens still further.

. . . . . .

Our diagnosis of the problem and our basic principles

1. There has been a decline this century in the extent to which we as people govern
ourselves. This has been the unintended consequence of five main trends in our
system of government which, for the most part, are still continuing.

2. First, there has been an enormous expansion and strengthening of the central
executive as it has assumed an ever increasing range of responsibilities. This has been
particularly marked since the Second World War. Then the government accepted
responsibility for the maintenance of full employment and the provision of comprehensive social services. Now we expect it to achieve such general economic aims
as a satisfactory rate of growth, stable prices and a healthy balance of payments.
Through nationalisation central government has become responsible for most of our
basic industries. It has assumed responsibility, too, for town and country planning.
The latest and perhaps most far-reaching duty we now call on our government to
perform is the general preservation and improvement of the environment; and this
has been signalised by the creation of a new 'giant' department — the Department
of the Environment.

3. These vastly enlarged responsibilities of central government are reflected in
the great increase in public expenditure — now rather more than £20,000 million a
year, over 43 per cent. of the gross national product and some £400 per head of
population, compared with just less than £100 million in 1870, when it was 9 per
cent. of the gross national product and £3 per head of population. They are
reflected, too, in the great increase in the number of civil servants employed in

central government. In 1900 there were about 50,000 civil servants; today there are over half a million. The fact that this century the number of civil servants has gone up not less than tenfold while the number of Ministers had doubled has fundamental implications for the problem of democratic control. There is reason to believe that the day to day burden on Ministers is now so great that they are unable to control adequately the full range of departmental business. If this is so the new balance of power gives bureaucracy the edge over democracy.

4. Alongside this growth and strengthening of the central executive, the second main development of the twentieth century has been a corresponding decline in the power of Parliament. Its staffing and procedures have failed to keep pace with the requirements of twentieth century democracy. The development of mass political parties and the attendant party discipline have also weakened the House of Commons as a check on the executive. The House as a whole no longer has the positive share in policy making that was the norm in the latter half of the nineteenth century.

5. Thirdly, there has also been a weakening of the other main arm of democracy — local government. Since 1945 local authorities have lost their responsibilities for a wide range of public services including hospitals, gas, electricity, trunk roads, etc. They are shortly to lose water, sewerage and what they had left of health. And under the new reorganisation of local government to be effective from 1st April, 1974, the number of elected representatives in England, Scotland and Wales is to be reduced from 37,510 to 23,950.

6. Many of the functions taken away from local government have been given to nominated *ad hoc* authorities of various kinds — e.g. Hospital Boards, Gas Boards, etc. Indeed, one of the main institutional developments since 1945 has been the proliferation of a wide range of *ad hoc* authorities. They have not been confined to duties previously the responsibility of local government. Many of the new tasks of central government have also been entrusted to *ad hoc* authorities. For the most part they have been set up in the cause of managerial efficiency. It was felt that this could be achieved only if responsibility for the functions concerned was entrusted to specially nominated (rather than elected) individuals who must be able to operate without being subjected to the detailed control of Parliament or local government. Often the effect has been to make the operations of these bodies largely independent of democratic supervision — certainly in their day to day impact on the life of the community.

7. The fifth major governmental development has been the extent to which the main central departments of government have set up their own regional and local structures. It is not a tidy picture. There is no uniformity, for example, in the number of regions into which England has been divided by departments for administrative purposes. In fact there are some twenty different departmental regional structures — only two of which are coterminous. More important, though, is the extent of this large scale decentralisation. Twice as many civil servants work in departmental regional and local offices as at departmental headquarters. This has serious implications for the problem of democratic control. In the interests of

efficiency departments have devolved a great deal of decision making to their regional and local outposts. There are, however, no regional ministers (apart from the Scottish and Welsh Secretaries of State) to give close supervision to the work of civil servants at these levels. So, in so far as these civil servants are involved in administrative decision making, they are operating without being subject to much close democratic supervision.

8. The general effect of the developments outlined above is that government appears to be, and is, remote from the people. Popular dissatisfaction expresses itself in a number of ways. There are nationalist movements in Scotland and Wales. Everywhere there is a growing 'we–they' syndrome – with an increasing recognition that 'they' control 'us', rather than 'we' control 'them'. Political parties and elections appear to do nothing to redress the balance. Hence people are increasingly alienated from the political process. And there is a growing tendency to resort to direct action as the only means of achieving political change.

9. Quite simply, the fact has to be faced that if we really believe that democracy means that the people and their representatives should have a real share in political power, our institutions do not make adequate provision for this today. And this at a time when a more educated citizenry has a greater capacity for playing a fuller part in the country's decision making processes than ever before in our history.

10. The evidence we received or obtained was mainly a natural and healthy democratic reaction to the trends outlined above. Clearly, there is a widespread and disturbing sense of powerlessness in the face of government. At the same time there is a clear demand that the people and their representatives should have a greater share in political power. Thus, in our view, the essential objectives of any scheme of constitutional reform must be:

(a) to reduce the present excessive burden on the institutions of central government;

(b) to increase the influence on decision making of the elected representatives of the people;

(c) to provide the people generally with more scope for sharing in, and influencing, governmental decision making at all levels;

(d) to provide adequate means for the redress of individual grievances.

In our view all the evidence makes it clear that it is just as important to achieve these objectives for the people in the different regions of England as for the people in Scotland and Wales.

11. United Kingdom membership of the Common Market makes the achievement of the objectives in paragraph 10 above even more urgent and important. This is because the constitutional and institutional consequences of our Common Market membership are so profound and far-reaching. They can be summed up as follows:

(a) important areas of decision making are increasingly moving to Brussels and will thus become more remote from the people of the United Kingdom and their elected representatives in Parliament;

(b) there will be a still further strengthening of the power of bureaucracy, both national and European;

(c) the two points at (a) and (b) above make it imperative that Parliament should become an effective countervailing force — developing the capacity to exercise the full influence of the British people on the decisions made in Brussels. Parliament must be the vehicle by which the will of the people prevails over the will of the bureaucrats;

(d) there will be a major increase in the load on our central machinery of government — on Parliament if it develops as envisaged at (c) above and on Ministers and the central departments of government as more and more major problems have to be decided in a European context and at a European level.

12. In our view our central institutions of government will not be able satisfactorily to cope with the Common Market dimension unless they devolve a substantial proportion of their present functions to subordinate units of government within the United Kingdom. At the same time our Common Market membership imposes serious constraints on the form and extent of any system of devolution that might be envisaged. For example, it would hardly be prudent to recommend a devolution of legislative power and autonomy to the 'different nations and regions of the United Kingdom' in any of the increasing range of subjects where legislative power is in fact moving to Brussels.

13. Before outlining the institutional changes we believe to be necessary to achieve the objectives in paragraph 10 above, we think it important to summarise the main principles on which we believe the restructuring of our system of government should be based. These are as follows:

(a) the essential features of our existing system of government should, as far as possible, be maintained and the necessary changes should be moulded into the existing framework;

(b) any necessary changes should not weaken the political and economic unity of the United Kingdom;

(c) there must be a substantial equality of political rights and obligations for the people in all parts of the United Kingdom;

(d) the basic and overriding principle that should govern any institutional change should be the maintenance and extension of democratic rights and freedoms;

(e) because of the supreme value we place on the individual in a democracy, the system of government must be sensitive and humane;

(f) the different levels of government in the United Kingdom should be linked closely together without at the same time restricting the freedom of the different levels to take independently the decisions appropriate for them to determine. A way of providing for this is to adopt what we have called the 'inter-locking principle' and to devise methods whereby elected representatives and officials at one level of government are able directly to participate in the decision-making process of the immediately superior level.

Our scheme

14. To modify our system of government in accordance with the principles and

objectives set out in paragraphs 10 and 13 above, the first major decision that must be taken is whether or not we need a tier of government in the United Kingdom between the local authority level on the one hand, and the central government level in Whitehall and Westminster on the other. In fact, though it has not been very generally appreciated, we already have a tier of government at this intermediate level. It consists essentially of two different types of organisation:

(*a*)   the direct outposts of central government, e.g. the Scottish Office, the Welsh Office, and the offices of the various central government departments in the different regions of England;

(*b*)   the regional organisations of the various *ad hoc* authorities — e.g. the Gas, Electricity and Hospital Boards etc.; thus, for example, from 1st April, 1974, England will have fourteen Area Health Authorities and a number of Regional Water Authorities.

15. Even with the new and enlarged units of local government operating from 1st April, 1974, it is clear that this existing intermediate level of government is not going to disappear. This is quite simply because there are a large number of important problems and functions which cannot be satisfactorily handled except by bodies operating at this level. But at this intermediate level:

(*a*)   we need in England to rationalise the jungle of boundaries and replace them if possible by one set of standard regional boundaries;

(*b*)   we need in England to create a centre of power in each region comparable with the Scottish and Welsh Offices so that decisions can be taken on the wide range of different functional problems about schools, hospitals, roads, housing, etc., which, together, comprise regional policy and strategy;

(*c*)   we need in Scotland and Wales and in the regions of England to devise arrangements so that the people in these areas can share in the decision making process and hold those who take decisions fully accountable; it should be democratic government, not bureaucratic government.

16. Accordingly, the essence of our scheme is to set up seven democratically elected Assemblies and Governments — one for Scotland, one for Wales and one for each of, say, five English regions. The Assemblies would be elected by the single transferable vote system of proportional representation. They would be given very substantial powers. Thus, these Assemblies and Governments would:

(*a*)   take over the control of, and responsibility for, virtually all the outposts of central government now operating in their areas. Thus, for example, the Scottish and Welsh Offices will be detached from Whitehall and Westminster and be placed instead under the full control of Scottish and Welsh Assemblies and Governments. Similarly, as far as the English regions are concerned, virtually all the outposts of central government like the Department of the Environment Regional Offices, etc., will be 'hived off' from their departmental headquarters and come under the control of English Regional Assemblies and Governments;

(*b*)   take over the functions of the non-commercial, non-industrial *ad hoc* authorities operating in their areas. Thus, for example, the functions of the projected Regional Health Authorities in England will be transferred to, and absorbed by, the Regional Assemblies and Governments; so will the functions of the projected Regional Water Authorities. Similarly in Scotland and Wales; the Scottish and Welsh Governments and Assemblies will take over the functions and responsibilities of all the non-commercial, non-industrial *ad hoc* authorities operating there;

(*c*) be given some supervisory responsibilities in respect of the various commercial and industrial *ad hoc* authorities (e.g. Gas Boards, Electricity Boards);

(*d*) be responsible for devising policies for the general welfare and good government of their respective areas within the framework of the legislation and overall policies of the United Kingdom Parliament and Government and, within the framework, too, of any regulations and directives emanating from the European Commission in Brussels. Clearly, an important aspect of the work of these intermediate level governments will be to draw up and regularly modify as necessary a strategic plan for the future physical, social and economic development of their areas and to decide within this what for them is the right balance of functional spend as between roads, hospitals, schools, housing, water, sewerage, etc. In this general context their duties will not be limited to any specific functions or duties conferred on them by Parliament; they will also have a general competence to act for the welfare and good government of the people in their areas;

(*e*) have some independent revenue raising powers and sufficient financial 'independence' of central government to give them the requisite degree of freedom in carrying out their duties and responsibilities — while still leaving central government with the tools it needs for the overall management of the economy.

17. It is an important part of the scheme that minority parties or groups in the intermediate level Assemblies should be closely associated with decision making at this level. Accordingly, it is envisaged that intermediate level governments will operate on lines similar to the present local authority committee system rather than on the Whitehall Ministerial pattern which denies opposition parties and groups any direct share in governmental decision making.

18. Each intermediate level government will have its own 'civil service'. As with local government now there would be a substantial uniformity of grades and conditions of service over the United Kingdom as a whole; and just as local government officials now move on their own initiative between different local authorities so there would be similar movements of officials between the different intermediate level governments. In our view there should also be a substantial vertical movement of officials between all the different levels of government in the United Kingdom. Thus all posts at all levels in the central departments of government should be open to appropriately qualified and experienced officials in intermediate level and local government; and it should be part of the normal career pattern of the most import-

ant officials at any level of government to have served in the other main levels of
government. This will be an important means of giving effect to the interlocking
principle referred to in paragraph 13.

19. There will be an Ombudsman associated with each intermediate level government. There will be provision for direct access to him by members of the public. He
will not be limited by a narrow interpretation of the concept of 'maladministration'.
He would have terms of reference similar to those of the New Zealand Ombudsman
and thus would be able to look at the merits of a decision and recommend redress
where any decision seems to him unreasonable in the light of all the facts presented.
The ambit of each Ombudsman's responsibilities will need to cover not only individual complaints against the intermediate level government itself, but also against
the local authorities in the area and all those who are concerned with the provision
of public services including, for example, the health service and the police.

20. There will be no change in the functions of local government; they will
remain broadly as set out in the Government's Local Government Act (1972) which
covers England and Wales and the Local Government Bill for Scotland. Local authorities, though, will lose their present day-to-day administrative contacts with the
departments of central government; they will deal instead with the Government and
Assembly in their area. In this connection, it is important to stress that they will
themselves be directly represented in this intermediate level of government in
accordance with the inter-locking principle referred to in paragraph 13 (*f*) above.

. . . . . .

118. Any necessary changes in our system of government should not weaken the
economic and political unity of the United Kingdom. There are two reasons for
this. The first is a historical one. Centuries of tradition should not be lightly abandoned. And in this context it is important to stress that any objective assessment of
the evidence before the Commission inevitably leads to the conclusion that over the
years all parts of the United Kingdom have derived substantial benefits from the
development of economic and political unity which might not otherwise have
accrued. And while the benefits might not have been equally shared among the different parts of the United Kingdom, that is not an argument for breaking up the
United Kingdom into separate political and economic entities; it is an argument for
improving the present constitutional, political and economic arrangements in such
a way that the needs of the different nations and regions which now form the
United Kingdom are more properly and effectively recognised and the benefits of
economic and political unity more fairly and equally shared among the different
parts. The second reason for maintaining the economic and political unity of the
United Kingdom is that to do otherwise would be to seek to run counter to the
main forces of our time. Under the impact of population growth, mass communications, aspirations for a better life, and modern technology the trends everywhere
are towards enlarging areas of unity not towards fragmenting existing ones. The
problem is to ensure that the needs of individuals, nations and regions are fully
served by these larger units and unities whose sole justification, after all, is the
enrichment of mankind.

119. To adapt our constitution to the needs of the latter part of the twentieth century, we have to consider those needs in the context of our system of government as a whole. Such an approach was clearly within our terms of reference. And inevitably, in our view, it involved considering, for example, such issues as the decline in the power of Parliament *vis-à-vis* the Executive in the central policy-making process; the power of the Civil Service in an inevitably increasing bureaucratic age and whether it is subject to adequate democratic control; whether the central government is now unduly overloaded with functions and responsibilities so that they cannot be properly or efficiently performed; whether there are adequate means available for the redress of individual grievances; whether there is too much central control of local government; the extent of the alleged demand for 'participation' and what it means; and so on. In considering such a range of problems the question of devolution and its nature could have been put in its proper perspective. Our colleagues, however, rejecting this interpretation of our terms of reference, chose to put the main (and almost sole) emphasis on considering the case for devolving power from the central government to the various countries and regions of the United Kingdom. This has led them to concentrate on, and to give an unbalanced prominence to, the case for devolution as far as Scotland and Wales are concerned, and to commend it in an extreme form; whereas the case for devolution should have been considered as one (among many other) possible alternative or complementary changes in our system of government as a whole. If there is a case for devolution (as we believe there is) it should be seen as part of a whole series of modifications which should now be made to our system of government. And if our colleagues had approached the task in this way, we doubt if they would have been led to put forward schemes of devolution for Scotland and Wales in such an extreme form, while virtually neglecting the essentially similar problems of the English regions. For they are seeking to achieve for Scotland and Wales by devolution alone what needs to be achieved for all parts of the United Kingdom (including the different regions of England) by a more moderate and balanced form of devolution coupled with other equally important changes. We have, therefore, taken a much broader and more comprehensive approach than our colleagues. Against the background of the present discontents we have considered what changes should be made in our system of government as a whole. In this way we hope that the question of devolution has been put in its proper perspective.

. . . . . .

121. A major objective of any scheme of reform must be to adapt United Kingdom institutions to the consequences of our membership of the Common Market. In our view, as we have shown in Chapter III, Common Market membership is likely to have a profound and far-reaching long-term impact on our main institutions of government. In particular, there will be a big increase in the burdens on Parliament and the main government departments. This, together with the removal of so much decision-making in so many spheres to Brussels, means both that Whitehall and Westminster will have to shed some of their present loads (so they can cope with the additional Common Market work), and also that the nature of the loads that

can be shed is limited. Thus, as we concluded in Chapter III, there is very little scope for any real devolution of any independent legislative power to the different nations and regions of the United Kingdom. So our objective here must be substantially to reduce the burdens on central government so that Whitehall and Westminster have the time to promote and watch over British interests in Brussels — but to do it without any significant devolution of legislative autonomy.

122. There is abundant evidence that even before our entry into the Common Market, Parliament, Ministries and Government Departments were heavily overloaded. Decisions often take too long and frequently are not properly considered. More fundamentally it has meant that Ministers, even though working an excessive number of hours a day, have not had the time to scrutinise with adequate care and evaluate fundamentally all the recommendations of their Civil Servants and thus exercise the full control of departmental and inter-departmental administration and policy-making which a democratic system demands. And Parliament has been able to consider only a small fraction of the departmental policies and decisions it is supposed to control. So, even before the new Common Market dimension, there was an urgent need to reduce substantially the burdens on central government. Thus an essential objective of any scheme of reform irrespective of any Common Market considerations must be that the decisions made at central government level must be limited to those which cannot, without obvious detriment to efficiency and to the economic and political unity of the United Kingdom, be made at a lower level. This will make it possible for Ministers and Parliament to exercise fuller control over central policy making and the work of the central departments of government.

123. Any reform of our system of government must recognise that one of the main developments of the twentieth century has been the vast expansion of bureaucracy. It is an expansion in numbers, power and range of operation — and is the inevitable consequence of the expansion in the functions of government, the growing complexity of the problems it has to handle and the increased sophistication in the techniques of decision-making. And whether these bureaucrats are employed by central government, local government, the nationalised industries or other *ad hoc* authorities, their common characteristic is that they are making policy recommendations or individual decisions which greatly affect most of us in our daily lives. And, as was shown in Chapter III, a likely consequence of our Common Market membership is to increase still more the influence of our central bureaucracy. So a major objective, therefore, of any reform of our system of government must be to ensure that this vastly expanded bureaucracy must be under adequate democratic control. Only if the people feel that they or their representatives control the bureaucrats will our system elicit the maximum consent of the governed to the acts of government. This means that bureaucrats everywhere must be the servants of the people in fact as well as in theory, not their masters. And to achieve this objective involves

    (*a*) reconsidering the relationship and power balance between Ministers, Parliament and Government Departments;

    (*b*) reconsidering the relationship between government at all levels on the one hand, and on the other hand the nationalised industries and other *ad hoc* authorities;

(c) reconsidering the relationship between local authorities and government departments and between local authorities and their staffs.

124. The evidence surveyed in Chapter II revealed a disturbing and widespread feeling of 'powerlessness' in the face of government. Detailed analysis showed it was compounded of three main ingredients:

(a) Lack of effective two-way communication between government and governed.

(b) A widespread concern for a greater share in, or influence on, government decision-making.

(c) Dissatisfaction arising from a large body of unresolved individual grievances against central and local government and the services for which central government has ultimate responsibility – the nationalised industries, the health service, etc.

The institutional changes we devise must provide an adequate counter to these ingredients of powerlessness.

125. Finally, we recognise that any reform of our institutions of government to meet the particular objectives in paragraphs 121 to 124 above, may not, in itself, be enough. This is because the agencies that operate our main institutions are the political parties. It might follow, therefore, that a democratic participatory system of government could be thwarted by the operations of oligarchically controlled and dominated political parties; or it could be that our parties have not the resources to work out realistic and practical policies which they can implement when in office. In any event, our constitutional arrangements cannot neglect the way our political parties operate. Our political parties, no less than our institutions of government, must provide for full popular participation in their operations; and they must be adequate instruments to meet all their responsibilities in a modern democratic system of government.

Our guiding principles and some of their implications

126. We have already stressed the importance we attach to maintaining the political unity of the United Kingdom. In our view an essential condition for maintaining this unity is that there must be a substantial equality of political rights and obligations for the peoples of its different nations and regions. This principle has far-reaching implications. For example, it means that normally in all parts of the United Kingdom:

(a) racial, religious or other minority groups should have the same political rights and obligations;

(b) there should be equal means for the redress of individual grievances;

(c) there should be equal rights to freedom of the press, freedom of speech and freedom of assembly;

(d) there should be available to all individuals equal rights and opportunities to participate in government.

And the justification for asserting this principle of the equality of political rights and obligations for all citizens of the United Kingdom is self-evident if we consider the implications of departing from it. Clearly, there would no longer be any reality to the concept of the political unity of the United Kingdom if individuals in one part of the United Kingdom had significantly greater or lesser political rights and obligations than those in another part.

127. This principle of a substantial equality of political rights and obligations throughout the United Kingdom carried with it, in our view, important economic and financial rights. This is because the ultimate purpose of political rights is to enable people to provide for themselves a fuller, freer and richer life than might otherwise be possible. It follows, therefore, that political rights are a hollow sham if people in some parts of the United Kingdom are too poor or ill-educated to make proper use of them. So the United Kingdom Government must continue to have the obligation of directing our economic resources and making its financial arrangements in such a way that all parts of the United Kingdom have the means of enjoying equality of standards in those services like health, education and so on which are now regarded as a responsibility of government. It does not necessarily follow from this that there will in fact be an absolute uniformity of standards in these matters throughout the United Kingdom. The people in the different parts of the country might wish to re-allocate expenditure between the different government services. But they must have the right to resources which could produce an equality of standards throughout the United Kingdom in those services the government provide.

128. The concepts of a substantial equality of political and economic rights and obligations throughout the United Kingdom have particularly important implications for any scheme of devolution. It means that we cannot offer rights to one part of the United Kingdom which we deny to another part. More specifically, if we think it is in the interests of 'the good government of our People under the Crown' (to quote from our terms of reference) that there should be elected Assemblies with legislative or other powers in Scotland and Wales and thus give the people in Scotland and Wales an extra vote and an extra 'say' in the way their affairs are conducted, then we cannot deny, as the majority of our colleagues wish to do, that extra vote and extra 'say' to the people of the different regions of England. Still less can we accept a second feature in the scheme of legislative devolution to Scotland and Wales proposed by our colleagues. Not only do they want to transfer legislative sovereignty in important fields like education, health, agriculture, etc., from the United Kingdom Parliament to Scottish and Welsh Assemblies, they also envisage that when the U.K. Parliament then legislates for England alone in the matters which have been transferred to Scottish and Welsh Assemblies, the 100 or so Scottish and Welsh M.P.s at Westminster should have a full share in the legislative process for England. While we agree that within the framework of their scheme there was no practical alternative, that does not commend their solution; it condemns the scheme. For it must be completely unacceptable not only to give the people in Scotland and Wales political rights which are denied to the people in the

various regions of England — but, in addition, to give to the people of Scotland and Wales a share in determining policies applying to England only, while denying the people of England any similar share in shaping policies in Scotland and Wales. There is surely a profound irony here; the scheme commended by the majority of our colleagues to give Scotland and Wales autonomy in certain specified fields would actually deny autonomy to England in those very same fields. This is no way to maintain the political and constitutional unity of the United Kingdom. And, anyway, it is a fundamental violation of the principle of the equality of political rights — of the basic democratic principle expounded by Bentham when he wrote: 'everybody to count for one, nobody to count for more than one'.

129. There are two further reasons why in our view there must be equality of political rights in all parts of the United Kingdom and why the people of Scotland and Wales should not have political rights denied to the people in the different regions of England:

(a) The claim to be a separate nation within the United Kingdom (even if it is true) does not entitle the people in Scotland or Wales to be better governed or to have more participation in the handling of their own affairs than is offered to the people of Yorkshire or Lancashire (to mention only counties with comparable populations).

(b) Scotland and Wales, like certain of the poorer regions of England, are now heavily subsidised by the richer regions of England. The concept of 'the right to equality of standards' outlined in paragraph 127 is the justification for this. And it is an essential feature of the economic and political unity of the United Kingdom. But it would neither be right nor just to deny the people in the richer regions of England equality of political rights with the people of Scotland and Wales while at the same time expecting them to continue to provide certainly for Wales and possibly for Scotland very substantial economic and financial support.

130. We have implied earlier in a number of places in our report that the basic and overriding principle that should govern any institutional change is the maintenance and extension of democratic rights and freedoms. This is vital, in our view for the health of the body politic; and it assumes particular importance in the United Kingdom today in view of all the evidence about the erosion of democracy — the decline in the extent to which we as a people govern ourselves. The application of this fundamental principle has widespread ramifications and implications which are developed in the following paragraphs. Here we wish to emphasise that in our view the essence of the principle means that the people or their directly elected representatives must have full control over the political decision-making processes. The more the people or their representatives share in making decisions, the more likely they are to accept them. People who feel they have had an adequate part in the decision-making process do not then usually find themselves as part of the forces of direct action at the barricades. So, in our view, this principle is fundamental to achieving the ultimate objective of a modern democracy — the maximum consent of the governed to acts of government.

48 THE MAJOR ALTERNATIVE SCHEMES

Extracts from *Democracy and Devolution: Proposals for Scotland and Wales* (Cmnd. 5732, 1974); reprinted by permission of H.M.S.O. This extract outlines the two major alternative schemes produced by the Majority Report (legislative devolution for Scotland and Wales) and the Memorandum of Dissent (elected assemblies for Scotland, Wales and five English regions).

A. LEGISLATIVE DEVOLUTION FOR SCOTLAND AND WALES

1. Legislative devolution was recommended for Scotland by eight of the thirteen members of the Commission and for Wales by six members.

General description

2. Responsibility for legislating on specifically defined matters would be transferred from the Westminster Parliament to directly elected Scottish and Welsh legislatures. In relation to the transferred subjects these legislatures would make such laws and policies as they saw fit, and would carry out all aspects of administration. The ultimate power and sovereignty of the United Kingdom Parliament would be preserved in all matters, but it would be a convention that in the ordinary course this power would not be used to legislate for Scotland or Wales on a transferred matter without the agreement of the Scottish or Welsh Government. The United Kingdom Government would also have the power, for use in exceptional circumstances, to determine, with the approval of the United Kingdom Parliament, that a Bill passed by the Scottish or Welsh legislature should not be submitted for the Royal Assent. The Scottish and Welsh executives would be composed of Ministers drawn from their respective assemblies who would then operate the traditional Cabinet system of government. It is the intention that the Scottish and Welsh Governments should have a large measure of financial independence, especially in matters of expenditure, but would be subject to such restraints as are necessary in the interests of the economic management of the United Kingdom as a whole.

Main features of the scheme

3. Legislative power in the following subjects would be transferred to the Scottish and Welsh legislative assemblies:

Local government
Town and country planning
New towns
Housing
Building control
Water supply and sewerage

Road passenger transport
Harbours
Other environmental services (*e.g.* prevention of pollution, coast protection and flood prevention)
Youth and community services

Ancient monuments and historic buildings

Roads (including the construction, use and licensing of vehicles)

Social work services (including, for Scotland, probation and after-care)

Health

Miscellaneous regulatory functions (including matters such as betting, gaming, and lotteries, obscene publications, shop hours and liquor licensing)

Education (probably excluding universities)

Sports and recreation

Arts and culture (including the Welsh and Gaelic languages)

Agriculture, fisheries and food (except price support and some other functions)

Forestry

Crown estates

Tourism

4. Legislative power in the following additional matters would be transferred to the Scottish Assembly only:

Police

Fire services

Criminal policy and administration

Prisons

Administration of justice

Legal matters, including law reform

Highlands and Islands development (including crofting)

Sea transport

5. In the subjects listed above the Westminster Parliament would normally cease to legislate for Scotland and Wales (though existing United Kingdom legislation in these fields would continue to apply initially). But the United Kingdom Parliament and Government would continue to be responsible for the international aspects of transferred matters. It is also envisaged that the Scottish and Welsh assemblies might have some limited powers in relation to consumer protection, road freight, civil aviation and broadcasting.

6. The legislative assemblies in Scotland and Wales would each have about 100 members directly elected for a fixed term of four years by the single transferable vote system of proportional representation, though in the more sparsely populated areas of Scotland the alternative vote system might be adopted. All matters relating to the franchise and to elections to the assembly (though not elections to local authorities) would be reserved to the United Kingdom Parliament.

7. The Scottish and Welsh executives would consist of Ministers drawn from their respective assemblies. Normally the leader of the majority party would be chief Minister (or Premier) and would form a Cabinet which would operate in accordance with the traditional Westminster principles of collective and ministerial responsibility. Scotland and Wales would each have a separate civil service.

8. Scotland and Wales would continue to be represented in the Westminster Parliament, but their representation in proportion to population would be the same as for England. This would probably reduce the number of Scottish MPs at Westminster from 71 to about 57; and the number of Welsh MPs from 36 to about 31.

9. The offices of Secretary of State for Scotland and Wales would disappear, but Scotland and Wales would each have a Minister with the special responsibility of representing its interests in the Cabinet.

10. There are detailed proposals for finance which the Report says are open to modification. The chief object would be to give the Scottish and Welsh Governments maximum freedom in expenditure. Each would have its 'fair share of United Kingdom resources' and freedom to allocate expenditure on the transferred services according to its own chosen priorities. Scotland and Wales might also have some limited powers of independent taxation, and perhaps a share of United Kingdom taxes. But the assemblies' income would come mainly from United Kingdom subventions. They might also be able to raise loans to meet capital expenditure.

11. The determination of Scotland's and Wales' 'fair share of United Kingdom resources' would be in the hands of a nominated Exchequer Board which would be independent of the Scottish, Welsh and United Kingdom Governments. Exceptionally the United Kingdom Government could reject the Board's recommendation with the approval of the United Kingdom Parliament.

B. A SCHEME FOR ELECTED ASSEMBLIES IN SCOTLAND, WALES AND THE ENGLISH REGIONS

12. This scheme of intermediate level governments was the main proposal in the Memorandum of Dissent signed by two members of the Commission.

General description

13. The scheme seeks to achieve a substantial measure of devolution of power from the central Government to Scotland, Wales and the English regions. It could, however, be considered for application to Scotland and Wales alone. Under the scheme the United Kingdom Parliament and Government would remain responsible for the framework of legislation and major policy on all matters, but directly elected Scottish and Welsh and English regional assemblies would be responsible for adjusting United Kingdom policies to the special needs of their areas and putting them into effect. The Scottish, Welsh and English regional Governments would be run on the local authority pattern with a functional committee structure and not on the Cabinet model as in the scheme of legislative devolution. They would assume control of all the regional outposts of central Government now operating in their areas including the Scottish and Welsh Offices in their present form and the regional and local offices of other central Government Departments. Thus these outposts, which employ very substantial numbers of civil servants, would be completely 'hived off' from central Government. The 'intermediate level' governments (*i.e.* the Scottish, Welsh and English regional governments) would also take over completely the functions of certain *ad hoc* authorities operating in their areas (*e.g.* health and water authorities); and they would be given some supervisory responsibilities in respect of the activities in their parts of the country of the various industrial and commercial authorities (*e.g.* gas and electricity boards). The 'intermediate level' governments would not be limited to the specific functions or duties conferred on them by Parliament; they would have a general residual competence to act for the welfare

and good government of the people in their areas. They would have some independent revenue-raising powers and sufficient financial 'independence' of central
Government to give them the requisite degree of freedom to carry out their duties
and responsibilities.

Main features of the scheme

14. The scheme envisages that the broad range of functions set out in paragraph 13
above would be devolved to an assembly and government in Scotland, in Wales and
in each of, say, five English regions. Each assembly would consist of about 100
members elected by the single transferable vote system of proportional representation for a fixed term of four years. The executive of each government would consist of a number of functional departments or divisions staffed by the authority's
own civil servants. There would be departments or divisions for such functions as
Finance, Education, Health and Social Security, the Environment, etc. Each department or division would be controlled by a committee drawn from the membership
of the assembly — reflecting the balance of party strengths.

15. Each assembly would be able to make 'ordinances':

(*a*) to implement United Kingdom policies and legislation and to adapt them to
    the special needs of the area; and

(*b*) to give effect to their residual power to act for the welfare and good govern-
    ment of the people in the area.

16. Each intermediate level government would have its own civil service and a
separate ombudsman. There would be no change in the functions of local authorities, although they would deal with the appropriate intermediate government
instead of with the central Government as at present. They would have direct
representation in the intermediate level governments.

17. The general financial arrangements are outlined at the end of paragraph 13
above. A possible development of these arrangements is outlined in Appendix B of
the Memorandum of Dissent. It is designed to give the intermediate level governments a considerable degree of financial and economic independence of central
Government; and to improve the ability of the central Government to achieve the
major objectives of national economic policy such as full employment, regionally
and nationally, and a satisfactory rate of economic growth.

18. At the centre, the scheme envisages that Members of Parliament, by being
relieved of a great deal of detail, would have time for a much greater share in
Government policy making including more influence on the decisions which United
Kingdom Ministers have to take in the Council of Ministers in Brussels; for these
purposes MPs would need to be organised in functional committees matching each
of the main Departments of Government. The composition of the House of Lords
might be altered to include members of the 'intermediate level' governments.

19. The Secretaries of State for Scotland and Wales would remain as members of
the United Kingdom Cabinet though their existing Departments would be taken
over by the Scottish and Welsh Governments. They would have the special responsi-

bility of safeguarding and promoting Scottish and Welsh interests in all Cabinet decisions. A third Cabinet Minister would perform a similar function for the English regions. There would be no reduction in the number of Scottish and Welsh MPs at Westminster.

. . . . . .

49 THE GOVERNMENT'S APPROACH

Extracts from *Our Changing Democracy: Devolution to Scotland and Wales* (Cmnd. 6348, 1975); reprinted by permission of H.M.S.O. The extracts below outline the Government's basic philosophy, the proposed composition and powers of the Assemblies (which would operate through the existing Parliamentary constituencies and would not affect Westminster membership), the structure and functions of the Executive, financial arrangements, the subjects to be devolved and complaints machinery. These proposals had not, at the time of writing, been given legislative effect.

9. Political and economic unity has been maintained and deepened throughout Great Britain for over two and a half centuries, giving its countries a common history, heritage and way of life richer than any of them could have enjoyed on its own.

10. The Government are firmly committed to maintaining this unity. It is a powerful and constructive force shaping the daily lives of us all; and those who advocate destroying the United Kingdom, for the sake of a real or imaginary short-term gain to some, brush aside the long-term loss to all. The Government reject entirely the idea of separation for Scotland and Wales and the break-up of the United Kingdom, and believe that the vast majority of Scottish and Welsh people endorse this rejection. As the Government made clear in the White Paper of September 1974, they agree wholeheartedly with the Kilbrandon Commission in rejecting also federalism within the United Kingdom.

11. Unity however is not uniformity. Within the United Kingdom Scotland and Wales have kept their own identities, with distinctive elements of tradition, culture and institutions. Respect for these diversities has strengthened the Union far more than an imposed conformity could have done.

12. This respect underlies the long tradition of decentralisation of Scottish government — that is, the practice whereby large areas of government work for Scotland are carried out not in London but in Edinburgh, under Ministers answerable to Parliament at Westminster but nevertheless distinctively Scottish. In 1964 the Government extended this system to Wales; and its scope in both countries has recently been widened by the transfer of new responsibilities in the industrial field to the two Secretaries of State.

13. Decentralisation remains a useful means of ensuring that administration in Scotland and Wales is founded on an understanding of the needs and wishes of these

countries; the Government will continue to use it and indeed in some respects to extend it, as Part V explains.

14. The Government believe however that something more is needed — the creation of elected as well as administrative institutions distinctive to Scotland and Wales. This is what devolution means. There will be new democratic bodies, directly chosen by and answerable to the Scottish and Welsh people for very wide fields of government.

15. The central task on which the Government have concentrated in developing the devolution schemes is to define those areas of activity where decisions affect primarily people living in Scotland and Wales. It would plainly be wrong to devolve to the Scottish and Welsh Assemblies powers over activities which substantially affect people elsewhere, or the well-being of the United Kingdom generally. The need is to achieve balance — to reconcile unity and diversity in a stronger and better system, offering more achievement and satisfaction to the parts while improving the efficiency and stability of the whole. In working this out the Government have observed the principles which flow from acceptance of the essential unity of the United Kingdom. They have also kept in mind the need for a consistent and coherent pattern of government, which will be clear and understandable to the people who work in it and the public whom they serve. The objective throughout has been the long-term advantage of the people of Scotland and Wales within the United Kingdom.

16. Under the Government's proposals, the Assemblies will control policies and spending priorities over a very wide field, including for example most aspects of local government, health, personal social services, education, housing, physical planning, the environment and roads, and many aspects of transport. They will have a very large block grant from the Exchequer and some power to supplement it from local taxation, and they will have the fullest possible freedom to decide how the money should be spent among the services they control. The Scottish Assembly will also be able to make new laws or amend present ones in these matters, and it will be responsible for most aspects of the distinctive private and criminal law of Scotland.

17. All these powers will enable the new Scottish and Welsh administrations to bring far-reaching influence to bear on the whole physical and social environment of their countries. That influence, together with the huge spending power which they will control, will enable them to have a very marked effect also on their economic environment.

18. The new powers will not however be conferred at the expense of the benefits which flow from the political and economic unity of the United Kingdom.

19. Political unity means that The Queen in Parliament, representing all the people, must remain sovereign over their affairs; and that the Government of the day must bear the main responsibility to Parliament for protecting and furthering the interests of all. In particular, the Government must be able to do whatever is needed for national security; they must conduct international relations, including those flowing from our membership of the European Community; and they must

maintain the national framework of law and order, guaranteeing the basic rights of the citizen throughout the United Kingdom.

20. Economic unity plainly means that the Government must manage the nation's external economic relations — the balance of payments, the exchange rate, external assets and liabilities, and economic, trading and other arrangements with other countries. But the principle reaches much further. The Government must be able to manage demand in the economy as a whole — to control national taxation, total public expenditure and the supply of money and credit. The Government must be able to regulate the framework of trade, so as to maintain a fair competitive balance for industry and commerce everywhere. Within the wider common market which the European Community is developing we already enjoy a common market throughout the United Kingdom, and any new and artificial barriers within that long-established market could be seriously damaging. And the Government must also keep the task of devising national policies to benefit particular parts of the United Kingdom, and of distributing resources among them according to relative need. This last point is the cardinal fact about our whole system of allocating public expenditure. Resources are distributed not according to where they come from but according to where they are needed. This applies between geographical areas just as much as between individuals.

. . . . . .

. . . Government cannot shed their responsibility for the interests of the United Kingdom as a whole. They must ensure that they and their successors remain able to act freely and promptly in those interests. Reserve powers are therefore built into the devolution proposals to enable the Government of the day to intervene, subject to the approval of Parliament, in actions by the devolved administrations which the Government judge seriously harmful.

27. It is impossible to predict what situations might lead to the use of these powers, and it is largely for this reason that the Government propose to provide them rather than attempt to deal specifically in the Act with every possible eventuality. Their use should not therefore be regarded as a last resort implying a serious confrontation. But if the schemes of devolution fulfil their objectives, the necessity to use reserve powers should not arise frequently and need not be a source of conflict. The future of us all turns to a great extent upon harmonious co-operation between all the people of the United Kingdom and their elected representatives, whether in Parliament or in the Assemblies.

. . . . . .

B. Constitutional arrangements

31. Many features of the constitutional scheme proposed are modelled on Parliament, where they are well tried and have evolved over the centuries in a practical blend of efficient government and democratic rights. Parliament must endow Scotland with a comparable blend. But the Government do not intend that the new Assembly should be forced to be a carbon copy of Westminster. Within the main

features which the Act must lay down and which only Parliament can change, the Scottish Assembly and the Executive answerable to it will be free to develop their own ways of working as they judge best.

The Scottish Assembly 32. There will be a single-chamber Scottish Assembly, initially with 142 members — two for each of the 71 Parliamentary constituencies in Scotland. There will not be time before the Assembly comes into being for the Boundary Commission for Scotland to complete the thorough scrutiny needed to divide the Parliamentary constituencies fairly. At the first election therefore each elector will be able to vote for two candidates, and in each Parliamentary constituency the two with most votes will become Assembly Members.

33. For later elections the Boundary Commission will divide Parliamentary constituencies as necessary into single-member Assembly constituencies, on a basis which will improve the fairness of the system by taking more account of the number of voters in each constituency. Each Parliamentary constituency will be allotted one, two or three Assembly seats, according to a formula based on the average size of Parliamentary electorates in Scotland . . .

. . . . . .

35. The Assembly will be elected for a normal fixed term of four years, but the Secretary of State will have power to make minor adjustments either way to give a convenient election day.

. . . . . .

The Scottish Executive 43. Executive powers in the devolved fields (including the power to make delegated legislation) will be exercised by a Scottish Executive. These powers will be vested in Members of the Executive, with each of them exercising whatever responsibilities are allocated by the head of the Executive — the Chief Executive.

44. The Executive will normally be formed after each election. The Secretary of State for Scotland will invite a prospective Chief Executive to form an Executive which will command the support of the Assembly; in the ordinary course he will invite the leader of the majority party. The prospective Chief Executive will submit the names of his proposed Executive to the Assembly, which will approve or reject them as a whole. If the Assembly approves, the Secretary of State for Scotland will formally appoint them as the Executive. If the Assembly rejects the proposed team, the Secretary of State will at his discretion invite the same person to try again, or someone else.

45. The Secretary of State will also appoint Assistants to the Executive, on the recommendation of the Chief Executive. These Assistants will be political in character but will not be members of the Executive, nor require Assembly approval.

46. Executive Members and Assistants will normally be members of the Assembly, but there will be no rigid rule about this. Some flexibility is desirable to leave room for possible appointments from outside the Assembly. It may be desirable to include a distinguished person, or one with special expertise (for example in

the law) who is not an Assembly Member; and there will be no second chamber upon which to draw, as there is at Westminster. Political pressures should ensure that the scope for appointing non-members to the Executive is not over-used. The Assembly's right to approve or reject the Executive as a whole will be a strong factor.

47. Executive Members and Assistants who are not Assembly members will be able to sit and speak in the Assembly, but not to vote.

48. Maximum numbers of Executive Members, and of Members and Assistants combined, will be laid down in the Act. The Secretary of State will have power to increase the numbers later by Order. The pay and allowances of Executive Members and Assistants will be set initially by the Secretary of State and thereafter by the Assembly.

49. Changes in the Executive (including dismissals) will be made formally by the Secretary of State on the recommendation of the Chief Executive; Assembly approval will not be required. If a Chief Executive misused his power of individual change to create a whole new team without Assembly approval, the Assembly could pass a vote of censure or no confidence. The members of the Executive will hold office formally at Her Majesty's pleasure, and the Secretary of State could in the last resort dismiss the Executive if he judged that it was holding on to office without commanding adequate support in the Assembly.

50. Any departure of the Chief Executive from office will entail the resignation of the whole Executive and the Assistants. The Secretary of State will have power, without needing Assembly approval, to appoint a 'caretaker' Executive to carry on business until a new Assembly-approved Executive can be appointed.

Scottish Assembly Legislation 51. In subjects not devolved, Parliament will continue to make and control legislation for the whole of the United Kingdom. In devolved subjects however the Scottish Assembly will become responsible for legislation. At the outset the Executive will administer the law as it now stands; but the Assembly will be free to amend or repeal existing law and to pass new laws of its own.

52. As at Westminster there will be two kinds of legislation — primary legislation in the form of Scottish Assembly Acts, and secondary legislation in the form of Scottish statutory instruments. These statutory instruments may be made under the authority either of Assembly Acts or of Westminster Acts still applying to Scotland.

53. There will be no second chamber. Within the Assembly however the procedure for introducing and considering Bills will be very similar to that at Westminster. Having passed through all their stages in the Assembly, Bills will be submitted for Assent by Her Majesty in Council through the Secretary of State for Scotland. The following paragraphs set out the process leading up to Assent.

54. Either the Executive or individual Assembly Members will be able to introduce Bills (though if Bills introduced by individual Members entail expenditure they will be able to proceed only with the Executive's agreement). Any differences in handling will be for the Assembly itself to settle. The Act will lay down in

broad terms various stages for the handling of legislation by the Assembly. There will be:

a. a general debate on each Bill, with an opportunity for Members to vote on its general principles;

b. consideration of, and an opportunity for Members to vote on and amend, the details of the Bill;

c. a final stage at which the Bill can be passed or rejected but not amended.

Further elaboration of the procedure will be left to the Assembly's own Standing Orders.

. . . . . .

56. The Assembly's presiding officer, on the advice of his counsel, will report to the Assembly on the *vires* of a Bill (that is, whether it falls within the devolved powers) when it is introduced, and again before the final Assembly stage; if the report is adverse it will not stop the Bill but will serve as a warning to the Assembly and the Executive. The Government will not be formally involved at these stages, but they will be aware of the Bill and the presiding officer's report and may wish to give informal warning of any difficulties about *vires* which they foresee. The Scottish authorities will be similarly free, if in doubt, to consult the Government informally.

57. When a Bill has passed its final stage in the Assembly it will be forwarded to the Secretary of State. The Government will then consider, with advice from the Law Officers, whether any part of the Bill is *ultra vires*. In accordance with normal legal principles, ancillary provisions reasonably incidental to a main purpose falling within a devolved field will be treated as *intra vires* even though they may not strictly relate wholly to devolved subjects. The Government will also consider whether the Bill is acceptable on general policy grounds.

58. In order to be submitted for Assent the Bill must be both *intra vires* and acceptable on policy grounds. If it contains *ultra vires* provisions, or is unacceptable on policy grounds, or both, the Secretary of State will send it back to the Assembly with a clear statement of the reasons.

59. It will be for the Assembly itself to decide how to handle any Bills referred back to it. If a Bill referred back as *ultra vires* is re-submitted to the Secretary of State in terms still adjudged to be *ultra vires*, he will tell the Assembly so and the Bill will not go forward for Assent. If a Bill referred back on policy grounds is re-submitted in terms which the Government are still not prepared to accept, they must within a set period from the Bill's receipt by the Secretary of State lay it before Parliament with a notice of motion praying for its rejection. If Parliament affirms this motion the Assembly will be told that the Bill will not be submitted for Assent. If Parliament rejects the motion the Bill will go forward.

. . . . . .

62. The Scottish Assembly will be constitutionally subordinate to Parliament. It will have been created by Parliament and will always remain subject to Parliament's laws, and it will not be free to change the devolution settlement. The Government intend however that the Scottish Assembly should effectively assume, in the devolved field, the task of making laws for Scotland. Bills of the Scottish Assembly

will be scrutinised, as explained in paragraphs 56—57, to see whether they are within the devolved powers. The question arises whether, after Assent has been given, an Assembly Act should be open to review in the courts on the grounds of *vires* — that is whether the courts should have jurisdiction to declare, at the instance of a litigant, that an Assembly Act goes outside the powers conferred by the devolution Act. The issue is more than just a legal technicality, and there are arguments both ways.

63. In favour of judicial review, it can be argued that this is a normal and natural accompaniment of the operation of a legislature whose powers are limited by law; that the right of the citizen to challenge in the courts any possible excessive use of power should not be abated; that the limits of what Parliament intended in the devolution Act should be subject to interpretation by the courts as specific situations arise in litigation, not merely by Government Ministers inevitably exposed to political pressures and making their judgements in the abstract before experience has been gained of how particular Assembly Acts will work in practical application; and that excluding judicial review will complicate the task of the courts, which will in any event have to take account of the devolution Act when they interpret Assembly Acts.

64. Against judicial review, it can be argued that its exclusion would have the merits of simplicity and finality and would therefore reduce doubt and room for argument, which might otherwise hamper good government, especially given the unavoidably complex division of responsibilities in the devolution scheme; that the Assembly will be taking over the normal practical responsibilities of Parliament, and the citizen should be able to rely on its laws as he now can on those of Parliament; that judicial review caused problems in the operation of the Government of Ireland Act 1920 and was therefore deliberately excluded by Parliament in enacting the Northern Ireland Constitution Act 1973; and that the three successive checks on *vires* before Assembly Bills become law (see paragraphs 56—57 above) should be a sufficient safeguard.

65. The Government would welcome public discussion before reaching a final decision.

. . . . . .

Delegated legislation 67. The Scottish Executive will be able to make delegated legislation under enabling powers contained either in Assembly Acts or in United Kingdom Acts still in force in the devolved fields.

. . . . . .

United Kingdom Reserve Powers in Executive Matters 71. Paragraphs 56—60 above have explained the arrangements there will be to ensure that in primary legislation the Assembly does not exceed its powers or act in a way that would be seriously harmful. Some similar provision is required to cover other actions — that is, executive acts or omissions. (For this purpose the term 'executive' includes delegated legislation.)

72. There is no point in devolving substantial powers and then maintaining detailed oversight from the centre. The Government could not monitor everything the Scottish administration do, nor indeed should they wish to. Nevertheless the Government must have power to step in where necessary, either because matters not devolved — such as defence — are being prejudiced, or for wider reasons of their ultimate responsibility for all the people of the United Kingdom.

73. The Government will have open to them three methods, for use either separately or in combination:

a. for actions in prospect, whether involving a proposed subordinate instrument or some other proposed executive act, they will be able to issue a direction prohibiting the action or requiring a particular course of action (including the reversal of a previous action), subject to an affirmative resolution of Parliament within a specified period;

b. for subordinate instruments already made, they will be able to make an annulment Order following an affirmative resolution of Parliament. In case of urgency the Order can be made without asking Parliament first, but subject to affirmative resolution within a specified period;

c. for other actions already taken, or for omissions, the Government will be able, if the Scottish administration decline to put the matter right, to resume responsibility for the devolved subject in question to the minimum extent necessary — for the required place, task or period — with power to require and direct the use of the administration's staff and facilities for the purpose. They will do this by Order, subject to affirmative resolution of Parliament. The powers which the Government will be able to take by such an Order will be any powers available within statute law applying to Scotland, though any requirement for Assembly approval (for example by affirmative resolution on a particular sort of subordinate instrument) will be suspended.

. . . . . .

Assembly committees 76. The Government believe it to be important for the success of the Assembly that all its Members should take a constructive part in the work devolved to the Scottish administration. The Assembly will therefore have a highly-developed system of committees to advise the Executive and investigate what it is doing.

77. There will be a committee of Assembly Members corresponding to each of the main subject fields of the Scottish Executive — education, health, and so on. The composition of these subject committees will broadly reflect the political balance of the Assembly as a whole; and they will be chaired by Assembly Members from outside the Executive. Their staff will answer to them and the Assembly, not to the Executive.

78. Before the introduction of major new policies or Bills, the Executive Member responsible will have to consult the relevant committee of the Assembly, except where the matter is especially urgent or confidential. Before a Bill is introduced the committee may discuss its principles and report on it to the Assembly, as a prelude

to general consideration of the Bill in plenary session. The Assembly may remit the detailed examination of a Bill (equivalent to the Committee stage at Westminster) to the main appropriate subject committee with arrangements to associate any other committees whose subjects are affected. The committee may also scrutinise statutory instruments in its particular field. It will have the right to offer suggestions to the Executive, to initiate discussion and enquiries on particular topics, and in general to oversee the work of the corresponding Executive department.

The Civil Service in Scotland 80. Members of the Executive will hold office under the Crown, and their officials will therefore be civil servants. The Government have considered whether these should constitute a separate Scottish civil service, or be part of the United Kingdom civil service. Most of them will in practice be people who are now United Kingdom civil servants in the Scottish Office.

81. The Kilbrandon Commission thought that there would have to be a separate civil service, on the grounds that a devolved administration would wish to choose its own senior officials, might not be content for general personnel matters to be handled by a Government Department, and would want to be able to rely on the undivided loyalty of their officials dealing with the Government, for example on the block grant.

. . . . . .

84. The Government believe that it will be in the best interests of all to keep a unified United Kingdom civil service.

. . . . . .

C. Finance and taxation

93. Financial arrangements lie at the heart of any scheme. Those which the Government have chosen reflect their general approach to devolution recognising continued political and economic unity and the need for close co-operation. Paragraphs 94–100 below explain the basic concepts, and paragraphs 101–113 set out their detailed application.

The basic concepts 94. The White Paper of September 1974 proposed that, as recommended by the Kilbrandon Commission, the financial allocation for the devolved services should be in the form of a block grant voted by Parliament, taking account both of local needs and of the desirability of some uniformity of standards and contributions in all parts of the United Kingdom; and that it should thereafter be for the Assemblies to judge among competing claims.

95. Further study has confirmed that this is inescapable. Economic unity requires a system which considers the expenditure needs of the whole United Kingdom, including the claims of regions with special problems. This requires a decision each year on public expenditure for all parts of the United Kingdom by the Government, answerable to Parliament.

96. In theory one might base public expenditure for Scotland on revenues arising

there. But even if they could be identified unequivocally, such a system would be quite incompatible with distribution according to need.

97. The Government are well aware that the discovery of major oilfields under the North Sea has given rise to ideas of a quite different kind. There are some who argue that oil revenues should be controlled directly by those parts of the United Kingdom off whose shores the oil is found, whatever the effect elsewhere. Let there be no misunderstanding such a proposal — whether its advocates realise this or not — would mean the break-up of the United Kingdom. The Government believe that oil must be treated in the same way as other national resources (like the big coal deposits recently found in England, and the natural gas off its shores) and the benefits brought into the national pool for distribution in accordance with relative needs. Any other course could destroy not only economic unity but also political unity. Those who wish to reserve to Scotland oil or other revenues arising there are in effect demanding a separate Scottish state. The circle cannot be squared: it is not possible for Scotland — or any other part of the United Kingdom — to enjoy rights which can only go with separatism yet not to have separatism itself.

98. For their part, the Government rule out separatism. Even if on a narrow economic calculation Scotland might be better off materially for a time by keeping the benefits of oil exclusively to itself — and such a calculation would be at best highly precarious, resting on limited reserves of a single commodity whose value varies with the world market — the Government are convinced that the Scottish people are overwhelmingly opposed to destroying the Union. The Government repeat their pledge that all the parts of the United Kingdom most in need will receive their full and fair share of the benefits from the energy resources of the continental shelf, which belong to the United Kingdom as a whole.

99. The Government accordingly intend that Scottish public expenditure should be settled as part of the annual public expenditure review for the United Kingdom as a whole. The amount will be a matter for political judgment, on the basis of an assessment of relative needs made jointly with the Scottish administration through close and continuous collaboration. Once the relative amounts of public expenditure are established, Parliament will be asked to vote the appropriate element for the devolved services in the form of a block grant. In 1974—75 public expenditure on the services proposed for devolution was about £2,000 million, with a further sum of more than £100 million met by local authorities as loan charges. Had the proposed financial arrangements been in operation this would have involved a block grant of more than £1,300 million, local authority taxation of £300 million and borrowing of about £500 million. Expenditure on the devolved services would have come to nearly three-fifths of total identifiable public expenditure in Scotland.

100. No neat formula could be devised to produce fair shares for Scotland (and for England, Wales and Northern Ireland) in varying circumstances from year to year. The task involves judgments of great complexity and political sensitivity. Nevertheless, objective information on standards and needs would help the Scottish administration, the Government and Parliament to make their judgments. Various

arrangements might be adopted for collecting such information, and the Government will discuss possibilities with the Scottish administration.

The block grant 101. Once the block grant has been voted by Parliament, it will be paid over at regular intervals during the financial year. Accountability for the expenditure will run not to Parliament but to the Assembly. The devolution Act must lay down certain basic features of the financial control system, but its running will be overseen by the Scottish Assembly.

102. The Scottish administration will have the fullest possible freedom to decide how the money from the block grant should be spent — how much, for example, should go on roads, houses, schools and hospitals, and where in Scotland it should be spent. As the figures in paragraph 99 demonstrate, this is a major economic as well as social power. It will give the administration a powerful new instrument for shaping developments over a wide range of services.

103. The Government's decision on the total amount for all the devolved services will not be a matter of simply imposing an arbitrary figure. It will be the outcome of a close and thorough process of consultation each year with the Scottish administration.

. . . . . .

Taxation 106. Scottish taxpayers will continue to pay United Kingdom taxes at United Kingdom rates, and these payments will contribute to the central pool of national resources from which the block grant and other national expenditure will be financed according to needs.

. . . . . .

108. The people of Scotland may not want to pay more taxes regularly year after year in order to finance more public expenditure than the assessment of their needs in the United Kingdom context provides. Nevertheless, some powers for the devolved administrations to levy additional taxation would give them greater freedom . . . The Government have concluded that the only tax power suitable for devolution is a general power to levy a surcharge on local authority taxation, whether on the rates as at present or on any new system introduced in the future (for example after the Committee of Inquiry into Local Government Finance — the Layfield Committee — has reported). No tax is popular, but a power of this kind would give the Scottish administration a useful degree of discretion. They will not have to use it unless they run into deficit or deliberately aim for a higher level of expenditure, for example to meet some particular Scottish priority for which they judge people would be willing to accept higher burdens.

109. Local authorities, who will run many of the devolved services, can settle their own levels of taxation, so that there will in any event be some flexibility in the total amount available for the services in Scotland. The Scottish administration will decide both how much of the block grant should be distributed to local government and how to allocate it among individual authorities. In calculating block grant the Government will in general assume that Scottish local authorities will receive, in

relation to their expenditure needs and their taxable resources, provision comparable with that for local authorities in England; whether they in fact levy more or less local tax, and are assigned more or less subsidy from the block grant, will be a matter to be settled in Scotland.

110. The sources of local authority taxation will be the same as in England. The Scottish Assembly will have legislative powers to adjust the application of the system of rating and valuation for rating to suit local conditions; but only Parliament will be able to authorise new forms of local taxation.

. . . . . .

D. The devolved subjects

The general approach 114. It is important to recognise what legislative devolution will mean. Where a subject field is devolved, responsibility for the activities of government in that field will be transferred to the Scottish administration. Devolving a subject field in Scotland will not however be like transferring functions between Government Departments or between local authorities; it will mean much more. The present law will be inherited, but the administration will be free to change it. They will not be confined to the activities going on now. They could end these activities, or run them in different ways, or create quite new activities.

115. The Government intend to apply this far-reaching concept to a massive hand-over of responsibility for Scotland's affairs.

116. The Act will devolve certain subjects; anything not shown as devolved will remain the direct responsibility of the Government and Parliament as at present. The Government have in general approached the task of deciding which subjects to devolve from the positive standpoint of devolving wherever possible, and keeping subjects back (or making exceptions within subjects otherwise devolved) only where there is cogent reason for doing so — for example where devolution might risk damaging basic unity and the fundamental rights of United Kingdom citizenship, or where wider uniformity is plainly needed, or where devolving or dividing a subject would be very awkward to work.

117. Paragraphs 119—168 below set out the effect of applying this approach, and Appendix D gives a tabular summary. The Government believe that the result is well suited to the interests of Scotland and of the United Kingdom as a whole, and that the scale and character of the devolved responsibilities will enable the Scottish administration to take a broad and comprehensive view of their tasks in serving the people of Scotland.

118. The responsibilities to be transferred on devolution in the various fields will be those which the Government now carry. The proposals do not entail any removal of current tasks or powers from local government.

Local government 119. Responsibility for central government supervision of most aspects of local government in Scotland will be devolved. The administration will oversee the work of local authorities in devolved matters, will allocate rate support grant to them, will control their capital investment in the devolved fields and will be responsible for the application of the local taxation system, as explained in paragraphs 109–110. The devolution Act will not change local government structure. The Government believe that it would not be in the interests of either the Assembly or Scottish local government for the new structure of local authorities and the distribution of functions among them to be radically revised again in the next few years. These must however be matters in future for the Assembly; and it will be empowered to legislate on local government administrative and electoral boundaries, the detailed application of the rating system and the division of devolved functions between local authorities and the Scottish Executive, as well as on the structure of local government itself.

120. Responsibility will not be devolved for determining the qualifications for voting in local government elections; the qualifications and disqualifications for membership of local authorities; the voting system for local government elections; and the frequency with which they are held. These basic democratic features of the local government system should remain under the direct authority of Parliament.

121. The Scottish administration will not of course be responsible for any functions which Scottish local authorities continue to carry out in matters not devolved; the responsibilities of central and local government in these matters will not be changed by the Act.

. . . . . .

PART IV: WALES

A. The background to devolution in Wales

172. Wales has been politically united with England for much longer than has Scotland, and has been more closely associated in matters of law and administration. Nevertheless, the distinctive traditions and needs of Wales have led to increasing pressure for separate governmental arrangements. More and more government work has been moved to Wales, and more and more bodies set up to deal with Welsh problems. In 1951 the office of Minister for Welsh Affairs was created and allocated to the Home Secretary alongside his other duties; and in 1964 the Government appointed the first Secretary of State for Wales. The work of his department, the Welsh Office, now covers such matters as housing and local government, some industrial development functions, town and country planning, highways, health, personal social services, and primary and secondary education; and he shares responsibility for agricultural policy and its execution. The Secretary of State also has a general role of keeping in touch with government work in Wales that is not his executive responsibility, and representing Wales's interests. This is particularly important in the economic field.

173. The presence of the Secretary of State in the Cabinet and Welsh Office representation on interdepartmental committees has brought great advantages to Wales. These advantages must not be lost. The Secretary of State will carry out

many important functions. But a Welsh Assembly is needed to administer a wide range of other major matters, so as to make government in Wales more open and more directly accountable to the Welsh people, and to preserve and foster the rich national heritage of the Principality.

174. Plans for the Welsh Assembly represent a major advance from the present position. That position is however not the same as in Scotland. There is no separate legal system and therefore no general problem about distinctive legislation needed for Wales. Moreover, the Government's consultations suggest that whereas public opinion in Scotland favours a legislative assembly, the situation in Wales is different. The desire is for better democratic control over the government already carried out in Wales, particularly by non-elected bodies.

175. The Government have therefore decided in favour of a Welsh Assembly with very substantial policy-making and executive powers and wide responsibility for democratic oversight. The Government believe that such a body will meet the needs and aspirations of the great majority of the people of Wales.

. . . . . .

B. Constitutional arrangements

The Welsh Assembly 177. There will be a single-chamber Welsh Assembly, initially with 72 members — two for each of the 36 Parliamentary constituencies in Wales. At the first election each elector will be able to vote for two candidates, and in each Parliamentary constituency the two with most votes will become Assembly Members. For later elections the Boundary Commission for Wales will divide Parliamentary constituencies as necessary into single-member Assembly constituencies. Each Parliamentary constituency will be allotted one, two or three Assembly seats, according to a formula based on the average size of Parliamentary electorates in Wales . . .

. . . . . .

179. The Assembly will be elected for a normal fixed term of four years, but the Secretary of State will have power to make minor adjustments either way to give a convenient election day.

. . . . . .

187. The use of the Welsh language in Assembly proceedings and working documents will be for the Assembly itself to decide.

Executive powers and Committees of the Welsh Assembly

188. Executive powers in the devolved matters will be vested in the Assembly as a corporate body (and a Crown body). This means that there will not be a sharp distinction between an Executive sponsoring policies and an Assembly discussing and questioning these policies. Instead all policy discussion and decision making will rest with the Assembly itself. Most of its work however will be carried out through standing committees set up to deal with particular devolved subjects, like health and education. The Assembly's powers will be exercised (like the Secretary of State's now)

in a variety of ways — political or administrative decision, the issuing of circulars, resolutions of the Assembly or committees, and delegated legislation.

189. This system, which is well suited to a body which will not have to deal with primary legislation, will allow wide democratic participation in making decisions, since all Members will have a positive role. The detailed pattern will to a great extent be for the Assembly itself to decide, but the Act will lay down the general framework.

190. The Act will empower the Assembly to delegate its functions to the committees. The Assembly will be required to set up committees to cover all the main devolved subjects, and to ensure that representation on the committees is broadly based, so as to reflect the political balance in the Assembly.

191. Each subject committee will have a chairman, to conduct the business impartially; there will also be a leader (to be known as the Executive Member), who will take the main initiative on policy and administration and will be the main link with the officials working on the committee's particular subject. A committee will be able to delegate powers to sub-committees or to the Executive Member.

192. The committee chairmen and the Executive Members will be appointed by the Assembly.

193. There will be a central co-ordinating committee (to be known as the Executive Committee) to oversee general policy and the allocation of resources. This will provide a body of manageable size to draw business together, to ensure that cohesive proposals are presented to the Assembly and to act for the Assembly as a whole on major issues affecting several subjects, including discussion with the Government on the size of the block grant.

194. The Executive Committee will comprise all the Executive Members from the major subject committees plus any other members (not exceeding a quarter of the total) specially appointed by the Assembly. The Assembly will also appoint the chairman, to be known as the Chief Executive. There will be no formal limits on the powers of the Executive Committee; but its main purpose will be to settle the allocation of resources between the services administered by the subject committees, and to see that policies are consistent.

. . . . . .

Legislation for Wales 196. Parliament will continue to legislate for Wales in the devolved subjects as well as in others. The Welsh Assembly will therefore work within the limits of Westminster Acts. But in controlling the devolved services it will take over whatever powers those Acts confer on central government, including the power to make delegated legislation.

197. This division of responsibility for primary legislation and for execution presents some problems. The formal position is quite clear: the Assembly will in general be able to do anything in relation to devolved matters that does not require new primary legislation. This means that its powers will vary from service to service, depending on how far primary legislation lays down detailed requirements. In some subjects Westminster Acts are in fairly general terms, leaving plenty of scope for

discretion in day-to-day administration; in others they are drawn more tightly. So the degree of freedom which the Assembly will enjoy at the start of its life will to some extent be uneven.

. . . . . .

Delegated legislation 201. In devolved matters the Welsh Assembly will have general responsibility for framing and passing delegated legislation under powers conferred by existing or future Acts of Parliament. There may be some exceptions, but they will be few. In general, the Welsh Assembly will deal with all classes of delegated legislation.

202. Where an Act applying to a devolved field lays down, in order to control expenditure, that delegated legislation shall be made jointly by two or more Ministers or with the consent of the Treasury or the Civil Service Department, the power to make instruments will pass simply to the Assembly. Where an Act confers a power exercisable by Order in Council, that power will become exercisable by Order of the Assembly.

. . . . . .

204. All delegated legislation which at Westminster would be subject to the affirmative or negative resolution procedure will require a resolution by the Welsh Assembly in plenary session. Some provision will be needed to enable subject committees to act, and report back later to the full Assembly, in specially urgent cases. The committees will in any case play an important part in framing statutory instruments and considering their merits.

205. Some equivalent is required also to Westminster's Joint Committee on Statutory Instruments. The Assembly will therefore be required to set up, for the general scrutiny of secondary legislation, a committee broadly representative of the Assembly as a whole and not including any member of the Executive Committee. The committee will thus be as independent as possible of those primarily responsible for promoting the statutory instruments which it will examine.

. . . . . .

C. Financial arrangements

222. Paragraphs 94–100 above explain the basic concepts for the financial arrangements underpinning devolution. These concepts are the same for Wales as for Scotland. Paragraphs 223–232 below set out their detailed application to Wales.

The block grant 223. Central governmental finance for the devolved services will be provided essentially by block grant voted by Parliament. The Assembly will have the fullest possible freedom to decide how the money should be spent — how much, for example, should go on roads, houses, schools and hospitals, and where in Wales it should be spent. This is a major economic as well as social power, and will give the Assembly a powerful new instrument for shaping developments over a wide range of services. In 1974–75 public expenditure on the services propsed for devolution was more than £850 million with a further sum of £60 million met by local authorities as loan charges. Had the proposed financial arrangements been in operation this would have involved a block grant of about £650 million, local authority taxation of £90 million and borrowing of about £170 million. Expenditure on the devolved services would have come to more than half of total identifiable public expenditure in Wales.

224. The Government's decision on the total amount for all the devolved services will not be a matter of simply imposing an arbitrary figure; it will be the outcome of a close and thorough process of discussion each year with the Assembly . . .

225. The Assembly will base its proposals on its view of Welsh needs in the devolved fields. But the Government must take account also of other needs, both elsewhere in the United Kingdom and in non-devolved fields within Wales. All these needs must then be related to what the United Kingdom can afford for public expenditure against other claims, including the balance of payments, private investment and private consumption, as well as the needs of public industries such as coal and steel which will continue to be very important to Wales.

. . . . . .

Taxation 227. Welsh taxpayers will continue to pay United Kingdom taxes at United Kingdom rates, and these payments will contribute to the central pool of national resources from which the block grant and other national expenditure will be financed according to needs.

228. Local authorities, who will run many of the devolved services, can settle their own levels of taxation, so that there will be some flexibility in the total amount available for the services in Wales. The Assembly will decide both how much of the block grant should be distributed to local government and how to allocate it among individual authorities. In calculating the block grant the Government will in general assume that Welsh local authorities will receive, in relation to their expenditure needs and their taxable resources, provision comparable with that for local authorities in England; whether they in fact levy more or less local tax, and are assigned more or less subsidy from the block grant, will be a matter to be settled in Wales.

229. The Assembly will have an optional power to make a surcharge on local authority taxation; but it will not have to use this unless it runs into deficit or deliberately aims for a higher level of expenditure, for example to meet some particular Welsh priority for which it judges people would be willing to accept higher burdens.

. . . . . .

COMPLAINTS MACHINERY IN SCOTLAND AND WALES

1. The existing complaints machinery (the 'Ombudsman' system) is an important protection for the citizen, and the Government will establish comparable machinery

to investigate complaints of maladministration by the Scottish and Welsh administrations in the devolved fields.

2. Scottish and Welsh Assembly Commissioners will be appointed by Her Majesty. Action will be initiated by a complaint to an Assembly Member which will then be passed to the Commissioner; in Wales, where the Assembly will be the executive and can itself be the body complained against, there will be additional provision for the Commissioner to accept a complaint direct from the public where an Assembly Member has declined to pass it on.

3. Subject to exclusions comparable to those applying to the Parliamentary Commissioner, the Scottish Assembly Commissioner will be able to investigate any action taken in the exercise of administrative functions by a department serving the Scottish Executive. The Welsh Assembly Commissioner will have a similar power in relation to action taken by or on behalf of the Welsh Assembly by Members, committees, or officers.

4. The Commissioners will make periodic general reports to the Assemblies. They will also be able to make special reports, for example on cases where the injustice has not been or will not be remedied.

5. The investigation of complaints about the activities of the Scottish and Welsh Offices and other Government Departments will remain the responsibility of the Parliamentary Commissioner.

6. Where a Government Department or one of the devolved administrations is acting as agent for the other, or where a complaint covers both devolved and non-devolved matters, the Government Department's actions will be investigated by the Parliamentary Commissioner and the administration's action by the appropriate Assembly Commissioner.

7. The complaints machinery for the health service in Scotland and Wales will continue, but with procedural modifications so that the Commissioners report to the devolved administrations. The complaints machinery for local government in Scotland and Wales will continue as at present.

8. Legislative responsibility for all these Commissioners will remain with Parliament. In the longer term, when the Government and the devolved administrations have had some experience of operating after devolution, there may be scope for them, in collaboration, to consider streamlining the present system.

. . . . . .

OUTLINE OF SUBJECT FIELDS TO BE DEVOLVED

Notes: a. The references to the main matters are to the functions as they exist now. The Scottish Assembly will be able to legislate to develop new or to modify or abolish existing functions within devolved fields. In Wales the Assembly will be able to act within the framework established by Acts of Parliament . . .

1. Local government The main devolved matters will be:

    i.   the general supervision of local government, including (in Scotland) the allocation among local authorities of functions in devolved fields and local government structure and administrative and electoral areas and boundaries;

   ii.   the financial arrangements of local government, including the amount and distribution of rate support grant, the approval of capital investment and the detailed application of the local tax system. (Power to legislate on the sources of local taxes and on borrowing will not be devolved.)

2. Health The main devolved matters will be:

    i.   the structure and operation of the National Health Service;

   ii.   policy on private practice (including its supervision) and private hospital facilities;

   iii.   general health matters, such as the prevention and notification of infectious diseases and control of nursing homes;

   iv.   policy on such matters as abortion and the use of dead bodies and organs;

    v.   radiological protection.

3. Personal social services (in Scotland, Social Work) The main devolved matters will be:

    i.   care and support of children (including the supervision of children who have been before the courts and, in Scotland, Children's Hearings), the handicapped and the elderly, and other groups in need of special care or support such as drug addicts and alcoholics;

   ii.   supervision of the standards of private provision in these fields, and grants to voluntary bodies.

4. Education and the arts The main devolved matters will be:

    i.   schools, including organisation, attendance requirements and curricula;

   ii.   further and higher education, except universities;

   iii.   certain awards to students;

   iv.   adult education;

    v.   youth and community services;

   vi.   national and local museums and libraries;

  vii.   the arts.

5. Housing The main devolved matters will be:

    i.   the provision, upkeep and improvement of housing accommodation by private owners and public authorities;

   ii.   public sector housing finance; subsidies to local authorities and housing associations; and control of rents in the public and private sectors.

6. Physical planning and the environment The main devolved matters will be:

    i.   land use and development, including protection of countryside amenity and landscape;

  ii. most executive aspects of the community land scheme;

 iii. environmental improvement, and rehabilitation of derelict land (including all the environmental functions of the Scottish and Welsh Development Agencies);

 iv. water, river management, arterial drainage and flooding, sewerage and sewage disposal and water recreation and amenity planning;

  v. new towns;

 vi. other environmental functions, including

    a. allotments

    b. ancient monuments and historic buildings

    c. buildings: design and construction standards and building regulations

    d. burial and cremation; and provision of mortuaries

    e. commons registration and management (applicable only to Wales)

    f. markets and fairs

    g. national parks (applicable only to Wales)

    h. protection of the environment generally, including the prevention of nuisances and control of noise and pollution of the atmosphere (except in relation to aircraft, motor vehicles and ships)

    i. provision and protection of public and civic amenities

    j. refuse collection and disposal

    k. sport and recreation, including the provision of parks and open spaces.

7. Roads and transport The main devolved matters will be:

   i. roads (including motorways) – planning, construction and standards;

  ii. the local application of rules for the management of road traffic (except on motorways) and, in Wales, the authorisation of bilingual traffic signs;

 iii. road safety publicity;

 iv. road service licensing, the appointment of Traffic Commissioners and appeals from Traffic Commissioners in cases involving services wholly within Scotland or Wales;

  v. local transport planning (including in Wales powers, concurrent with those exercised by local authorities, for the Assembly to subsidise bus and rail passenger services);

 vi. bus and shipping services operated by the Scottish Transport Group;

 vii. payment of new bus grants;

viii. payment of bus fuel duty rebate;

 ix. subsidies for Scottish internal air and shipping services;

  x. local authority airports (arrangements for devolving other publicly-owned airports in Scotland will be discussed with the Scottish administration);

 xi. inland waterways.

8. Development and industry The main devolved matters will be:

   i. factory building by the Scottish and Welsh Development Agencies and the

Highlands and Islands Development Board, new town corporations and local authorities (subject to Government control of the terms of disposal);

ii.   all other functions of the Highlands and Islands Development Board (subject to retention of the Board and to Government control in certain fields).

9. Natural resources The main devolved matters will be:

i.   forestry functions, except for fiscal, regulatory and international aspects, and subject to retention of the Forestry Commission;

ii.   management of the agricultural estates now vested in the Secretaries of State for Scotland and Wales;

iii.   smallholdings;

iv.   crofting (Scotland only);

v.   agricultural landlord/tenant relationships;

vi.   improvement of fisheries harbours (Scotland only);

vii.   freshwater fisheries.

10. Scottish law functions The main devolved matters will be:

i.   as much of private law as proves on further study, to be compatible with consistency in matters of wider United Kingdom interest, including the maintenance of a common framework for trade;

ii.   the general criminal law (except for offences concerning the security of the state, matters for which uniformity is important — eg explosives, firearms and dangerous drugs and poisons — and matters relating to subject fields which will not be devolved, such as tax and motoring offences);

iii.   the treatment of offenders;

iv.   executive responsibility for the Scottish Law Commission.

Responsibility for the supreme courts, the sheriff courts, the district courts and related matters needs further consideration.

11. Tourism Responsibility for tourism in Scotland and Wales will be devolved, subject to the retention of the British Tourist Authority for overseas promotion.

12. Other matters The devolved matters will include:

i.   fire services;

ii.   miscellaneous regulatory functions: licensing of taxis, liquor and places of entertainment; shop hours;

iii.   betting, gaming and lotteries;

iv.   the fixing of public holidays and summer time;

v.   registration of births, marriages and deaths;

vi.   records and archives;

vii.   byelaws in devolved fields.

The devolution of government: Northern Ireland

'Ireland does not enjoy the advantages of the British Constitution, nor the free principles of the English Law.'

(Isaac Butt, 1874)

Devolution is not a concept that is new to British constitutional thought; Northern Ireland provided an example long before the debate on Scotland and Wales. But devolution there was a response to the particular historical problem of the Irish question, and the continuation of political divisions rooted both in that historical context and in religious differences makes Northern Ireland so different from Scotland and Wales as to offer little real contribution to the current devolution debate. But it does underline three points. First, that serious political divisions in the devolved legislature can prejudice the acceptability of legislative and executive devolution; secondly, that Westminster always retains the ability to vary devolution arrangements or suspend devolution altogether; thirdly, that constitutional arrangements ultimately depend upon widespread agreement in a society about their nature and operation. If parts of the society feel that constitutional rules are framed to their disadvantage, they will feel impelled to resort to unconstitutional actions. Constitutions are only as strong, or as weak, as the degree of political consensus in the system.

In consequence of a breakdown in this consensus in Northern Ireland, and a related breakdown in law and order, the British Government suspended Stormont (the Northern Ireland Government and Parliament) in May 1972, reverting to direct rule from Westminster. Since then, constant attempts have been made to negotiate a return to devolved government, albeit in a form which would better reflect political realities than the original system. In the process, several constitutional innovations were attempted in the search for a formula which would command general acceptance, and the opportunity was taken to correct past abuses. Local government was reorganised and, in effect, lost many of its former powers; housing, education and other significant social services were taken out of direct control by elected local representatives; elections both to the new local authorities and to a new Assembly in 1973 were held under the single transferable vote method of proportional representation; a new power-sharing executive was briefly formed under a new Constitution in which, however, the Northern Ireland executive was more subordinate to Westminster/Whitehall (in the person of the Secretary of State for Northern Ireland) than under the original arrangements. But the power-sharing executive did not involve the less moderate 'loyalist' Unionists, who in the February 1974 General Election demonstrated, by winning all except one of the Northern Ireland seats in the British Parliament, that they reflected majority opinion in

Northern Ireland. This political inbalance quickly undermined the existing arrangements, and enforced a return to direct rule in May 1974 (**50**). The British Government continued to search for an acceptable formula, but were insistent that any solution must satisfy criteria fundamental to any system of devolution (**51**). The system of government established by the Northern Ireland (Constitution) Act 1973 remained in force, except for the suspension of the provisions dealing with the Assembly and the Administration (**50, 52**). The British Government next decided to form a Constitutional Convention as a means of obtaining a constitutional settlement agreed by Northern Ireland political representatives (**53**). The elections to this Convention, on a single transferable vote basis, gave a clear overall majority to the loyalist coalition (the United Ulster Unionist Coalition) with the Social Democratic Labour Party as the largest single minority party. Not surprisingly, the political majority had its way, and the Convention Report was no more than the majority party's endorsement of its own policy document (**54**). This document resisted any move towards giving minority groups a place in any future executive, and since this breached the established criteria for devolution (**51**), the Report was in principle unacceptable to the British Government, who nonetheless tried to build on the measures of agreement in less significant areas by reconvening the Convention (**55**). The attempt foundered on the loyalist majority's determination to avoid an effective power-sharing system, and the prospects for an agreed return to a devolved system of government in Northern Ireland seem bleak at the moment.

50 CONSTITUTIONAL DEVELOPMENTS, 1972–4

Extracts from *The Northern Ireland Constitution* (Cmnd. 5675, 1974); reprinted by permission of H.M.S.O. This extract outlines the constitutional and political developments between the institution of direct rule in March 1972 and its reintroduction in May 1974 after an experiment with a new 'power-sharing' executive operating under a new constitution.

THE CONSTITUTION OF 1973

6. In March 1972 a period of 'direct rule' was instituted, with the support of the three major parties in the Westminster Parliament. It was made clear that the new system of government was intended to be transitional. The aim was to allow all concerned to discuss how to bring into being a more permanent system commanding the broadest possible support.

7. The consultative document 'The Future of Northern Ireland: A Paper for Discussion' (October 1972) and the White Paper 'Northern Ireland Constitutional Proposals' (Cmnd. 5259, March 1973) record the various discussions which took place. In summary the consultative process involved the following stages:

    (*a*) intensive discussions between the then Secretary of State for Northern

Ireland — political parties, community groups, representatives of social, economic and other interests;

(b) an invitation to individual citizens in Northern Ireland to submit proposals and suggestions;

(c) an invitation to each of the seven political parties which had representation in the prorogued Northern Ireland Parliament to take part in a conference to discuss suggestions for the future. Three parties attended this conference, held at Darlington in September 1972, and put forward proposals for discussion. Other parties and groups also published suggestions for the future;

(d) a comprehensive consultative document 'The Future of Northern Ireland: A Paper for Discussion' was published in October 1972, and formed the basis for further discussions with representatives of a wide range of interests;

(e) the people of Northern Ireland were given an opportunity, in the Border Poll of March 1973, to indicate by their votes whether they wanted Northern Ireland to remain part of the United Kingdom or to be joined with the Republic of Ireland, outside the United Kingdom. An overwhelming majority of those who voted, and a clear majority of the electorate as a whole, voted to remain within the United Kingdom;

(f) in the White Paper of March 1973, the then Government set out fully its proposals for the constitutional future of Northern Ireland. The Northern Ireland Assembly Act 1973 and the Northern Ireland Constitution Act 1973 were published and then passed into law in Westminster.

8. Throughout this process great efforts were made to find common ground between the Northern Ireland parties. This was made more difficult by the decisions taken by various interests at various times not to participate in discussions.

9. After the Assembly elections held at the end of June 1973, a further stage of consultation got under way. All the parties represented in the Assembly were asked to take part in discussions as to how a broadly-based Executive, likely to be widely accepted throughout the community, might be formed. Under section 2 of the Northern Ireland Constitution Act 1973, the ability to bring such an Executive into being was a prerequisite of devolution of legislative and executive powers to the new Northern Ireland institutions.

10. Paragraph 72 of the White Paper (Cmnd. 5259) referring to the formal appointment of political Heads of Departments in Northern Ireland made it clear that: 'when an agreed understanding on the formation of an Executive is reached in discussion with elected representatives, it would be the intention to make appointments in accordance with that understanding'.

Certain of the parties and members returned to the new Northern Ireland Assembly stated that they were opposed in principle to the formation of an Executive on the basis laid down in the Constitution Act. They therefore refused to take part in any discussions, either with the then Secretary of State or with other Northern Ireland parties, to seek an agreed understanding on the formation of an Executive. The Alliance Party, the Social Democratic and Labour Party and the then Official Unionist members, representing between them almost two-thirds of the total membership of the Assembly, eventually agreed to consider together whether such an understanding could be reached. Discussions were initiated upon the basis that all concerned fully accepted the Northern Ireland Constitution Act 1973, and continued for a period of seven weeks.

11. Finally, on November 22 1973, the then Secretary of State for Northern Ireland was able to report to the House of Commons that substantial progress had been made. The three Northern Ireland parties had reached agreement on a statement of aims and policies in the social and economic sphere and on the shape and balance of an Executive and Administration in which they would be prepared to serve together. This required a small amendment to Section 8(3) of the Northern Ireland Constitution Act 1973. This progress had made possible the nomination of an Executive-designate. It had, however, always been understood among the parties engaged in these discussions that it would be undesirable actually to form an Executive unless and until there was agreement on all the major issues under discussion.

12. One of these matters was the possible formation of a Council of Ireland, which required discussions with the Government of the Republic of Ireland. The Secretary of State therefore informed the House of Commons (Official Report, November 22 1973, Col. 1576):

'If we are to make the advances on a Council of Ireland to which I have referred, it is essential that there should now be urgent discussions between representatives of the Government of Ireland and those persons who will be members of the Northern Ireland Executive. This conference will be held as soon as possible and will, I hope, reach a clear understanding. I also intend to invite the leaders of those parties in the Northern Ireland Assembly who have indicated that they are not prepared to participate in an Executive to discuss with me their views on a Council of Ireland, so that these will be known at the time of the conference. It will be necessary, therefore, to hold a formal conference between Her Majesty's Government, the Government of the Republic and the Northern Ireland Executive, which will have been appointed by then.'

13. The leaders of those parties who had indicated they were not prepared to take part in an Executive, the Democratic Unionist Party and the Vanguard Unionist Party, protested that their parties should be invited to participate in the conference on the same basis as the other Assembly parties. They argued, as did the then leader of unofficial Unionists opposed to official Unionist policies, that the terms of paragraph 112 of the White Paper (Cmnd. 5259) were not being fulfilled. This had stated that:

'following elections to the Northern Ireland Assembly, the Government will invite the Government of the Republic of Ireland and the leaders of the elected representatives of Northern Ireland opinion to participate with them in a conference . . .'

Those leaders did not accept the proposal that they should discuss their views on a Council of Ireland with the Secretary of State. On December 5 1972, the leaders of the Democratic Unionist Party and the Vanguard Unionist Party were invited to attend the first session of the conference and to address it. This too was unacceptable to them.

14. The Sunningdale Conference took place, from December 6 to 9 1973, between representatives of Her Majesty's Government, of the Government of the Republic of Ireland and of the three parties involved in the Northern Ireland Executive-designate. The principal features of an Agreed Communique issued on December 9 were:

(*a*) declarations by Her Majesty's Government and by the Government of the Republic of Ireland on the constitutional status of Northern Ireland. These were to be incorporated in a formal agreement to be signed at the formal stage of the Conference and registered at the United Nations;

(*b*) outline agreement on the basis for setting up a Council of Ireland, to be implemented after further detailed study of functions and finance;

(*c*) agreement to establish a joint British-Irish Commission to recommend, as a matter of extreme urgency, the most effective means of dealing with those who commit crimes of violence, however motivated, in any part of Ireland.

(*d*) agreement to give a Council of Ireland a recommendatory role in relation to human rights in Ireland, and a consultative role in relation to appointments to Police Authorities, North and South;

(*e*) a re-affirmation by Her Majesty's Government of its firm commitment to bring detention to an end in Northern Ireland for all sections of the community as soon as the security situation permitted;

(*f*) Parliament would be asked to devolve full powers to the Northern Ireland Assembly and Executive as soon as possible. The formal appointment of the Executive would then be made;

(*g*) early in the New Year the British and Irish Governments and the Northern Ireland Executive would hold a formal conference 'to consider reports on the studies which have been commissioned and to sign the agreement reached.'

THE NORTHERN IRELAND EXECUTIVE, JANUARY–MAY 1974

15. By a Devolution Order, January 1 1974 was appointed as the day for the devolution to the Northern Ireland Assembly of legislative powers over a very wide range of matters, and to the Northern Ireland Executive and Administration of executive powers relating to these matters. At a ceremony on December 31 1973, the 11 members of the Executive and the four additional members of the Administration took the Oath or made the Affirmation required by law to:

'uphold the laws of Northern Ireland and conscientiously fulfil my duties under the Northern Ireland Constitution Act 1973 in the interests of Northern Ireland and its people'.

The following day, for the first time in the history of Northern Ireland, elected representatives of the majority and minority communities took up office as a government. While all those participating retained their long-term aspirations, they all accepted the principle embodied in section 1 of the Constitution Act, that Northern Ireland would not cease to be a part of the United Kingdom without the consent of a majority of its people.

16. The newly-appointed Executive at once took two important decisions which were communicated to the Assembly by the Chief Executive on January 24 1974. The first was that, although the Constitution Act did not so provide in terms, the Executive would hold itself responsible to the Assembly, and would therefore at once seek a Vote of Confidence there. The second was that the Executive would be bound by the principle of collective responsibility.

17. On January 24 1974, the statement of social and economic aims agreed during the inter-party talks was published. As soon as it took up office the new Executive set about the task of converting these broad policy objectives into comprehensive proposals for the future development of Northern Ireland. The new Heads of Departments assumed control of the various services for which they were responsible, and from the earliest days the new system showed itself capable of coping with difficult, controversial and potentially divisive matters.

18. The Assembly members of the 'loyalist coalition' refused to play any part in much of the business of the Assembly and did not take up their role as the Opposition in the lawfully constituted Assembly.

19. The agreement reached at the Sunningdale Conference became the centre of deepening political controversy . . .

. . . . . .

22. The comparatively slow progress in these respects meant that, when the United Kingdom General Election took place on February 28 1974, a number of important aspects of 'Sunningdale' remained unresolved, and the formal Conference, which had been envisaged as taking place 'early in the New Year', had not been held. Candidates in Northern Ireland opposed to the Sunningdale agreement and particularly the Council of Ireland received over 50 per cent of the vote and won 11 out of the 12 seats.

23. The Executive discussions on how to make progress in implementing the Sunningdale agreement were still in progress when, on May 16, a vote in the Assembly to reject a 'loyalist coalition' Motion calling for re-negotiation of the constitutional arrangements was made the occasion for a general stoppage of work by the non-elected Ulster Workers' Council. This started in the electricity industry and spread into other essential services. The Executive brought to a successful conclusion its discussions on implementing the Sunningdale agreement on May 22, when the Chief Executive announced in the Assembly that the Executive now proposed that the agreement should be implemented in two phases. In the first, immediate phase, a Council of Ministers would be established as a forum for consultation, co-operation and co-ordination of action between the Northern Ireland Executive and the Government of the Republic of Ireland in relation to various social and economic matters. The other aspects of the Council of Ireland scheme — a 'second tier' Consultative Assembly; transfers of functions to the Council;

appointment of a Secretary General, etc. – would be part of a second phase, to be introduced only after the opinion of the people of Northern Ireland had been tested at a further general election to the Assembly.

24. Her Majesty's Government had been faced in the weeks before the strike by a renewed bombing campaign by the IRA. It made it clear that the IRA would not be allowed to bomb its way to the conference table. Similarly, throughout the stoppage, it held firmly to the principle that there could be no negotiation on constitutional issues with those who had not been elected as part of the normal democratic processes. The stoppage of work continued with the Ulster Workers' Council, the various para-military associations, and the 'loyalist coalition' politicians associated with them demanding early Assembly elections as a basis for re-negotiating the constitutional arrangements. The effects of the stoppage were severe. A large part of the labour force, particularly in urban areas, stopped work and many business and commercial undertakings co-operated with those who had brought about the stoppage. The organisers progressively reduced the electrical power output; secured a virtual stranglehold upon the distribution of petrol and oil; and gained virtual control of other vital services and supplies. Many main and minor roads were blocked. The Army re-opened the main traffic routes and, on Monday May 27, successfully took over control of the main petrol and oil depots together with the means of distribution. The Army then began to distribute petrol and oil, with great competence, to essential users.

25. In response to this action taken by Her Majesty's Government following requests received from the Executive, the organisers of the stoppage started to shut down completely the electricity system and withdraw labour from other essential services. On Tuesday May 28 the Chief Executive informed the Secretary of State that he, and his Unionist colleagues on the Executive, had come to the conclusion that some form of negotiation or mediation must be considered, and that if this could not be agreed, they should resign. The Alliance Party also favoured mediation, but not resignation. The SDLP members remained opposed to negotiation or mediation. The Secretary of State told Mr. Faulkner that the principle which had animated the Government's conduct must be maintained and Mr. Faulkner then offered his own resignation and that of his Unionist colleagues. The necessary broad basis for maintenance of the Executive accordingly ceased to exist, and on May 29 the Warrants of the remaining members of the Executive and Administration were revoked.

26. In plain terms the Ulster Workers' Council in association with the para-military organisations brought down the Executive, which, in a spirit of partnership, had undertaken the tasks of government in Northern Ireland since January 1. In the political history of these islands, few men had ever undertaken a more arduous yet honourable task, with a full awareness of the political and even personal dangers to which they were exposing themselves. What they attempted to do was undoubtedly distorted and misrepresented and they found it difficult to establish themselves and their policies against a background of continuing violence. The unremitting campaign of the Provisional IRA and the violent actions of other extremist organisations,

including the sectarian murders of Roman Catholics, created an atmosphere of growing polarisation and distrust, unreceptive to the politics of conciliation and compromise. Yet, if the Executive failed, the men who served in it did not fail. They disproved for ever the idea that it is not possible for Protestant and Roman Catholic to work together for the good of Northern Ireland and its people.

51 CRITERIA FOR DEVOLUTION

Extracts from *Northern Ireland Constitutional Proposals* (Cmnd. 5259, 1973); reprinted by permission of H.M.S.O. These extracts from the White Paper outlining the 1973 Constitution set out the criteria which the British government feel must be met prior to the reintroduction of devolved government in Northern Ireland.

1. In October 1972 the Government published 'The Future of Northern Ireland: A Paper for Discussion'. This Paper reviewed the background, set out the proposals made up to that time by the Northern Ireland parties and other interests, together with the wide range of theoretical options, established the basic facts — political, economic and security — which would have to be taken into account in moving towards a settlement, and stated the criteria which firm proposals for the future must meet.

   2. These fundamental criteria were set out in paragraph 79 of the Paper as follows:

'(a) In accordance with the specific pledges given by successive United Kingdom Governments, Northern Ireland must and will remain part of the United Kingdom for as long as that is the wish of the majority of the people; but that status does not preclude the necessary taking into account of what has been described in this Paper as the 'Irish Dimension'.

(b) As long as Northern Ireland remains part of the United Kingdom the sovereignty of the United Kingdom Parliament must be acknowledged, and due provision made for the United Kingdom Government to have an effective and continuing voice in Northern Ireland's affairs, commensurate with the commitment of financial, economic and military resources in the Province.

(c) Any division of powers and responsibilities between the national and the regional authorities must be logical, open and clearly understood. Ambiguity in the relationship is a prescription for confusion and misunderstanding. Any necessary checks, balances or controls must be apparent on the face of a new constitutional scheme.

(d) The two primary purposes of any new institutions must be first to seek a much wider consensus than has hitherto existed; and second to be such as will work efficiently and will be capable of providing the concrete results of good government: peace and order, physical development, social and economic progress. This is fundamental because Northern Ireland's problems flow not just from a clash of national aspirations or from friction between the communities, but also from social and economic conditions such as inadequate housing and unemployment.

(e) Any new institutions must be of a simple and businesslike character, appropriate to the powers and functions of a regional authority.

(f) A Northern Ireland assembly or authority must be capable of involving all its members constructively in ways which satisfy them and those they represent that the whole community has a part to play in the government of the Province. As a minimum this would involve assuring minority groups of an effective voice and a real influence; but there are strong arguments that the objective of real participation should be achieved by giving minority interests a share in the exercise of executive power if this can be achieved by means which are not unduly complex or artificial, and which do not represent an obstacle to effective government.

(g) There must be an assurance, built into any new structures, that there will be absolute fairness and equality of opportunity for all. The future administration of Northern Ireland must be seen to be completely even-handed both in law and in fact.

(h) It is of great importance that future arrangements for security and public order in Northern Ireland must command public confidence, both in Northern Ireland itself, and in the United Kingdom as a whole. If they are to do so they must be seen in practice to be as impartial and effective as possible in restoring and maintaining peace and public order. In any situation such as that which obtains at present, where the Army and the civilian police force are both involved in maintaining law and order and combating terrorism, it is essential that there should be a single source of direct responsibility. Since Westminster alone can control the Armed Forces of the Crown this unified control must mean Westminster control. For the future any arrangements must ensure that the United Kingdom Government has an effective and a determining voice in relation to any circumstances which involve, or may involve in the future, the commitment of the Armed Forces, the use of emergency powers, or repercussions at international level.'

. . . . . .

CONDITIONS FOR A SETTLEMENT

Essential conditions

11. Successive United Kingdom Governments have affirmed that Northern Ireland will continue to be part of the United Kingdom unless and until its people decide otherwise, and a majority of the people in Northern Ireland have voted in favour of the present status of Northern Ireland as part of the United Kingdom. It is the responsibility of the United Kingdom Parliament to determine how Northern Ireland shall be governed as a part of the United Kingdom.

12. There is a three-fold pattern of obligations:

(*a*) The United Kingdom as a whole has an obligation to those of its citizens who live in Northern Ireland to afford them the fullest protection of the rule of law; to secure their fundamental rights and freedoms; and to work towards the realisation for them of the United Kingdom standards of living, employment and social conditions.

(*b*) Those who live in Northern Ireland as part of the United Kingdom have an obligation to respect the decisions of the Crown in Parliament and to play their part in creating and upholding an equitable political settlement.

(*c*) Those who wish to see the achievement of Irish unity, which can only be on a basis of consent, have an obligation to accept that such consent does not at present exist, and — without prejudice to their aspirations — to assist in the achievement on a constitutional basis of peace, equality and prosperity.

13. Any significant advance towards a settlement in Northern Ireland at this stage must be consistent with this pattern of obligations. In deciding what the shape of a settlement should be, the United Kingdom Government has refrained from seeking to impose on Northern Ireland a rigidly defined and detailed scheme for its future which could not be done at the present time without assumptions about the wishes of its people. This approach requires that no interest in Northern Ireland should refuse constructive co-operation in working out the details of such a scheme. The United Kingdom Government for its part must have regard to the interests of all the peoples in the United Kingdom including the communities in Northern Ireland. All these interests must be brought as nearly as possible into a state of reconciliation. The true interests of the whole community in Northern Ireland require that the majority should not fail in fairness and generosity towards all their fellow citizens and that the minority should play a truly constructive part which it is the United Kingdom Government's firm determination should be made available to them.

. . . . . .

Secretary of State for Northern Ireland

48. There will continue to be a Secretary of State for Northern Ireland who will be a member of the United Kingdom Cabinet. His role will naturally be different from what it has been under direct rule during which the Secretary of State has had executive responsibility for the full range of public services. He must, however, continue to have charge of a Department, with offices both in London and in Northern Ireland, so organised as to discharge his responsibilities both to Parliament and to Northern Ireland itself.

49. It is of the greatest importance, in a situation where wide powers are to be devolved upon Northern Ireland institutions and others reserved to Parliament and the United Kingdom Government, that the two sets of authorities should not work in separate compartments or to conflicting objectives. The best interests of the

people of Northern Ireland will only be served if, from the start, their duties are regarded as complementary in character.

50. Accordingly, the Secretary of State will have the following main areas of responsibility in relation to Northern Ireland:

(*a*) he will undertake the necessary consultations with the elected representatives of Northern Ireland to determine how an acceptable basis for devolution of powers may speedily be achieved.

(*b*) thereafter, he will exercise direct ministerial responsibility in relation to certain reserved services administered either by his own Department or, where appropriate, by Northern Ireland Departments acting as his agents.

(*c*) he will represent Northern Ireland's interests in the United Kingdom Government, both generally and in relation to the allocation of financial resources to Northern Ireland.

Conditions for devolution of powers

51. As soon as the Assembly has been elected, the Secretary of State will discuss with representatives of the parties how devolution on a basis of government by consent may take place. Hitherto, the executive dispositions in Northern Ireland have been made by the Governor under the Act of 1920 and in accordance with the current British constitutional conventions. But those conventions have been applied to Northern Ireland in a situation where:

(*a*) the same party has been the majority party after each General Election; and

(*b*) that party has never returned to Parliament in the course of half a century a member from the minority community which comprises more than a third of the population.

It is from this situation that there flows the problem, as described in the Paper for Discussion, of 'binding the minority to the support of new political arrangements in Northern Ireland'.

Formation of the Executive

52. There is no future for devolved institutions of government in Northern Ireland unless majority and minority alike can be so bound. This is not to say that any 'right of veto' can be conceded to violent, subversive or unconstructive elements determined, if they can, to undermine any new system from the outset. But the Government does not believe that this is the wish of the overwhelming majority in either community. What has to be found — through their representatives — is a system of exercising executive power in Northern Ireland which is broadly acceptable to them. One important means of ensuring this will be more effective participation by the Assembly as a whole, through its structure of committees, in the development of policy; but it is the view of the Government that the Executive itself can no longer be solely based upon any single party, if that party draws its

support and its elected representation virtually entirely from only one section of a divided community. The Executive must be composed of persons who are prepared to work together by peaceful means for the benefit of the community. Members of the Executive will be required to take an appropriate form of official oath or make an affirmation on taking up their appointment.

53. It is this central issue which, after the election of the Assembly, the Secretary of State will urgently discuss with its elected leaders. The objective of the discussions will be to seek an agreed understanding which the United Kingdom Government can with confidence recommend to Parliament as a fair and viable basis for the devolution of power. When the Government is satisfied:

(*a*) that the procedures of the Assembly and the proposed method of exercising executive powers will, taken together, be a reasonable basis for the establishment of government by consent (that is to say, with substantially wider support from the community as a whole than would necessarily be indicated by a simple majority in the Assembly).

(*b*) in particular, that executive powers will not be concentrated in elected representatives from one community only; and

(*c*) that any proposed arrangements will represent not just a theoretical framework for fair and acceptable government, but a system which can and will be worked effectively by those concerned,

it will seek the approval of Parliament for the devolution by subordinate instrument of extensive law-making powers to the Assembly, and for a broadly corresponding devolution of executive powers to a Northern Ireland Executive, which will be constituted in accordance with the arrangements that have been agreed.

52 THE 1973 STRUCTURE OF GOVERNMENT

Extracts from *Northern Ireland Discussion Paper 3: Government of Northern Ireland* (H.M.S.O., 1975); reprinted by permission of H.M.S.O. This extract sets out the basic structure of government under the Northern Ireland Constitution Act, which remains fully in force, except for the suspension of the provisions dealing with the Assembly and the Administration.

9. The basic constitutional law is the Northern Ireland Constitution Act 1973. Those parts of the Act which deal with the Assembly and Administration are, for the moment, suspended by the Northern Ireland Act 1974, but they have not been repealed, and all the other provisions of the Act remain in full force and effect.

10. The scheme of the 1973 Act is one of a division of powers between the sovereign national Parliament and the United Kingdom Government and the regional Assembly and Administration. Under this scheme, powers are divided in the following way:

'EXCEPTED' MATTERS (Schedule 2): These are national, as distinct from regional, matters in respect of which the Westminster Parliament has retained the *sole* right to make laws for Northern Ireland. They include elections and the franchise, all existing taxation, and the appointment of all members of the judiciary. The responsibility for taking decisions about these subjects is correspondingly retained by the United Kingdom Ministers (for example, judicial appointments by the Lord Chancellor, taxation by the Chancellor of the Exchequer, and elections and franchise by the Secretary of State for Northern Ireland).

'RESERVED' MATTERS (Schedule 3): these, also, are matters in respect of which Parliament has retained law-making powers for itself. The distinction between this category and the 'excepted' category is that laws in these fields may also be made by the regional Assembly with the consent of the Secretary of State for Northern Ireland (and subject to eventual Parliamentary approval at Westminster); and that, at a later time, these law-making powers may be given by Parliament to the Assembly, free from this restraint. The 'reserved' matters include criminal law, the maintenance of public order and the police. While they remain 'reserved', the responsibility for taking decisions about these subjects is also retained by the Secretary of State for Northern Ireland and other United Kingdom Ministers.

'TRANSFERRED' MATTERS: These are all matters other than those 'excepted' or 'reserved', in practice covering the great bulk of civil government functions in Northern Ireland. In respect of them the regional Assembly could make laws and the regional Administration take decisions . . .

11. The Northern Ireland Assembly consists of seventy-eight members, elected from the twelve Parliamentary constituencies in Northern Ireland by the Single Transferable Vote method of proportional representation.

12. Sections 7(4) and 25(4) to 25(7) required the Assembly to establish, for each Department of the regional government, a consultative committee to be chaired by the political Head of that Department, who had a duty to consult it when formulating policy and proposing new legislation. These committees, taken as a whole, were required by statute to reflect in their membership the respective strengths of the parties in the Assembly.

13. The services controlled by the regional government were to be operated by the nine Northern Ireland Departments – Finance; Health and Social Services; Manpower Services; Education; Agriculture; Commerce; Housing, Local Government and Planning; Environment and Community Relations – each under the direction of a political Head. Collectively these Heads of Departments, together with others appointed without specific departmental responsibilities, would form the Northern Ireland Administration, whose directing core would be the Executive, presided over by the Chief Executive Member.

14. Appointments to the Administration were to be made by the Secretary of State for Northern Ireland on behalf of Her Majesty The Queen, Section 2(1) of the Act of 1973 required the Secretary of State, in making such appointments, to be satisfied

'that a Northern Ireland Executive can be formed which, having regard to the support it commands in the Assembly and to the electorate on which that support is based, is likely to be widely accepted throughout the community, and that having regard to these matters there is a reasonable basis for the establishment in Northern Ireland of government by consent.'

The Act thus required the Secretary of State, in making his appointments, to apply a series of tests. The regional government appointed by him had to represent a reasonable basis for government by consent. How was this likelihood to be assessed? By the presence of widespread acceptance throughout the community. What were to be the indications of such widespread acceptance? The extent and nature of support in the Assembly and amongst the electorate.

15. The foregoing provisions of the Act of 1973 operated from January to June 1974. An Executive was appointed with effect from 1 January consisting of the Chief Executive, his Deputy, the Heads of seven of the Departments, and two others. The Administration of fifteen was completed by the Heads of the other two Departments and two further office-holders. The Administration collapsed at the end of May and the Assembly was prorogued. The effect of the Northern Ireland Act 1974 was to provide that for an interim period, initially one year from July 1974, the legislative functions of the Northern Ireland Assembly would be suspended and laws made for Northern Ireland by Orders-in-Council; no appointments to a Northern Ireland Administration would be made; and the Northern Ireland Departments would discharge their functions subject to the direction and control of the Secretary of State for Northern Ireland.

16. Other provisions of the Act of 1973 are unaffected. These include in particular the extensive provision made by Part III of the Act for the prevention of religious and political discrimination.

17. First, Section 17 of the Act provided that any legislative Measure of the Assembly should, to the extent that it discriminated against any person or class of persons on the ground of religious or political belief, be void. Moreover, Section 18 made special provision for legislation alleged to be discriminatory to be tested before the Judicial Committee of the Privy Council. During the interim period these procedures apply to Orders-in-Council as they applied to Measures.

18. Second, Section 19 of the Act made unlawful any discriminatory act by a Minister, Department or public body, and it provided that a person who believed himself to be a victim of such discrimination should have the right to bring a court action against the authority concerned.

19. Third, Section 20 of the Act provided for the appointment of a Standing Advisory Commission on Human Rights, for the purpose of:

(*a*) advising the Secretary of State on the adequacy and effectiveness of the law for the time being in force in preventing discrimination on the ground of religious belief or political opinion and in providing redress for persons aggrieved by discrimination on either ground;

(*b*) keeping the Secretary of State informed as to the extent to which the persons, authorities and bodies mentioned (ie the various Ministers, Departments, public bodies, etc) have prevented discrimination on either ground by persons or bodies not prohibited from discriminating by that law.

This Commission, whose chairman is Lord Feather, is at work.

20. These provisions of the 1973 Act supplemented other provision already made for the protection of human rights in Northern Ireland, including the creation of the offices of Parliamentary Commissioner for Administration and Commissioner for Complaints.

53 THE CONVENTION PROPOSAL

Extracts from *The Northern Ireland Constitution* (Cmnd. 5675, 1974); reprinted by permission of H.M.S.O. The Convention here proposed was elected on the basis of proportional representation and reflected faithfully the existing political balance with a clear 'loyalist' majority. The Convention had a neutral Chairman in Sir Robert Lowry, the Lord Chief Justice of Northern Ireland.

... Political structures should not be confused with political relationships. If the Northern Ireland community can reach a broad consensus of agreement any one of a number of possible patterns of government might well be workable. If agreement is not reached, the troubles in Northern Ireland will not only remain but could intensify. No-one will be able to turn this defeat into a victory. That is reality.

45. It is only part of the reality which must also include recognition of a number of facts:

(*a*) history has caused divisions within the Northern Ireland community. Events of the past few years have amply demonstrated that no part of that community can, let alone should, be coerced into accepting the others' view. Events have also shown that a consensus can be obtained on the basis of serving the interests of the whole community. There must be some form of power-sharing and partnership because no political system will survive, or be supported, unless there is widespread acceptance of it within the community. There must be participation by the whole community;

(*b*) any pattern of government must be acceptable to the people of the United Kingdom as a whole and to Parliament at Westminster. Citizenship confers not only rights and privileges but also obligations;

(*c*) Northern Ireland, unlike the rest of the United Kingdom, shares a common land frontier and a special relationship with another country, the Republic of Ireland. Any political arrangements must recognise and provide for this special relationship. There is an Irish dimension.

46. It would be premature at this stage to say that the approach embodied in the Constitution Act 1973 is untenable. Indeed, much of the content of that Act is not a matter for dispute. What is apparent is that there is little prospect of forming from

the present Northern Ireland Assembly another Executive which meets the terms of that Act.

. . . . . .

48. The Government continues to believe that the best and most desirable basis for political progress in Northern Ireland would be the establishment of local institutions enjoying broadly-based support throughout the community. It has always been recognised that there is no means to impose such a system upon Northern Ireland if substantial sections of its population are determined to oppose it. Indeed, the final paragraph of the White Paper of March 1973 (Cmnd. 5259) included these words:

'These, then, are the Government's proposals to Parliament, to the country, and above all to the people of Northern Ireland themselves for a way forward out of the present violence and instability. At every point, they require the co-operation of these people themselves if they are to have any prospect of success. They can be frustrated if interests in Northern Ireland refuse to allow them to be tried or if any section of the community is determined to impose its will on another.'

49. Local institutions in Northern Ireland cannot be established on a basis unacceptable to broad sections of opinion there; equally they cannot be established on a basis unacceptable to the United Kingdom as a whole or to Parliament as representing it. Any system which results in the permanent exclusion from any real and substantial influence in public affairs of a whole section of the community is inherently unstable and would be unacceptable to Her Majesty's Government.

50. Against this background the Government proposes to introduce legislation for the election of a Constitutional Convention, to consider what provisions for the government of Northern Ireland would be likely to command the most widespread acceptance throughout the community there.

51. The legislation will provide for the Convention to be based upon the constituencies and the methods of election prescribed by the Northern Ireland Assembly Act 1973. It will accordingly consist of 78 members, elected on a multi-member basis from the 12 parliamentary constituencies in Northern Ireland by the Single Transferable Vote system.

52. The Convention will be required to make a report or reports on its conclusions which will be laid before Parliament. It will be dissolved on the date of laying its final report, or six months from the date of its first meeting, whichever is the earlier; but the dissolution may be postponed or further postponed by order subject to parliamentary control for periods not exceeding three months at a time. Provision will also be made for re-convening the Convention within six months of its dissolution, if it appears desirable that any matter should be considered or further considered.

53. The Government proposes that there should be an independent Chairman of the Convention, a person of high standing and impartiality from Northern Ireland. He will not be a member of the Convention . . .

54. The intention is that the Convention will be entirely a forum for elected

representatives of the people of Northern Ireland. The Government will play no part in its proceedings but will, of course, be willing to make available factual information and to assist the Convention in any way which is likely to bring its deliberations to a successful conclusion.

55. In the event of the Convention producing recommendations which command majority and widespread support from its members, the Government will give the most serious consideration to them. In any event, it may prove to be desirable for the Government to test directly the opinion of the Northern Ireland electorate on their attitude to particular or to alternative proposals before any course is recommended to Parliament. The proposed legislation will therefore make provision for the Secretary of State to direct the holding of a referendum or referenda on questions arising out of the work of the Convention.

54 THE CONVENTION'S RECOMMENDATIONS

Extracts from *Report of the Northern Ireland Constitutional Convention* (H.C. 1, 1976); reprinted by permission of H.M.S.O. The Convention operated largely through informal inter-party talks and formal debates, on the basis of outline policy documents produced by each party. The Convention finally voted by 42 to 31 to recommend to the Secretary of State as the Convention Report, the report of the majority party, the United Ulster Unionist Coalition, which resisted proposals for a power-sharing or coalition system in favour of a conventional Parliamentary system.

Consistent with Section 2(1) of the Northern Ireland Act 1974 the Convention worked for the provision of a government of Northern Ireland on the basis of the only constraint therein i.e., that likely to command the most widespread acceptance throughout the community in Northern Ireland.

It was noted with approval that in the Northern Ireland Act 1974 the United Kingdom Parliament did not impose any constraints such as power-sharing in an executive or all-Ireland institutions.

Therefore it concluded.

1. That Northern Ireland should be administered by an elected body and an executive empowered to legislate and govern and to be known as the Parliament and Government of Northern Ireland.

2. That legislation affecting devolved matters should be enacted by the Queen in Parliament and Her Majesty should be represented in Northern Ireland by a Governor appointed by Her Majesty to exercise such constitutional function and perform such ceremonial duties as She is not able to fulfil in person.

3. That there should be a Privy Council of Northern Ireland in which some places should be offered to leading members of major opposition parties.

4. That the number of Northern Ireland Members of Parliament at Westminster should be increased to between 20 and 24, the boundaries and exact number of the

constituencies to be determined by judicial commission on a basis and scale similar to comparable parts of the United Kingdom.

5. That the office of the Secretary of State for Northern Ireland should lapse and those services not directly administered by the devolved administration should be the concern of a Secretary of State for the devolved regions or other senior Cabinet Minister.

6. That the Parliament of Northern Ireland should be unicameral and a term should not exceed five years. The Chamber should consist of not less than 78 and not more than 100 members who are British citizens.

7. That the Parliament of Northern Ireland should be able to legislate in matters affecting the franchise, elections and disqualification for membership of that Parliament.

8. That the devolved government for Northern Ireland should have powers broadly similar to those conferred by the Government of Ireland Act 1920.

9. That the formation and operation of the executive should conform to the practices and precedents of the Parliament of the United Kingdom.

10. That the Queen's Representative should invite the leader of the largest parliamentary party or group to form a government.

11. That the selection and dismissal of ministers should be at the discretion of the Prime Minister, who should not be compelled to include members of any particular party or group.

12. That no country ought to be forced to have in its Cabinet any person whose political philosophy and attitudes have revealed his opposition to the very existence of that State.

13. That the Government should be responsible to Parliament and the Cabinet should be collectively responsible for its decisions.

14. That the Prime Minister should be entitled to remain in office until he has ceased to retain the support of a majority in Parliament.

15. That the number of Cabinet Ministers should not exceed eight.

16. That a Committee system should be devised to give real and substantial influence to an opposition and to make Parliament more effective.

17. That covering each Department of Government there should be a Departmental Committee of 8 or 10 backbenchers drawn equally from Government and opposition supporters with normal parliamentary voting rights.

18. That each Committee would be involved in the legislative process and scrutiny of Government action relating to its Department.

19. That there should be a Rules Committee drawn from the whole House.

20. That it should be a rôle of a strong regional government to deal with economic and social problems.

21. That it should be the responsibility of a strong regional government to determine economic and social priorities.

22. That the systems which existed in the latter years of the Northern Ireland Parliament and during the brief lifetime of the Northern Ireland Assembly were unduly restrictive and inhibited local variations.

23. That there should be provision for divergences in approach to spending as compared to the rest of the United Kingdom.

24. That there should be supplementary financial assistance related to Northern Ireland needs from the United Kingdom Government.

25. That there should be scope for some Northern Ireland variations in taxation.

26. That there should be a Bill of Constitutional Rights to guarantee the stability and integrity of the Northern Ireland Constitution and a general Bill of Rights and Duties to protect the rights of the individual citizen.

27. That external relations should be the responsibility of the Government at Westminster in consultation with the Government of Northern Ireland.

28. That good neighbourly relations should be welcome but that imposed institutionalised associations with the Republic of Ireland should be rejected.

29. That Her Majesty's Government should make all haste to end the political vacuum, defeat terrorism, and, recognising the political realities, restore devolved Government to Northern Ireland: in the interim the Convention should continue in being as a representative forum of the people of Northern Ireland until the administration is formed, and tender advice to the Secretary of State.

55 THE BRITISH GOVERNMENT'S RESPONSE

Extracts from *Letter from the Secretary of State for Northern Ireland to the Chairman of the Convention* (Cmnd. 6387, 1976); reprinted by permission of H.M.S.O. The British Government were unable to accept the Convention Report, but indicated a continuing determination to return power to a Northern Ireland government, and reconvened the Convention on 3 February 1976 to reconsider the possibilities of building on existing measures of agreement to produce a solution, if need be a temporary one, which would command widespread acceptance in Northern Ireland and provide a stable system of government. But the resumed Convention discussions were fruitless and the Convention was wound up on 5 March 1976.

1. Parliament at Westminster set up the Constitutional Convention under the terms of the Northern Ireland Act 1974. Its task was to consider 'what provision for the government of Northern Ireland is likely to command the most widespread acceptance throughout the community there'. The Convention was not empowered to make decisions but was asked to put forward its conclusions to the Government. Decisions are a matter for Parliament at Westminster.

2. The Convention first met on 8 May 1975. On 7 November 1975 you transmitted to me the Report of the Northern Ireland Convention; the Convention was dissolved at the end of that day, and the Report was duly laid before Parliament on 20 November. Following this I met groups from all the political parties in the Convention. These talks were solely for purposes of seeking explanation and elucidation since it was to Parliament at Westminster that the Government had the responsibility and the duty to put forward its proposals for the next steps in Northern Ireland. This it did on 12 January 1976.

3. The purpose of this letter is first to outline the views of the Government on some of the major issues arising from the Report of the Convention and second to indicate the matters on which further consideration is desirable.

4. The Report follows the draft put forward by the United Ulster Unionist Coalition. The Government welcomes the fact that the Convention decided that the draft reports of all other parties in the Convention should be included in an Appendix to the Report.

. . . . . .

6. The Government accepts that from its foundation and for reasons of history, geography and tradition there are a number of differences between Northern Ireland and the rest of the United Kingdom. Nevertheless, as part of the United Kingdom, Northern Ireland like the rest of the United Kingdom must remain subject to the authority of The Queen in Parliament at Westminster. Indeed, as the White Paper of July 1974 stated:

'any pattern of government must be acceptable to the people of the United Kingdom as a whole and to Parliament at Westminster. Citizenship confers not only rights and privileges but also obligations'.

7. Northern Ireland has been unique in the United Kingdom in having had a distinct system of government for 50 years. There is a further and crucial way in which Northern Ireland is different. The community in Northern Ireland is divided in ways which cannot be ignored. Experience in recent years has made it plain that no system of government within Northern Ireland will be stable or effective unless both parts of the community acquiesce in that system, and are willing to work to support it. It is clear that such support is not at present forthcoming for the system proposed in the Report.

8. The Government shares with the Convention the strong desire that direct rule may be brought to an end and that a new system of government may be established within Northern Ireland. The Government, however, takes the view that the proposals for a system of government within Northern Ireland contained in the Report do not command sufficiently widespread acceptance throughout the community there for a system based solely upon them to provide stable and effective government.

9. There are a number of points arising from the Report of the Convention on which the Government has now reached conclusions.

The system of government

10. Provided the necessary agreement can be reached, the Government accepts in principle the Convention's recommendation that power should be returned to a government within Northern Ireland. This would involve the creation in Northern Ireland of a separate unicameral legislature and a government with power to legislate for, and administer, a wide range of matters within Northern Ireland. The Government also accepts that the transferred subjects could include all those transferred in

1974, under the Northern Ireland Constitution Act 1973. Responsibility for law and order is discussed separately below.

Collective responsibility

11. The Government agrees with the view expressed in the Report on the importance of collective responsibility and accepts the need for an oath in the terms recommended in the Report to be taken by all members of the Northern Ireland legislature and the Northern Ireland Government.

Committee system

12. The Government has noted the importance attached in the Report of the Convention to a committee system and that there were widely differing views within the Convention on the way the system would work in practice and on its effectiveness — whether the committees would have any real power or, at the other extreme, whether they would have so much power as seriously to hamper government. The Government also recognises that a committee system represents a constructive attempt to involve opposition parties more closely in government. The Government considers that a committee system might be of value as part of a wider and acceptable constitutional framework which provides adequately for partnership and participation on a basis which commands the most widespread acceptance. It is a matter which merits further examination. The Government would not, however, wish to see the responsibility of a Public Accounts Committee dispersed among a number of functional or departmental committees.

Parliamentary representation

13. The Government is aware of the strong views held by many on the question of Parliamentary representation at Westminster. It is also aware that in the past 50 years some members elected to the Westminster Parliament have not taken their seats — another reflection of a divided community. The Government does not feel able to recommend re-examination of the question of the number of Northern Ireland constituencies returning members to the United Kingdom Parliament in advance of an agreement on a system of government commanding the most widespread acceptance.
. . . . . .

Law and order

15. The parties in the Convention agree in principle that a future Northern Ireland administration should have responsibility for law and order in the Province. The Government considers that an essential prerequisite for membership of a Northern

Ireland Government is public support of the security forces. Subject to this, the Government accepts this broad aim in principle though there are a number of matters which it would be inappropriate to transfer. These include all judicial appointments and the administration of the courts. Transfer of responsibility for law and order would necessarily be gradual and the Government will consider how best to give a meaningful role to a Northern Ireland administration on security matters until such time as transfer is complete. The phrase 'law and order' covers a wide range of subjects:

(i) *The Armed Forces:* These are under the control of a Minister accountable direct to Parliament and will remain so. So long as they are involved in internal security in Northern Ireland, the Secretary of State must remain responsible for security policy. It is the policy of the Government to bring about a situation in which there can be a progressive reduction in the present commitment of the Armed Forces, both in numbers and in the scale of activity, to a point where they have ceased to be involved in internal security. But this depends upon civil policing by the RUC playing an increasing role. Above all, it depends upon reduction in the scale of violence, for which the GOC and his forces and the Chief Constable and his police officers are constantly striving.

As I announced in Parliament on 12 January, I shall examine, with my Ministerial colleagues from other Departments, action and resources required for the next few years to maintain law and order in Northern Ireland. This will include how best to achieve the primacy of the police; the size and role of locally recruited forces; and the progressive reduction of the Armed Forces as soon as is safely practicable. I shall be inviting the parties in the Convention to make their views on these matters known to me in writing.

(ii) *Emergency Legislation:* So long as the Secretary of State remains responsible for security policy, responsibility for emergency legislation would remain with the United Kingdom Parliament.

(iii) *Police:* Once the Armed Forces in Northern Ireland have been reduced to peace-time level — which depends on the level of violence — the Government will be prepared to transfer responsibility for the police to a new Northern Ireland legislature and executive. Parliament would expect that the practices observed in Northern Ireland would continue to follow the standards and traditions which are common to the whole of the United Kingdom and, in particular, that the independence and responsibilities of the Chief Constable should in no way be diminished. The police are responsible to the law and it has always been my aim to ensure that this position is preserved and maintained at all times.

It is clear that close liaison between the Secretary of State and a Northern Ireland executive on internal security would be necessary. The Government sees a continuing role for an independent Police Authority with significant powers and is prepared to consider any suggestions that the parties in the Convention may wish to put forward to me in writing about its responsibilities and composition, which are at present based on the provisions of the Police Act (Northern Ireland) 1970.

(iv) *Prisons:* The Government would be prepared to transfer responsibility for administration of the prison service and for treatment of offenders generally not later than the transfer of responsibility for the police.

16. The Government has noted the views of the Convention on the financial arrangements which should be created for any new Northern Ireland administration. It would be the intention of the Government to give to such an administration as wide a discretion as would be consistent with maintaining the unity of the United Kingdom economy and with the Government's retaining the powers necessary to manage the economy as a whole. These powers must include the power to determine the total amount of public expenditure in the United Kingdom, the proportion of different categories of expenditure within that total and, after appropriate consultation, the share of public expenditure allocated to meeting the needs of Northern Ireland. The Government is conscious of the special economic and social problems of Northern Ireland and of the need for them to be taken into account when allocations of expenditure are determined; those decisions must be taken by the United Kingdom Cabinet in the light of the needs of all parts of the United Kingdom.

17. The financial powers that the Government would be willing to see exercised by a Northern Ireland administration are matters that the Government will itself determine in due course. It envisages, however, that many important financial decisions would fall within the Northern Ireland administration's discretion including, in particular, the determination of priorities among the various transferred services. Any system of government proposed by the Convention will have to be capable of resolving such problems which will span the complete range of functions of the Northern Ireland administration. There must, moreover, be arrangements for co-operation on economic and financial matters with the Government at Westminster.

Bill of Rights

18. The Government recognises that there is a consensus that there should be further legislation on human rights and will consider how best to make appropriate statutory provision in the light of the detailed study currently being undertaken by the Standing Advisory Commission on Human Rights.

Reconvening the Convention

19. It is against this background, and in accordance with the wishes of Parliament, that I have decided to reconvene the Convention so as to give it an opportunity, through discussion and further exchanges of view, to reach that wider area of agreement which is essential if there is to be an effective transfer of power, the ending of direct rule and a basis for stable government. The Government hopes that the Convention will not feel constrained by the limits of earlier — and not completed — discussions, and that it will be able to build on the principles on which there is already

a wide measure of agreement. The prime requirement is for more widespread acceptance of any proposed system of government, providing for a form of partnership and participation. No political system in Northern Ireland will work, let alone survive, without it. The Government wishes further consideration to be given to this matter of a system of government commanding the most widespread acceptance throughout the community, and in both parts of it.

20. The Government shares the view expressed in the Report that the aim should be to achieve agreement on a permanent arrangement for a system of government. It will be for the Government to translate this into constitutional and legislative form and to turn it into reality through Parliament at Westminster. The greater the measure of support for any proposed system of government within Northern Ireland, the more likely it is that Parliament would be prepared to approve the necessary legislation.

21. Other, wider, considerations are relevant to the timescale of future political development. For example, there is force in the view that hasty action in the past may have exacerbated some of the problems of Northern Ireland. Six years of violence taken together with the divisions in the community are going to make the transition to a new system of government particularly difficult. Political development cannot be divorced from the security situation and a political agreement would make a major contribution towards dealing with the security problems in Northern Ireland.

22. Furthermore, Northern Ireland is facing serious social and economic problems — not least unemployment. An early political agreement would lead to the more productive employment of the energies of those who have local knowledge and interest, and would create a community united in its devotion to the task of finding a solution to these urgent problems.

23. The Government would therefore wish the Convention to consider the matter of whether progress could best be made on the basis of setting up a system of government which, though not temporary, is capable of evolving over a period of time into permanent and agreed constitutional arrangements.

24. Accordingly, by virtue of the powers conferred on me by paragraph 15(4) of Schedule 2 to the Northern Ireland Act 1974, I hereby reconvene the Convention as if it had not been dissolved, in order that it may consider and report on the following matters:

(a) how best agreement can be reached on a system of government built on the principles on which there is already widespread agreement, and providing for a form of partnership and participation, and which will command the most widespread acceptance throughout the whole of the community in Northern Ireland and in both parts of that community; (see paragraphs 6, 7 and 19 of this letter)

(b) whether a committee system might be of value as part of a wider and acceptable constitutional framework; (paragraph 12)

(c) whether progress could best be made on the basis of setting up a system of government which, though not temporary, is capable of evolving over a period of time into permanent and agreed constitutional arrangements; (paragraph 23).

Section IX
The impact of the European Community

'The Common Market? First left, past the church.'   (Anonymous)

The question of British entry into the European Economic Community was a major focus of political controversy in the 1960s and 1970s, and entry became a fact on 1 January 1973 (56). Part of the controversy focussed on the effects of entry upon the British system of government. There is little doubt that the implications of membership for traditional constitutional arrangements (57, 59) were played down not only by supporters of entry, but even by a British government intent on renegotiation of what it regarded as unfavourable terms of entry (58). The principal constitutional impact was upon the sovereignty of Parliament, hitherto the fount of all statute law in Britain, but now unable to intervene in the legislation which flows from Brussels in the form of regulations made by the European Council of Ministers. All that the British Parliament can do is to examine these regulations in draft and attempt to secure modifications through the British Ministers on the Council. The mass and complexity of this legislation is a formidable obstacle to effective scrutiny, and Parliament established both Lords and Commons Committees to deal with this problem, but a review of the work of the Commons Scrutiny Committee by the Select Committee on Procedure highlighted the major problem that it is difficult to find Parliamentary time to debate draft E.E.C. legislation which the Scrutiny Committee recommends for further consideration by the House; moreover, provisions of any urgency have to be put into effect without any opportunity for prior Parliamentary consideration (60). These problems would seem to justify the unease felt by critics of British entry into Europe about 'government from Brussels'.

Other constitutional innovations associated with Europe are the use of a referendum and the prospect of direct elections to the European Assembly. The Labour Government elected in 1974 came into office electorally committed to the renegotiation of the terms on which Britain had entered the Community in 1973. The entire Labour movement and its political leadership were seriously divided on the issue of involvement in Europe, and the decision to hold a referendum was an astute means of lowering the political temperature by placing responsibility for the decision on the country as a whole; at the same time, the Government declared themselves on one side of the question and were able to use their resources and machinery in aid of their position. Participation in the referendum was high, and it is possible that this form of consultation could be used again whenever controversial constitutional issues arise (61).

Part of the political development of the Community is a move towards the introduction of direct elections to the European Assembly, possibly as early as mid-1978.

371

The proposals (62) envisage that Britain would have 67 representatives, who would be elected at a fixed time and for a fixed period of five years, on the basis of electoral arrangements similar to those for the British Parliament (except for the drawing of special constituencies). The European Assembly has a limited, largely consultative role, with some power of control over the European Commission and the Community Budget.

56 THE FACTS

Extracts from *Britain 1974: An Official Handbook* (H.M.S.O., 1975); reprinted by permission of H.M.S.O.

On 1st January 1973, Britain, together with the Irish Republic and Denmark, joined the original six countries — Belgium, France, the Federal Republic of Germany, Italy, Luxembourg and the Netherlands — in the European Community. The Treaty of Accession was signed by the applicant countries and the original member states in January 1972.

The enlarged Community forms a trading area of over 250 million people and accounts for some 40 per cent of world trade. At a meeting of the nine heads of state or government held in Paris in October 1972, guide-lines and a timetable were agreed for the development of Community policies to bring about a European Union, including the establishment of economic and monetary union, by the end of 1980.

European Communities Act

The European Communities Act became law in October 1972 and made the legislative changes necessary to comply with Britain's obligations under the Treaty of Accession to make provision for the application of future Community decisions and to exercise the rights of membership. The Act gave the force of law in Britain to that part of Community law which is directly applicable in member states. It also contained detailed legislation (in part repealing or amending existing statutes) to implement Community obligations. Other Community obligations are being met under existing powers to make subordinate legislation, introduced as the measures become applicable.

FORMATION OF THE EUROPEAN COMMUNITIES

The European Community consists of three communities set up by separate treaties — the European Coal and Steel Community, the European Economic Community and the European Atomic Energy Community . . .

The European Coal and Steel Community

The European Coal and Steel Community (ECSC) was established in 1952, by bringing together the coal and steel resources of the six member countries, and formed the model for the 'community' approach to economic integration.

The European Economic Community

The European Economic Community (EEC) was created by the Treaty of Rome signed by the six countries in 1957, and aimed to promote the continued and balanced expansion of the members' economies by their progressive harmonisation and integration. The preamble to the treaty included among the basic objectives of the EEC the establishment of the foundations for a growing unity among European peoples, the improvement of their working and living conditions, the progressive abolition of restrictions on trade, and the development of the prosperity of overseas countries. The initial steps towards the attainment of these objectives were the creation of a customs union, abolition of internal tariffs and other barriers to trade and establishment of a common external tariff, the development of a common policy for agriculture, and the introduction of measures to establish the free movement of labour, capital and services. At the same time, provision was made for the overseas countries which had special links with the member countries to have an associate status with the EEC, with preferential treatment in aid and the development of trade.

At the Paris meeting in 1972 it was agreed that transition to economic and monetary union should involve parallel progress in regional, social, industrial, scientific and technological, environmental and energy policies. Joint action in external relations, particularly trade, and the reinforcement of Community institutions were also discussed.

The European Atomic Energy Community

The European Atomic Energy Community (Euratom) was set up by a second treaty signed in Rome in 1957 which provided for the co-ordinated development of members' atomic energy industries and of their other peaceful nuclear activities . . .

Institutions

The separate institutions established by the treaties for each of the three Communities were merged in 1967. The Community institutions, comprising the Council of Ministers, the Commission, the Court of Justice, the Assembly or European Parliament and others including a number dealing with specific subjects, provide a framework (see diagram overpage) within which the interests of the member states may be effectively represented and reconciled and common policies

Institutions of the European Community

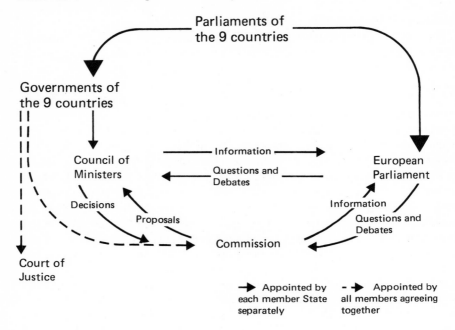

formulated and administered while national institutions and identities are fully safe-guarded.

In each of the institutions Britain has a position equal to that of France, the Federal Republic of Germany or Italy. English is one of the official languages of the Community.

The Council of Ministers is the decision-making body for all major questions, and is the only institution whose members, usually the foreign minister or other ministers appropriate to the subject of discussion, directly represent each member country. Most Council decisions are taken on the basis of a proposal by the Commission. Although provision is made in the Treaty of Rome for certain matters to be decided by a qualified majority, using a system of weighted voting, in practice decisions are taken on the basis of consensus. On all matters of major importance, affecting vital national interests, decisions are taken on the basis of unanimity.

The Commission is responsible for formulating policy proposals for submission to the Council of Ministers, for promoting the Community interest and attempting to reconcile national viewpoints and for implementing the provisions of the treaties and Community measures. It is composed of 13 commissioners nominated by the member governments; two are from Britain. Each commissioner is responsible for one or more of the main Community activities. The Commission is pledged to act in complete independence of national or sectional interests and to formulate its proposals and administer policy in the interests of the Community as a whole. Its proposals are made only after extensive consultation with officials of the national governments and with such organisations as producers, trade unions, employers' associations and many others.

The Court of Justice interprets and adjudicates on the meaning of the treaties and of any measures taken by the Council and Commission under them, hears complaints and appeals brought by or against the Communities' institutions, member states or individuals and gives preliminary rulings on questions referred to it by courts in the member states. As a court of final appeal its procedure in such cases is broadly similar to that of the highest courts in member states; its rulings are binding on member countries, Community institutions and individuals. The Court of Justice is being enlarged to consist of nine judges, assisted by four advocates-general.

The Assembly or European Parliament is composed of nominated members of the parliaments of member states, sitting according to party affiliation and not nationality. Britain is entitled to nominate 36 members out of a total of 198. The parliament is consulted on and debates all the major policy issues of the Communities. It also examines and approves the Communities' budget. Members of the parliament may question the Council and Commission and have the power to dismiss the Commission by a two-thirds majority.

The Committee of Permanent Representatives consists of representatives of the member states, of ambassadorial rank, whose task is to prepare for the meetings of the Council and perform whatever additional functions it might delegate.

. . . . . .

The Community budget

All member countries contribute to a common budget for certain specific purposes, such as agricultural support (administered by the European Agricultural Guidance and Guarantee Fund, often known by its French initials, FEOGA), the European Social Fund (used for occupational re-training and re-adaptation programmes and programmes designed to further manpower mobility), and administrative costs. Under the direct income system, which came into effect for the original members in January 1971, the Community is progressively drawing a greater proportion of the finance for this budget directly from the revenue of customs duties and of levies on agricultural imports . . .

57 IMPLICATIONS FOR THE BRITISH MACHINERY OF GOVERNMENT

Extracts from *The Royal Commission on The Constitution, 1969–73, Vol. 2, Memorandum of Dissent* (Cmnd. 5460, I, 1973); reprinted by permission of H.M.S.O. The dissenting members of the Commission believed that too little thought had been given to the consequences of membership of the European Community for British government, and they set out here their view of these consequences.

101. The first and clearest consequence of Common Market membership is that in many fields (not limited to Agriculture, Finance, Trade and Economics) important areas of decision making will inevitably be moved still further away from the citizens of the United Kingdom. Major policies will now be determined in Brussels, not London. This has a second important implication for what hitherto has been a vital feature of our system of government – the clear-cut nature of political responsibility. Hitherto, Parliament and the electorate have, in theory, at any rate, been able to hold a particular Minister or Government fully responsible for major policy decisions. This will now be changed. In future major policy in many fields will emanate from the Council of Ministers . . . There will, inevitably, therefore, be many instances when United Kingdom Ministers will have to tell Parliament that a particular policy is the best they could get rather than what they really wanted. So, with decision making moving still further away from the British people and with Parliament and the electorate unable in the future to hold Ministers or even the Government as fully responsible as now for major policy decisions, all this will give a still further impetus to the trend away from democratic control . . . unless we develop the appropriate countervailing forces.

102. The most obvious potential countervailing force is Parliament. And there is no doubt that in this respect it could have a major role to play. Thirty-six of its members are, of course, also members of the European Parliament. But while this will place an immense extra burden on them it can hardly produce much British impact on Brussels policy making – primarily because the European Parliament in Strasbourg . . . has virtually no power. So if United Kingdom Parliamentarians are to exercise any control of, or influence on, the European Commission and the Council of Ministers it will have to be done from London not Strasbourg. And even if the European Parliament manages to increase its powers, nevertheless United Kingdom Ministers in the Council of Ministers must remain accountable for their actions to the United Kingdom Parliament.

103. It is generally recognised that there is only one possible and satisfactory way for the United Kingdom Parliament to make its impact on the Brussels decision-making processes. This is for Parliament to be able to put its views to United Kingdom Ministers on the issues coming up for decision in the Council of Ministers. This means that M.P.s must be able to know in advance what proposals are in fact coming from the European Commission to the Council of Ministers. The pattern that probably ought to be followed here is that adopted in Western Germany. There the Federal Government is required to inform the West German Parliament (both the Bundestag and the Bundesrat) of any legislative proposals (i.e. proposed regulations or directives) being made by the Commission to the Council of Ministers which, if approved, would necessitate changes in German law. The proposals are then considered by the appropriate functional committees of the Bundestag (e.g. the Committee on Agriculture, etc.; each German Ministry has its counterpart specialised committee in the Bundestag). This has enabled committees of the Bundestag to investigate the proposals being made and to comment on them before the West German Government itself has to take a final decision for the meeting of the Council

of Ministers. The comments made by the Bundestag committees, including recommendations for change and improvement to the proposals being considered, are summarised in a report which then undergoes the formality of acceptance by the Bundestag itself. Only in a few exceptional cases have these reports been debated.

104. If the United Kingdom Parliament eventually adopts something broadly on the lines of the West German Parliament, this will, of course, add to its present burdens. It is important, therefore, to know how great that extra burden might be. In 1971 the Community made 2,900 Regulations and 410 Directives and Decisions. But over 90 per cent. of the Regulations represented autonomous Commission action . . . thus, while these Regulations have the direct force of law in member countries, they are in effect the detailed implementation by the Commission of broad policies already agreed on by the Council of Ministers. It could be argued, therefore, that this category of Regulations should not be scrutinised by the United Kingdom Parliament; certainly, Parliament could do no more than take note of them since normally, they are law from the date they are published. That still leaves, however, all the other Regulations and Directives. How many of these ought to be scrutinised by Parliament it is difficult to say. The guiding principle ought to be that all proposals made by the Commission to the Council of Ministers for decision should be submitted to Parliament for prior scrutiny and report by a Select Committee . . .

105. To scrutinise by some new Select Committee or Committees something like 200 proposed Common Market instruments a year is undoubtedly the least that Parliament should do if it is to exert some sort of democratic control and influence on what happens in Brussels. Many people would argue that Parliament should, indeed, go much further than this. For example, it has been suggested that by the time the Commission submits its proposed Regulations and Directives to the Council of Ministers, they are in too final a form to admit of much amendment. Thus there is a case for the Commission consulting with member Parliaments as it formulates the proposals it will eventually lay before the Council of Ministers. After all, at this stage the Commission has consultations with all the various international and national pressure groups which may be affected by its proposals. And no doubt the Commission officials will also at this stage be in informal contact with British Civil Servants. So why should the elected representatives of the people be excluded from the act? And then there is the problem of all those Regulations emanating directly from the Commission and having the force of law in member countries without scrutiny or approval by the Council of Ministers, the European Parliament or, at present, by any national Parliaments. Perhaps the European Parliament or the national Parliaments have a role to play here — if only in a post-mortem capacity?

106. Whatever final answers are given to the questions raised in paragraph 105 . . . three facts are clear beyond all reasonable doubt. Membership of the Common Market will:

(*a*) remove important areas of decision making still further away from the British people;

(*b*) further weaken the doctrine of ministerial responsibility. For decisions taken in the complex negotiating sessions in Brussels, it will be illogical and impractical to seek to pin responsibility for them on the British Government of the day. The British Government will have made its contribution, and no doubt have argued for solutions acceptable to this country. But the final result will be a compromise. Whilst Parliament will be justified in asking whether the British Government or individual ministers have played their cards well and pursued intelligent policies, it will be pointless to react as if the Government and its ministers were acting as independent agents;

(*c*) increase even more the power of officials. The Commission bureaucracy is the power-house of the Common Market. The interlocking contacts which are sure to develop between United Kingdom Civil Servants and their counterparts in the Commission and other member countries will add to the difficulties of ministerial control.

If the United Kingdom Parliament is to develop as an adequate countervailing force to the still further potential erosions of democracy involved in (*a*), (*b*) and (*c*) above, the fact has to be faced that Parliament will be taking on a very big additional burden. And if Parliament does not develop in this way, then the House of Commons Select Committee on Procedure was no doubt right when it reached this conclusion:

'Your Committee conclude that the entry of Britain into the Communities presents a profound challenge to many of the established procedures of Parliament *which, if not adequately dealt with, could leave Parliament substantially weaker vis-à-vis the executive*'.

107. Whatever Parliament does to meet this particular challenge, another certain consequence of Common Market membership will be the greatly increased burden of work which will be placed on United Kingdom Ministers and their departments ... at least some part of the responsibilities of every main home department of government are or will be affected by the new European dimension. As Sir Christopher Soames has emphasised, 'basically each Minister and each department will be responsible for its own European thinking ... Whole departments must now be learning to think European and to take account at all times of the obligations imposed by Community Membership. This will apply, too, in differing degrees to those government departments and to certain facets of local government which so far have had little or no responsibilities beyond our shores, but whose work will be found to have a European content'.

58 THE ROLE OF PARLIAMENT

Extracts from *Membership of the European Community: Report on Renegotiation* (Cmnd. 6003, 1975); reprinted by permission of H.M.S.O. A main argument by critics of entry to the European community was that membership would entail a dilution of the key constitutional principle of Parliamentary sovereignty. This extract expresses the Government's view of this problem.

133. [It was earlier] pointed out that one of the distinctive and fundamental features of the Community was the system of directly applicable Community law. This system provided an effective means of implementing and enforcing the collective agreements of governments in the Council. National courts are required to apply directly applicable Community law and to give it priority should it conflict with national legislation.

134. Thus membership of the Community raises for us the problem of reconciling this system of directly applicable law made by the Community with our constitutional principle that Parliament is the sovereign legislator and can make or unmake any law whatsoever. That principle remains unaltered by our membership of the Community: Parliament retains its ultimate right to legislate on any matter. The situation was fully analysed in the White Paper published by the Labour Government in May 1967:

'[If this country became a member of the European Communities,] it would be necessary to pass legislation giving the force of law to those provisions of the Treaties and Community instruments which are intended to take direct internal effect within the Member States. This legislation would be needed because, under our constitutional law, adherence to a treaty does not of itself have the effect of changing our internal law even where provisions of the treaty are intended to have direct internal effect as law within the participating States. The legislation would have to cover both provisions in force when we joined and those coming into force subsequently as a result of instruments issued by the Community institutions. No new problem would be created by the provisions which were in force at the time we became a member of the Communities. The constitutional innovation would lie in the acceptance in advance as part of the law of the United Kingdom of provisions to be made in the future by instruments issued by the Community institutions – a situation for which there is no precedent in this country. However, these instruments, like ordinary delegated legislation, would derive their force under the law of the United Kingdom from the original enactment passed by Parliament . . .

It would also follow that within the fields occupied by the Community law Parliament would have to refrain from passing fresh legislation inconsistent with that law as for the time being in force.'

135. The problem therefore has to be considered from two aspects: first, the general issue of whether the ultimate sovereignty of Parliament has been weakened, and secondly, whether Parliament can play an effective role in the making of any particular new Community law. On the general issue, Parliament by the European Communities Act 1972 authorised the application in this country of directly applicable Community law and to that extent has delegated its powers. Parliament has however the undoubted power to repeal that Act, on which our ability to fulfil

our Treaty obligations still depends. Thus our membership of the Community in the future depends on the continuing assent of Parliament.

136. At the level of the day-to-day legislative activity of the Community there is a range of legislative instruments, from the purely technical and regulatory to items of major policy significance. Apart from the instruments made by the Commission in specific areas . . . all items of Community law are contained in instruments adopted by the Council, in whose discussions and decisions United Kingdom Ministers necessarily take part. Parliament, by passing the 1972 Act, in effect remitted to the Government responsibility for safeguarding United Kingdom interests in the Council deliberations which result in directly applicable Community law. United Kingdom Ministers remain directly answerable to Parliament, since the continuance of any Government depends on Parliament's support. Parliament thus operates in the Community law-making process by exercising its traditional role of controlling and restraining the Government against the background of the ultimate sanction of withdrawal of confidence. This applies to Ministers when they are sitting in the Council in Brussels as much as when they are taking decisions solely as members of the Government of the United Kingdom.

137. For Parliament to exercise this control and restraint it is essential that it should have sufficient information and the opportunity to make its views known to Ministers. The Government have been concerned since they took office in 1974 to ensure that these requirements are met.

138. Following the recommendations of Select Committees of both Houses of Parliament, and on the initiative of the Government, Scrutiny Committees were set up with the status of Select Committees in both Houses in April and May 1974. The Scrutiny Committees have the task of examining all Commission proposals for Council legislation and other documents published by the Commission for submission to the Council, and of reporting in particular on those which should be debated in Parliament because of the political or legal issues which they raise. The Government have undertaken to supply the Committees with the information which they need and to find time for debates which they recommend. They have further undertaken to ensure, consistently with the national interest, that final decisions are not taken in the Council of Ministers on proposals recommended for debate in Parliament until the debate has taken place.

139. Over the whole range of Council instruments the Community's practice is to publish proposals so that they are available for public examination and discussion some time before they come up for discussion in the Council of Ministers. In many cases therefore Parliament is able to consider proposals at a much earlier stage in the policy-making process than if the proposals were for United Kingdom subordinate legislation. Moreover, the supervision exercised by Parliament extends over a wider range of subjects, in greater detail, because the Community practice is to include in legal instruments decisions which we might take administratively.

140. From the date of their being set up to 21 March 1975, the House of Commons Scrutiny Committee considered and reported on 366 Community documents and the House of Lords Committee on 397 documents. Of these the Commons

Committee identified 58 documents as raising issues of sufficient importance to warrant their being debated by the House, and the Lords Committee similarly identified 21 documents. Up to the same date 35 of these documents were debated in the Commons and 11 in the Lords; the remainder will be debated in due course. In these debates Members have expressed their views on Community proposals. On a number of occasions the debates in the House of Commons have led to resolutions committing the Government to a particular course of action in subsequent negotiations in the Council of Ministers.

141. The Government intend to continue to develop these arrangements so as to make them more effective and to enable Parliament to express its views on draft Community legislation in the most appropriate way. The House of Commons Select Committee on Procedure has been asked to consider the despatch of business relating to European secondary legislation, which brings additional pressure to an already crowded Parliamentary timetable. The Government propose to improve the arrangements in the light of the Procedure Committee's report which is expected shortly.

59 COMMON LAW OR COMMON MARKET?

Extracts from Lord Chief Justice Scarman, 'Common Law or Common Market?', published in *The Listener*, 31 October 1974; reprinted by permission of the author. The Lord Chief Justice describes European entry as constituting a 'legal revolution'.

Momentous legal events have a way of happening in our society without anyone troubling much about them at the time. Later, when the event is beyond recall, and its consequences seen, the debate begins. The way that we slipped into a new legal world on 1 January 1973, when the European Communities Act 1972 came into force, is a good illustration. The economics and politics of entry into the Common Market were fiercely debated at the time: voices, notably that of Enoch Powell, were heard in protest at the consequences of entry for the legislative sovereignty of Parliament.

But the general public were not told, and few, very few, of the legal profession realised that the English were entering not only a new market but a different legal system, which springs from the Roman law — from which we have kept aloof ever since the end of the Roman occupation of Britain . . .

Lawyers, civil servants, politicians and academics are still playing down the legal revolution to which we are committed by international obligation and by Act of Parliament. 'Community law operates only in the fields covered by the European Treaties, and its immediate consequences are economic.' So says the majority of the Kilbrandon Commission on the Constitution; they then proceed to dismiss from their consideration the constitutional implications of entry as being 'largely questions for the future'. The minority report is more realistic: it contains a chapter entitled 'The Common Market Dimension' in which it is argued — surely, correctly — that there are features of the Common Market which seem likely to have profound consequences for our main institutions of government.

The three European Treaties are part of the law of England; they establish three communities, the Coal and Steel Community, the Euratom Community, and the Economic Community. They are wide-ranging, covering indirect taxation (for instance, the VAT), agriculture, fisheries, movement of labour, services and capital, transport, monopolies, restrictive practices, state aid for industry, the coal, steel and nuclear energy industries. Community legislation and Community judicial decisions will affect us in all these areas of social, economic and industrial activity. In these fields the Community makes law; and the Community decides what the laws mean. The role of our courts is to apply the law as made by Community institutions.

The system works in this way. The European Treaties are part of the law of the land: for Parliament has so enacted. Each treaty — and I will take the economic treaty, the Treaty of Rome, as my example — empowers the Community to legislate to give effect to the Treaties. The legislative power belongs to the Council of Ministers, who act upon the initiative of the European Commission and, sometimes but not invariably, after consultation with the European Parliament. From the deliberations of these bodies there emerge various sorts of Community enactments — regulations, directives, decision. Regulations have direct effect within members states: that is to say, they are part of the law of the land to be applied and enforced by our courts . . . Directives are not necessarily part of the law when made — though they may be, if they are so interpreted by the European Court of Justice.

By these various types of instruments, Community institutions make legal rules which bind us, and must be enforced by our courts. Their drafting — indeed all the work of their preparation — is the task of the Commission, the appointed body of high-powered European officials, who work full time for the Community in Brussels. The British Parliament plays no part in the preparation of Community legislation. Parliament completed its job when it enacted in 1972 that the Treaties and Community legislation deriving from them were to be part of English law, and that the courts were to accept the European Court of Justice as their authoritative interpreter. No doubt, Parliament will create some means of scrutiny and consultation before the Community issues new legislation; but this will not alter the legal position. We now have a new source of law.

The Common Market Treaties leave a lot to the judges to do; an English Act of Parliament leaves as little as possible. The Treaty of Rome imposes upon the European Court of Justice the duty of ensuring the effectual implementation of the Treaty. On all questions as to the meaning of the Treaties, and their derivative legislation, this is a Supreme Court. It is continental in style, outlook and procedure: its attitude to the Treaties is — absolutely properly, I think — activist. It will interpret them and the regulations made under them in a way that helps to achieve their purpose. If there is an omission the Court is prepared to remedy it. If words are capable of more than one meaning, they will assign to them the meaning most consistent with the overall purpose of the Treaties — even if the meaning be a strained one.

It is, of course, for the Court to say what is the purpose of the Treaties, and what the intention of the regulations. Because of their broad declarations of principle, the task is not really very difficult, so far as the Treaties are concerned. But finding out the intention of a regulation could be a real problem. It is, however, greatly simplified, because regulations are preceded by recitals or preambles which direct attention to all sorts of matters — specific articles of the Treaties, memoranda, records of discussions, and so on — to which the Court may look for a proper understanding of the meaning. Finally — an immense power — the European Court can invalidate Community legislation, if in its opinion it infringes the Treaty, or its preparation and issue have been irregular.

Lord Denning put it mildly when he said that we lawyers have to learn a new system. The Common Market presents us not only with a new-style legislation but with a new and challenging role for the courts. Our courts accept a strict discipline when confronted with an Act of Parliament: within its context they are obedient to the letter of the law, but they will not extend its operation to situations not covered by the Act, even though it would seem right in principle to do so. Parliament's mistakes and omissions are for Parliament, not the courts, to remedy. But this is not the approach of the European Court of Justice to the legislation of the Communities. It exercises great freedom in the interpretation of the legislation so as to ensure that the principles of the Common Market are fully developed, not frustrated, in its jurisprudence. We now have to follow the European Court: and subject always to its ultimate ruling, our judges will have a freedom and power when dealing with Community legislation that they do not have with Acts of Parliament.

Is this the beginning of a new legal era? It could be. I do not think the judges will relish applying one set of standards to Community legislation and another to Acts of Parliament. If we remain part of the Common Market, I would expect European methods and approach to enacted law to triumph over that of the common law. This would be a breath of fresh air, greatly to the advantage of the law in the United Kingdom. But whatever the future, the law will never be quite the same again.

We have learnt a new approach to enacted law: new ways of writing it, of interpreting its meaning and effect, and of handling it. We are, at this moment, part of a legal system which not only confers a right but imposes a duty on the courts in certain circumstances to invalidate legislation: that is, to quash it. Compare this alone with the unquestioning obedience of our courts to the enacted word of Parliament, and you will see why I suggest that, on 1 January 1973, there occurred, unheralded and unnoticed, a legal revolution.

60 PARLIAMENTARY SCRUTINY OF EUROPEAN SECONDARY LEGISLATION

Extracts from the *First Report of the Select Committee on Procedure: European*

Secondary Legislation (H.C. 294, 1974–5); reprinted by permission of H.M.S.O.
Extract (a) defines European secondary legislation. Extract (b) describes the proposals of the Foster Committee (the Commons Select Committee on European
Community Secondary Legislation, specially appointed to advise how Parliament
should handle European legislation) for a new Scrutiny Committee which would
sift draft European legislation, and other relevant documents, and draw to the
attention of the House any matters of legal or political importance. This new Select
Committee on European Secondary Legislation was established in May 1974 under
the chairmanship of Mr John Davies and has 16 members; extract (c) gives an
account of its work. Extract (d) is from the 1974–5 Procedure Committee's review
of these scrutiny arrangements, which many parliamentarians regard as unsatisfactory.

(a)

3. The secondary legislation of the Communities was defined by the Foster Committee as:
    (i)   regulations, made by the Council or the Commission which are of general
           application, binding in their entirety and directly applicable in all Member
           states;
    (ii)   directives, issued by the Council or the Commission, which are binding as
           to the result to be achieved but which leave the choice of form and
           methods to the Member states;
    (iii)   decisions, taken by the Council or the Commission, which are binding in
           their entirety upon those to whom they are addressed;
    (iv)   the general budget, a preliminary draft of which must be submitted by the
           Commission to the Council by 1st September each year, and which must
           thereafter be sent to the European Assembly by 5th October, and returned
           to the Council for final decision before 31st December.
    (v)   instruments, made by the Council, concluding Treaties negotiated by the
           Community institutions, for example Treaties between the EEC and third
           parties (this excludes Treaties to which the Member states of the EEC are
           signatories as individual states).

4. It will be noted that some legislation is made by the Council and some by the
Commission. The latter legislation made by the Commission is made under powers
delegated by the Council and forms the overwhelming bulk of the legislation, in the
region of 90 per cent. The legislation that is deemed to be more important is made
by the Council on the proposal of the Commission and amounts to approximately
300–400 documents a year. The European Secondary Legislation etc. Committee
only deals with Council-made legislation and it is only in regard to this type of
legislation that special arrangements have been made for debate in the House. Since
the order of reference of the Procedure Committee only deals with legislation considered by the European Secondary Legislation etc. Committee, no further mention
is made of the legislation made directly by the Commission without reference to the

Council; further evidence could however be given on this, if background information is required.

5. Although the Procedure Committee's order of reference is only concerned with European legislation, they may wish to know by way of background information that the Scrutiny Committee does not deal with secondary legislation alone. Their order of reference both in the sole Session of the last Parliament, and in this Session, requires them to consider not only secondary legislation but 'other documents published by the Commission for submission to the Council of Ministers'. Within this heading the present Scrutiny Committee would include:

(i)   policy guidelines and draft resolutions,

(ii)   draft directives and other documents relating to mandates for trade negotiations (which the Foster Committee included in its definition of secondary legislation).

(iii) communications from the Commission to the Council regarding occasions when Commission Management and Regulation Committees have dissented from decisions by the Commission within the field of its delegated authority.

(iv) communications from the Commission to the Council of Ministers regarding requests by individual member countries for action by the Commission within the field of its delegated authority which it has rejected.

(b)

THE SECOND REPORT OF THE FOSTER COMMITTEE

7. In their Second Report the Foster Committee noted that as the consequence of membership of the Communities substantial and important parts of the UK law would now be made in new and different ways and with new and different consequences. In their view it remained central to the UK concept and structure of parliamentary democracy that control of the law making processes lay with Parliament — and ultimately with the elected Members of it. It followed therefore that new and special procedures were necessary, to make good so far as might be done, inroads made into that concept and structure by the new methods of making law. In the view of the Foster Committee the objective must be to restore to Parliament responsibilities for, and opportunities to exercise its constitutional rights in respect of, the making of these laws — involving as that must, acceptance:

(i)   by the Government that it necessarily followed that that must be at the expense of the freedom of action enjoyed by the Executive since UK entry into the EEC; and

(ii)   by Parliament that the scope, means and degree of scrutiny and control must all be attuned to the fact that it was dealing with a new way of making laws which was very different from that to which it had been accustomed.

8. The Foster Committee proceeded on the assumption that, on the basis of at least 300 to 400 proposals made by the Commission to the Council for legislation a year, it would obviously be necessary to have a sifting process to select the more important proposals for consideration by the House. They envisaged a preliminary sifting by a Minister responsible for European Community affairs and a new third law officer, assisted by a committee of Civil Service officials. The duty of the officials would be to isolate all proposals which they considered to be unimportant and report to the two Ministers concerned. The Ministers and the new law officer would then lay the results of their sifting before a new Committee composed of Members of the House of Commons.

9. The Committee would be a new and different type of Committee, for its functions and duties would be of a new and different kind. Its working procedures would be as determined by it, and as varied by it as considered necessary to deal with each situation, and could therefore be at all times as formal or informal as the Committee considered appropriate to the occasion. It was envisaged that the new Committee would meet at least fortnightly during the sittings of the House and perhaps once or twice during the summer recess. It would be served by the Clerks of the House and would have the assistance of the Civil Service officials referred to in paragraph 8 above. It was further recommended that the services of a House of Commons official of the status and qualifications of the Speaker's Counsel should be available to the members of the Committee.

10. The Foster Committee thought that on the basis of a fortnightly intake of some 30 proposals each member of the new Scrutiny Committee would receive copies of all 30 proposals with accompanying explanatory statements. In addition to examining legislative proposals, it was essential in their view that the new Committee (and through it the House) should receive as much early warning as possible of major policy documents, so that appropriate action could be taken to consider their probable impact on the Constitution, law and practice of the UK.

11. The object of the new Scrutiny Committee was to be to inform the House as to any proposals of legal or political importance and to make recommendations as to their further consideration. Its task would not be to debate the reasons for or against a proposal, but to give the House the fullest information as to why it considered a particular proposal of importance and to point out the matter of principle or policy which it affected and the changes in UK law involved.

12. The new Scrutiny Committee would have power to report at any time. Thus, proposals which it reported to be only of lesser importance would require no special procedure for their further consideration by the House; i.e. it would be open to any Member to table a motion rejecting or amending them. But a proposal reported by the new Committee to be of major importance should be referred to the House for consideration and debate well before the expected decision of the Council of Ministers upon the proposal. Furthermore a proposal reported by the Committee to be of extreme urgency and importance should be debated by the House within two weeks of the report unless an earlier debate during the course of normal business included the subject matter of the proposal.

. . . . . .

15. As regards implementation the Foster Committee said that it might be considered desirable, perhaps even in some instances necessary, to make some additions to or changes in Standing Orders or otherwise to secure the effective implementation of their recommendations. It seemed however to the Foster Committee to be entirely within the power of a Government to give full effect to the recommendations without any such changes, e.g. by the Government undertaking to provide, and in fact providing, time as required by the recommendations of the Committee. The Government should further accept that it would not cause or permit the law of the UK to be changed contrary to a Resolution of the House . . .

16. The Foster Committee also considered that some EEC matters might be of sufficient importance to warrant a debate in the House, either because they affected a number of constituencies or because they were of importance to certain groups. In some cases these might be proposals for secondary legislation which had not been characterised by the Scrutiny Committee as important, sometimes perhaps because matters changing the degree of importance of the proposal had arisen because of subsequent events . . .

17. The Foster Committee made further recommendations on the debates on Community matters in general. These are not directly relevant to the matters referred to the Procedure Committee, but since they have relevance to the total time made available for consideration of European Community affairs, a brief mention is made of them. It was recommended that the Government should make a report to Parliament each six months on EEC matters generally and that two days each Session should be provided by the Government to debate these reports. The Foster Committee also considered that specific provision should be made by Sessional or Standing Order to enable debates on EEC matters in general to be held on a certain number of days each Session. They recommended that four days should be so provided (in addition to the two days for debating the six monthly reports). The subject for debate should be chosen on two of the days by the Government and on two by the Opposition and they could be split up for shorter debates if required.

(c)

THE WORK OF THE SCRUTINY COMMITTEE

31. The European Secondary Legislation Committee (the Scrutiny Committee) were first set up on 7th May 1974 in the last Parliament. They were set up again as a permanent Committee for the remainder of the Parliament (i.e. their existence is not terminated by the end of a Session) on 18th November 1974. Their order of reference is as follows:

'to consider draft proposals by the Commission of the European Economic Communities for secondary legislation and other documents published by the Commission for submission to the Council of Ministers, and to report their opinion as to whether such proposals or other documents raise questions of legal or political importance, to give their reasons for their opinion, to report what matters of principle or policy may be affected thereby, and to what extent they may affect the law of the United Kingdom, and to make recommendations for the further consideration of such proposals and other documents by the House.'

32. There are 16 members of the Committee which has the usual powers of a Select Committee including the power to appoint specialist advisers and to appoint Sub-Committees . . .

. . . . . .

34. In their Reports to the House the Scrutiny Committee usually interpret their order of reference so as to note secondary legislation under the following headings:

(i)	They may report that proposals for legislation do *not* raise questions of either legal or political importance.

(ii)	They may report that proposals for legislation *do* raise questions of either legal or political importance or both, *without* recommending that they should be considered by the House.

(iii)	They may report that proposals for legislation *do* raise questions of either legal or political importance or both, stating that they have *suspended judgement* on whether or not the proposals should be considered by the House, pending further information or further developments.

(iv)	They may report that proposals for legislation *do* raise questions of either political or legal importance or both and *should* be considered by the House.

35. In their Second Special Report of 1974 (paragraph 20), the Scrutiny Committee observed that the fact that a proposal or document had been classed as in their opinion unimportant, i.e., came within the category mentioned in head (i) of the previous paragraph of this memorandum, did not of course preclude any Member of the House (or of the Committee) from raising it in question or debate or from pressing the Government for it to be debated, on the floor of the House. They added that this was 'the more so when the Committee finds a document politically or legally important but makes no recommendation for its further consideration by the House' — i.e. when the Committee had reported a document or proposal under heading (ii) of the previous paragraph of this memorandum. They hoped however that Members of the House with an interest in a particular document would make their opinion known to the Committee.

36. The Scrutiny Committee acknowledged in their second Special Report of 1974 (para. 31) that they ought, under their terms of reference, to give reasons for their opinions and to report 'what matters of principle or policy may be affected' by Community documents. Owing to the lack both of time and of expert staff, they had hitherto been unable to perform these tasks. They saw their duty, and that of their successors in the future, to be the provision of Reports, in good time for the House to hold debates (or for individual Members to pursue the matter) before final decisions were taken in the Council. These reports should contain reasons why a document was important, and why in the appropriate cases it

required debate, together with explanations of the matters of principle or policy involved.

. . . . . .

40. By the end of last Session the Scrutiny Committee had effectively considered 117 documents; they were unable to consider some 75 more, because the proposals for legislation concerned had been agreed to by the Council before they could be scrutinised by the Committee. Of the 117 documents considered, 21 were specifically recommended for debate . . .

41. The number of documents recommended for debate forms just under 20 per cent. of the total number scrutinised. The Scrutiny Committee also classified 25 additional documents as raising questions of political or legal importance or both, without recommending consideration by the House.

. . . . . .

49. Certainly if the proportion of documents recommended for debate in the House by the Scrutiny Committee remains at the level that has obtained since May 1974, the House faces a formidable task in finding time for debate. It has already been stated that the Scrutiny Committee have listed 20 per cent. of the documents scrutinised as important and recommended for debate, and if the figures of those listed as important but not necessarily recommended for debate is included, the percentage is 41 per cent. Taking 350 . . . as the mean of the documents to be scrutinised in an average year when the backlog has disappeared, this would mean that 143 documents would be listed as important on this basis, and 70 specifically recommended for debate. Assuming that only 70 documents were in fact debated, that they were grouped in pairs for the purpose of debate and that each debate lasted for 1½ hours, a total of 54 hours, or the equivalent of 9 parliamentary days of 6 hours (i.e. 4pm—10pm) would be required for debate.

. . . . . .

. . . One thing appears to be certain. If the situation is left as it is, those documents listed as important but not carrying the obligation of debate have a very slight chance indeed of being debated, despite the Scrutiny Committee's general observations that they are candidates, though not obligatory ones, for consideration by the House . . .

(d)

. . . . . .

. . . European Secondary Legislation is a term which Your Committee have found it convenient to use to describe legislation proposed by the European Commission for submission to the Council of Ministers. It does not cover the legislative instruments made by the Commission which have effect without approval by the Council. This latter class of instruments do not come before the Select Committee on European Secondary Legislation, &c., and are therefore not brought to the attention of the House.

5. Successive Governments have accepted the main proposals of the Foster Com-

mittee, subject to minor reservations and modifications. The arrangements at present in force were set out in the statement of Government policy by the Leader of the House on 2nd May, 1974. They can be summarised very briefly as follows: a Select Committee on European Secondary Legislation, &c., has been appointed, to carry out the sifting process recommended by the Foster Committee; proposals for Community legislation (including consultative documents) published by the European Commission for submission to the Council of Ministers are transmitted by the Government to the Select Committee together with explanatory memoranda; the Committee examine the proposals and report to the House whether legal or political importance (or both) attach to each, recommending that certain of the more important should be further considered by the House. The Government have undertaken to provide time for the consideration of all proposals so recommended; they have also undertaken to arrange for six days in each Session to be set aside for debates on general Community matters. On a number of occasions since 2nd May, 1974, the Government have given assurances that, if the Select Committee report that a European Commission legislative proposal should be further considered by the House, U.K. Ministers will not (except in extreme urgency) permit that proposal to pass the Council of Ministers until it has been so considered . . .

. . . . . .

Presentation of documents 8. Your Committee acknowledge the strenuous efforts made by the Government and the Vote Office to ensure that Commission documents and explanatory memoranda are available to Members. They nevertheless consider that further action is required to assist Members and the House in dealing with these voluminous and complex papers. The documents should, so far as practicable, be produced for the House in a standard format and should be numbered systematically so that they can be easily identified, listed and indexed. Where possible each document should bear an explanatory note describing its genesis and status and the relative urgency attaching to it. Moreover, since the effectiveness of debate in the House frequently depends upon consultation with outside interests, it is desirable that documents which have been recommended for debate and any relevant explanatory notes should be made readily available to the public in time to allow for representations to be made to Members.

. . . . . .

11. The regular provision of up-to-date documents in time for their consideration by the Select Committee on European Secondary Legislation, &c., and the House is made more difficult by the working methods of the Community. On a number of occasions the Government has been unable to provide the documents in time for the Select Committee to consider proposals before their adoption by the Council of Ministers. Moreover, a Commission proposal is subject to amendment as a result of negotiations between individual member States and the Commission right up to the moment when it comes before the Council. It is difficult for the Select Committee or the House to obtain full and up-to-date information on these developments, particularly since the Government normally treats the amendments proposed by

themselves and other Governments as confidential. By the time the House comes to consider the matter, the proposal may differ considerably from the original document on which the Select Committee have already reported; and the version which finally comes before the Council of Ministers may differ still further. The informal links which the Select Committee have established with the Commission, the Council and the British Permanent Representatives in Brussels should, with the assistance of H.M. Government, be strengthened and formalised so that the Committee received earlier warning not only of Commission proposals but also of amendments proposed thereto. Your Committee welcome the intention of the Select Committee to report as early as possible on the original instrument and to take a second look in all cases where instruments had subsequently been substantially amended.

. . . . . .

CONSIDERATION OF THE COMMISSION DOCUMENTS IN THE HOUSE

13. It is impossible accurately to forecast how many legislative proposals and consultative documents will be put forward by the European Commission in any year, but between 650 and 700 seems likely. In Session 1974, of the 192 documents considered by the Committee on European Secondary Legislation 21 were recommended for further consideration by the House, and of these 5 were considered . . .

14. Most of the debates on Commission documents, in last Session and this (up till the end of February), have taken place on Motions (moved by Ministers) to take note of a document or group of documents. In one instance the Motion proposed to approve the document, in four others, to take note with reservations. In one case, the debate has taken place on a Motion for the Adjournment of the House. On several occasions Amendments have been proposed, two of which were agreed to. In all but four cases, the proceedings have been entered upon after Ten o'clock, and in all but two the Government have moved to suspend the rule so as to enable the debate to continue for one and a half hours. On three occasions the time available has elapsed without a decision being reached, and the Debate has stood adjourned and has not been resumed.

15. Of the six days per Session which are to be allotted to consideration of general Community matters (including two days on half yearly reports by the Government on developments in the Communities) only two have so far been taken up . . .

16. All the evidence given to Your Committee was to the effect that the arrangements and procedure for the House's further consideration of Commission documents have been unsatisfactory in various ways. This evidence has been supported by many complaints made in the House in the course of debate. Some at least of the difficulties might be overcome by referring certain Commission documents to Committees, who would report to the House on the merits of the proposals . . . Your Committee recommend that amendments which are of substance and which

affect the United Kingdom should be set out in an up-to-date explanatory memorandum to be laid before the House, and that there should be an opportunity for
them to be considered, either in the House or (on the initiative of a private Member)
in a Standing Committee. This arrangement would enable the House to consider
and express a view on documents in their original form at an early date, if so
desired, but would provide a safeguard in cases where the final form of the document was materially different. Your Committee do not consider that such further
consideration should be made compulsory by Standing Order, since in their view
this would be too inflexible a way of dealing with very varied circumstances. The
Select Committee on European Secondary Legislation, &c., propose to examine and
report on documents which have been substantially amended. Their subsequent
report and recommendation will guide the House in any decision whether, and how,
such amendments should be further considered.

. . . . . .

Retrospective consideration 19. There will necessarily be occasions when the Council
of Ministers deals with proposals at extremely short notice, and H.M. Government
must act in the Council without the House having had an opportunity to consider
the proposal (or amendments thereto) . . . Your Committee consider that it would
be of assistance to the House if the Select Committee were to make a practice of
reporting whether any, and which, of the proposals which have passed the Council
in this way are of major political or legal importance, and whether such a proposal
should be further considered by the House. In reaching their decision, the Select
Committee would no doubt take into account any representations from Members
regarding the action of the Minister concerned. Your Committee consider that
documents recommended for retrospective consideration in this way would come
within the Government's undertaking to provide time in the House. Your Committee believe that the occasions for such consideration would be extremely rare.

. . . . . .

22. Your Committee consider that one or more of the six days per Session which
the Government have undertaken to make available for debates on general Community matters should be used for the consideration of Commission documents of
major importance. Those documents which are largely or entirely consultative
rather than legislative would seem particularly suitable for such an arrangement. By
separating consultative documents the House will be better able to concentrate on
purely legislative proposals on other occasions. Your Committee also suggest that
those who manage the business of the House should consider the further possibility
of dividing one or more of the six days into half days to suit debates on particular
documents or groups of documents.

Form of Motion and opportunity for decision 23. Your Committee have referred,
in paragraph 4, to the basic proposition put forward by the Foster Committee in
their Report of Session 1972–73, that the House can, by insisting on the accountability of United Kingdom Ministers to the United Kingdom Parliament, exercise a

degree of control over certain European legislation comparable to that exercised by the House over United Kingdom delegated legislation. The extent of the House's control over U.K. delegated legislation is an absolute constitutional power to accept or reject it. In the case of European Secondary Legislation, it is open to the House to pass a Resolution instructing U.K. Ministers, through the use of the veto, to secure the rejection of the legislative proposals at the Council of Ministers. It is also possible for the House by Resolution to instruct U.K. Ministers to attempt to obtain changes in the proposals of the Commission (on the assumption that they would use the threat of an eventual veto to secure agreement to such changes).

24. Clearly, a Resolution of the House in regard to European Legislation has not the force of law in the same sense as a Resolution approving or annulling a Statutory Instrument. Although the Government have accepted that they cannot, in this matter, disregard the Resolutions of the House, such an undertaking has no legal effect. The final effectiveness of the House's control may depend upon the extent to which it is prepared to insist upon its wishes. The Clerk Assistant put the point in this way: 'Ministers ignore resolutions of the House at their peril. If they do ignore them, motion of censure can be put down. If motions of censure are ignored, Supply could be refused to the department concerned'. Your Committee assume, however, that in any foreseeable circumstances, a Resolution requiring the Minister concerned to take certain action in the Council of Ministers would be complied with. Such a Resolution is therefore the most important step in the House's influence over European Secondary Legislation.

61 THE REFERENDUM

Extracts from *Referendum on U.K. Membership of the European Community* (Cmnd. 5295, 1975); reprinted by permission of H.M.S.O. A referendum on renegotiation of British membership of the European community was held on 5 June 1975. These extracts describe the arrangements, and indicate that individual Ministers were permitted to ignore the requirements of collective Ministerial responsibility during the campaign. The referendum was decisively in favour of continued membership of the European community (67.2% against 32.8%).

It is the declared policy of the Government that, once the outcome of our renegotiation of the terms of membership is known, the British people should have the right to decide, through the ballot box, by means either of a General Election or of a referendum, whether Britain should continue in membership of the European Community or should withdraw.

The Government have decided that this should be done by means of a referendum.

. . . . . .

When the outcome of renegotiation is known, the Government will decide upon their own recommendation to the country, whether for continued membership of the Community on the basis of the renegotiated terms, or for withdrawal, and will announce their decision to the House in due course. That announcement will provide an opportunity for the House to debate the question of substance. That does not, of course, preclude debates at any earlier time, subject to the convenience of the House.

The circumstances of this referendum are unique, and the issue to be decided is one on which strong views have long been held which cross party lines. The Cabinet has, therefore, decided that if, when the time comes, there are members of the Government, including members of the Cabinet, who do not feel able to accept and support the Government's recommendation, whatever it may be, they will, once the recommendation has been announced, be free to support and speak in favour of a different conclusion in the referendum campaign.

. . . . . .

2. The poll and the Question

5. The Government's general approach to the organisation of the referendum is that the familiar procedures and practices applied to normal United Kingdom elections should be used as far as possible. The same approach applies to the more general questions of the size of the poll and of the majority required to provide a decisive result; these are discussed below.

Size of Poll and Majority 6. The Government have agreed to be bound by the verdict of the British people as expressed in the referendum result. They have considered whether that result should be subject to any special conditions in terms of the size of the poll or the extent of the majority.

7. It may be argued that a verdict of such importance should not depend on a simple majority — theoretically a single vote in an electorate of 40 million . . .

8. The Government are concerned that the size of the poll should be adequate, and they are confident that it will be so. They also consider it to be of great importance that the verdict of the poll should be clear and conclusive. In the circumstances they believe that it will be best to follow the normal electoral practice and accept that the referendum result should rest on a simple majority — without qualifications or conditions of any kind.

The Question of the Ballot Paper 9. It has been suggested that more than one question should be posed on the ballot paper, and that the questions should include one asking if the voters would prefer to leave the issue to Parliament. But the Prime Minister has made it clear on several occasions that the referendum will ask for a simple 'Yes' or 'No' to a single straight-forward question about staying in or leaving the Community in the light of the renegotiated terms of membership, and the Government believe that the advantage lies with simplicity. The question will be embodied in the Referendum Bill itself and will therefore be approved by Parliament.

10. Some argue that the precise wording of the question can have a significant effect upon the result. Although there is no reliable evidence to support this view, the Government will seek to ensure that the words on the ballot paper are as free from bias as possible . . .

. . . . . .

Electorate 12. In the Government's view the electorate should include those on the current Parliamentary election register which came into force earlier this month, together with peers (who are registered for local government elections but cannot vote in Parliamentary elections).

. . . . . .

GOVERNMENT INFORMATION ACTIVITIES

25. The Government have given careful consideration to the part they should play in providing information to the public about the issue of continued membership of the European Community and about the referendum itself. The question of membership has been debated many times in the last 15 years and a massive Government information campaign would be inappropriate. The campaigning organisations, the press, radio and television can all be expected to provide an ample supply of information about the Community.

26. The Government will however ensure that the outcome of the renegotiation and their own recommendation whether to stay in the Community or not are explained fully to the voters by the publication of a White Paper (which will be debated in Parliament) and of a popular version containing a less technical account of the renegotiated terms and the Government's recommendation.

27. The referendum itself will be unfamiliar to the public and the Government will take appropriate steps to publicise the date of the poll and the procedures for voting.

28. The Government will accordingly arrange for the delivery to every household of the popular version of the White Paper and an explanation of the way in which the referendum will be conducted.

29. A large number of bodies will be engaged in the campaign and the Government have explored the possibility of ensuring that a clear statement of both sides of the case is readily available to the voters. In Parliamentary elections a basic form of information is the 'election address' issued by candidates. It would be appropriate to ensure that something analogous is provided for the referendum.

30. In the Government's view the best way of achieving this would be to deliver to every household at public expense (at the same time as the separate document described in paragraph 28) a single document containing a statement of between 1,000 and 2,000 words of each of the opposing views, together with answers given by each side to the same sets of questions. This document would best be prepared by representatives of the main campaigning organisations representing the two points of view.

31. It is to be expected that there will be a substantial additional flow of requests to the Government for factual information, interpretation of the renegotiated terms and the like from the press, radio, television and interested organisations and individuals. The Government therefore propose to establish for the period before the poll a special information unit to deal with such requests.

. . . . . .

Other activities 35. There is concern that the organisations favouring one course will have greater resources than those favouring another. It is already clear that any such imbalance, if it exists, is not preventing both sides from obtaining wide coverage of their views. The Government are convinced that any attempt to limit total expenditure by the two sides would be impracticable — not least because it could apply only after legislation had received Royal Assent.

36. The Government believe however that it is a matter of legitimate public interest to know how much money has been spent on the campaign by major organisations and interests and the sources of their income. Although this can be known only after the event, it could exercise a restraining influence. The Government are therefore considering how far it is possible to require that this information should be disclosed.

. . . . . .

Assistance from public funds 40. The Government have received representations that a fair and effective referendum requires assistance from public funds to the campaigning organisations. This would require statutory authority. The Government are prepared to consider providing limited financial assistance, to be equally divided between the two sides, if it is possible to identify two organisations which adequately represent those campaigning for and against continued membership of the Community.

62 DIRECT ELECTIONS TO THE EUROPEAN ASSEMBLY

Extracts from *Direct Elections to the European Assembly* (Cmnd. 6399, 1976); reprinted by permission of H.M.S.O. This Green Paper sets out proposals relating to the introduction of a system of direct election of British representatives to the European Assembly; the suggestion that the normal majority 'first-past-the-post' system should operate is likely to be challenged by the Liberals and other minority parties, since it will favour the two major parties in the same way as the national system for elections to Parliament.

Introduction

1. At present Members of the European Assembly are nominated by national Parliaments from among their members. The Treaty of Rome provides in Article 138(3)

(see Annex A) for the introduction of direct elections to the European Assembly. No agreement was reached during the first 18 years after the signature of the Treaty to put Article 138(3) into effect. There is now a strong feeling in the Community that the time has come to do this.

2. HMG regard the introduction of direct elections as an important matter. Consultation with the political parties is already in progress. Debates in Parliament must precede any firm commitment by the Government to any of the detailed arrangements for, or the timing of, the introduction of direct elections. Thereafter, once agreement has been reached on the questions which are to be decided by the Nine Member States, a Convention or Treaty will need to be signed and ratified and it will be necessary to introduce a bill making provision for the holding of the elections.

3. This timing means that decisions will need to be taken at two different stages, first in the Community and then in the United Kingdom. Part II of this Paper indicates the matters on which the Government will need to take a position in discussion with Community Governments and, subject to consultation and debate, the position they propose to take. It will be necessary for HMG to be able to put forward British views on these issues at the next meeting of the European Council in April 1976. Part III of the Paper briefly sets out the main questions which will fall to be decided by the British Parliament when it comes to consider draft legislation providing for direct elections to be held in this country. Decisions on Part III matters are not required immediately. Indeed some of them, such as the drawing of constituency boundaries, cannot be settled until after agreement has been reached among the Nine on such questions as the number and distribution of seats in the new European Assembly.

4. In considering this problem the Government have naturally had in mind the relationship between the question of direct elections to the European Assembly and the creation of Scots and Welsh Assemblies. Their preliminary view is that the issues involved can and should be kept separate. The timing of direct elections would have to be consistent with the plans which the Government are considering for setting up Scots and Welsh Assemblies. The Government will at every stage ensure that those who are working on the two questions remain in close touch in order to avoid any possible complications or conflicting arrangements. The future system of government in Northern Ireland is also a separate matter. Again, direct elections to the European Assembly should not cut across arrangements for the establishment or election of any new legislative body in Northern Ireland.

The present situation

5. Article 138(1) of the Treaty of Rome provides that, for what was envisaged as an interim period, 'the Assembly shall consist of delegates who shall be designated by the respective Parliaments from among their members in accordance with the procedure laid down by each Member State'. This is the system at present used. Article

138(3) provides for the introduction of a system of elections 'by direct universal suffrage in accordance with a uniform procedure in all Member States'.

6. In 1960, the Assembly drew up and adopted a draft Convention for Direct Elections in accordance with Article 138(3). This was not however acted on by the Council at the time, and for the following fourteen years there was disagreement on the subject among the original members of the Community. However, at the Heads of Government meeting in Paris on 9 and 10 December 1974, seven of the Nine agreed, in the words of the Communiqué 'that the election of the European Assembly by universal suffrage, one of the objectives laid down in the Treaty, should be achieved as soon as possible. In this connection, they await with interest the proposals of the European Assembly, on which they wish the Council to act in 1976. On this assumption, elections by direct universal suffrage could take place at any time in or after 1978' . . .

7. A number of ideas have so far been put forward as to what a draft Convention on direct elections might contain; the Government are not committed to any of them. Among these proposals were certain new ones produced by the European Assembly in January 1975. These were in the form of a resolution embodying a draft Convention . . .

8. In the course of . . . discussions it became clear that there exists a general recognition that the difficulties of reaching agreement between the Member Governments would be so great that it would be unwise at this stage to try to implement Article 138(3) in full by attempting to lay down a uniform electoral procedure in all the Member States. The consensus is that as many questions as possible should be left to national decision, including the fundamental one of the electoral system to be used for each Member State.

9. Heads of Government . . . agreed that elections to the European Assembly should take place on a single date in May or June 1978, but that any country which at that date is unable to hold direct elections should be allowed to continue to appoint its representatives from amongst the members of its national Parliament. . . . . . .

The powers of the European Assembly

12. There are at present no specific proposals before the Council for granting increased powers to the European Assembly. The Assembly acquired additional powers regarding the adoption of the Community Budget with effect from 1 January 1975. Some detailed improvements in the budget procedures have subsequently been agreed among the Member States, although the Treaty to this effect, signed in July 1975, has yet to be ratified by all Member States. In addition, 1975 saw the introduction of a conciliation procedure, whereby the Assembly and the Council agreed to try to resolve differences over draft legislation which has major financial implications. It is the Government's view that the immediate need is for the Council and the Assembly to establish a sound working relationship in the

exercise of their existing powers and that these powers should be the basis on which the first direct elections are held.

Matters for Community decision

13. There is a general consensus within the Community that certain issues must be determined on a Community-wide basis, of which the most important are the size of the European Assembly, together with the distribution of seats between Member States; whether the elections should be held on the same day throughout the Community (or within a few days) or at the same time as national elections; whether the Assembly should be elected for a fixed period (the Assembly have suggested five years) and whether it should be a requirement that members of the European Assembly should also be members of national Parliaments. Until agreement has been reached on these, Member Governments and national Parliaments cannot take decisions on the matters which will fall to be decided nationally.
. . . . . .

Size and composition of the European Assembly

15. The most difficult issue on which agreement among the Nine is required is the number and distribution of seats in the new Assembly. At present it consists of 198 members including 36 British members . . . The Assembly's draft Convention proposes a larger Assembly of 355 members of whom 67 would be from the United Kingdom.

16. The Assembly's draft proposals allocate seats on the following basis:
— up to a population of 1 million, each State receives 6 seats,
— States with a population between 1 million and 2.5 million are given 6 further seats,
— up to a population of 5 million, each State receives 1 further seat for each additional 500,000 inhabitants,
— for a population between 5 million and 10 million each State receives 1 further seat for each additional 750,000
— for a population between 10 million and 50 million each State receives 1 further seat for each additional 1 million inhabitants or part thereof,
— above 50 million, each State receives 1 further seat for each additional 1.5 million inhabitants or part thereof.

. . . there is a need to ensure a certain level of minimum representation for the smaller Member States, in particular Luxembourg. At the present stage of the Community's development, a provision of this kind seems essential. All Member States, even those with a small population, must be represented in the Assembly. On the other hand the relationship between their representation and that of the constituent parts of the larger Member States must be taken into account. It remains to be decided what the minimum number should be and the degree to which the remaining seats are distributed in proportion to population.

19. The precise size of the directly elected Assembly and the allocation of seats between Member States will be the subject of intergovernmental negotiation before the text of the Convention can be finalised. The government's own preliminary views are that an Assembly of about the size put forward in the Assembly's own Convention would be acceptable, subject to paragraph 18 above. In considering the number of seats to be allocated to the United Kingdom and to other Community countries Her Majesty's Government will aim for a solution which, given the situation described above, tends as far as possible in the direction of relating the number of seats allotted to each country to its population. The distribution of the United Kingdom allocation of seats will be a matter for national decision (see paragraph 33 below).

Date for elections

20. The European Assembly's draft Convention proposes that elections should take place on the same day throughout the Member States. The Council Working Group, however, considered two possibilities: a single date provided that this principle was interpreted flexibly to take account of national customs by allowing voting to be completed in a short space of time, such as a given number of days; alternatively that elections to the European Assembly should take place on the same dates as elections to national Parliaments. Heads of Government at the European Council in Rome came down in favour of the first alternative. (The Prime Minister made it clear that the Government would not be prepared to consider the holding of elections to the European Assembly on a Sunday in the United Kingdom). On balance it seems best to have the whole European Assembly elected at the same time (*i.e.* within a few days to allow for different national traditions about the appropriate day for voting) for a fixed period rather than electing each country's delegation whenever there happen to be national elections. There is much to be said for the Assembly having its own distinct life-span, for if national groups are elected at different times this would be likely to have an undesirable effect on the smooth functioning of the Assembly. And it would be difficult for the political parties to give due attention to the European Assembly elections if they were at the same time fighting a national election. The Government would, however, see advantage in holding the European Assembly elections in May at the same time as local authority elections if this can conveniently be arranged.

. . . . . .

22. As regards the period for which the Assembly should be elected, Her Majesty's Government agree with the Assembly's proposal that it should be five years. There seems to be a broad consensus on this point in the Community.

Status of members of the European Assembly

23. An important issue which will fall to be considered in this category is the question of the so-called dual mandate, that is whether members of the European

Assembly should at the same time be members of national Parliaments (as is the case with the existing arrangements), whether they should be excluded from membership of national Parliaments, or whether it should be left to the discretion of individual members if they wish to stand for election to both their national Parliament and the European Assembly. The existing arrangements impose a heavy burden on those Members who carry out seriously their responsibilities as members of national Parliaments and their responsibilities as members of the European Assembly. This is felt particularly severely by members of the House of Commons who traditionally have close links with their constituencies and who devote a lot of their time to constituency business. As against that, however, the view has been expressed that it is desirable to maintain close links between the national Parliament and the European Assembly. The Government of Denmark believe that they may wish to retain a compulsory dual mandate in Denmark. But among other Governments there was a general consensus that the dual mandate should be optional, *i.e.* that Members of Parliament should be free to stand for the European Assembly if they wish and vice versa. The Government share this view.

. . . . . .

Eligibility

26. In the course of their discussions, the Working Group distinguished between two types of 'incompatibility' with membership of the European Assembly, *i.e.* what categories of persons would be ineligible to stand for election: 'incompatibility' arising from national legislation, which would be left to the discretion of each Member State, and 'Community incompatibility', which would be agreed at Community level. The two lists would apply simultaneously. The European Assembly's suggested list for 'Community incompatibility' is contained in Article 6 of the draft Convention: it provides that such functions as membership of the Government of a Member State, of the Commission of the European Communities and a number of other official bodies of the Communities shall be incompatible with membership of the European Assembly. The Government see no reason to object to this proposal.

. . . . . .

Provisions for the future

28. In their proposals, the Assembly set themselves the task of putting forward further proposals by 1980 for the introduction of a uniform electoral procedure to complete the implementation of Article 138(3). No date was however set for the adoption of such a procedure by the Member States. The difficulties of reaching agreement on a uniform procedure between the Member States, who have widely different traditions in such matters, are likely to remain great. The prospect is therefore that the provisions to be established in the Convention will remain in force for a considerable number of years.

. . . . . .

Matters for decision by the British Parliament

30. It is proposed that it should be for the Government and Parliament of each Member State to decide on their own electoral system and procedures. From the discussions which have taken place so far in the Community, it seems clear that as many of the detailed arrangements as possible will, in fact, be left for national decision in this way.

31. Legislation will be required to provide for all the essential details of the electoral arrangements in this country. This will be preceded by full consultations between the parties and with those who will be concerned with the organisation and conduct of the elections, and there will be ample opportunity for the details to be debated in Parliament. This will also be the time to consider any proposals for *ex officio* links between Parliament and the directly elected British members of the European Assembly.

32. Certain adaptations to arrangements for Parliamentary elections will be necessary, some of which are mentioned below.

Constituencies

33. It will be necessary to decide how the seats which are eventually allocated to the United Kingdom under the Convention are to be distributed. There will be many fewer constituencies than for Westminster, and they will be much larger. The intention will be to maintain the electoral integrity of the several parts of the United Kingdom.

34. It would seem appropriate that in ordinary circumstances the Parliamentary Boundary Commission should be responsible for reviewing, and making recommendations about, the boundaries of the Assembly constituencies, in accordance with principles and procedures laid down in legislation. But if the general Community view is in favour of holding the first elections in 1978 and Parliament concludes that the United Kingdom ought to participate at the same time, special arrangements for drawing the initial boundaries will probably be needed, and Parliament can consider in the legislation what arrangements should be made.

Franchise and candidature

35. The existing franchise for Parliamentary elections could, in general, be maintained, with the addition of Peers. Consideration can be given to special extensions of the normal franchise, *e.g.* to nationals of the other Member States resident here, subject to the avoidance of double voting.

36. Subject to the provisions of the Convention about disqualification on grounds of 'Community incompatibility' (paragraph 26 above) it seems that the

rules governing candidature for Westminster election could be adopted, though Peers might in addition be eligible.

......

38. Registers for the Assembly elections could be constructed on the basis of the existing electoral canvass and Parliamentary registers, supplemented to cover any extensions in the franchise and amalgamated to cover the new constituencies. There would be a consequential reallocation of responsibilities among returning officers. Provisions on postal and proxy voting would be needed.

......

41. In addition, a number of new arrangements will need to be made which do not involve legislation. The political parties will presumably want to consider the local arrangements to be made for the selection of candidates and handling the campaign. Appropriate provision will need to be made for broadcasting time.

ANNEX A

Treaty establishing The European Economic Community, Rome, 25 March 1957

Article 138 1. The Assembly shall consist of delegates who shall be designated by the respective Parliaments from among their members in accordance with the procedure laid down by each Member State.

2. The number of these delegates shall be as follows:

Belgium	14
Denmark	10
Germany	36
France	36
Ireland	10
Italy	36
Luxembourg	6
Netherlands	14
United Kingdom	36

3. The Assembly shall draw up proposals for elections by direct universal suffrage in accordance with a uniform procedure in all Member States.

The Council shall, acting unanimously, lay down the appropriate provisions, which it shall recommend to Member States for adoption in accordance with their respective constitutional requirements.

ANNEX B

A number of ideas have so far been put forward as to what a draft Convention on direct elections might contain. Among these proposals are ones put forward by the European Assembly at the beginning of 1975 in the form of a draft Convention containing, in addition to its preamble, 17 Articles.

The main features of this draft are as follows.

Numbers The Assembly would contain 355 members as compared with the present total of 198. Seats would be distributed as follows (existing distribution in brackets):

Belgium	23	(14)
Denmark	17	(10)
Germany	71	(36)
France	65	(36)
Ireland	13	(10)
Italy	66	(36)
Luxembourg	6	(6)
Netherlands	27	(14)
UK	67	(36)

Term of Office The draft Convention provides for representatives to be elected for a five year period, each outgoing parliament remaining in office until the first sitting of its successor.

Status of Members Representatives are to vote on an individual and personal basis accepting neither instructions nor any binding mandate. On parliamentary immunities and eligibility to stand for election, the draft Convention envisages that the provisions governing national elections should apply (though it would also be made incompatible with Assembly membership to hold office in the Community institutions or in the Government of a Member State). Membership of the European Parliament would be compatible with that of a national parliament (*i.e.* the Convention would neither make the so-called dual mandate obligatory nor rule it out).

Electoral system The Assembly recognises the difficulty of going all the way to direct elections on a Community-wide uniform basis in one step as Article 138(3) of the Rome Treaty envisages. The draft Convention provides that the Assembly should put forward a proposal for a uniform electoral system by 1980. The appropriate provisions would be for unanimous decision by the Council which would recommend them to the Member States for adoption.

Select bibliography

Note. This bibliography is in sections which have an approximate correspondence to the documentary sections. Under each heading is listed first the most relevant official publications followed by selected secondary texts, and then particularly helpful journal articles. These sources are listed in reverse date order, i.e. the most recently published are listed first, since texts date rapidly in this field.

GENERAL

Official publications

The Royal Commission on the Constitution, 1969–73 (The Kilbrandon Report). Cmnd. 5460 and Cmnd. 5460–I, 1973.

Books

Geoffrey Wilson. *Cases and Materials on Constitutional and Administrative Law*, 2nd ed. Cambridge University Press, 1976.

T. C. Hartley and J. A. G. Griffith. *Government and Law: An Introduction to the Working of the Constitution in Britain*. Weidenfeld & Nicolson, 1975.

Frank Stacey. *British Government, 1966–75*. Oxford University Press, 1975.

P. A. Bromhead. *Britain's Developing Constitution*. Allen & Unwin, 1974.

O. Hood Phillips. *Constitutional and Administrative Law*, 5th ed. Sweet & Maxwell, 1973.

A. H. Hanson and M. Walles. *Governing Britain*. Fontana, 1970.

E. C. S. Wade and G. G. Phillips. *Constitutional Law*, 8th ed. by E. C. S. Wade and A. W. Bradley. Longman, 1970.

Frank Stacey. *The Government of Modern Britain*. Clarendon, 1968.

R. M. Punnett. *British Government and Politics*. Heinemann Educational Books, 1968.

S. B. Chrimes. *English Constitutional History*, 4th ed. Oxford University Press, 1967.

G. Marshall and G. C. Moodie. *Some Problems of the Constitution*. Hutchinson, 1967.

W. Bagehot. *The English Constitution*, with an Introduction by R. H. S. Crossman. Fontana, 1963.

W. C. Costin and J. Steven Watson. *The Law and Working of the Constitution: Documents 1660–1914*, 2nd ed. A. & C. Black, 1961.

H. J. Laski. *Reflections on the Constitution*. Manchester University Press, 1951.

PARLIAMENT

Official publications

The Preparation of Legislation (The Renton Report). Cmnd. 6053, 1975.
Report of the Select Committee on Members' Interests (Declaration). H.C. 102, 1974—5.
Report, Select Committee on Parliamentary Questions. H.C. 393, 1971—2.
Report from Joint Committee on Delegated Legislation. H.C. 475, 1971—2.
Second Report, Select Committee on Procedure: The Process of Legislation. H.C. 538, 1970—1.
Select Committees of the House of Commons. Cmnd. 4507, 1970.
Fourth Report, Select Committee on Procedure. H.C. 303, 1964—5.
First Report, Select Committee on Procedure: Scrutiny of Public Expenditure and Administration. H.C. 410, 1968—9.
House of Lords Reform. Cmnd. 3799, 1968.

Books

J. P. Morgan. *The House of Lords and the Labour Government 1964—70*. Clarendon, 1975.
P. Pulzer. *Political Representation and Elections in Britain*, 3rd ed. Allen & Unwin, 1975.
C.O.I. *The British Parliament*. C.O.I., 1974.
J. A. G. Griffith. *Parliamentary Scrutiny of Government Bills*. Allen & Unwin, 1974.
The Times. *The Times Guide to the House of Commons 1974*. Times, 1974.
D. Leonard and V. Herman. *The Backbencher and Parliament*. Macmillan, 1972.
P. G. Richards. *The Backbenchers*. Faber, 1972.
E. Taylor. *The House of Commons at Work*. Penguin, 1971.
A. P. Barker and M. Rush. *The Member of Parliament and his Information*. Allen & Unwin, 1970.
A. H. Hanson and B. Crick. *The Commons in Transition*. Fontana, 1970.
A. Morris (ed). *The Growth of Parliamentary Scrutiny by Committee*. Pergamon, 1970.
P. G. Richards. *Parliament and Conscience*. Allen & Unwin, 1970.
J. P. Mackintosh. *Specialist Committees of the House of Commons: Have They Failed?* Edinburgh University Press, 1969.
B. Crick. *The Reform of Parliament*, 2nd ed. Weidenfeld & Nicolson, 1968.
Hansard Society. *Parliamentary Reform 1933—60*. Cassell, 1967.
N. Johnson. *Parliament and Administration: The Estimates Committee 1945—65*. Allen & Unwin, 1966.
H. V. Wiseman. *Parliament and the Executive: Readings*. Routledge & Kegan Paul, 1966.
Study of Parliament Group. *Reforming the Commons*. P.E.P., 1965.
A. H. Birch. *Representative and Responsible Government*. Allen & Unwin, 1964.
A. Hill and A. Whichelow. *What's Wrong with Parliament?* Penguin, 1964.
D. E. Butler. *The Electoral System in Britain since 1918*, 2nd ed. Oxford University Press, 1963.

R. T. McKenzie. *British Political Parties*, 2nd ed. Heinemann, 1963.
D. N. Chester and N. Bowring. *Questions in Parliament*. Oxford University Press, 1962.
Sir Ivor Jennings. *Parliament*. Cambridge University Press, 1957.

Articles

Arnold Silkin. 'The Expenditure Committee: A New Development', *Public Administration*, 1975, 45—66.
Sir Richard Clarke. 'Parliament and Public Expenditure', *Political Quarterly*, 1973, 137—53.
G. Drewry. 'Reform of the Legislative Process: Some Neglected Questions', *Parliamentary Affairs*, 1972, 286—302.
Sir S. Goldman. 'The Presentation of Public Expenditure Proposals to Parliament', *Public Administration*, 1970, 247—62.
J. M. Lee. 'Select Committees and the Constitution', *Political Quarterly*, 1970, 182—94.
G. T. Popham and D. Greengrass. 'The Role and Functions of the Select Committee on Agriculture', *Public Administration*, 1970, 127—52.
C. K. Seymour-Ure. 'Proposed Reform of Parliamentary Privileges: An Assessment in the Light of Recent Cases', *Parliamentary Affairs*, 1970.
D. R. Shell. 'Specialist Select Committees', *Parliamentary Affairs*, 1970, 380—404.
G. K. Fry. 'Thoughts on the Present State of Ministerial Responsibility', *Parliamentary Affairs*, 1969—70, 10—20.
J. R. Vincent. 'The House of Lords', *Parliamentary Affairs*, 1966, 475—85.

CABINET, PRIME MINISTER, MACHINERY OF CENTRAL GOVERNMENT

Official publications

Sir R. Clarke. *New Trends in Government*. Civil Service Department, 1971.
The Reorganisation of Central Government. Cmnd. 4506, 1970.

Books

R. H. S. Crossman. *Diaries of a Cabinet Minister, vol. 1*. Hamilton, 1975.
R. H. S. Crossman. *Inside View*. Cape, 1972.
P. Gordon Walker. *The Cabinet*. Heinemann Educational Books, 1972.
Lord George-Brown. *In My Way*. Gollancz, 1971.
H. Wilson. *The Labour Government 1964—70*. Michael Joseph, 1971.
A. King (ed). *The British Prime Minister: A Reader*. Macmillan, 1969.
H. Berkeley (ed). *The Power of the Prime Minister*. Allen & Unwin, 1968.
J. P. Mackintosh. *The British Cabinet*, 2nd ed. Stevens, 1968.
F. M. G. Wilson. *The Organisation of British Central Government 1914—1964*, 2nd ed. Allen & Unwin, 1968.
R. K. Alderman and J. A. Cross. *The Tactics of Resignation*. Routledge, 1967.
Norman Hunt. *Whitehall and Beyond*. B.B.C. Publications, 1964.
H. Daalder. *Cabinet Reform in Britain 1914—63*. Oxford University Press, 1964.

H. Morrison. *Government and Parliament*, 3rd ed. Oxford University Press, 1964.

Articles

C. Pollitt. 'The Central Policy Review Staff, 1970–74', *Public Administration*, vol. 52, 1974, 375–95.
Sir R. Clarke. 'The Number and Size of Government Departments', *Political Quarterly*, 1972.
B. C. Smith. 'Reform and Change in British Central Administration', *Political Studies*, June 1971.

PUBLIC EXPENDITURE PLANNING

Official publications

12th Report, Expenditure Committee, 1974–5: Cash Limit Control of Public Expenditure. H.C. 535, 1974–5.
Sir S. Goldman. *The Developing System of Public Expenditure Management and Control*. H.M.S.O., 1973.
Programme Analysis Review. H.C. 147, 1972.
The Public Expenditure Survey System. The Treasury, 1971.
Public Expenditure Survey Committee. H.C. 549, 1970–1.
New Policies for Public Expenditure. Cmnd. 4515, 1970.
Public Expenditure: A New Presentation. Cmnd. 4017, 1968–9.
Public Expenditure: Planning and Control. Cmnd. 2915, 1966.
The Control of Public Expenditure (The Plowden Report). Cmnd. 1432, 1961.

Books

H. Heclo and A. Wildavsky. *The Private Government of Public Money*. Macmillan, 1974.
E. L. Normanton. *The Accountability and Audit of Governments*. Manchester University Press, 1967.

Articles

'The Plowden Report', *Public Administration*, Spring 1963.

GOVERNMENT OF THE PUBLIC SECTOR

Official publications

British Steel Corporation: Organisation Review. H.M.S.O., 1975.
National Consumers' Agency. Cmnd. 5726, 1974.
The Regeneration of British Industry. Cmnd. 5710, 1974.
British Railways Board: Report on Organisation. H.C. 50, 1969.
The Government's Reply to H.C. 371–I, 1967–8. Cmnd. 4027, 1969.
Report from the Select Committee on Nationalised Industries: Ministerial Control of the Nationalised Industries. H.C. 371–I, 1967–8.
The Task Ahead: Economic Assessment to 1972. H.M.S.O., 1969.

Reorganisation of the Post Office. Cmnd. 3233, 1967.
Nationalised Industries: a Review of Economic and Financial Objectives. Cmnd. 3437, 1967.
The Industrial Reorganisation Corporation. Cmnd. 2889, 1966.
Financial and Economic Obligations of the Nationalised Industries. Cmnd. 1337, 1961.

Books

L. Tivey (ed). *The Nationalised Industries Since 1960: A Book of Readings.* Allen & Unwin, 1973.
W. Thornhill. *The Nationalised Industries.* Nelson, 1968.
D. Coombes. *The Member of Parliament and the Administration: The Case of the Select Committee on Nationalised Industries.* Allen & Unwin, 1966.
A. H. Hanson. *Parliament and Public Ownership.* Cassell, 1961.

Articles

A. H. Hanson. 'Ministers and Boards', *Public Administration*, 1969, 65–74.
Sir R. Clarke. 'The Machinery for Economic Planning: The Public Sector', *Public Administration*, 1966, 61–72.
D. Coombes. 'The Scrutiny of Ministers' Powers by the Select Committee on Nationalised Industries', *Public Law*, 1965, 9–29.
Sir T. Low. 'The Select Committee on Nationalised Industries', *Public Administration*, 1962, 1–16.
G. H. Daniel. 'Public Accountability of the Nationalised Industries', *Public Administration*, 1960, 27–34.
A. H. Hanson. 'Parliamentary Control of the Nationalised Industries', *Parliamentary Affairs*, 1957–8, 328–40.

THE CIVIL SERVICE

Official publications

Civil Servants and Change: Report of the Wider Issues Review Team. C.S.D., 1975.
Civil Service Training: Report by R. N. Heaton and Sir Leslie Williams. C.S.D., 1974.
Fulton: The Reshaping of the Civil Service. National Whitley Council, 1971.
Fulton: A Framework for the Future. N.W.C., 1970.
Developments on Fulton. N.W.C., 1969.
The Method II System of Selection for the Administrative Class. Cmnd. 4156, 1969.
The Committee on the Civil Service (The Fulton Committee). Cmnd. 3638, 1968:
    Vol. 1. Report
    Vol. 2. Report of a Management Consultancy Group
    Vol. 3, (1) and (2). Surveys and Investigations
    Vol. 4. Factual, Statistical and Explanatory Papers
    Vol. 5, (1) and (2). Proposals and Opinions
6th Report of the Estimates Committee, 1964–5: Recruitment to the Civil Service. H.C. 308, 1965.
Royal Commission on the Civil Service. Cmnd. 9613, 1955, 1953–5.

Books

J. Garrett. *The Management of Government*. Penguin, 1972.
D. Keeling. *Management in Government*. Allen & Unwin, 1972.
R. Chapman and A. Dunsire (eds). *Style in Administration*. Allen & Unwin, 1971.
R. G. S. Brown. *The Administrative Process in Britain*. Methuen, 1970.
R. A. Chapman. *The Higher Civil Service in Britain*. Constable, 1970.
H. Parris. *Constitutional Bureaucracy*. Allen & Unwin, 1969.
H. Thomas (ed). *The Crisis in the Civil Service*. Anthony Blond, 1968.
Max Nicolson. *The System*. Hodder & Stoughton, 1967.
B. Chapman. *British Government Observed*. Allen & Unwin, 1963.

Articles

R. A. Chapman. 'The Vehicle and General Affair: Some Reflections for Public
Administration in Britain', *Public Administration*, Autumn, 1973.
M. Wright. 'The Professional Conduct of Civil Servants', *Public Administration*,
1973, 1–16.
L. Gunn. 'Politicians and Officials: Who is Answerable?', *Political Quarterly*, 1972,
253–60.
D. Keeling. 'The Development of Central Training in the Civil Service, 1963–70',
Public Administration, 1971–2.
'The Fulton Report', *Public Administration*, 1969, 1–64.
R. G. S. Brown. 'Organisation Theory and Civil Service Reform', *Public Adminis-
tration*, 1965, 313–30.
'Who are the Policy-makers?', *Public Administration*, 1965, 251–88.

THE CONTROL OF GOVERNMENT

Official publications

Report of the Committee of Privy Councillors on Ministerial Memoirs. Cmnd. 6386,
1976.
The Red Lion Square Disorders of 15 June 1974. Cmnd. 5919, 1975.
First Report, Standing Advisory Commission on Human Rights in Northern Ireland.
Annual Report, 1974–5.
Report of the Gardiner Committee on Terrorism in Northern Ireland. Cmnd. 5487,
1975.
First Report of the Health Service Commissioner. H.C. 161, 1974.
Prevention of Terrorism (Temporary Provisions) Act 1974.
The Franks Report on Sections 1 and 2 of the Official Secrets Act. Cmnd. 5104,
1972.
Remedies in Administrative Law. Law Commission Working Paper No. 13, 1971.
Lords and Commons Joint Committee on Delegated Legislation. H.C. 475, 1971–2.
Law Commission Report on Administrative Law, 1969. Cmnd. 4059, 1969.
Information and the Public Interest. Cmnd. 4089, 1969.

The Parliamentary Commissioner for Administration: Annual Report for 1968.
H.C. 129, 1969.
Third Report of the Parliamentary Commissioner for Administration (on Sachsen-hausen). H.C. 54, 1967–8.
Parliamentary Commissioner Act 1967.
The Parliamentary Commissioner for Administration. Cmnd. 2767, 1965.
Report from the Committee on Administrative Tribunals and Enquiries. The Franks Report, Cmnd. 218, 1957.
Report of the Committee on Ministers' Powers (The Donoughmore Report). Cmnd. 4060, 1932.

Books

R. Gregory and P. G. Hutchesson. *The Parliamentary Ombudsman: A Study in the Control of Administrative Action.* Allen & Unwin, 1975.
Frank Stacey. *A New Bill of Rights for Britain.* David & Charles, 1973.
K. C. Wheare. *Maladministration and its Remedies.* Stevens, 1973.
R. E. Wraith and P. G. Hutchesson. *Administrative Tribunals.* Allen & Unwin, 1973.
S. A. de Smith. *Constitutional and Administrative Law.* Penguin, 1971.
Frank Stacey. *The British Ombudsman.* Oxford University Press, 1971.
R. E. Wraith and G. Lamb. *Public Inquiries as an Instrument of Government.* Allen & Unwin, 1971.
K. Bell. *Tribunals in the Social Services.* Routledge, 1969.
H. J. Elcock. *Administrative Justice.* Longman, 1969.
H. Street. *Justice in the Welfare State.* Stevens, 1968.
G. Marshall. *Police and Government.* Methuen, 1965.
Harry Street. *Freedom, the Individual, and the Law.* Pelican, 1963.
Justice. *The Citizen and the Administration: The Redress of Grievances.* Stevens, 1961.
J. E. Kersell. *Parliamentary Supervision of Delegated Legislation.* Stevens, 1960.
R. D. Brown. *The Battle of Crichel Down.* Bodley Head, 1955.
H. J. Laski. *Liberty in the Modern State.* Pelican, 1937.
Lord Hewart. *The New Despotism.* Benn, 1929.

Articles

G. Marshall. 'Maladministration', *Public Law*, 1973, 32–44.
R. Gregory and A. Alexander. 'Our Parliamentary Ombudsman', *Public Administration*, 1972, 313–31; 1973, 41–59.
J. D. B. Mitchell. 'Administrative Law and Parliamentary Control', *Political Quarterly*, 1967, 360–74.
J. D. B. Mitchell. 'The Causes and Effects of the Absence of a System of Public Law in the United Kingdom', *Public Law*, Summer 1965, 95–118.
K. C. Wheare. 'The Redress of Grievances', *Public Administration*, 1962, 125–8.
H. W. R. Wade. 'The Council on Tribunals', *Public Law*, 1960, 351–66.
G. Marshall. 'Tribunals and Enquiries: Developments since the Franks Report', *Public Administration*, 1958, 261–70.

THE DEVOLUTION OF GOVERNMENT (SCOTLAND AND WALES)

Official publications

Our Changing Democracy: Devolution to Scotland and Wales. Cmnd. 6348, 1975.
Democracy and Devolution: Proposals for Scotland and Wales. Cmnd. 5732, 1974.
Devolution Within the United Kingdom: Some Alternatives for Discussion. 1974.
The Royal Commission on the Constitution, 1969–73 (The Kilbrandon Report) 1973:
    Vol. 1. Report. Cmnd. 5460.
    Vol. 2. Memorandum of Dissent by Lord Crowther-Hunt and Professor A. T. Peacock. Cmnd. 5460–I.

Books

J. G. Kellas. *The Scottish Political System*, 2nd ed. Cambridge University Press, 1975.
J. N. Wolfe (ed). *Government and Nationalism in Scotland.* Edinburgh University Press, 1969.
J. P. Mackintosh. *The Devolution of Power.* Penguin, 1968.

Articles

J. Stanyer. 'Nationalism, Regionalism, and the British System of Government', *Social and Economic Administration*, 1974, 136–57.

DEVOLUTION OF GOVERNMENT: NORTHERN IRELAND

Official publications

Letter from the Secretary of State for Northern Ireland to the Chairman of the Convention. Cmnd. 6387, 1976.
Report of the Northern Ireland Constitutional Convention. H.C. 1, 1976.
Northern Ireland Discussion Paper 3: Government of Northern Ireland. H.M.S.O., 1975.
The Northern Ireland Constitution. Cmnd. 5675, 1974.
The Northern Ireland (Constitution) Act 1973.
Northern Ireland Constitutional Proposals. Cmnd. 5259, 1973.

Other

J. Magee. *Northern Ireland: Crisis and Conflict.* Routledge & Kegan Paul, 1974.

THE EUROPEAN COMMUNITY

Official publications

Direct Elections to the European Assembly. Cmnd. 6399, 1976.

Referendum on U.K. Membership of the European Community. Cmnd. 5295, 1975.

Membership of the European Community: Report on Renegotiation. Cmnd. 6003, 1975.

Financial Control in the European Community. Cmnd. 6360, 1975.

First Report, Select Committee on Procedure: European Secondary Legislation. H.C. 294, 1974–5.

Special Report, House of Lords European Communities Committee. H.C. 139, 1974.

First and Second Reports, Select Committee on European Community Secondary Legislation. H.C. 143, and 463–1, 1972–3.

The United Kingdom and the European Communities. Cmnd. 4715, 1971.

Other

Lord Chief Justice Scarman. 'Common Law or Common Market', *Listener*, 31 October 1974.